ALSO BY MICHAEL T. KAUFMAN

The Decline and Fall of the Soviet Empire (with Bernard Gwertzman)

The Collapse of Communism (with Bernard Gwertzman)

Mad Dreams, Saving Graces: Poland, a Nation in Conspiracy

In Their Own Good Time

Rooftops and Alleys

SOROS

SOROS

THE LIFE AND TIMES OF A
MESSIANIC BILLIONAIRE

MICHAEL T. KAUFMAN

ALFRED A. KNOPF   NEW YORK

2002

THIS IS A BORZOI BOOK
PUBLISHED BY ALFRED A. KNOPF

Copyright © 2002 by Michael T. Kaufman
All rights reserved under International and Pan-American
Copyright Conventions. Published in the United States by
Alfred A. Knopf, a division of Random House, Inc., New York,
and simultaneously in Canada by Random
House of Canada Limited, Toronto.
Distributed by Random House, Inc., New York.
www.aaknopf.com

Knopf, Borzoi Books, and the colophon are
registered trademarks of Random House, Inc.

All photographs, unless otherwise noted, are courtesy of George Soros.

Library of Congress Cataloging-in-Publication Data
Kaufman, Michael T.
Soros: The Life and Times of a Messianic Billionaire / Michael T. Kaufman.
p.   cm.
Includes bibliographical references and index.
ISBN 0-375-40585-2 (alk. paper)
1. Soros, George. 2. Capitalists and financiers—Biography.
3. Investments.   I. Title.

HG172.S63 K38   2001
332.6'092—dc21   2001032661
[B]

Manufactured in the United States of America
First Edition

For my children, Susan, Seth, and Noah

In practical matters the end is not mere speculative knowledge of what is to be done, but rather the doing of it. It is not enough to know about virtue, then, but we must endeavor to possess it, and to use it, or to take any other steps that may make us good.

—Aristotle, *Nicomachean Ethics*

Contents

PART III: GIVING IT AWAY

Introduction

IT IS MY HOPE, as it doubtlessly is with every author, that the story in this book is far better and more compelling than the story of this book. Nonetheless, it seems sensible at the outset to explain how this book came to be written and, more particularly, to describe my relationship to George Soros, the subject of this biography.

Briefly: I had known about Soros and been intrigued by him for more than a decade, when in the spring of 1995 I received a phone call from his Open Society Institute asking whether I would be willing to move to Prague and edit a magazine. The publication, financed by Soros, was called *Transitions*, and it covered the social, political, and economic transformations then underway in some thirty countries emerging from Communism. At the time of the totally unexpected offer, I was finishing my third year happily writing an unabashedly sentimental column for the *New York Times* called "About New York," which focused on the often remarkable lives of unknown New Yorkers. It was quite a reach to go from that to *Transitions*, but the people who made the proposal knew that I had covered Eastern Europe for the *Times* in the mid-eighties and that, as the paper's deputy foreign editor from 1989 to 1992, I had helped organize its coverage of Communism's spectacular collapse. They were also aware of a book about Poland I had written in 1988 that had anticipated at least some of the democratic changes that were soon to occur in the dissolving eastern bloc.

In any case, Soros's people had their reasons for offering the position to me and I had reasons for accepting. After thirty-eight years with the *Times*, fourteen of them as a foreign correspondent, I was growing aware that my future at the paper was unlikely to be as interesting as my past and I wanted at least one more adventure. The job itself also seemed challenging and worthwhile: to edit a serious publication dealing with a region undergoing profound, though little understood, changes. In a sense it was like having an opportunity to cover an epoch, like the Reformation or the Enlightenment. And Prague, I knew, was beautiful.

There was, however, another incentive. By taking the job, I would be able to learn a good deal about the Open Society's network of do-gooding enterprises and more particularly about its billionaire founder, George Soros. At the time I had no thoughts of writing about him, though I had come to consider him a fascinating and elusive figure.

My first awareness of him came when I was living in Warsaw. Dissidents throughout Eastern Europe, who were my sources and my friends, were telling me about a mysterious American who was using his own money to support them in their struggles against dictatorial Communism. According to their sketchy accounts, Soros was a wealthy financial speculator who did not welcome publicity about himself or his projects. My friends told me he had been born Jewish in Budapest, where as a boy he had survived the Nazi occupation. Then, after the war, as the Soviets tightened their control over Hungary, Soros, then a teenager, managed to slip under the descending Iron Curtain and make his way to England. There, he studied at the London School of Economics. In the mid-fifties he came to the United States, to begin a career on Wall Street.

I found the few details enticing, and I remember looking up Soros in *Who's Who* only to discover that he had no listing. But during the next few years I was able to learn a little more about him. He was funneling his money to Solidarity in Poland, to Charta 77 in Czechoslovakia, to dissident groups in Moscow. Later, he opened a foundation in Communist Hungary, and he was providing hundreds of scholarships to bring academics from the East to study and travel in the West.

In 1986 I met Soros briefly, exchanging a handshake with him at a hall in New York where I had been invited to lecture to a group of Hungarian-Americans. They had asked me to elaborate on a story I had written about a secret section of a Budapest cemetery where the remains of several hundred people executed in the anti-Soviet uprising of 1956 lay in unmarked graves. After I flew back to Europe, I learned that Soros had paid for my airfare.

Three years later, I was back in New York on the *Times* foreign desk tracking the revolutionary events in Europe. By then, though Soros's name was still widely unknown, I would hear it mentioned more and more often by those engaged in work on human rights and those monitoring Communism's decay. His Hungarian foundation soon gave rise to others, in Poland, Czechoslovakia, Ukraine, the Baltic, Russia, and the Balkans. He was planning to build an international university. In those days I would sometimes be visited by my former dissident friends who would tell me about playing chess and discussing philosophy with Soros at his summer home on Long Island's Atlantic shore. They described him as a worldly and knowledgeable intellectual who seemed to prefer their company to that of other businessmen.

At the time, Soros was still zealously guarding his privacy. As a financier he had learned to shun publicity, superstitiously fearful that his exposure might jinx the performance of his pace-setting hedge fund, the Quantum Fund. So as he steadily expanded his philanthropic activities, he habitually kept to the shadows, and into the nineties Soros remained largely unrecognized by an American public that could easily identify, and often celebrated, far lesser plutocrats.

All that changed after September 16, 1992, when the British government abandoned its earlier commitment to prop up the value of the pound. Soros was hardly the only speculator to make a fortune on what Britons came to call Black Wednesday, but he was among the biggest winners and he ended up being the one most prominently exposed by the British press. Once his smiling stock photograph looked out at the suddenly poorer readers of the tabloids, the prospect of further anonymity vanished. Besieged by the Fleet Street journalists, Soros decided to talk openly about what he had done, in finance as well as in philanthropy. He made a conscious decision to exploit his new notoriety as "The Man Who Broke the Bank of England" to gain influence among world leaders and to become what he has since described as a stateless statesman.

His earliest public urgings to reform the World Bank and organize a version of the Marshall Plan to help Eastern Europe were spurned and even openly ridiculed. But in time his reputation rose steadily as his philanthropies successfully took on bold and risky tasks that even powerful sovereign governments would have found intimidating. Eventually he did gain access to world leaders, and in the words of Morton Abramowitz of the Carnegie Endowment for Peace, Soros became the "only private citizen who had his own foreign policy." By the end of the century he was annually being nominated for the Nobel Peace Prize.

Among his most imaginative policy interventions was his expenditure of $50 million to help the citizens of Sarajevo withstand a deadly siege during the Bosnian war. As part of this project he underwrote the remarkable installation in wartime of a water filtration plant that provided tap water to a city where Serb snipers on the high ground regularly killed women as they filled jugs at wells. In another spectacular program, Soros spent more than $100 million to rescue Soviet science from looming bankruptcy.

At the same time that such projects were gaining attention, Soros was also becoming known as one of the world's richest people. Throughout the 1990s he would regularly be cited in annual magazine listings of the world's highest earners, the wealthiest and the most generous. In terms of charity, it was not merely the size of his contributions that differentiated Soros from others. His personal involvement in his projects was unlike that of any other living philanthropists; it evoked comparisons to Andrew Carnegie and John D. Rockefeller. Soros didn't simply fund his projects; he helped devise them, monitored them, tinkered with them, and, when they seemed to be ineffective, shut them down. He worked at it with the same energy, and often the same tactics, that he had employed in finance. Moreover, he had his own rationale for all his contributions, drawing upon the teachings of his mentor, the philosopher Karl Popper, to aid and abet the formation of "open societies" where they did not exist and protect them from their enemies where they did. When he was asked how he wanted to be identified at an award ceremony at Oxford, he suggested the following descriptive phrase: "George Soros, a financial, philanthropic, and philosophical speculator."

By the time I went to Prague, I knew at least some of these things. I had seen the magazine profiles and the television interviews. I had read several of Soros's books and a number of his newspaper and magazine articles. But as I suspected, once I took up my new job, the view of Soros available within his altruistic empire turned out to be very different—far richer and more paradoxical—than that conveyed by the media.

Within that network the atmosphere was dizzying. Everything was in perpetual flux, with people and programs and ideas constantly coming and going. Mission statements were routinely rejected and revised. Yet the lead time between the conception of an idea and its implementation was extraordinarily short, even for a journalist who had spent his professional life working under daily deadlines. And this frenetic tempo was being set by Soros himself. A half-page memo could inspire him to start a $100-million project as soon as he read it. Within the network people would jokingly note that if Soros sat next to you on a plane for more than an hour, he would probably appoint you president of one of his foundations, only to fire you within a few weeks. Another widely circulated phrase held that "Soros must be a Hungarian word for changing one's mind." There were frequent mentions of "flavors of the month," references to people or ideas that had aroused strong but hardly enduring enthusiasms in Soros. Far rarer were those people whom Soros designated as "doers," his highest accolade. He was always looking for "doers."

Chaos was common and disasters often loomed. Some projects capsized or were melded into others. There were conflicts with national leaders, and there were also cases of scandal and corruption within the network. And yet, somehow, despite the turmoil and the feverish pace—or perhaps because of it—Soros was compiling an extraordinary record of successful philanthropy. In addition to the Sarajevo campaign and the rescue of Soviet science, his more expansive projects came to include the reform of early childhood education in more than thirty countries, the introduction of modern social sciences to large parts of the globe where they had long shriveled in the shadow of Marxist dogma, the retraining of thousands of Communist military officers for civilian life in privatized economies, and the irrevocable linking of scores of Soviet bloc universities to the Internet.

During the two and a half years I spent at *Transitions,* I was able to watch Soros in large and small gatherings, and I met hundreds of people who worked with or for him, or who were foundation grantees. I attended the so-called jamborees to which Soros annually summoned Open Society staff from Haiti to Uzbekistan, to discuss what they were doing, should be doing, or could be doing. At the Budapest jamborees and at other smaller gatherings, the delegates would mingle and spend much of their free time talking about Soros, who was referred to simply as George.

Such conversations would usually begin with a reference to something Soros had said or done, but then they quickly gravitated toward gossip and speculation. For example, was Soros turning his philanthropic interests away from Europe to America? Did he want to give away all his money before he died? Did anyone really believe that he would rather write a great philosophical text than make more money? Was it true that his wife didn't like Hungary? Why didn't he have a private plane? Did he have any rich friends? Was he really a social democrat at heart? With all the countries he had helped, why had he never helped Israel? And why, given all the corruption and scandals in Moscow, was he still so committed to helping Russia? Did he really think that the struggle against corruption could be the global issue of the late nineties just as human rights had been the issue of the eighties? How serious was he in challenging American anti-drug policies? Was he really going to build a university in Warsaw in addition to the one he had founded in Budapest? What was his favorite lesser-known project of the moment—the loan guarantee scheme that was providing housing for hundreds of thousands of black South Africans or perhaps the Albanian project that focused on school construction to build communities and civil society? Was he more European or American? Was he a good father? Was he shy or arrogant? How much ego did he have? Did his philosophy—or, for that matter, Karl Popper's—really make sense? And, above all, who was he? Where did he come from? What made him?

I participated in dozens of sessions of this kind, where hypotheses and anecdotes about Soros were exchanged late into the night. However the views of Soros might differ, there was always general agreement that he was quite definitely not just another rich man.

Often in these wine-assisted conversations, people would reach for historical analogies to explain him to each other and to themselves; Rockefeller and Carnegie were the most common benchmarks but there was talk, too, of engaged intellectuals and moralizing activists like Albert Schweitzer, Mahatma Gandhi, Bertrand Russell, and André Malraux, or the rich men who dabbled in world affairs like the oil magnate Armand Hammer, the Canadian pacifist Cyrus Eaton, and Bernard Baruch, the investor who had advised American presidents.

Literary allusions sometimes seemed even more appropriate. Someone would offer up the prototype of Aristotle's philosopher king, who like Soros linked wisdom, means, and great autonomy. Or else Don Quixote would be suggested as sharing both Soros's moralistic naïveté as well as his fondness for high-risk ventures. From pop culture came Daddy Warbucks, the cynical protector of the perpetually innocent Orphan Annie, the Wizard of Oz, and even Goldfinger, James Bond's plutocratic nemesis who overreached himself turning money into power and vice versa.

During one such evening it was suggested that the reason Soros's life held such fascination for so many who came to know him was that it represented the ultimate fulfillment of the great lottery dream, which, the proponent of this view contended, had to be the most common fantasy in the modern world. In its basic version, the dreamer envisions winning a huge lottery and then using his or her bounty to make the world a better place. The first steps were clear—providing for one's family—but after that, what? Where would one begin? Soros, it was alleged, was so compelling to so many precisely because he had moved far beyond the first step, perhaps as well as anyone in real life or literature.

In the spring of 1998, I finished my stint at *Transitions* and returned to New York where I rejoined the *Times* as the senior obituary writer, preparing biographical articles on well-known living figures that would be used when they died. In connection with this work, I was reading many biographies and it quite naturally occurred to me that Soros's life would make a rich subject for a book. I learned, however, that another writer had already been commissioned to write such a biography. Then, a few months later, friends from Europe who had known of my interest in Soros advised me that this writer had abandoned the project, and they urged me to take it on.

I was very interested, but there were some problems. For one thing I clearly liked and admired Soros. Though I had never quite thought of him as a friend, I had stopped addressing him as Mr. Soros and, like everyone else in his ambit, called him George. Obviously I could not even pretend to be starting out with my mind a clear slate. Then too, Soros had paid my salary at *Transitions*. Would such circumstances strain my credibility? Ultimately, I concluded that they would be offset by the habits and reflexes acquired in forty years as a journalist, which I was certain would compel me to follow the story wherever it led.

There were also questions of access. Would Soros be willing to provide me with the kind of information I would need? When I went to see him to talk about it, he explained that he had cut off his contacts with the original writer, who then gave up his efforts. Soros said that after originally giving the writer information and permitting him to accompany him on trips, he began to feel uncomfortable. Soros emphasized that the writer had every right to look at his life from whatever perspective he chose and to produce whatever kind of book about him he wanted, but he added that he did not feel himself obliged to help someone who did not have his trust. As for my proposal, he said he was willing to extend his full cooperation.

I told him that I would be professionally bound to look for skeletons in his closets and bring them to light if they existed. He said he understood that. I also told him that I had been raised to believe that it was impossible for a really rich man to be a really good man. He answered that so had he, and that this was a reasonable position to take.

A few days later he sent me the following note: "This is to confirm in writing what I told you in person. If you get a book contract, I shall be ready to cooperate with you and encourage others to cooperate with you. I do not want to influence the content of the book in any way and I should like to see it clearly stated that this is not an authorized biography."

So let me now emphasize in my own voice that this is not an authorized biography. It is my book and not George Soros's. It is also a book about the life of a living man who, seventy years of age when this book was written, was still very active and fully capable of more surprises and achievements.

I also want to state clearly that Soros fulfilled his commitment to me. He sat for numerous interviews, allowed me to accompany him to Russia and to Hungary and to attend meetings of the Open Society board. He provided personal documents, including correspondence and unpublished manuscripts he wrote as a young man, and he interceded with members of his family, old friends, and business associates, urging them to talk to me.

—*MTK, April 2001*

PART I

ORIGINS

CHAPTER I

ERZEBET AND TIVADAR

IN 1985, George Soros arranged for his mother to dictate her recollections and for them to be taped and transcribed. That way his children would have access to them and he would be able to check his own memories against hers. Erzebet Soros was then an eighty-two-year-old widow with failing eyesight who had repeatedly rejected offers by her two very rich sons to house her in a grand style with maids and a driver. She preferred her modest two-room apartment in Manhattan near Columbus Circle, with its mismatched furniture, paintings by Hungarian artist friends, and small African animal carvings. At her death in 1989 she willed the apartment to George Soros's Open Society Institute to be used as accommodations for visitors from overseas who were in New York for brief periods. Though many people have stayed there, the place has remained quite the way it was when she lived in it, shelves filled with dog-eared books in several languages, including works by Kierkegaard, Paul Tillich, and Martin Buber, as well as several Bibles.

In this setting Erzebet recorded her story and that of her family. Her tone was basically reportorial, with very few rhapsodic flights of pride. Instead, with often rich detail, she described how her family had endured the vicissitudes of war, separation, and displacement. She told of the prewar years when the upper-middle-class family pursued an unconventional and bohemian lifestyle. She recounted how, once the Nazis came, she, her husband Tivadar, and their sons, Paul and George, lived under false names and Christian identities. In her down-to-earth chronicle she went on to tell of the time when George, then barely seventeen, escaped from Communist Hungary to a life in the West, with the entire family assuming that they would never again be reunited. Then, as she explained, in 1956, in the wake of the Soviet suppression of the Hungarian uprising, she and her husband were able to walk away from their native land to join their sons in New York, where the boys were becoming successful. "So," as she said in her Hungarian-accented English, "that is the story; that is how we loved each other and how we grew."

Though the telling was for the most part as prosaically modest as her apartment, her story clearly had its hero. Over and over, during the months that she talked into the tape recorder, she spoke in worshipful terms of her husband and his profound role in shaping the life of the family, assuring its survival and determining its unfolding destiny through the rearing of his sons. She mentioned how once when George was a child of seven or eight, he had written a poem in which he had portrayed his father, Tivadar, as Zeus, or, as she added, "the father God." The impact of her husband's life upon the family had been so powerful, she declared, that even then, as she was taping her memories years after his death in New York, Tivadar continued to dominate the thoughts and feelings of those he had loved most and who in turn had loved him so intensely.

"George really has now the problem," she said. "I think that is the reason he is going to a shrink, to find out how to get completely rid of his father."

When, fifteen years later, this passage was pointed out to George, he laughed, recalling that at the time, "if anything, I was trying to get rid of my mother." Nevertheless, he conceded that Erzebet's overall point was valid. Tivadar was indeed the central and dominant figure in the saga. It was he who shaped the family, defined its character, and instilled in its members a loyalty to each other that superseded all other identities, whether of a wider family, friends, religion, class, nationality, or citizenship. "There was definitely an awareness that we were different," said Soros. He does not remember the poem he wrote about Zeus, but as he talked at length about his youth, Tivadar emerged both as a loving and innovative father and a Platonic demiurge, a man who, using what life had taught him, prepared his sons for the unpredictable and unforeseen and set everything in motion.

Then on the verge of seventy, George Soros gave the impression that his dialogue with his long-dead father was far from over. During long conversations at his baronial Westchester County estate, he would digress into what appeared to be lifelong musings about Tivadar. "I guess he could be best described by the German word *lebenkunstler*, or artist of life," he observed. "Was he a strong man or a weak man? Even to this day I am in doubt. On the one hand, he was very strong and this had to do with his First World War experience when he obviously went through very trying times as a prisoner in Siberia and then witnessing the Russian civil war. People were getting killed and he went through hell. Obviously, the very fact that he lived through it may have marked him so powerfully that maybe he didn't want that kind of exposure again. And so he may have bought himself a comfortable life by marrying my mother. Here there was a sense that he had withdrawn, lost ambition."

As Soros weighed such judgments his thoughts moved forward to 1944, the most instructive year of his own adolescence and perhaps of his entire life, when Tivadar, no longer simply an artist of life, drew upon his experiences of Siberian rigors to make sure that his immediate family, as well as many other endangered Hungarian Jews, would escape the Nazis and their Hungarian Arrow Cross henchmen. Here Tivadar had undoubtedly been strong, and his son would later write of that year, when Budapest was in flames and when people like him were being deported or taken to the Danube and shot, that it had been "the happiest of his life," for it had provided him with an opportunity to observe a man he adored and admired act bravely and well.

Clearly, Tivadar has persisted as a dominating presence in George's mind, and on a wintry day in 1999, as he sat in the sun room of his resplendently furnished home, surrounded by paintings by Winslow Homer, Mary Cassatt, and Childe Hassam, the multibillionaire and pioneering global philanthropist casually found parallels between Tivadar's life and his own, seemingly questioning how he had measured up.

He explained how he had experienced the lowest point in his own life, or his own Siberia, when after leaving Hungary he found himself a seventeen-year-old in England, without money, friends, or likely prospects. "I had the feeling that I had touched bottom, and that I could only rise from there. That is a strong thing. It has also marked me for life, because I don't ever want to be there again. I have a bit of a phobia about having to live through it again. Why do you think I made so much money? I may not feel menaced now but there is a feeling in me that if I were in that position again, or if I were in the position that my father was in in 1944, that I would not actually survive, that I am no longer in condition, no longer in training. I've gotten soft, you know."

Tivadar was born in 1893 into an Orthodox Jewish family, whose name was not Soros but Schwartz, in Nyirbakta, a rural village not far from Hungary's border with Ukraine. His own father had a general store and sold farm equipment. The business prospered, and when Tivadar, the second of eight children, was still quite young the family moved to Nyiregyhaza, the regional center in northeastern Hungary. By giving their oldest son a typically Hungarian name like Tivadar instead of its German equivalent, Teodor, his parents were reflecting the respectful identification that many successful, rising, and assimilating Jews were showing for the Hungarian part of the Austro-Hungarian dual monarchy. Though the family had roots in Jewish piety, by the time Tivadar and his siblings were born, many of its members were becoming less visibly devout. George believes his paternal grandparents spoke Yiddish, and he remembers being amused when as a child he noticed that one of his father's sisters was bald. The traditional wig that as a married Jewish woman she wore over her shaved head had slipped as she dozed on the living room couch while she visited her brother's family in Budapest. Tivadar, who has left separate biographical accounts of his experiences in each of the century's world wars, noted in one of them that his father had lost his religious zeal but that he kept this from his friends and neighbors in the interest of community harmony and continued to regularly attend synagogue.

Tivadar himself grew openly less religious and more assimilated than his brothers and sisters, though he too never broke ties with the more religious part of his family, nor they with him. In *Maskerado: Dancing around Death in Nazi Hungary,** a memoir he wrote in Esperanto, Tivadar reflected on his religious beliefs, saying that there were periods in his youth "when the problems of god and religion and of mankind and the universe were foremost in my mind," with the "preoccupation strongest around the age of thirteen." He added that he had been particularly interested in the problem of death and afterlife. However, he added that after much reading, he ultimately concluded that "not only did God make man in his own image, but also man imagines God in his own human way. The anthropomorphic nature of the deity frightened me away from organized religion. Instead of going to services I was happier worrying about human lives. Understanding, a love of people, tolerance—these were the virtues I cultivated." With a touch of self-mockery he added that such tolerance was soon tested since his Erzebet was an "enthusiast for all kinds of religious mysticism."

---

*Edinburgh: Canongate, 2000.

During the latter part of the nineteenth century Jews in Hungary had grown markedly in numbers, prosperity, and prominence. They fared better under Magyar rule than virtually anywhere else in Europe, and Soros's grandfather Schwartz was among the Jewish merchants who benefited as capitalism and the industrial age continued to alter a fading world of agrarian and feudal values. Though anti-Semitism was hardly unknown, Tivadar grew to manhood in a period of boom in which liberal and tolerant attitudes dominated. He would recall as a child being taunted by cries of "Hep! Hep!" which he was told was an acronym for *Hierusolyma est perdita*, Latin for "Jerusalem is lost." He also remembered that when he was a boy there was a blood libel case in the nearby town of Tiszaeszlar where Jews were falsely accused of murdering a Christian girl and using her blood for rituals. He could even recall the words of an anti-Semitic song that related to the trial.

> *Hundred Jews in a row*
> *March on to Hell below*
> *Nathan is the leader*
> *A sack on his shoulder*
> *Hundred Jews in a row.*

Yet, while outrages occurred, Jews were at the same time entering almost all levels of Hungarian society, and by the late 1880s they were significantly represented in all the professions. Many of the country's industrialists, the so-called magnates, were of Jewish origin, though among these a large percentage had converted to Christianity. Alone among Central and Eastern European countries, Hungary had even elevated some Jews to noble status, raising a number of the magnates and even a rabbi to the rank of baron and seating them in the upper house of the legislature. The upsurge of remarkably capable Hungarian Jews in this period is perhaps best reflected in the realm of science, where Jews of Tivadar's generation were soon to achieve international fame. Among the best known of these were the mathematician John von Neumann, who among other things helped to establish the computer age, and the nuclear physicists Leo Szilard and Edward Teller, whose work led to the development of both the atomic and the hydrogen bombs. Similar high accomplishments in the humanities, the social sciences, the professions, commerce, and industry by Hungarians of Jewish origin have been the subject of much academic scrutiny of a kind that is succinctly expressed in the title of a highly intriguing and illuminating book by William O. McCagg Jr., *Jewish Nobles and Geniuses in Modern Hungary.*

WHETHER TIVADAR SCHWARTZ of Nyiregyhaza as a young man might have qualified as one such potential "Jewish genius" is moot, but certainly he was very bright and gifted, showing both promise and ambition. His father, having moved the family and his business from rural hamlet to regional center, realized his eldest son's capabilities and singled him out to receive a university education. He was even willing to invest the tuition and boarding fees to send Tivadar to Sarospatak, a prestigious and elitist private boarding school that had been founded by Protestant churchmen in 1698. From Sarospatak, Tivadar went on to study law at the university in Cluj, in what was then Hungarian Transylvania. He traveled in Central Europe and spent some time auditing courses at Heidelberg. By all family accounts he was hard-working and eager to make a notable career.

Then in 1914, Gavrilo Princip, a Serbian nationalist terrorist, shot and killed the Austrian archduke Franz Ferdinand in Sarajevo. By August all the European powers were at war, and very shortly thereafter Tivadar, who was twenty years old and still in university, enlisted in the Austro-Hungarian army. He would later write that he did not take up arms in any spasm of patriotism but rather because of his belief that the war would prove to be a worthwhile adventure and that he felt he had better hurry because it would probably end quickly. It is also likely he calculated that volunteering would prove advantageous for his future legal career. As things turned out, he was wrong in all his assumptions.

He was commissioned as the lowest ranking of officers. At first, in the trenches on the eastern front, he had time to read law books and even supplied a few dispatches for Hungary's major news agency. He occasionally returned home on leave, and on one of these visits he called upon the family of his father's second cousin, Mor Szucz, in Budapest. It was not a particularly memorable visit for him, but the Szuczes' daughter, Erzebet, had reason to remember it. After Tivadar left she claimed she had fallen in love with him. He presumably wore his uniform. She was then eleven years old.

At the time, Mor Szucz was on his own way to fortune. He had been born in a small hamlet in what his daughter would later describe for her sons as a hut with an earthen floor. His own father had been a poor man, whose original family name, also Schwartz, had been changed to reflect what he did for a living. In Hungarian, *szucz* means "furrier," but Erzebet in her eighty-second year carefully explained that her grandfather had never sewn fur coats of precious skins for rich customers. Instead his craft was to make the crude sheepskin jackets that peasants and country people wore in the Carpathian regions. His son Mor, she said, had left his birthplace at thirteen for Budapest, where he worked first as a stock clerk and then for many years as a salesman in shops that sold fabrics. Erzebet recalled how, as his jobs improved, the family had moved from an apartment where they shared a hall toilet with other tenants to one in which they had their own bathroom. But around the time that Tivadar was heading for war, Szucz was making a much greater leap to prosperity. Using money he had received as an inheritance from an older brother, he formed a partnership with a wealthy merchant named Markus to establish a fabric shop, Markus and Szucz, on Petofi Street, the most fashionable thoroughfare of then booming Budapest. The store sold silk and other fabrics that well-to-do women bought to have their dresses made. It was to become quite well known, the most prestigious such store in the city, and provided both partners with great profits for quite a long time.

Indeed, Markus and Szucz may well have been the prototype for the store that was the setting of the 1940 Ernst Lubitsch film comedy, *The Shop around the Corner*, which stars Jimmy Stewart and Margaret Sullavan. Not only was the shop in the film set on a fashionable street in Budapest, but the storyline, by Hungarian Nikolaus Laszlo, used a comic subplot that seemed to elaborate on the at times tense and troubled relationship of the partners.

By the end of 1914, Tivadar had other things on his mind than his father's second cousin's daughter, who thought she loved him. War had become painfully less boring. The tsar's troops had crossed the Carpathians to advance within 125 miles of Budapest. Many years later, when Tivadar told his sons about combat, he pointedly played down the glory, tempering bravado with mockery. In one such story that George Soros recalls, his father told him how as a commander of a small unit he once asked for volunteers for a dangerous mission. Many years later, after the Second World War, when Tivadar wrote his memoir, which dealt mostly with the period when the Nazis were energetically seeking out and deporting Jews to death camps, he parenthetically included the battlefield story that George vividly remembered. With a blend of cynical realism and lofty idealism that is often heard in George Soros's own pronouncements, Tivadar described the incident in this way:

> Then there was the occasion when, as commander of a small
> stretch of the front, I was ordered to send a soldier over the top

to find out what the enemy was doing. In my opinion the order was stupid: we were within spitting distance of the Russians and nothing new could be discovered on the ground. But as a soldier I knew that an order was an order. I read my instructions to my men.

"Who wants to volunteer?"

A tall thin soldier stepped forward. We exchanged a few words.

"You can't go," I said decisively.

"Why not?" he asked in fearful surprise.

"Because you're afraid. I can see that you are trembling."

He could hardly deny it.

"But, sir, for God's sake let me go. I'm only a lady's dressmaker, but I want to be an artist. I am good at drawing. I can't stand the roughness and brutality of an ordinary soldier's life. If my mission succeeds, I'm sure to be promoted, right? So give me a chance."

I have a soft heart. I let him go.

He got down on his belly and crawled forward. He had covered no more than five or six yards when, bam!, he was hit by a bullet and lay still.

"Do I have a volunteer to bring our comrade back?"

An uneasy silence. No one volunteered.

"Do you expect *me* to do it?"

Silly question. No reply. In seconds I would have to decide. It dawned on me rather too late that it's better to give orders to one's men, rather than asking them questions. But now it was too late for an order. I had to do something. I quickly got down on my belly and crawled toward my wounded comrade. It took me only a few minutes to drag him back to our trenches, but by that time he was dead of a bullet to the head.

Tivadar included the vignette as a flashback setting the stage for his actions as a fifty-year-old man in a Budapest invaded by Nazis. He included it in the manuscript that in 1965 was published as one of a series of Esperanto books printed in the Canary Islands. With the help of Paul and George Soros this volume was translated into English by Humphrey Tonkin, an Esperanto scholar. George Soros has read his father's work, but he is sure that when his father first told him the story in 1937 he included two elements that were not in the written account. His father said he had received some minor decoration for the act, and he had also included a punch line expressing the lesson he assumed his father was trying to get across: "He told me that medal or not, he learned he would never do something so foolish again."

Tivadar told that story to George in Budapest, at the indoor swimming pool on Margaret Island, where George would meet him almost daily after school. It was at the swimming pool where Tivadar, using the ceramic wall tiles to depict battlefield positions, described how some five months into the war, the Russians had overrun Austro-Hungarian positions and taken him prisoner along with thousands of disarmed Czechs, Slovaks, Croats, Germans, and Magyars. Along with these men, he was shunted from one slow-moving train to another and slowly transported five thousand miles across the entire width of Russia to a prison camp near Khabarovsk, three hundred miles north of Vladivostok and forty miles east of Russia's border with Manchuria.

When he first arrived at the camp, which would at times hold as many as twenty thousand prisoners, it was administered by officers of a tsarist Russia that was fighting as an ally of Britain and France. In 1917, the Russian Revolution flared, effectively taking Russia out of the world war that was dragging on so far away from the prison camp. But even after Tivadar's captors withdrew to contend with revolution and civil war, little changed for the captured lieutenant, who had so avidly hoped to return from a quick war to participate in the boom and progress of the still new century. Instead he was ending his second year in the camp he would refer to as "that unhappy graveyard," sharing a densely crowded barrack with more than seventy men, many of them sick.

More sad ironies, more unforeseeable consequences were yet to come. In 1918, the armistice ended the war. Now it was not only tsarist Russia, which had taken him prisoner, that ceased to exist; Austro-Hungary, for which he had fought, also disappeared from the political map of Europe. And still he remained a prisoner. To the west of the camp a Russian civil war was being fought by Reds and Whites, and the Great Powers had intervened in the chaos. At first the Russian administration of the camp was replaced by Americans, part of a perfunctory expeditionary force. When the Americans pulled out, Japanese took their place. Through it all, Tivadar looked for ways to keep busy. At one point he put out a camp newspaper called *The Plank*, which was hand-written in Hungarian and posted on a wooden board in the central area—hence the name. He and his associates would stand behind the fence and listen to the comments their articles evoked. He studied Russian, and he learned from a fellow prisoner how to be a locksmith.

He also learned lifelong lessons about the cost of ambition, and acquired what he later claimed was a tendency to laziness, which George Soros has spoken of as his father's weakness. In the second of his published memoirs Tivadar wrote:

> Over the years, I tried to justify my natural laziness with a philosophy that was especially developed for the purpose: it doesn't pay to be prominent. You become identified with the ideas or opinions you hold and, if those ideas are attacked, you have to sacrifice either the opinions or yourself. As I had no wish to become a martyr I preferred to stay in the background. I used to tell my wife how as a prisoner of war in Siberia in World War I, I had led a campaign to improve living conditions in the camp. When our effort was successful, the major who was in charge of the camp offered me an official position as the "Prisoners' Representative." It carried with it various small privileges and represented the highest position a prisoner of war could attain.
>
> I refused because I felt the offer was a bribe.
>
> Shortly afterwards there was a new wave of agitation which broke into violence and the Prisoners' Representative was executed as an example to the men.

The story, like many of the cautionary tales Tivadar would tell his sons, fused pragmatism and honor. He had, as a matter of ethical conduct, rejected what he recognized to be a bribe. But it was the shunning of prominence, the abdication of ambition, that assured him of the ultimate reward: survival. Once more, virtues like bravery, honor, and compassion were not really scorned, but they were put into the context of a life that would inevitably be challenged by unpredictable events. In much of his writing Tivadar emerges as a man constantly learning about life's chaotic dynamism. In these discoveries he establishes his personality, and if he becomes a hero at all, he is a hero in spite of himself.

His involvement with Esperanto also dated from the years in the prison camp. It was from fellow inmates that he learned the synthetic language that Ludwik Zamenhof, a Jewish physician, had devised during the 1880s in Warsaw by grafting a vocabulary adapted from Romance, Slavic, and Germanic roots onto a logically consistent grammar. Esperanto embodied and reflected the internationalism, anti-sectarianism and cosmopolitanism that Tivadar valued. It was this general outlook that George Soros would reflect in his own passion for "open societies," though without his father's enthusiasm for linguistic reform. At one time, however, George could read and speak the language, and Esperanto would play a small but significant role in his own flight from Communist Hungary.

Esperanto became more than a hobby for Tivadar. When he eventually made his way arduously into western Siberia, he remained long enough in the city of Irkutsk to help establish an Esperanto club there. And when Tivadar died in New York on February 23, 1968, he was eulogized at his funeral at the Ethical Culture Society by several Esperantists, one of whom declared that "instead of egotism, nationalism, and chauvinism, he had thought of universal man."

Beyond the ideals that Esperanto symbolized for Tivadar, it also served him as a practical tool for business and a focal point of his social life. When after his long trek westward across war-torn Russia he managed finally to return to Hungary, he established an Esperanto magazine, *Literatura Mondo*. In its June 1923 issue there appeared a long article he wrote called "Crusoes in Siberia." This account centered on the spring and summer months of 1920, after he had finally walked away from the camp to embark on a painful and adventurous journey home.

Appearing three years after the events it described, the article blends a melancholy tone with often caustic and ironic commentary. It was a "Robinsonade," one of those long, fashionable, and entertaining tales of travails and persistence inspired by Daniel Defoe's classic. But there was another more prophetic element as well. "My aim is simple," wrote Tivadar, "to provide a remembrance of human pain and suffering, experienced in this twentieth century, the so-called century of humanity." While much of Tivadar's writing foreshadowed the more horrifying literary testimony that would emerge from the century's gulags and death camps, he often resorted to humor and self-mockery to describe his westward trek through the taiga and forests. He portrayed his fellow wanderers and those they met along the way—Cossack brigands, reindeer herders, goldminers, partisans, renegades, and deserters—in generally compassionate terms. They were more or less all victims of the same sort of unforeseen and unforeseeable consequences that had disordered his own plans.

He had finally left the camp on March 3, 1920. With twenty others Tivadar made his way by train, raft, foot, mule, and pony. There were many pauses and detours as he and the others built bridges and rafted down rivers in the wrong direction. At some stops they mined for gold, or lay low while the battling of White and Red militias prevented their own slow advance.

After nine months, Tivadar finally reached Moscow, but as he sought to complete his journey home and have himself repatriated, he was once again thwarted by the vicissitudes of global politics. In 1919, Hungarian Communists, led by Béla Kun, had taken power in Hungary, installing a Soviet-style government and imposing a period of Red Terror. But now the Hungarian Communists had been routed and replaced by the regency of Miklosi Horthy, a right-wing admiral who rode to power on a white horse.

Now it was the ousted Communists and those thought to be their sympathizers who were the targets of a retaliatory White Terror. While Tivadar had no fondness for either side, or any great knowledge of what had happened in Budapest in his absence, his journey homeward was stalled because no Soviet bureaucrat would issue papers to a former Hungarian officer seeking to return to a land considered to be in the throes of an anti-Communist campaign. Ultimately, Tivadar devised yet one more ploy: he would become Austrian. He spoke German very well, and he found a guide book to the city of Linz, memorizing its streetplan well enough to claim it as his hometown in any interrogation. He was placed on a train to Vienna and from there he had no trouble finding his way home. Two days before Christmas in 1920, after an absence of almost seven years, he was back in Budapest.

CHAPTER 2

FAMILY VALUES

SOMETIME AFTER Tivadar returned, he and Erzebet became lovers. He was completing the exams he needed to pass to qualify as a lawyer and she was then studying languages, hoping to become a teacher of French and German. But, as she would recall, "instead of going to school I went to his apartment, and that is how I started, how I tasted life with him." In 1924 they married. She was twenty-two years old and he was thirty-two. By this time, the ambition that had propelled him through school had slackened. The years on the battlefield and in the prison camp had diminished his yearning for conventional success and his taste for work. As his widow would later recall, "He was just looking for harmony, for peace, morality, just to earn enough for a good life with no high pretensions."

As for her own views at the time, they were considerably more materialistic. "I was still a young girl who had been brought up in affluence. I had a normal bourgeois upbringing and it took me a while until I accepted his morality. As a young girl I cared a good deal about the opinion of other people." From the start, they traveled often, going on hiking and skiing holidays in the Alps. When Markus, her father's partner, gave them a generous wedding gift of money, earmarking it for a Persian rug, Tivadar spent it on a honeymoon trip to Italy. She spent many hours looking at paintings, particularly the Giottos, and Tivadar lectured her, urging her to stop paying so much attention to so many paintings as if she were a schoolgirl preparing a term paper. She remembered that he had instructed her, "Stop where you have a strong liking but don't go page by page." In Florence the newlyweds received a telegram from Erzebet's mother asking them to come home because Mor Szucz had become very sick.

The sickness, it turned out, was paranoid schizophrenia. It had surfaced violently one night when Szucz tried to strangle his wife, screaming at her and calling her a whore. In *The Shop around the Corner*, there is a bit of comic byplay based on an affair that a clerk, played by Joseph Schildkraut, is having with the wife of one of the store owners. In the real store, there was nothing funny about Mr. Szucz's unsupported but obsessive suspicions about his wife and his partner. A man of careful, even meticulous habits, he had developed a fixation on the idea that his wife, a woman whom George Soros remembers as highly conventional, boringly straitlaced and repressed, was romantically involved with Markus, a lifelong bachelor. The schizophrenia, which persisted, manifested itself only in his mania about his wife's alleged infidelities with his partner. When distracted from this subject, or when out of sight of either wife or partner, Szucz remained a soft-spoken, well-mannered man who was an interesting and pleasant conversationalist. Erzebet had always adored him. Toward the end of her life she even said, "He was the one I loved the most, the most in my life, and when he died I had the feeling that I didn't like my children that much, not my husband." Struggling to adapt to the "bohemian" ways of her new husband, Erzebet was staggered by the onset of her father's illness and had no idea how to cope with his idée fixe and the rages it provoked. In one of these, soon after she and her husband came home from their shortened wedding trip, he had waved a pistol and threatened to shoot Markus. For his part, Tivadar had always gotten on well with his father-in-law, and his years in Russia had heightened his interpersonal skills. He quickly took command and set about stabilizing the business and domestic matters.

The situation persisted until Mor Szucz died of cancer in 1935, when George Soros was five years old. Soros remembers the old man as a much more pleasant figure than his grandmother, whom he knew much better, and he does not believe that as a child he was aware of the mental illness, only that his mother was extremely devoted to the old man. In one family photograph, a rosy-cheeked George, probably less than two, is sitting in his grandfather's lap smiling quite happily. However, as an adult, he absorbed the story of Mor's illness with characteristic introspection and has discussed it quite openly. In an interview used in a full-length television profile aired by Britain's Channel 4 in 1994, Soros was asked whether the "messianic" tendencies and fantasies that he has admitted having at various times in his life might be signs of irrationality or madness. The thought clearly amused him and with an eruption of the sort of spontaneous and provocative candor that his public relations advisers have learned to dread, he smilingly agreed. "Absolutely," he said, and then he volunteered: "and in this regard you should know that one of my grandfathers was a paranoid schizophrenic."

As a consequence of Szucz's illness, Tivadar, who was building up an eclectic but not overly time-consuming private legal practice, took over the management of the Szucz family's financial interests, which in addition to the store included real estate holdings in Budapest, Vienna, and Berlin. During the interwar period he would add to these investments, acquiring buildings for himself as well as for his wife's family. For the work he did for his in-laws he received a management fee that provided a significant portion of his income. None of the work seemed very taxing and, according to his sons, Tivadar soon developed a routine in which, aside from court appearances, he devoted only two hours a day, usually between 12 and 2, to office work. It was also around this time that he established *Literatura Mondo*, the Esperanto magazine, in partnership with several poets and writers. Soros thinks there could not have been much money in the venture, and that his father undertook it primarily as a labor of love until he withdrew from its management in 1926. He would travel to Esperanto conventions with Erzebet, frequently combining such trips with skiing or hiking excursions. He was gregarious and friendly and at one point performed in an Esperanto cabaret. Through the magazine he was introduced to a widening circle of artistic free spirits that extended beyond Esperantists to include writers, poets, artists, and architects. Meanwhile, through his law practice, he came to acquire a wide range of acquaintances, from the rich investor with whom he regularly played bridge, to pickpockets, con men, and grifters down on their luck.

In 1926, Erzebet gave birth to her first child, Paul. George was born on August 12, 1930. Both births were difficult, involving particularly long labor and long periods of recovery. Erzebet suffered a pelvic injury as a result of Paul's birth, and after George arrived, she and Tivadar decided there would be no more children, even though Tivadar, from the very start, took to fatherhood as a passionate calling. Erzebet maintained that watching Tivadar with the infant Paul had been one of the great joyous surprises of her life. "I was amazed to find in my husband such a loving father. I was ashamed that as a mother I didn't have this motherly feeling that he had; he slept with his child in his arms and I really, honestly, never saw a man love a baby so much." It was the same when George came along, and the tactile closeness between father and sons extended beyond infancy.

George remembers that even when he was already going to school, he would begin his day by running into his father's bed.

"It was Tivadar's art that he would always be on their level," recalled Erzebet, expressing admiration for the way her husband had raised his sons and for the gentle manner in which he educated her in his views of childrearing. She recalled how when Paul was born, she had been reluctant to have the boy circumcised as Jewish custom required. "I thought it was a stigma. I really didn't mean to break with Jewishness." She explained that she thought circumcision was cruel and potentially traumatizing and that she then felt religions should emphasize moral teachings rather than rituals. At that time, her reservations were not primarily based on a fear that her children might seriously suffer for being Jews. Though anti-Semitism had been gaining, no one in Hungary or anywhere else could have foreseen in 1926 or 1930 that in slightly more than a decade, the absence of a foreskin would be enough to condemn boys and men to death, or that Tivadar, who had persuaded her to follow tradition, would then obtain forged certificates attesting that his sons had been circumcised for medical reasons, because of a condition known as phymosis.

George Soros does not have any particular memories of his toddler years. His mother claimed that from infancy Paul was stubborn and George was far more tractable. "George," she recalled in her dictated reminiscences, "was more round faced and happier. He got very much love from me because it was easy to love him. He was not resisting or stubborn like Paul. So later on, Paul was his father's favorite and George was mine in the family, which didn't mean that we had special treatments for them, but when, for example we were making a boat trip, George would be sitting next to me, leaning on me, and Paul was next to his father." In his seventh decade, George saw the relationship somewhat differently, saying that there had always been tension between Paul and his mother and so Paul naturally sat with his father and that he consequently ended up next to his mother on the boat. But George never felt shortchanged by his father. "I didn't feel any lack of love from my father. I did not feel that I was in any way excluded. I felt very close to him physically."

Paul drew pictures from an early age and skied by the time he was four; George also skied as a very young child, but in his case the achievement drew less comment since his brother had already established the standard for precociousness. Paul would sometimes use his four-year age advantage to pummel his younger brother, but George was not rendered docile. Istvan Eorsi, a Hungarian playwright and director, distinctly remembers his first meeting with George in a playground sandbox near the Danube in

1935. George approached him and without any explanation punched him in the mouth, knocking out two baby teeth. Soros remembers this event pretty much the same way. A friendship of sorts developed between the two through elementary and high school, and many decades later, years after Eorsi had served a five-year prison term for his role in the Hungarian uprising of 1956, Soros brought Eorsi to the United States on a traveling scholarship. George remembers that at the time he knocked out Eorsi's teeth he also developed a reputation for lifting girls' dresses, not out of sexual curiosity, which he says he did not have, but to make the girls shriek.

In 1936, the lives of the Schwartz family changed significantly in three ways. For one thing they moved. After the death of Mor Szucz in 1935, Erzebet's mother was able to return to her six-room apartment on Esku Square, on the Pest side of the Danube, which she had abandoned when Mor went mad. Tivadar then moved his wife and two children to a third-floor apartment at Kossuth Square, facing the Hungarian Parliament building, which the historian John Lukacs has aptly described as "an eclectic combination of Magyar-medieval, French-Renaissance, Westminsterian neo-Gothic, with a neobaroque ground plan." The windows in the new apartment looked out at the fanciful massive gray building, which was built in 1902, when more was still definitely more. It was at that time the largest parliament building in the world, and the view it presented with the Danube behind it was impressive enough to make the new Soros home and neighborhood very desirable. The apartment itself was large enough to accommodate the family and Tivadar's office. There was one maid to do the cooking and another to help with the children. George remembers that there was an elevator with facing mirrors whose reverberating images exposed him to the notion of infinity before he could fully grasp it.

The second big change, which occurred when George was six, was the family's acquisition of a summer house on Lupa Island, a narrow sliver of land in the Danube that lay just beyond the capital's northern limits. The house was designed in Bauhaus style by George Farkas, the architect husband of Erzebet's sister, Clara. Originally the two families had intended to share it, though it was quite small, but a family argument upset that plan. Farkas had come upon Tivadar as he strolled along Budapest's riverside promenade arm in arm with a handsome woman. According to Erzebet's recollections, Farkas then approached his mother-in-law and denounced Tivadar as untrustworthy and fickle. In her oral history, Erzebet quoted Farkas as having said, "Mother, you should not place unlimited faith in Tivadar. He will run after beautiful women and walk with them on the Danube quay and he will leave the whole family and elope with one of them." Erzebet went on to say that her mother, who had been grateful for the way that Tivadar looked after the family when her husband lost his equilibrium, told Tivadar about what Farkas had told her.

Angered, Tivadar paid for the entire house on the island. "So," Erzebet continued, "we divided, we separated and we never invited them and they didn't invite us." The Farkases left Hungary in 1938, first for England and then, in 1940, for the United States. They settled in Miami. As for Tivadar's womanizing, it remained an aspect of the marriage, at times raising the tensions between husband and wife considerably but never quite fracturing the family bond.

George remembers one occasion when his mother, clearly upset about one of Tivadar's flirtations, left the summer place and set off by herself in a rowboat, sitting alone and drifting in the river's flow. In her memoir, she spoke of the trips her husband liked to take on his own, and she noted how George, when he was eight, had once told their neighbors that his father was "a married bachelor." In her recollections, dictated when she had long been a widow, Erzebet noted, "I didn't mind it, honestly. It was a pause, I had time to recover myself. His pace was always faster than mine. Later on I used to say I was running after him like a doggy on a leash, but I liked to do it so I'm not complaining. Staying home for me was a time to recover and for him it was a time of adventures."

But for George, the incident with the rowboat was painful enough that he remembered half a century later how angry it had made him. "I went after her and brought her back. And I expressed it at the time to my parents, saying I loved them both—but I really disapproved of my father for the way he treated my mother. You see, that was the one thing I held against him. There were big fights between them. And there was sexual tension, because my father was a man-about-town, and loved to flirt with other women. You see, the way I saw it was that my father gave in to my mother's love. He kind of compromised himself by actually marrying her. You know, he was really a free spirit, and then he wasn't. In actual fact, it was a great boon to him, because she gave him the financial base on which to carry on his *lebenkunstler* life."

The house at Lupa was to become extremely important. For eight years after the family acquired it, they moved there every spring and returned in the fall. There was a fireman's pole outside the boys' window that they slid down to the river's edge in the morning, thus avoiding the stairs in an area where their parents slept. After learning the river's tricky currents at an early age they were allowed to swim without supervision, a sight that often alarmed strangers in passing boats. The boys had their own rowboat, and they learned to play tennis on the courts across the path from their house. Tivadar hired a professional coach for Paul and George, who was left-handed in all things but writing.

The island contained the summer homes of about forty families, of whom about half were Jewish. The Lupa Jews tended to be cosmopolitan and assimilated, and their Gentile neighbors were also typically liberal. Though the families did not see much of each other during the colder months, the community they established in the warm months was strongly cohesive. Tivadar had taught his boys and the other Lupa children to greet each other with their own islanders' salute, the cry of "Paaapuuuaa!" They would also shout "Paaapuuuaa" when they were on the mainland shore and wanted someone on Lupa to row over and pick them up. In Erzebet's recollections, Tivadar was one of the boys of Lupa, playing with the children, telling and listening to stories and exchanging the shouted greetings. "He was like a child, another one of my children," she said several times in her oral history. "My sons and the other children on the island didn't feel the difference in age and they were all on very, very friendly terms."

One of Tivadar's pastimes was the telling of an ongoing story, a sort of serial soap opera called "Amosarega" after a miraculous machine that took its name from the beginning of the words for "airplane," "motorcycle," "car," and "garage," since the device could be commanded to turn into any of these. Tivadar would, for example, inform the boys that he had received a call from Mahatma Gandhi in India who, it seemed, needed their help. In that case, as he told it, he and the brothers first flew to Central Asia and then, after turning Amosarega into a car, drove over the Hindu Kush, talking their way out of difficulties among the fierce Pathans as they headed toward their rendezvous with Gandhi. The fanciful Amosarega tales would be spun in the evening. They were very different from Tivadar's descriptions of his experiences in Russia, which he would tell George after school at the swimming pool.

According to George, none of the stories were sermons. There was obviously moral content but it was conveyed subtly and indirectly. He says he never had the sense that his father was instructing him to emulate him, or to implant any guidelines or beliefs. The stories, he says, were not vain. "He was very modest, not a show-off at all, and he was not trying to impress me." George says the accounts never left him with the feeling that he would have to match his father's adventures, nor was he intimidated by his father's exploits, fearful that he might never be capable of such things. "No, I never felt that. On the contrary I even felt that I could do better than my father. At the time I had this somewhat blind confidence in myself." He paused and added, "But I think my own children have that feeling, you know, that I convey to them that they couldn't do all the things that I have done."

While Tivadar spent much time talking with his sons, he consciously avoided steering them into any particular career. "He never suggested a profession for us. Though it was clear that we were not destined for money-making. I mean, what we got from him was that money is a means to an end and is not to be taken that seriously. That's not what life is about, you know." George offered these recollections with eyes and facial expression reflecting an amused awareness of the ironies that time had wrought.

"As for his stories, it was just communication," said Soros, acknowledging, though, that they have had a lifelong impact. "I really grew up having vicariously lived through his experiences of Russia. So much so that when so many years later I dealt with Russia as a philanthropist and an investor, I felt very much at home."

If Tivadar shied away from dictating thoughts and beliefs, there were values and traits that he wanted his sons to acquire, the most notable being self-confidence and independence. And such things, he felt, were best implanted by indirection. "My father was not didactic at all," George explained. "I mean, his way of guiding us was so indirect that I had no idea he was doing it, you see? And yet he was there." Once, when George was eleven years old, his father asked that they meet at a ski resort and George, taking his skis, set off first by bus and then by train on a journey of four or five hours. He arrived feeling extremely proud of himself for making the trip on his own and was warmly congratulated by his father for the resourcefulness and maturity he had shown. It was not until many years later that he learned that his father had paid a streetwise acquaintance to follow his son and make sure that all went well.

This was Tivadar's basic educational approach: to encourage confidence and curiosity, to stimulate initiative, and to help his sons prepare for inevitable unanticipated challenges by developing such survival skills as good judgment, athletic ability, and a sense of responsibility. "It is clear that it was a deliberate policy on his part to bring us up this way, and he went to considerable trouble to do it," said George, adding that it was precisely this upbringing by his father that more than anything else contributed to his later success.

Paul agrees, adding that his father's pedagogical philosophy included some idiosyncratic elements. When, for example, it was time for Paul to go to elementary school, Tivadar sought out the worst school he could find for his firstborn son. This reflected Tivadar's prison camp experience, which taught him the importance of getting along with all sorts of people in stressful conditions. He concluded that in the mid-1930s even the worst elementary school in the city would teach Paul to read and do basic mathematics while at the same time exposing him to the greatest variety of classmates. George, who went to a different elementary school, said that he was not aware of this particular idea, but it struck him as exactly the kind of notion that his father would have conceived.

George remembers quite clearly the emphasis on sport and fresh air, which his father believed would increase his sons' height. Having sons taller than he was an important objective. A second theory involved sex education, or rather the lack of it. Tivadar, said George, believed in keeping his sons in the dark for as long as possible, in the belief that sustained ignorance in this regard would encourage growth in other spheres. In his memoir of the Nazi period, Tivadar described how a few years earlier Paul had approached his mother and asked, "Mother, what does the father do to make the baby?"

Tivadar wrote that his wife directed the boy to him, and Tivadar rose to the occasion.

> "Have you studied the Patriarchs in your religious education," I asked.
>
> "Yes."
>
> "Well then, you know that Abraham begat Isaac, Isaac begat Esau, and Jacob begat Joseph. This begetting is the father's part. Get it?"
>
> "Yes," he said and that was that.

But of all the changes the family experienced in 1936, the most momentous and lasting was the replacement of Schwartz with Soros as the family name. Even though George was then only six, he remembers how his father had involved the entire family in searching for a new name, bringing home a big book with thousands of possibilities and debating various choices at the dinner table. The change was undertaken, significantly, just as George was going to school for the first time and Paul was entering gymnasium, the upper school. And while it would be another two years before Hungary passed the first of several laws restricting Jews in their activities, the policies of the Nazis in Germany were ominous. Two years earlier, the Nazis had engineered the murder of Engelbert Dollfuss, the chancellor of Austria. And that summer the Olympics were taking place in Nuremberg under the sign of the swastika. Erzebet had long wanted to change their name, fearing that it might stigmatize her sons as Jews, but also as something less than Hungarian. Paradoxically, the name Schwartz could indicate either a German or Jewish identity.

But why Soros?

The name is not common in Hungary, and George has never heard of anyone outside the family who bears it. His father, however, found it suitable and meaningful. George recalled that his father "liked the idea that it was a palindrome, and he liked the idea that it was a name he thought could be pronounced the same way in every language." This proved to be an error since according to Magyar phonics the name should be pronounced "Shorosh." Now, years after George has made the name famous while living in England and America, he has become accustomed to being addressed as Soros, with *ess* sounds at both ends and more or less rhyming with "morose." George also noted that his father liked the idea that "the word had a meaning and he liked the meaning that it had."

According to Magyar-English dictionaries, *soros* means "the one who is next in line," in the sense of the designated successor, or the duty officer on call to take up responsibilities. Clearly, by choosing this designation Tivadar was making an emphatic statement. But who was it that "was next in line," who, in his estimation, was standing in the wings, waiting to come into his own? Given his repeated references to his own lapsed ambitions he surely was not referring to himself, a man who limited his work to a few hours a day. Once George, as a child, drew a laugh from family friends when he told them that unlike other fathers Tivadar "did not have a real job but just made money." If he saw himself as the others did, and there is every sign that he did, then he knew that his own turn had come and gone while he was in detention. So it must have been his sons, the only other males named Soros, whom he had in mind. The name had yet another meaning of which Tivadar must have been aware. *Soros* is also a word in Esperanto—the future tense of the verb "to soar."

"Obviously he was projecting on us," said George. "You could see it in the way he pushed my brother in sports. He remembered his ambitions as a young man. He felt he was an old man, having lived through the war and so on, so he wanted us as young men to have his ambition as it had been. He definitely programmed us, and pushed us and spent a lot of effort. I mean, all the effort that didn't go into his own achievements or career went into the education of his children."

There exists one contemporary record of Tivadar's subtle guidance of George, which has the further significance of also being the first account of George as a philanthropist. It is an article published on December 23,

1939, in a Budapest newspaper called *8 Orai ujsag*, or *8 o'Clock News*. Bearing the headline "George Soros Brings a Donation," it recounted his response to the paper's donation appeal for the Finns who were resisting an invasion by Soviet forces. Finland, like Hungary, is a small country, and linguistically Finnish and Magyar are distantly related. It is not unlikely that Tivadar, who had imaginatively invoked Amosarega to help Mahatma Gandhi, may have told his son about the valor of the Finns and their ski troops. In any case, this is what the newspaper reported:

> A guest arrives in our editorial office. He enters the room and skillfully shuts the door behind him. Standing on tiptoes, he reaches up to the high doorknob and turns it comfortably. Hatless but with a leather bag flung over his shoulders, our smiling guest is a ray of sunshine in the office.
>
> "My name is George Soros," he says, clicking his heels.
>
> We admit that it is not every day that we have dealings with young gentlemen from the fourth grade of elementary school.
>
> "I just dropped in after school," says George and slides open the wooden dual-compartment pencil case clutched in his palm. From an assortment of erasers and pen wipers he digs out two pieces of paper the size of a standard postage stamp. Two tiny hands start unfolding the pieces and place two ten-pengo notes on the counter. "There you go!"
>
> "George," I address him sternly. "What is this supposed to mean? What do you intend to do with all this money?"
>
> With his angelically mischievous blue eyes sparkling, he turns to me. "I brought this money for the Finnish people. There is a war in Finland at the moment, Daddy told me."
>
> I begin to cross-examine George in the sternest fashion. Compliantly and withstanding the interrogations of an adult, George tells me the money belongs to him. No, oh, no, he was not given it by Daddy, nor by Mummy. The money is his. He earned it! How? Well, back in the summer, every summer, he is the editor-in-chief, publisher, and news vendor of a newspaper. His family always spends their summer holidays on Lupa Island and that is when George publishes his paper, "The Lupa News." It is mostly adults who buy the paper.
>
> This is his way of earning money and he has only just decided to take his Christmas savings out of his plaster pear-shaped piggy bank. The plaster powder stuck to the crumbled worn-out banknotes bore evidence to George's method of sav-

ing. He smashed the piggy bank open and brought the money in
for the Finns.

George Soros, the fourth grader who had five B's in his last
school report, our ever-smiling rosy red-cheeked guest, the
editor-in-chief of "The Lupa News," the little Hungarian with
a heart of gold, seems relieved only when I take his money. He
swiftly slides his pencil case shut, clicks his heels. "Good day,
sir," he says and steps out of the room. All of a sudden, the
room becomes empty. Only our hearts are full. This is how it
happened. It was so beautiful there was no need to change or
embellish the story.

Asked about the story, an adult George said, "I don't remember it very
clearly but I think my father probably put me up to it."

CHAPTER 3

WAR

O N MARCH 19, 1944, a Sunday, George Soros, who was then thirteen years old and, briefly, interested in modern art, went to look at
paintings in a museum. On his way home he saw German tanks and German soldiers in front of a police station, and he rushed home to tell his
father about it. But Tivadar had already learned that the Germans had
invaded their Hungarian allies. He had gone for a late breakfast at one of
his regular cafés, where a waiter handed him a newspaper and leaned over
to whisper, "Have you heard? During the night, the Germans took over."

From the war's outset, Horthy's Hungary had been Hitler's ally. Hungarian troops had fought alongside German forces and the country had
shaped its economy to fill the needs of the Reich, providing the Nazis with
armaments. Hungary was an authoritarian, anti-Semitic, discriminatory,
and pro-Nazi state, but its rulers were not Nazis. There had been periodic
rumors during the previous four years that the Germans would occupy the
country. Though the governments appointed by Horthy did draw up discriminatory laws and seize Jewish property, the Germans were displeased
there had been no massive roundups of Hungary's Jews or any steady
deportations to concentration camps similar to those that were taking
place in other lands controlled by the Nazis and their puppets.

Even before the war, the Soros family wondered what Hitler's rise to
power might mean for European Jews beyond Germany's borders. In
1938, soon after Austria was incorporated into Germany in the Anschluss,
a Jewish lawyer came to Budapest from Vienna and asked Tivadar for
money to help him get his family to the West. When Tivadar offered a

modest contribution, his colleague told him, "You give as if the money were still yours." Tivadar realized that his visitor was telling him that it was only a matter of time before Hungary's Jews were as vulnerable as those of Austria.

Some months after this episode the Soros family went on a skiing vacation to Garmisch-Partenkirchen in southern Bavaria, where for the first time they saw signs at restaurants saying "No Jews Allowed." Erzebet was profoundly shocked and wanted to leave, but Tivadar laughed and led her and the children to tables in the posted establishments. He told his wife that the exclusion did not apply to them. "You are a foreigner, it's not for you." Erzebet, however, could not stop worrying and soon began to suffer ulcer attacks.

Later in 1939, Tivadar traveled to the United States to negotiate a deal for a Czech client. According to Paul, he was also seeking to conclude a sale of a large apartment complex in Berlin that his mother-in-law had inherited from her husband. As it turned out, his mother-in-law rejected the sale terms as too low; the building would soon be seized by the Nazis as Jewish property. On the way back from America, Tivadar arranged to meet his wife and sons in Geneva. Despite the bravado he had shown in the face of the "No Jews Allowed" signs, he was sufficiently apprehensive to have obtained United States visas for his wife and sons. He felt that Erzebet and the boys should stay for now in neutral Switzerland, but if and when the situation in Europe deteriorated they should leave for the United States. As for himself, he would return to Budapest to conduct his business.

In Geneva, Erzebet made it very clear that she wanted no part of this plan, which years later George learned had an ulterior motive. "My father had an intense love affair in Budapest, so he arranged for us to go to America, with my mother. My mother refused to be parted from him. It may have been a situation in which she knew and did not know, or did not want to know." In any case, despite thickening war clouds and her worsening ulcers, Erzebet refused to leave her husband alone in Budapest. "My mother said, 'No, we are a family, and we must stick together.' "

The life they lived during the first years of war proved to be not very much different than it had been before. The boys continued their studies and sports, Tivadar worked and played as he had, and the entire family made use of the house on Lupa during the warmer months. Paul claims that the most significant difference in those years was that they had to make do with inferior tennis balls. "We could no longer get the Dunlaps from England and instead had to use balls from Spain." He exaggerates, for in fact there were changes that Jewish Hungarians couldn't avoid feeling. In 1938 Hungary passed a law that defined who was and who was not a Jew and limited Jewish participation in the professions to 20 percent. The following year that quota was reduced to 6 percent. By 1941, when George entered Berzsenyi Gymnasium, Jewish pupils were put into separate classes. Paul, who had been going to the Bolyai Gymnasium, had to transfer to a newly formed Jewish school. To conform with yet another law Tivadar was obliged to find an Aryan partner for his law office.

But such changes took place incrementally, and except for Erzebet's continuing ulcer attacks, the family adapted without apparent anxiety. Indeed, as Tivadar explained in his memoir, until the arrival of the Germans in Budapest in 1944 the fears and apprehensions that were first aroused in 1938 had been steadily abating. "Word of mass shootings, slave labor, and the Jewish rebellion in the Warsaw Ghetto became more and more frequent, but we preferred not to believe such things. Untouched directly by such calamities, we felt that we were somehow above them."

Meanwhile, George, an indifferent student ranking consistently toward the top of the lower half of his classes, was fully engaged in playing sports and games, among them Kapital, a cousin of Monopoly. He would also spin amorphous fantasies of great achievements. His lackluster performance in school did not lessen his self-confidence. "Quite honestly I always considered myself exceptional," he said, recalling his adolescence. He did particularly poorly in mathematics, having fallen behind when he missed several weeks of school because of scarlet fever. Tutors were sporadically hired to coach him for his English and French classes. He already spoke and read German quite well and had picked up smatterings of Latin and Esperanto. At the time, his career interests, while vague, tended to involve history or journalism or some form of writing. He read adventure stories, mythology, and Hungarian classics, enjoying the works of Jules Verne and Karl May, the German who wrote about American Indians he had never seen. From grade school on George wrote poems and short stories that his mother saved for many years, one of them an allegory about a group of farm animals in which a donkey named Peaceful ended a war of barnyard beasts.

When he was twelve he began reading a philosophical text that was above his head and that he never finished. "It may have been Aristotle, but the idea that I got from it was this concept that man, who may have been created in God's image, certainly created God in his own image. I thought that was an important idea and I remember thinking about it a great deal." Indeed, it may have been Aristotle who inspired such thinking but it is more likely to have been Tivadar. In *Maskerado*, the elder Soros had included a chapter called "A Little Jewish Philosophy," and in it he wrote how as a young man he had come to the identical momentous conclusion after reading the Koran and the Bhagavad Gita as well as Giovanni Papini's *The Story of Christ* and Martin Buber's *Jewish Legends.*

George's brief period of religious interest occurred during 1942 and 1943. On his own he attended Hebrew classes, where he asked questions about death and afterlife and received what he regards as unsatisfactory answers. Still, the ties to religion were strong enough for him to decide on his own to have a bar mitzvah when he turned thirteen in the fall of 1943. It was a modest event, but on the appointed day in the midst of war he went to a synagogue where he read a section of scripture and passed through the rite of Jewish manhood.

During these years, while the worst horrors remained obscure and distant, Tivadar tried to read between the lines of newspapers and began each day by listening to the radio, mostly the German service of the BBC. He was anticipating and hoping for rapid Allied advances. One report alleged that in 1941 a number of Jews who were unable to prove their Hungarian nationality had been driven eastward into Ukraine, forced into a river, and shot by Nazis. George recalls that this news had been brought to his father by a man who had escaped from the group and made his way back to Budapest. The witness was a professional boxer named Adler whom George knew and who would later teach him to box. The account he had provided almost certainly relates to the seizure of eleven thousand Jews and their execution in Ukraine in 1941 on orders of Nazi SS officers. George was then unaware of the death camps and crematoria and had no pictorial images of Jewish roundups available to him; Adler's testimony remained his most frightening image of war until the German tanks arrived.

The issue of Hungary's Jews was of great importance to the Nazis in Berlin. Within days of their March 19 invasion, Adolf Eichmann, the head of the Gestapo's Jewish section, arrived in Budapest to oversee the destruction of the 750,000 Jews then living in the country. But there were other reasons beyond the Jewish question that had led the Germans to invade and occupy their friendly Hungarian ally.

On the day before the German tanks appeared, Tivadar had heard on the BBC that Russian forces had reached into Romania. The German position on the eastern front had seriously weakened and American bombardment of Germany was intensifying. In this situation, Hungary's strategic importance for the Nazis was increasing. The country was a vital land bridge for military supply lines to German armies in Romania, Yugoslavia,

Bulgaria, Greece, and Albania. The Nazi command was worried that under pressure of Russian advances and American bombardments, Horthy might be tempted to proclaim neutrality or even switch sides. To strengthen his resolve, they summoned him to Austria for an Ides of March meeting with Hitler. And while the Hungarian regent was out of the country, German tanks took up menacing positions in the capital. By the time Horthy's train arrived back in Budapest, the Nazis and their enthusiastic and rabidly anti-Semitic Hungarian supporters from the Arrow Cross movement had gained the upper hand. While Horthy technically remained the country's leader, his autonomy and his bargaining power with his allies had been sharply diminished.

Quite abruptly, the arrival of the German forces on March 19 had changed everything. After the breakfast where the waiter had told him the news, Tivadar walked to the castle where Hungary's old kings had resided and noticed a single German tank parked in an alley. He wrote, "This battered little tank, it seemed, had taken Budapest." That afternoon as guests showed up for the bridge game that the Soroses hosted every Sunday, rumors were exchanged, and in the evening Tivadar listened to the short-wave radio and heard an appeal by President Roosevelt asking the Hungarian people to do what they could to help Jews who now faced death under German occupation. Tivadar called the words "a poignant and human statement, the first touch of humanity I had heard all day."

Then, as he described it, his thoughts turned to practical matters.

> I turned the radio off. My wife and I were alone in the stillness of the night. The children were sleeping and the maid had the day off. The silence was disconcerting. In the past, our comfortable apartment had always seemed a refuge from the turmoil of the outside world, but suddenly it felt more like a trap. It was laid out so poorly! There was only one exit, no fire escape at the back, no secret doors, no underground hiding place. If they were to come in the middle of the night to take us away, where would we hide? I examined the place carefully in a way I had never done before. In the process I made a surprising discovery: there was a double ceiling above the dining room, with a space big enough for all four of us to hide. We could put some boxes in front so we wouldn't be noticed. But the beds would be warm and that would give us away. And what should we do about our maid? Should we take her into our confidence? Or let her go? My wife could hardly imagine life without domestic help. But

even if we let the maid go, there was still the problem of the
superintendent. No, we really could not hide ourselves in the
house.

Tivadar began to think strategically and tactically. From the easygoing
lebenkunstler he quickly reverted to the survival specialist he had been in
Siberia.

George, meanwhile, began working as a courier for the Jewish Council,
which had quickly been established by Eichmann. As in other cities where
the Nazis had set up such organizations, the council was intended as a first
step leading to the identification and registration of Jews, which would be
followed by herding them into ghettos and ultimately by their deportation
to forced labor and death.

Pupils from Jewish classes at certain gymnasiums were sent to the
council offices to work as messengers; George was one of these children.
After his second day he told his father that in the afternoon he had been
sent to carry mimeographed messages to people in several parts of the city.

When his father asked him if had read the messages, George reached
into his pocket and pulled out several slips printed in blue ink. He said he
thought his father should read them before he delivered them the next
morning. It turned out the slips were summonses ordering people to
report at the rabbinical seminary on Rokk Szilard Street. Each addressee
was to bring a blanket and food for two days. Tivadar asked thirteen-year-
old George if he knew what the message meant.

"I can guess," George replied with great seriousness. "They'll be in-
terned."

George remembers the incident in vivid detail. "There were five or six
such notices and my father realized that the names were taken from an
alphabetical list of Jewish lawyers. My father looked at the pieces of paper
and said these people are deporting lawyers. The names were at the front
of the alphabet, starting with A or B, which gave him warning that within
a short period they would get around to S and order him to report. He told
me to deliver the notices, but to tell the people that if they reported they
would be deported."

The next day George followed his father's instructions. "I remember
one man I went to see who told me, 'You know, I have always been a law-
abiding citizen—I haven't done anything wrong—so I have no reason to
disobey this order, and I am sure that nothing terrible can happen to me.'
And when I went back and told my father about it, we had another conversation about rules, what rules you obey, and what rules you break."

Years after the war, the Budapest bar association put up a plaque in its offices bearing the names of more than six hundred Jewish lawyers who perished after responding to the summonses of 1944. After George delivered his handful of messages Tivadar ordered him to stop working at the council.

George had liked the excitement of being a courier but he obeyed his father without complaint. Tivadar had taken command. "From the very beginning, my father was in charge," said George. "When the Germans came, almost immediately he called all of us together and he said something like this: All the normal rules are suspended. This is an emergency. If we remain law-abiding citizens and continue our current existence, we are going to perish. So we have to make alternative arrangements."

On March 29 a decree was issued calling for all Jews above the age of six to wear a Jewish star on a yellow patch measuring six by four inches. Even though by this time Tivadar was preparing to have the family hide as Gentiles, he decided to see what it felt like to wear the star and to assess the reactions of his fellow citizens. Erzebet sewed on the patches and Tivadar took George on an outing. Tivadar later wrote that at one point in the walk he overheard two pedestrians discussing George; one of them said, "I would have never guessed that blond kid was Jewish." Tivadar recalled that in light of the plans he was making, the remark pleased him. George remembers the day as much more of an adventure than a humiliation. "We went out to reconnoiter, to see what the reaction of people might be. On the streets some people wore stars. Nothing much happened but when we were at a tram stop a man getting off a tram shouted, 'Get out of my way, piglet face.' It was a pejorative expression but my father and I then had a sort of kidding discussion as to who the man had really meant to insult. My father contended that because he had used the term piglet, he must have had me in mind, for if he had been the target the man would have no doubt said 'pig face.' " In his own version of this episode, Tivadar referred to the slur uttered by the man as "son of a pig," and claimed that George had chided him by asking, "If I am the son of a pig, so who is the pig I am supposed to be the son of."

In those spring days that followed, Tivadar met with his friends and associates, many of whom held out hopes for a rapid defeat of Hitler. Some contended that under military pressure the Reich would moderate or even abandon its persecution of Jews. He disagreed. "I concluded that we have nothing to protect us against Hitler's threats; there is nobody we can turn to; we are on our own. We must fight for ourselves. And since we can't stand up to Hitler's fury, we must hide from it."

His own primary obligation would be to provide for the safety and survival of five people: himself, his wife, his two sons, and his mother-in-law. He decided that if he could help others he would, but only if the risks were moderate. The first requirement was to obtain new, Christian identities for his family members. He drew up a long list of friends, acquaintances, former clients, former neighbors, and friends of his sons, weighing who might help. The best, most convincing sort of identification, he realized, would be real documents rather than photostats. He reasoned that the actual person to whom they referred, being a Gentile, had less to fear and thus could rely on copies while the Jew who was passing would need as much authenticity as possible. A number of people expressed sympathy but turned him down. Meanwhile, pressure mounted as the summonses for Jewish lawyers were still being sent out. Moreover, Paul was approaching his eighteenth birthday, when the authorities would almost certainly come to conscript him for the Jewish labor battalions that were providing construction laborers for the army.

Ultimately, he thought of Balazs, the superintendent of the building at No. 3 Esku Square, the building that his mother-in-law owned and where she lived. Several months before the German occupation one of the tenants had made a formal complaint that the building was not being properly heated. Tivadar was summoned to the police along with Balazs. The police magistrate treated Tivadar respectfully but snobbishly sneered at the janitor. Tivadar tried to defend his employee saying he had merely carried out Tividar's quite proper instructions to reduce the heat at night in order to economize on fuel. Though the magistrate continued to insult Balazs, in the end he dismissed the case. As the two men walked away Tivadar said he was sorry he had not been more forceful. "It was kind of you, sir, to defend me," Balazs told him. "It's a shame what they are doing to the Jews. If there's anything I can do for you, you can always count on me."

Several months later Tivadar went to see Balazs, who proved as good as his word. He had a son Paul's age, and he turned over all of the young man's original documents, birth certificates, confirmation records, school documents, and records of inoculations. Tivadar had copies made and returned those to the super's son. Paul would survive the war as Janos Balazs.

The real Janos Balazs was a scout leader, and when he learned of Soros's need for more documents, he came up with the papers of one of his troop members. The papers were for a young man named Sandor Kiss, who had been born into a Hungarian family in Romania and who had made his way to Hungary after the war started. Those papers and the identity they attested to went to George.

As for Erzebet, with the help of some real and some forged documents she was to become Julia Besany, adopting the maiden name of Mrs. Balazs. The birth, school, and baptismal records she received from the super's wife would soon help save her life.

Balazs was to provide one more service for Tivadar. It was while visiting him that Tivadar realized what a useful hideout could be constructed in his mother-in-law's building. As he wrote, "the manager and his family could be trusted. On the ground floor, next to the courtyard and the entrance to the air raid shelter, there was a tiny windowless room." He contacted an old friend, Lajos Kozma, suggesting they hide there together for the duration of the war. Kozma, an architect and an officer in World War I, agreed and with Balazs's help quickly and surreptitiously remodeled the windowless room, providing it with electricity, ventilation, a sink and toilet, and, most important, two exits. He rigged up a simple buzzer system by which Balazs could warn them of unwanted visitors and signal which exit they should use to escape.

By the time the hideout was being finished, Tivadar was already obtaining and distributing documents beyond family members, an enterprise he continued for the remainder of the war. He had established contact with a master forger and would soon locate others who could provide blank forms and rubber stamps and make new paper look old. It is not clear how many clients Tivadar helped during the war, but George thinks he rendered services to about fifty people. Some received documents, others help in finding housing or changing jewelry into foreign currency, although that came later. Some simply sought his advice on survival.

With more and more people coming to him for documents, Tivadar evolved a three-tier system. As he explained it in his memoir: "First I gave the documents completely free to people who were very close to me or in desperate straits. Second, for those people to whom I felt a moral obligation not to make a profit at their expense, I simply asked for my actual expenses, without consideration for the trouble or risk involved. Third, from my wealthy clients I asked for whatever the market would bear. In fact I had no particular limits for this category, or as they say, there was no ceiling on the prices. Sometimes I received as much as twenty times the actual cost." Among his wealthy clients, he numbered Christian nobles with Jewish grandparents, financiers, and Okanyi Schwartz, whose name, he wrote, "means as much in Hungary as Rothschild does in the rest of Europe."

By the time he had moved into the secret room at Esku Square, Tivadar also had a new name and identity. He had become Elek Szabo. The real Szabo, a retired army officer, had once worked for Tivadar's father. He had turned the papers over to Tivadar's brother, who sent them from Nyiregy-haza. The brother had urged Tivadar to use the documentation to return to his hometown, arguing that his chances of survival would be greater in the countryside. In fact, Nyiregyhaza lay in the Carpathian zone, the first of the Hungarian regions where Eichmann ordered ghettoes to be estab-lished. Within a month of the German arrival, the Jews of Nyiregyhaza were herded into specified streets, and two months after that, by June 7, residents of the sub-Carpathian ghettoes, including Tivadar's brother and his family, were put on trains for Auschwitz.

By April 1944, all members of Tivadar's immediate family had new names and identities. They all memorized their names, their new birth dates, their alleged old addresses, the dates of their baptisms and gradua-tions. Now they needed new residences where no one who knew them by their real names could give them away. In his planning, Tivadar had come to the conclusion that for the sake of security it would be best if all family members lived separately. That way, he reasoned, if any one of them was seized, there was less chance that any of the others would be compromised.

Paul, alias Janos Balazs, was the first to go. Tivadar had instructed him to spend his time in libraries and movies and to meet him in the mornings at a little-used swimming pool at the Rudas baths. He took a rucksack and rented a room in a poor part of town. That first night he was so bothered by bedbugs that he checked out and returned home in the morning. The next day, he found a room with fewer vermin and started following Tivadar's instructions. Tivadar placed his mother-in-law in a residential hotel, but the old woman, refusing to see any danger, returned to her home after several weeks. She also did not understand why she needed to use another name or pretend she was not Jewish. Erzebet found a place on the outskirts of the capital with the family of a traveling salesman.

With the help of his barber, Tivadar found a place for George with a man named Baumbach, an employee of the Ministry of Agriculture. Baumbach, who was of German origin, had a Jewish wife and was paying to have her hidden in the countryside. Tivadar paid him to take George into his home, ostensibly as his godson. Tivadar turned over the apartment facing Parliament to his Gentile secretary and moved into the secret room.

Within days of arriving at Baumbach's, George went for a walk into the Buda hills, where lost in a daydream he moved beyond the city limits. When he turned back, he was stopped by Hungarian gendarmes. "I remember it quite clearly," he recalled. "I had just arrived at Baumbach's . . . I had walked too far. I was frightened but nothing happened. It was the first test of my using a false name and I passed it."

While he was living with Baumbach as Sandor Kiss, an event occurred that more than half a century later would become the basis of charges that George Soros, the international financier and billionaire, had somehow collaborated with the Nazi occupiers of his homeland and had exploited his fellow Jews. The issue was raised in a bizarre television profile and interview of Soros aired on the CBS television program *60 Minutes* in December of 1998. In the segment, Steve Kroft, the interviewer, noted with prosecutorial gusto that George's father had "bribed a government official to swear that you were his godson," and added that this survival strategy "carried a heavy price tag." For, he continued, "as hundreds of thousands of Jews were being shipped off to the Nazi death camps, a thirteen-year-old George Soros accompanied his phony godfather on his rounds, confiscating property from the Jews." Visibly dumbfounded by the line of questioning, Soros could only manage to say that he had no role in the seizure of property and was merely a spectator. To underscore Kroft's point, film footage showed masses of Hungarian Jews being led away at gunpoint.

This is what actually happened. Shortly after George went to live with Baumbach, the man was assigned to take inventory on the vast estate of Mor Kornfeld, an extremely wealthy aristocrat of Jewish origin. The Kornfeld family had the wealth, wisdom, and connections to be able to leave some of its belongings behind in exchange for permission to make their way to Lisbon. Baumbach was ordered to go to the Kornfeld estate and inventory the artworks, furnishings, and other property. Rather than leave his "godson" behind in Budapest for three days, he took the boy with him. As Baumbach itemized the material, George walked around the grounds and spent time with Kornfeld's staff. It was his first visit to such a mansion, and the first time he rode a horse. He collaborated with no one and he paid attention to what he understood to be his primary responsibility: making sure that no one doubted that he was Sandor Kiss. Among his practical concerns was to make sure that no one saw him pee.

Shortly after he returned to Budapest, George went out on the balcony of Baumbach's apartment, where he was spotted by an old school friend who lived across the street. The boy called out, "George!" and the two chatted briefly between buildings. The next morning he met his father at the Ruda baths, and told him what had happened. Tivadar decided George would have to move elsewhere. Tivadar said that eventually he would find some place for him, but at that moment, with summer approaching, George should visit his mother at the lake resort where she was then living.

In the months after the family split up, it was Erzebet, the most timid and psychologically vulnerable, who experienced the closest call. She had been so frightened and frail when the Germans arrived that in devising her identity as Julia Besany, Tivadar put together a sheaf of documents that described a forty-year-old unmarried secretary who had worked in Germany and who returned to Budapest suffering from a nervous breakdown brought on by the Allied bombings of Berlin. For a while she lived with the family of a traveling salesman who agreed to take her in for payment, but their apartment was very small and she then moved to an empty cabin on the outskirts of Budapest, which also belonged to the salesman. One day, she spotted two men in uniform with distinctive feathers in their hats, riding bicycles up the forest track. She knew they were looking for her. The men interviewed her on the small porch of the cabin. She gave short answers to their questions and showed them her documents, particularly the references from her fictive former German employers that Tivadar had produced. They asked her to translate the letter and she did. The policemen were impressed, so much so that they read her the denunciation that had led them to look for her. A neighbor of the traveling salesman had labeled her a Jewess and a Communist and someone who was hiding typed scripts. She laughed and asked the men if they wanted to search the house. Eventually, the men told her the denunciation was plainly false and they left saying she would not be bothered.

That confrontation was to have immense significance for Erzebet. For the rest of her life she would talk of it as the moment when she confronted danger with perfect calm and control. "That was really the first test in my life. I was all alone, without husband, without anybody helping me, just God and this funny feeling that I was watching myself." But that night, panic set in and she made her way back to Budapest, where she met Tivadar at the swimming pool the next morning and told him what had happened. He concluded that since the feathered policemen had exonerated her, she would be safest back at the cabin. She answered that she was too nervous to return there. It did not help her state of mind that during this short stay in Budapest, while sitting at a café with her husband, she could see a group of Jews with yellow stars being led down the street. Particularly haunting was the sight of a young woman in the front holding an infant in one arm while her other hand was raised in submission. Tivadar sought to calm his wife. For some days he put her up in a spa, then he suggested that she look up Jutka, a sixteen-year-old girl who had been Paul's girlfriend. Provided with false papers by Tivadar, Jutka had gone to Almadi, a resort on the shore of Balaton, Hungary's largest lake, to find Elsa Brandeisz, who had been her modern dance teacher in Budapest.

In 1998, Brandeisz was a ninety-two-year-old woman living alone in the Hungarian city of Sopran, not far from the Austrian border. On her walls were many photographs, some of them showing her as a leaping, lithe dancer in the twenties and thirties; others were of Erzebet, who in that summer of 1944 became her best friend. Still other photographs showed Jutka, and some were of George Soros, whom she also met that summer. Prominently on display was the picture of the new building that replaced the high school where she taught after the war. The Communists had not let her teach modern dance so she taught gymnastics until she retired. Soros, she said, had provided much of the money to build this new school. But that was when he was already one of the richest men in the world. When she first saw him he was thirteen, though the age on his papers was fifteen.

"He was then Sandor Kiss and one day in July he showed up at Almadi. His mother was already living with us. She came to find Jutka and she took a room and then we met and she came to live with me and my mother and my blind father in our little house. It was so little that Erzebet and I slept head to toe on the couch," she explained.

Her mother had been very religious and thought it her duty to save Jews, whom she regarded as the chosen people of the Bible, so she quite happily invited Erzebet to live in the cottage. Elsa herself was not particularly religious. As a young woman she had been impressed by modern dance, by Isadora Duncan and Martha Graham. Jutka was already staying in an empty summer cabin by a vineyard that Elsa's family found for her. After Erzebet came to them, she learned to cook from Elsa's mother and to sew. She went to nearby farms to trade yarn and cigarettes, which Tivadar sent from Budapest, for milk and cheese. She also happily joined Elsa's mother in Bible studies and mystical pursuits like séances, indulging a passion for Christian-based spirituality that would fascinate her until her death more than four decades later.

George arrived unannounced, with instructions from his father that he was to find a place apart from his mother. He was to pass as her godson, though Elsa said that Erzebet confided the truth to her. He had made the trip to Almadi on his own, sharing the train with men in uniform, any of whom could have detained him if they suspected him of being a Jew. There was tension, but George enjoyed the enterprise and the adventure and was proud of the composure he showed. That first day they had him move into the cabin with Jutka. But before that, Erzebet took George aside and informed him about sex, filling him in on what Tivadar had so steadfastly avoided. George remembers the lecture and remembers also that when she brought him to Jutka's, his mother told the girl, "Be careful, he's just been enlightened about sex and he may be tempted to experiment."

For the next three months George spent his time in a peculiar summer idyll. The Russians were battling from the East. The Germans tightened their hold on Hungary. Jews were being placed into ghettoes and moved into specially designated Jewish houses in Budapest. Because of Eichmann's bureaucratic efficiency, the deportations soared above 350,000. And by shallow Lake Balaton, George Soros spent his days with Jutka and Gabor, a seventeen-year-old boy with a club foot who took care of a rich man's sailboat. Both boys had crushes on the girl, who George guessed might be ill because she could not swim as long as he could. In fact, she had contracted tuberculosis, which would kill her soon after the war ended. George would take walks and go to church with his mother, always addressing her as Julianeni, the "neni" being an honorific for "auntie." They would cross themselves in front of a church until Elsa's mother told them that it was a Lutheran church and only Catholics did that.

At one point George ran a very high fever, but Erzebet made sure that no doctor was called lest anyone notice anatomical proof of her "godson"'s origins. Luckily, after a few days the fever broke.

Erzebet continued to grow bolder. At one point in autumn, after George had returned to Budapest, several German officials settled in town, among them a physician, and Erzebet often spoke with them in her excellent German. One day, as she was waiting in a line to enter a store, an elderly man who had earlier trusted her enough to reveal his Social Democratic views, quietly told her that he needed her help. It seemed a local farmer was married to a Jewish woman who had been denounced. The police were in her house looking for her, but the woman had been alerted and was hiding in an outhouse. He asked Erzebet to go to the outhouse, knock on the door, and tell the woman to make her way to a nearby road where other people were waiting to help. The man had no idea that Erzebet herself was Jewish, but she agreed and went to deliver the message. The woman inside the outhouse was so frightened that without waiting for Erzebet to leave she bolted and ran. Fortunately no one saw the two women racing suspiciously across the fields. The woman was taken to the house of a brother-in-law, where she survived the war hiding in a secret room behind a wardrobe. Elsa laughed as she recalled the episode. "For Erzebet it became the story of how one Jew saved another."

Elsa said that the old Social Democrat had grown very fond of Mrs. Soros, and after the war he even tried to get her to return to Almadi and run for the town council. During that summer of 1944, he gave George books to read, among them Thomas More's *Utopia* and *In Praise of Folly* by Erasmus. George tried to read them but mostly he swam and sailed with Jutka and listened as the crippled boy raised arguments about who was worse, the Germans or the Russians. George did complete Dostoyevsky's *Crime and Punishment.* Shortly after his fourteenth birthday, which passed without celebration, he again took the train to return to the capital. There he moved in with the Prohaszka family in the Buda hills. Mr. Prohaszka was a lower-ranking official in the Agriculture Ministry, an assistant to Baumbach. He had a wife and two young children and by conviction was a monarchist. The house contained portraits of the Hapsburgs and he even named his infant son Otto after the last of the Austro-Hungarian monarchs. Unlike Baumbach, Prohaszka and his wife, a former schoolteacher, took George in not for money but because of their moral beliefs and the obligations of decency. George lived with them through the early part of the fall and was there on October 15, the date that marked the second brutal intensification of the war in Hungary and in Budapest.

In early October, the Red Army broke into southern Hungary, bringing its tanks only a hundred miles from the capital. Two months earlier, in neighboring Romania, after a similar advance by the Soviets, the Romanian king did what the Germans had feared Horthy might do back in March: informed the Germans he was seeking an armistice with Moscow and issued an ultimatum to the Germans to remove their forces within three days. When Berlin rejected the demand, Romanian troops switched sides and joined with the Russians. By October, a similar scenario seemed to be playing out in Hungary. Horthy and Prime Minister Geza Lakatos had been seeking to pressure the Germans, trying, among other things, to have them slow down their accelerated campaign against the Jews. Horthy issued a declaration saying he had advised the representatives of the Reich that he would seek an armistice with the Allies. It was read on the radio on October 14 and, in response, on that same day the Germans sent forty Tiger tanks into the capital with instructions to overthrow Horthy and Lakatos. Two days later Horthy capitulated and the Germans installed the Arrow Cross leader Ferenc Szalasi as their puppet. This led to the greatly accelerated deportation and murder of Budapest's Jews, the intensifying bombardment of the city, and months of siege and bitter house-to-house fighting.

Budapest's fate was sealed, coincidentally, at Esku Square, in the house next door to the one where Tivadar and his friend Kozma had holed up in the secret room. There, on October 15, 1944, Horthy's son was kidnapped by the SS as he was going to the residence of a prominent cleric for what he thought was a clandestine meeting with representatives of Marshal Tito's Yugoslav partisans. The abduction of the young Horthy, and German threats to kill him, ended all efforts by the regent to challenge the Nazis and forced him to step aside for the Arrow Cross leaders, whose anti-Semitism was much more virulent than his own.

A DAY after the kidnapping, Balazs, the superintendent, showed Tivadar bloodstains on the pavement. Tivadar and Kozma had by then moved from Esku Square to a large ground-floor room at 2 Vasar Street, but Tivadar had gone back to the old hideout to pick up a few gold coins and some paper bills he had tucked behind some loose bricks.

Now the war became less abstract. As Tivadar wrote: "The air raids grew more frequent. Russian planes were now involved and they did considerable damage to the brick buildings. The frequent air raids also damaged the electric power lines, so the streetcar service deteriorated, and, more to the point, all the lights went out. I concluded the time had come for my sons to move in with me, because it was getting more dangerous to be out on the street." In November, after George had made his way to his father's place by a long and circuitous route, Tivadar did not let him return to the Prohaszkas.

Bodies of men and horses lay on the streets. Once George noticed a Russian plane flying low and pointed out red dots in time for his father to push him into a doorway to take cover against the strafing. On Joszef Avenue near their apartment two bodies hung from lampposts, one with a sign saying "This is what happens to a Jew who hides," and the other with a sign declaring "This is what happens to a Christian who hides Jews." Jutka, who had come back from the countryside, moved into the room as well. A doctor came every day to see her, but as she weakened there was little that could be done. George's main job was to bring buckets of water up from the basement of a nearby market.

They gambled to pass the time, betting cookies on geography questions, chess games, and predictions of what time the electricity would be restored. When the power was on they listened to the radio, and on

Christmas Eve they heard the announcer read yet another decree: "Everyone sixteen or older must report for military service. Anyone who fails to obey this general mobilization is to be shot. Anyone who hides Jews is to be shot. Anyone who hoards merchandise, or sells at a high price, is to be shot." They knew the Germans were losing and that the Russians were very close. In fact, the siege of Budapest started on Christmas, beginning weeks of conflict in which the two largest armies in the world, the Soviet and the German, battled neighborhood by neighborhood and at times house by house for the city.

At one point, a month before the siege began, Tivadar learned that his mother-in-law had once again left the rooms where he had placed her and moved into one of the Jewish houses in the ghetto. He hired a young man to get her out and installed her in an exclusive hotel. At another point, Tivadar organized a raid on his mother-in-law's pantry at Esku Square, convinced there would be cans of food dating back to his own wedding. They found several tins, including a large one without a label that turned out to contain pineapple chunks, an unimaginable delicacy, which very quickly went bad after the tin was opened.

And then there was the morning when they heard a loud crash. George investigated and reported that there was a German soldier in the bathroom.

"We all went in and there stood a fair-haired, blue-eyed German boy in full military equipment, his chin smooth as a baby's," wrote Tivadar.

> The bathroom window, which had frosted glass in it, was normally never opened. Now it stood open.
>
> Chance had so arranged things that this solitary German soldier, representative of the power and might of Germany, now stood before four Jews, who had the opportunity to treat him with the same senseless barbarity and malice that the Germans had used on millions of Jews. With his blue eyes and blond hair he seemed the very embodiment of that Aryanness whose fanatical adherents had sought to enslave people and exterminate races. Should the *lex talionis*, the principle of compensation, of an eye for an eye and a tooth for a tooth apply? Was he himself guilty? Was it right to punish him for something he had perhaps not done himself, or even approved of?
>
> We did the boy no harm.
>
> "How old are you?" This was my first question.
>
> "I'm 17."

"Do you smoke?"

"Yes."

He took my offered cigarette, lit it, and inhaled eagerly. He explained that there was a Russian tank in front of our building. He ran into the air shaft and tumbled into our room. We talked for perhaps a quarter of an hour. The question then was what to do with him.

The eyes of my fourteen-year-old son seemed filled with tears. I put a handful of cigarettes into the Aryan soldier's fist and gave him his orders: "You're to go out the same way you came in."

The boys helped him climb on to the windowsill and the armed representative of the German Reich exited Jewish-occupied territory.

It was January 12, 1945. Later that day, at around 2 p.m., three bedraggled Russian officers presented themselves at No. 2 Vasar Street. Using the Russian he had learned in Siberia, Tivadar invited them to have tea. The war, it seemed, had ended.

CHAPTER 4

PEACE

THE IMMEDIATE AREA around Vasar Street was freed of Germans, but it would be another four days before all of Pest was under Russian control. That was when the Germans fled to the Buda side of the river, blowing all the bridges across the Danube behind them. They would remain dug in on the heights around the castle until February 14, when the last garrison of Germans and Arrow Cross forces surrendered to the Russians. Even though the occupants of the Vasar Street room realized that the tide had turned, the rejoicing was subdued: there was no power, no running water, and food was scarce, although Paul had found a place on the outskirts of the city where he could trade sweaters for potatoes. The temperature remained below freezing. Windows were shattered and George tried to replace the panes with cloth and cardboard. Corpses littered the streets.

And then there were the Russians. "They were liberators to us," George recalled. His father chatted with the Red Army soldiers who kept coming by. Once, two who showed up at the apartment made it clear that they wanted the two girls who were living in the room, the ailing Jutka and a friend of hers who had arrived highly distraught after being raped by a Russian soldier. "My father talked them out of it," George recalled. "Actually he took them to a nearby whorehouse."

George, his father, and Paul went on walks, observing the ruin and damage and losing wristwatches to Russians who demanded them at gunpoint. After a few days, Tivadar and his sons set off to look for Erzebet's mother, a venture that led to what George remembers as "perhaps the weirdest thirty-six hours" of his life:

> We went to the Hotel Hungaria, near the river, where my father had placed my grandmother when he had her pulled out of the ghetto. We got there in the early afternoon and found that she was alive and healthy. Then, as we wanted to leave, it became clear that the entire hotel had been taken over by Russians, all of them former officers who were recently liberated after having been held by the Germans as prisoners of war.
>
> As we start to leave one Russian tells us we cannot go because there is a curfew. My father says the curfew starts at dusk and that the sun was still in the sky. The guard agrees but says that by the time we will be in the street the sun will be setting. He says he will shoot us if we go outside. Then he accuses my father of being a spy and accuses me and my brother of being parachutists. Apparently my father is a spy because he speaks Russian and we are parachutists because we do not speak Russian.

The three Soroses were asked to produce their papers, and of course the only documents they had were the ones for their assumed identities. George's grandmother was summoned to identify them. But while she insisted that the boys were her grandsons and the man was her son-in-law she could not remember their names, at least not the ones on their identification papers.

"We spent the night in the cellar and the collection of people there was remarkably strange," said George. "You can imagine what kind of people had lived through the siege in a luxury hotel. You had fascists and you had resistance people. There was a couple who had brought people out of the ghetto and who showed us the marks of the beatings they had received from the Arrow Cross. And there was a Russian soldier who fell in love with a woman who had been bringing out Jews. He fell asleep holding her hand. When he woke up in the morning he found he had overslept. He became very angry and shouted that he had been tricked. He pulled out a grenade and said he was going to blow all of us up. It was crazy, like in the movies."

As George described this day, he became much more animated than he had when talking about his months of hiding. It was as if, reliving a cathartic experience, he evoked a time that stood out in sharp and polychromatic relief after all the earlier tense but drably similar days when emotions had to be held in check. "In the morning we left my grandmother after arranging for her to be taken to her home, and we started back to Vasar Street and that's when we saw an awful lot of corpses. When I got home I actually got sick, not throwing up, but I felt ill. I mean, I had seen corpses before, but this was really gruesome. Maybe it was more the sight of the horses than the men, but I remember seeing somebody with his hands tied behind his back and the skull squashed. Not a nice sight, you know, though the smell was not yet so bad because of the cold."

They had almost made it back to the apartment when they were stopped by Russian soldiers, who asked that Paul go with them for "*mala rabota*," which Tivadar, understanding the words to mean "small work," assumed meant tasks such as removing the charred hulks of trucks and tanks that blocked the streets. Teasingly, he said that he did not think small works would do his eldest son much harm. Paul was marched off under armed guard with other young men. In those early days of occupation, the Soviets announced that they had captured 110,000 German and Hungarian prisoners of war. The number of actual combatants seized was considerably lower; the difference was made up of able-bodied young men taken from the streets to be used as forced laborers in the Soviet Union. Some of these returned after many years, and some never came back.

Paul did not know any of this at the time, but he realized quickly that his guards had more in mind for him than "small work." After camping out overnight, the group was being escorted to what Paul realized was a suburban train yard. He moved energetically to the front and when the road turned sharply, he bolted into the forest. He made it back to Vasar Street.

In late January, even before the German garrison had surrendered across the river in Buda, Tivadar and his sons returned to their prewar apartment on Kossuth Square. The Gentile housekeeper to whom they had entrusted the place more than ten months earlier had kept the furniture dusted as best she could, but one small Russian bomb had scored a direct hit on the kitchen. "It was more or less swept away," said George. "We had to cook in the living room and there was also a hole in my father's office. My mother was out of communication so it was my idea to bring my grandmother to cook for us and look after us, but that did not turn out to be a happy arrangement since my father and brother really detested her."

At that time Erzebet was in Almadi living with the Brandeisz family. She knew Budapest had been taken by the Russians, but the Germans, though visibly jittery, still remained in control of the Balaton region. In her taped recollections she said that it was already spring when someone came to the house and said that the Russian army was about to arrive and that the Germans were fleeing. She said that the news set off a panic and that for reasons she never understood, she and Elsa found themselves fleeing with many others. Having survived the Germans, they were running, along with Gabor, the limping young man with the deformed foot, to a wild forest region where the youth had relatives who were woodcutters. "Why did we do it? I have no idea. Elsa says it was a kind of war insanity." She described the rush of people with bundles on the road and told how she and Elsa made their way to the house of the woodcutter, where they spent the night. The next day the Russians arrived in that region, and she was raped.

War had changed her, toughened her. She had learned to cook, sew, and bake. The woman whose husband had wondered whether she could survive without domestic help had endured separation from him and her sons, survived interrogation, and endured violation.

When she returned to Kossuth Square, it was Easter and the kitchen had been patched up. She ran up the stairs to find Tivadar, the boys, and her mother. She did not tell George what had happened by the haystack where the two Russian soldiers attacked her. Indeed, he did not learn of the rape until many years later.

George remembers that first postwar year as a continuation of the threatening excitement he had experienced since the Germans first arrived. Before then, by his own account, he had been a brooding and meditative adolescent, very much taken by a Hungarian novel, *Golyavar* (Stork's Castle), that deals with a character's parallel lives, one lived and one dreamed. At that time while in school, he once reached out to touch a wall to convince himself that he existed. In early adolescence, even before he saw any corpses, he had been preoccupied and depressed by the idea of death, his own and that of his parents. And then, with war, contemplation gave way to action.

"For me, this was the most exciting time of my life," a mature George said, referring to his years from thirteen to fifteen. "For an adolescent to be in real danger, having a feeling he is inviolate, having a father whom he adored acting as a hero and having an evil confronting you and getting the better of it, I mean, being in command of the situation, even though you're in danger, but basically maneuvering successfully, what more can you ask for?" He added that none of the risks he has taken as an adult, none of the bets he made on currencies or market movements, were greater than the ones he and his father took when he was fourteen. But clearly there is a connection.

The sense of exhilaration continued into 1945. "The early stages of the Russian occupation were as exciting and interesting—in many ways even more interesting and adventurous—than the German occupation, because you had to build up life from nothing." George's first financial ventures took place in the last months of the war, when he was living with his father on Vasar Street. There was a crowded café nearby called the Mienk, where a black market flourished. His father would send him there to change money and trade jewelry because a fourteen-year-old was less likely to arouse suspicion than an older man.

"That was my little fun, to try to get the best rate," he said, recalling how British five- and ten-pound notes forged by the Germans were circulating so widely that they forced down the rate for all pound notes by 75 percent. Gold, he explained, was traded in three grades: fashion, piece, and broken. Technically, a bracelet or a pin was fashion, a watch case was piece, and broken could be a tooth filling or a jewelry fragment. George observed that in practice, "When you wanted to buy it, it was fashion, and when you wanted to sell it, it became piece."

Among the black marketeers in the Mienk were a group of French prisoners of war who had managed to escape and were living a shadowy existence. On one occasion George dealt with one of these Frenchmen as he carried out his father's instructions to sell a heavy gold bracelet. The dealer took him to another café and then went off with the bracelet after leaving George with five thousand British pounds as security. George sat in the café and waited, tormented by the thought that perhaps the security was counterfeit and that the Frenchman had fled with the jewelry. The man came back and the deal went through. The money George brought home and that his father turned over to his clients was authentic. The sense of his thrill was apparent in his recollection.

With the Russian occupation came new financial challenges and new opportunities. There was a demand for everything and access to anything of value could be advantageously leveraged. Tivadar's brother Zoltan, who unlike several of their sisters had survived deportation, obtained cigarette papers and after selling them at a street stand quickly established a chain of subcontracting dealers. Tivadar parlayed his knowledge of Russian into a position as a translator and consultant for the Swiss diplomats, who in the absence of a United States embassy were handling American interests. When the Americans arrived several months later, Tivadar, ever fearful of too much prominence and exposure, left the job. It was one thing to work for the Swiss, even if they were dealing with American interests in a Hungary under increasing Russian control, and quite another to work directly for Americans. But in the short period he worked for the Swiss he gained access to foreign money and continued to deal in currencies and jewelry, often acting for others with the help of his young son.

By the time George returned to school in September, hyperinflation had reached the highest levels recorded anywhere. So dizzily did the pengo drop in value that at one time the authorities printed pengo bills in denominations of quintillions, a number followed by eighteen zeros. It was not uncommon for the currency to lose two-thirds of its value overnight. At the same time a family could live comfortably for a week on one U.S. dollar. All of this proved highly educational to a fifteen-year-old gymnasium student who spent some of his after-school hours changing money for his father's clients and watching his uncle become a cigarette paper baron.

He learned one of the many lessons that impressed him when the father of a friend commissioned him to change a significant sum. "He asked me to change some dollars and being conscientious I went to the pain of visiting both of the two markets for this sort of thing, the old Stock Exchange and an orthodox synagogue in another part of town. It turned out that there was a significant difference in the exchange rate, and I was able to get some 20 percent more at the synagogue than at the Stock Market, which was the only rate that my friend's father knew about. So I brought him the larger amount and said that I deserved a higher cut, but he refused.

"He said, 'You are a broker and it's your job to get the best rate, that is what you are getting paid for.' I remembered that years later when I became a market maker in over-the-counter securities," George observed whimsically. "Because if you are a market maker and can make someone an extra 20 percent and raise your own cut by a half a percent that's different and better than being just a broker. So in the end by his refusal to raise my compensation he encouraged me to be a market maker rather than a broker, which turned out to be quite useful and I suppose I was paid for that experience."

He was also gaining broader economic insight. He became aware that the inflation was being deliberately engineered by those in power. He even intuited the Communists' rationale for the inflation policy. "They wanted to wipe out all the savings and they set out to buy everything of value with paper money that they printed in great abundance." Later, after the Communists had acquired and nationalized what they wanted, they stabilized the situation by introducing a new currency, the forint, which they kept extremely scarce, driving up interest rates to usurious levels and driving out whatever pockets of private business had survived. "There was this very dramatic shift, from totally worthless currency to extremely scarce," said George, describing his early practical observations in political economy.

But in the immediate aftermath of the war George had no intention of pursuing a business career. "Making money was purely avocational. It was tied to survival, or rather to the family tradition of managing and coping in the sense of the French word *débrouiller*, you know, trying to come out on top no matter what happens around you. But though it was a time of adolescent fantasies, I had absolutely no fantasy of becoming a financier. It was not in my field of vision. Philosophy, politics, journalism, writing, those were the things I thought about."

The money he earned went into the family's common pot, and despite the economic turmoil the household fortunes improved. The bomb damage in the apartment was repaired and a maid was hired. The house on Lupa had suffered flood and ice damage, but that too was repaired and in the summer the family returned there. A few of the other families never returned, and some of the children had lost one or both parents in the war; when school started, six or seven boys in George's class were missing, killed by the Germans or their Arrow Cross accomplices.

During the summer of 1945 George swam, played tennis, rowed, and learned a little Russian, talking to the Russian soldiers who would visit the island from a nearby camp looking for booty. His vocabulary was sparse, though somewhat larger than the five words or phrases that his father jokingly claimed were all one needed to know to maintain basic conversations with Russians. These were *davai* (give me), *harasho* (good), *nichevo* (nothing, or it doesn't matter), *syechas* (right now), and *yob tvayu maht* (I fuck your mother).

School, when it began, was not for George a very happy place. There were the missing students. Then, too, though the old classes that segregated Jews and Gentiles were merged, "there was tension between the two groups," with a core of four or five of the Christian youngsters being "physically more aggressive and ruling the roost." George challenged one of these to a boxing match. He had been taught some basic moves by Adler, the man who had escaped from the roundup of Jews in Ukraine in 1941. George won.

He also challenged higher authority with a newspaper he produced on his own. It was a single-copy wall newspaper that he typed and posted on a bulletin board. "This was a period of wall newspapers, the Communist party encouraged them, there was even a kind of cult," George explained. But he was quite consciously emulating *The Plank*, the paper his father had prepared as a prisoner in Siberia. George does not remember the name he chose, but said "it was like *The Plank*, and obviously it was an acting out of the *Plank* story."

The paper was aggressive in tone. "It attacked everybody. I attacked my history teacher. I accused him of corruption because he used to sell a magazine in class and everybody was expected to subscribe. When I didn't he failed me." So in a box prominently displayed on the first of two pages, he wrote: "A good grade for a bank note. Only from Professor Takacs."

The main article in the paper, the subject of which George can no longer remember, also stirred controversy by its last word, "Amen." George had meant simply to express the idea "so be it." This led to a group of students expressing outrage and demanding the paper be taken down. The students, who George believed were inspired by the corrupt and offended teacher, claimed that the use of "Amen" had violated their religious feelings and constituted a sacrilege.

School dragged on and the economy settled down while the Russians entrenched themselves and their system. By the middle of 1946, the sense of heightened excitement and adventure was disappearing and George began to feel a psychological letdown. He talked to his father about leaving. His father asked him where he wanted to go.

"I said, I'd like to go to Moscow, to find out about Communism. I mean that's where the power is. I'd like to know more about it. Or maybe go to England because of the BBC, which we listened to."

Tivadar discouraged Moscow as a destination, telling his son that he himself had found out everything about the Soviet Union and would be happy to share his knowledge. As for London, the family had some distant relatives there and he urged his son to write to one of them, a man named George Frank, to see what he could do about having George admitted to a school. At his father's suggestion, George sent weekly postcards with lines such as "looking forward to seeing you soon." Eventually Frank sent a certificate saying that George had been registered in a polytechnic, a junior college.

Now George needed to obtain a passport, acquire a British visa, and placate Erzebet. On March 5, 1946, in a speech in the United States, Winston Churchill coined the expression "iron curtain," declaring that the Soviets had lowered it across the European continent. Tivadar, who was both experienced and perspicacious, realized what the Cold War division of Europe, engineered by Stalin, could mean and felt it important that both his sons leave Hungary before leaving became impossible. Erzebet agreed with her husband's gloomy assessment, but the thought of being separated from her youngest son, perhaps for good, was devastating. In the months that followed, Tivadar was encouraging and hopeful while she despaired. George found her sorrow tedious.

He was then sixteen and was about to complete the seventh, or next to last, grade of gymnasium. Each day after classes he would go to the passport office to line up with hundreds of people. Following his father's advice he asked to speak to the supervisor. It did not work. He also applied for a British visa and was eventually issued a letter saying that if he got a passport, a visa for England would be issued to him. School ended for the summer and he still kept going to the office, standing in line. An Esperanto conference was to be held shortly in Bern, and both he and his father had registered as delegates. His father received his passport and went to the meeting, while George still waited. Finally, soon after his seventeenth birthday in August of 1947, he was issued the necessary document. His brother gave him his favorite suit, a green tweed. His mother fought back tears and George left by train for what was then the Russian sector of Austria. There he switched trains for an uneventful ride to Bern.

By the time he arrived, the Esperanto conference was ending, and his father gave him some money he had managed to keep in Lichtenstein. It was not much but it would have to last George for however long it took the British consulate to issue him the visa promised in the letter he carried. His father instructed him to look for accommodations in boarding houses run by temperance organizations. As Tivadar returned to Budapest, George found one such place where for pennies a night he slept in the breakfast room. During the days he swam in the Aar and visited the zoo. He was recapturing some of the sense of adventure that had vanished with peacetime. It took two weeks for the visa to come, but, having economized successfully, he still had most of the money his father had left him. He used it to buy two Swiss wristwatches and with great enthusiasm left by train for Paris, where he assumed another relative would send him on his way to London. The relative was out of town. Resourcefully he approached a man he thought might buy a Swiss watch.

"I explained that I wanted to go to London," says George. "At the time I was very bold, like a street kid. I said it's worth a lot more than I was asking and then when he said he didn't have that much, I said just give me what you've got and send me the rest. Of course he never did but I got the money for the ticket. I got back at least what I had paid for the watch. It was a good deal."

Enthusiastic and eager to seize the day, George Soros, then barely seventeen years old, left for London.

CHAPTER 5

DOWN AND OUT
IN LONDON

GEORGE SOROS remained in London for the next nine years. There he acquired his formal education, eventually obtaining a degree from the prestigious London School of Economics. Also in London he developed his basic ideas about philosophy and economics and absorbed the rudiments of finance that have made him rich, famous, and internationally influential. He read great books, considered great ideas, and dreamed great dreams, and yearned to lead a life of intellectual activism.

And yet when Soros thinks back to the first years in England, his memories are painful, filled with frustration, loneliness, and rejection. This was his time of trial, comparable in his mind to his father's years in Siberia. Some of the despair was simply the brooding dissatisfactions of adolescence, but much of it was specific to the place and the period.

George's memories of his youth often clash with conventional expectations. For example, when he talks of his life during the Nazi period and the Soviet occupation he reveals more exhilaration and pride than despondency. His account of his arrival in England contains far more resentment than gratitude. For his altered prospects and even his material environment, he should have been thankful, for though life in postwar Britain was austere, it was better than what Budapest offered. Surely he was supposed to feel the appreciation of the refugee who has reached sanctuary. But he felt more unhappy than ever before in his life.

The Franks, the distant relatives he had written to, let him sleep on the couch but had not welcomed him with open arms. He was an awkward seventeen-year-old boy whom they had never met before. He did not speak English very well, and he combined a confidence that verged on arrogance with the naïveté of a country bumpkin. He was as he has remained, both aggressive and shy. A few days after he arrived, he jumped aboard a bus just as he had done in Budapest, only to be admonished by passengers who told him that in England people queued up and waited their turn. He listened in silence but seethed at the superior tone of his scolding elders; for years he would use the incident to describe the austere aloofness of Britain and convey the coldness of his welcome. He found the British pay phones mystifying and was unable to figure out which button he was supposed to push to enable two-way conversation once he heard the voice at the other end.

As the summer rolled on, he left his relatives' couch and headed to an Esperanto youth conference in Ipswich, where two matronly schoolteachers invited him to spend a week in southern Wales. He liked them well enough but drinking tea in a cottage in Wales was a far cry from selling piece gold in cafés to straggling French soldiers.

Back in London he signed up for a course in English for foreigners. His father had sent him a little money, which he knew would have to last him for a long time, so in a little book he kept track of his weekly expenses. He found a bed and breakfast on Liberia Road in Islington for thirty shillings a day, the first of many such places where he lived. He spent days walking the streets, learning the city while saving on carfare. At the time it was still something of a game, and he was proud when he was able to reduce his weekly outlay from four pounds to three.

But once school started and the weather turned bitter, the dreariness and loneliness of his life sapped all spirit of adventure. Forty years later when he was courting Susan Weber, who would become his second wife, he flew her from St. Moritz to London in a private plane specifically to show her the landmarks of this dismal time: the bed and breakfasts; the places he had worked as dishwasher, house painter, busboy; the mannikin-fabricating workshop where he was fired; the swimming pool where he was a lifeguard and the fancy restaurant where the headwaiter once told him that if he worked hard he might one day end up as his assistant. Susan felt the tour was meant to expunge old humiliations. She recalled that after showing her these sites from the windows of a Rolls-Royce, Soros, who normally scorns ostentatious extravagance, retreated to a hotel suite so overwhelmingly grand and spacious that it made Susan uncomfortable. She said he had picked the palatial suite quite intentionally, as if to wash away his experiences of the city from more than thirty years earlier.

In those first months George spent the day at his English course, then returned to his bed and breakfast to study and to write letters home assuring Tivadar and Erzebet that everything was fine. "That was the beginning of my low period," said George. "I had thought that everybody would be terribly interested in this brilliant, clever young man who had lived through so much and in reality nobody gave a damn.

"I used to go to Marble Arch, trying to pick up girls. I had no experience with women at the time. I was a virgin but very interested and so I tried to pick up girls on the street without success. The lack of sexual contact was painful, because sex was my main interest and all that gave me complexes that it took me a long time to shed."

Everything about his existence reinforced the sense of being an unwelcome outsider. His fellow students, though also foreigners, seemed much less alienated. In the evening he would go out with other rooming-house tenants, bachelors working as clerks in shops. Somewhere, he suspected, was a world of excitement and worthwhile challenges, but he had not found it. His sense of his own singularity and his family's distinctiveness did not help. To be shunned as he felt he was was a hurtful injustice. There was also the nagging thought that by failing to find a way out of his humdrum anonymity, George was not living up to Tivadar's expectations, as he was yearning to do. The downward spiral of brooding despair lasted at least a year and a half. It has marked him for much longer than that. He acknowledges that he later experienced similar episodes of dejection and doubt, in the United States in the early sixties and the early eighties, but the first of them, in London, was the most enduring and painful.

The exclusion Soros felt in law-abiding, decent, civilized London was psychologically more traumatic than the anti-Semitism that led him to be called a Jewish piglet as he walked through Budapest with the required yellow star on his shirt. "I knew about that kind of insult, but then I had never wanted to be friends with Nazis or Hungarian anti-Semites. Being excluded, and trying to break into a closed society as an outsider, that was new and painful. Most of the people I had to deal with had a life of their own, so they were not that receptive. There was also the artificiality of trying to make contact, finding some excuse or ulterior motive, that made me feel very uncomfortable. And of course there was the lack of money. It was still a time of rationing and the English were at that time very regimented and I thought they were distant, cold, and absorbed in their own lives and not interested in mine and, of course, I thought they ought to be terribly interested."

Against this tide of indifference, George tried to affirm himself as best he could. He had a tepid flirtation with a Norwegian girl, a fellow student, that went nowhere. Desperate for human contact, he even spoke at the Speakers Corner in Hyde Park. There, among the eccentrics and propounders of various doctrines, he spoke at the Esperanto stand, testifying for the utility of an international language in Esperanto and English. In December he sat for his matriculation exams, hoping to be admitted to the London School of Economics (LSE). He passed all the subjects but English, which meant he would have to take the exam again. As if to punish himself, he brought his weekly expenses to their lowest point, two and a half pounds.

Very soon afterward he took a skiing vacation in Switzerland. In trying to recall his motives in this period, Soros believes that in his adolescent confusion, he used the ski trip to affirm his sense of honor, or, more accurately, to punish one of his British relatives—a second cousin of both his parents, an ophthalmologist with two daughters. Soros understood that the doctor feared George might become a burden, but he also thought him stingy. At their first meeting the cousin took George to lunch at the Ophthalmological Society. At the end of the meal he gave George a one-pound note and told him to buy some chocolates. George tried to turn down the gift but the man insisted and George left the meal feeling outraged.

"I was an obnoxious, conceited, sensitive seventeen-year-old. I knew that my father had helped him to get a job as a doctor in the Jewish Hospital in Budapest and I took it amiss that he would give me a single pound in this offhanded way when I was living in poverty."

He brooded for some time and then, after failing the English exam, approached the cousin, asking him, "I want to go skiing in Switzerland, could you lend me a hundred pounds?" From the perspective of a half-century later, Soros claimed he asked for the money to chastise an adult who he felt had acted improperly, like the history teacher who had offered higher grades to students who bought his magazine subscriptions. "It was a childish thing but it sticks in my mind. I knew that he was under an obligation to my father. So I asked him for the hundred pounds and used it to go skiing when I was living on three pounds a week. I was able to return the money in a month, but you see, I was still a little clone of my father's. I might have been poor and had just failed the English exam, but the important thing was the idea that I should go skiing, that such things and not money were the important things in life."

In fact, money, or rather the lack of it, was becoming tremendously important. Soon after he returned from Switzerland, George found himself sitting in a Lyons Corner House near the Tottenham Court Road with just enough money to buy a pot of tea. He was overcome with mixed

feelings—dark despair that he had reached a nadir, along with an awareness that since he had reached the bottom the only direction he could go
was up.

Some money arrived from Tivadar but George's life remained one of
dreary solitude, with neither friends nor distractions beyond daydreams
and fantasies. He took the matriculation examination again, and passed all
parts of it, though his score was not good enough to enter the LSE.
Instead he was accepted into Kentish Town Polytechnic, a commuter college without reputation or cachet. He would start there in September, a
joyless prospect. Meanwhile he had heard of a program sponsored by the
Labour government called Lend a Hand on the Land, in which people
from cities helped farmers with their harvest. The participants were
mostly civil servants who received an extra week of holiday if they signed
up to pick crops, but Soros learned that he too was eligible even under the
restrictive terms of his visa.

He set off for the camp by hitchhiking and, rather remarkably, was
picked up by a police officer whose duty that day was to observe and guard
the Queen Mother as she shopped for antiques. The idea of a poor immigrant student being driven to a job picking apples by an officer who was
guarding royalty struck him as amusing and something that could only
happen in England. He took it as a rare stroke of fortune when the policeman dropped him off at Sandringham, near the camp.

There some of the dreariness that had settled on George began to fade.
For one thing there were young people in the camp, including women: sex
seemed a possibility. "That was the beginning of a little bit of romance,
meeting girls, and my first real affair grew out of one of these contacts,
when I went back to London and kept in touch with a girl I met there who
was a civil servant."

There was also some money to be made. The auxiliary farm workers
were initially paid three pounds a week. They were housed in a former
military barracks and were taken to nearby orchards to pick apples. It was
a big crop and in order to stimulate harvesting the managers introduced a
system of piecework, offering an additional shilling for each large box.
After some weeks, when the workers were switched to pick pears, the camp
bosses decided to cut that rate in half, to sixpence a box. Again, George
found himself pitted against authority. He was vulnerable both as an immigrant and as a poor student who was dependent on his earnings for his
existence. He was also not quite eighteen. Nonetheless he organized a
strike, persuading his co-workers to stay away from the orchards unless the
old rate was restored.

The episode sparked commercial impulses that had been dormant since his days at the Café Mienk. While the quasi-vacationing fruit pickers hiked and flirted at their rent-free barracks, George found an independent farm labor contractor. With local farmers desperate to complete the harvesting, this man was quite willing to pay the full shilling a box, and so within a few days George, with some others, resumed gathering pears. They lived in the barracks, subsidized by the government program, but they received their higher wages from private contractors who understood the urgent needs of the market and the desire of farmers to have their pears plucked before they fell and rotted. George understood the local pear and labor market and had intervened to his advantage. At the time he was certain he was simply acting out of moral outrage, angered by the decision of the Lend a Hand people to rescind the incentive. The supervisors of George's barracks identified him as a troublemaking ringleader, and asked him to leave, but he had no trouble finding a cot at another camp nearby. He spent the rest of the summer picking pears by day and making additional money by working in a cannery at night. These were his best months since he left home.

He returned to London with some money and with the address of that civil servant, Pearl, who though not his first choice that summer, had welcomed his attentions. Before he went to pick fruit, while speaking one weekend at the Esperanto stand at Hyde Park, he had been approached by a man a few years older than he who said that he too was Hungarian. His name was Andrew Herskovitz and he became George's first "English" friend. The two of them and a Dutch student now rented an apartment together.

Herskovitz, whose nickname was Bandi, had a number of impressive traits. "He was much more of a *débrouillard* than I was," explained Soros, using the term he often uses to describe Tivadar. "In the war he had been deported by the Nazis and had gone through Auschwitz. He was more experienced than I was, sexually and in other ways. He was also much more unscrupulous."

The apartment was not far from the Kentish Town college, where classes proved to be uninspiring. George was enrolled with a major in basic economics, taking five compulsory courses. There was no discussion in the classes or afterward. In British constitutional history, the professor, a Scotsman, talked at dictating speed and expected the students to take down exactly what he said and memorize it. Among his dictums was "the state is like a ship and government is its rudder."

None of this pleased Soros. In his mind, he was an intelligent, worldly young man who had read Erasmus and Aristotle and who had experienced war and seen its corpses. Listening to the prattle of lecturers in what he took to be a third-rate academy was not the destiny he had in mind. He began to cut school regularly and sneak into lectures at the London School of Economics. There he heard Harold Laski, the preeminent professor of government and chairman of the Labour Party, deliver a lecture on British constitutional tradition. In contrast to the polytechnic, George found the atmosphere and the talk at the LSE to be far more stimulating. This is where he felt he belonged. But he was a stowaway, and when he had the bad luck to be noticed by a geography professor from Kentish Town who also lectured at LSE, the sighting was reported to the principal of the polytechnic. Soros was summoned to the man's office. "He told me: 'Obviously you don't think much of us; you don't attend the classes. You're seen at LSE—you don't belong here.' So I was thrown out of Kentish Town."

The expulsion drove George further down the academic food chain. Now his only prospect was to join other bottom-feeders by enrolling in a correspondence division of the University of London. It was a blow, but he was not as dejected as he would have been earlier. The long depression was waning. He was seeing girls, and he was impressed by the cunning and the survivalist skills of Herskovitz, who for some time remained practically his only friend. Herskovitz was not exactly a student. He lived on the charity of Jewish philanthropy, receiving stipends as an apprentice learning a trade. Actually, he saw to it that his apprenticeships never quite worked out and he moved from one training program to another, receiving new stipends with each change of vocation. George also applied to the Jewish Board of Guardians for a stipend and was angered when he was turned down on the grounds that the board did not provide money for students seeking a higher education, only those learning specific trades.

So as the money from Budapest dried up, Soros was forced to move from one menial job to another, mostly in violation of his visa. He washed dishes at a diner called The Better 'Ole on the Great Western Road. It was hard work and soon he came down with a high fever. He worked in the mannikin factory, where they made papier-mâché figures and where he was fired for failing to attach wigs properly to the mannikins' scalps. He painted apartments. In the spring of 1949, he took another set of examinations and this time passed with a score that was good enough to gain him admission to the LSE. He could start in September.

After moving to several different apartments with Herskovitz, he had ended up on his own in an attic room in Chiswick, not far from the Thames. On the same floor there lived an LSE student with an extensive library of significant books that George could read. In another lucky break George found a job as an attendant and lifeguard at a swimming pool. Swimming pools, it seems, have always played significant roles in his life; from the one where his father would meet him after school to the one where he had kept in touch with his father and brother during the war. Now in the months before he began what he anticipated would be the beginning of his real studies and enter a world of worthy intellectual pursuits, he had a job that allowed him to read. The pool was not very well used and there were long periods when he could sit and read the books he borrowed from his neighbor and from a library. Soros is a very slow reader. Susan, his wife, wonders whether he unknowingly suffers from dyslexia. Still, at the swimming pool he had plenty of time to go through the works of Adam Smith, Hobbes, Ricardo, Bergson, and Machiavelli, among others. He read about great ideas and he felt that finally he was on the right track. When he began classes at the London School of Economics, he would find sophisticated students and sophisticated teachers who had more on their minds than comparing states to ships and governments to rudders.

Many years later, sometime after he made his first billion, Soros would claim that this was one of the very best summers of his life.

CHAPTER 6

THE LONDON SCHOOL
OF ECONOMICS

IN THE AUTUMN OF 1949, when George Soros began legally attending lectures and seminars at the London School of Economics on
Houghton Street, in the heart of Dickensian London, he was still an outsider. Without fully realizing it, however, he was crossing into a remarkable, though short-lived, intellectual epoch whose features would help
mold his aspirations and achievements for the rest of his life.

So soon after the war, intellectuals were still intent on rebuilding and re-
imagining a badly damaged world. It was a time of optimism and eclectic
inquiry when thoughtful people, among them victims of Nazism, refugees
from Communism, and new elites from countries then emerging from
colonial rule, had flocked to Britain. In that time, before the intellectual
specialization that C. P. Snow would soon describe and deplore in his
famous essay about "two cultures," inquiring minds ranged freely across
disciplines, trespassing over boundaries of art and science. There was an
appetite for "general" theories; broad, transcendent explanations were
sought to account for and predict human experience. Marxism was the most
widely asserted and debated of doctrines, but there were other provocative
ideas—Freudian theories, Keynesian theories, Social Darwinism—and
while some felt passionately that history ought to be deterministic, quantum physicists thrilled to the concept of indeterminacy. There was an
abundance of metaphors.

It was not enough for intellectuals merely to analyze and conceptualize;
they also had an obligation to do things in the real world, to test and
implement their notions, to accelerate progress, to make the world better.

Many of them had rallied in one way or another to defeat Nazism, and some were attracted to or repelled by Marxist and utopian guidelines. Hadn't the theoretical formulations of Einstein and others led to the powerful bomb that brought peace and threatened destruction? Hadn't Keynes gone beyond explaining the Great Depression to provide strategies for escaping it?

It was also a time when much of Europe was benefiting from the Marshall Plan, America's generous program for postwar reconstruction, while, more visible in London, Britain's Labour party was turning social theories into social programs and transforming the country into a welfare state.

The impact this period had on Soros's later philanthropic work would be evident in his emphasis on "big" ideas to change profoundly the way people live, and in the boldness with which his foundations would implement massive programs as Communism first shuddered and then fell.

But at nineteen Soros did not recognize the period as particularly distinctive or instructive. He was still grumbling about his cool reception by an England he thought to be unfeeling and austere. Yet at the same time, he was being made aware of an intellectual world of impressive polymaths, whom he openly envied: renaissance men who shuttled quite comfortably between disciplines, languages, cultures, and often countries. They were men like Ludwig Wittgenstein, who defined and then redefined twentieth-century philosophy, by tying it first to mathematical principles and then to the problems of language. He had been trained as an engineer. Or Bertrand Russell, Wittgenstein's early ally and mentor, was preeminent both as a mathematician and as a philosopher, while also dabbling passionately in politics. There was Snow, the prominent physicist and a popular novelist. And there had been John Maynard Keynes, who before he died in 1946 had recast economic thinking, advised governments, administered a university, speculated in stocks, and been a friend and mentor to the artists and writers of Bloomsbury. Of all these figures it was Keynes whom Soros most admired, dreaming that one day he too might make a similar mark on the world. He particularly remembers reading an early biography of Keynes by Roy Harrod, a Cambridge disciple of his hero.

"His whole career appealed to me, including the connection with Bloomsbury and the Apostles at Cambridge," Soros said, referring to the intertwined fraternities of brilliant friends that had been so important for the economist. "I read a great deal about Bloomsbury."

Soros could not have failed to notice the markedly international flavor of the intellectual life in postwar Britain. There were so many prominent figures who like himself had come from elsewhere. Wittgenstein and Karl

Popper, Soros's future mentor, were from Vienna. So were the economist
Friedrich Hayek and the art historian Ernst Gombrich. Michael Polanyi,
like Soros a Hungarian Jew, was carrying out investigations of science,
economics, and philosophy at the University of Manchester. Karl Mann-
heim, a historical sociologist and another Hungarian, had completed a critique of Marxism, at the University of London. The novelist Arthur
Koestler, originally from Budapest, was living in London. Despite what
Soros saw as Britain's coldness, at least some people who shared his origins
and love of ideas were thriving in the country.

As for the London School of Economics, in 1949 it was unquestionably
one of Britain's most prominent centers of expansive, internationalist, and
activist scholarship. Created at the turn of the century as an academy to
provide technocratic cadres in the manner of France's École Libre des Sciences Politiques, the school had become a bastion of both establishment
and anti-establishment elites. It had been largely created by Sidney and
Beatrice Webb, the patrons of Fabian Socialism, who themselves had
mixed socially prominent pedigrees with political beliefs that many of
their class thought threatening.

If the LSE lacked the hoary traditions of Oxford and Cambridge, it
could boast of its influence on contemporary social and political thinking.
Its basic values were enshrined in what were called the five E's: education,
economics, efficiency, equality, and empire—"empire" referred to the task
of training people from the colonies to struggle for and assume the
responsibilities of self-government.

Architecturally the main building was uninspiring, and Robert Mackenzie, a student in Soros's time who would later teach there, referred to it
as "a cheerless place, like the head office of an insurance company, hidden
away in a back street." But it was not the charm of its buildings that provided the school's cachet, but rather its faculty and students.

For many years, its most dynamic personification was Laski, a spell-
binding lecturer who had persistently sought to reconcile Marxism with
democracy. He retired from the LSE in 1949, but Soros, having gate-
crashed his lecture a year earlier, could join in the boast of older grads that
they had "heard Laski." Though profound, Laski's influence was hardly
monopolistic. In keeping with the Webbs' urging the faculty was ideolog-
ically diverse and there was also a prominent right wing. Its chief luminary
was Hayek, an eventual Nobel laureate whose book, *The Road to Serfdom*,
challenged Marxist theory and the policy interventions it had spawned.
Hayek taught that the common interest of society should be perceived
as the unintended by-product of people acting in their individual self-

interest. He also predicted that huge bureaucracies like the Soviet Communist party would necessarily collapse because the small elitist leaderships upon which they depended would never be able to effectively comprehend or effectively respond to the complex information they zealously sought to monopolize. Another LSE conservative whose lectures Soros attended was the economist Lionel Robbins, a longtime critic of Keynes.

For the youthful George Soros, being in proximity to such men as Laski, Hayek, and Robbins was clearly an improvement from Kentish Town Polytechnic. Here were important people whose ideas dealt with the major issues facing the contemporary world: decolonization, social justice, totalitarianism, free markets, and the benefits and drawbacks of the welfare state. Robert Mackenzie would recall "the sense of excitement of being at LSE when a government of social reform had come to power." Anne Bohn, another student there at the time, described the years from 1945 to 1950 as "the golden age of graduate students." And Ralf Dahrendorf, the sociologist who would serve as the LSE's director from 1974 to 1984, noted in his history of the school that it was during his own student years, which overlapped with Soros's, that "the myth of the L.S.E. was born." From such testimony one might assume that Soros also was excited and enthusiastic.

But he was not. While Soros was stimulated by the big names and big ideas swirling off in the distance, he was unimpressed by his more immediate environment. He found no counterpart to the Cambridge Apostles and his classmates struck him as a generally dull lot driven by petty ambitions.

"I made some friends, but intellectually I found the environment disappointing. Mostly the student body consisted of ex-servicemen who were older than me and concerned about their future. I was too, but I felt that I had a bigger intellectual curiosity than they had. I certainly didn't find the sort of intellectual ferment that I expected. These were rather drab people who were concerned with passing their exams and finding a job. Most of them were the first generation of their families to go to university, so they had no real background, or let's say they did not have the kind of carefree, aristocratic confidence that I associated with Cambridge. I felt that something was lacking. There wasn't that much student life, and of course, I was also preoccupied with survival."

The major problem continued to be money. Soon after he started his first term, George was distressed to learn that despite the expansion of the welfare state, he was one of very few students who were not receiving any financial aid. Because his parents were not resident in the United Kingdom, he was ineligible for the local council grants that British students were getting, nor was he being maintained by any foreign government. His parents could no longer send money. To support himself he had to rely on casual jobs. In addition to working, he went to lectures, stayed in the library reading until it closed at 9:15 p.m., and occasionally ended his days by sneaking into nearby theaters to catch a final act.

He had picked economics as his field of study, and that too was an unsatisfying choice. "I was compromising between my philosophical interests and my interest in getting on in the world. And I really did not take to economics, because I'm not good at math. I sort of struggled through it, though at times my intellectual curiosity would be aroused in addressing the foundations of economics, like the assumptions of perfect competition. I tried to draw some curves that other people had not drawn yet, but I did not succeed. I was vocal in class but really I had no academic triumphs."

Toward the end of the first term, an unexpected event changed Soros's personal fortunes on several levels. It would also significantly shape his attitude toward philanthropy. He broke his leg. The story, as Soros tells it, reveals his appreciation of paradox: a bad thing led to a good thing—or, as he might have explained it later, in his Wall Street days, an event unforeseen and unforeseeable signaled the end of a bust and the advent of a boom.

During the Christmas break he had taken a temporary job as a railroad porter, beginning very early in the morning at the Willesden Junction station. One day, about a week into the job, he was lifting a crate of ice cream from a freight car while standing on a wheelbarrow. The wheelbarrow rolled back and his leg became wedged beneath the carriage, causing a longitudinal fracture of the lower leg. At the hospital doctors joined the bone with two screws that have remained in place ever since.

Just before his operation, he chatted with a young and brassy Irish nurse, who boldly told him that she would look after him after his surgery. When a friend from LSE came to visit him, George mentioned the exchange. The friend on his own wrote to the nurse in George's name, saying he remembered her as an apparition that appeared before consciousness was lost and that he had been dreaming of her ever since. "It worked," said Soros, and an affair of sorts blossomed in the orthopedic ward. As he lay in the hospital Soros even developed a theory about the disproportional flourishing of romance—or romance and lust—around broken bones in hospitals. He concluded that nurses, like other humans, are repulsed by sickness, and that consequently in a hospital full of sick people they are attracted to men in casts, who were healthy but for their broken and knitting bones. In any case, his recovery went well and he was able to spend New Year's Eve with the nurse in his apartment. For the short while that it lasted, the relationship was "a nice episode."

But another consequence of his accident had a far more meaningful impact. Once he could get around on crutches, Soros hobbled his way up four flights of stairs to the office of the Jewish Board of Guardians, where his earlier requests for stipends had been turned down. His mission this time was to get money on what he knew to be deceitful grounds. His situation was hardly as perilous as the Nazi invasion of Budapest, which had led his father to announce that in the interest of survival the family would suspend its respect for law. Still, the idea rankled, that his classmates could study without working at odd jobs while he could not. To some degree it seemed that his own survival as a student was at stake and that he, too, needed to act like a *débrouillard*.

His plan was to obtain two streams of compensation for his accident: one from the state agency that provided payments for on-the-job disabilities and the other from the Jewish charity. "I wanted to double-dip," he said simply.

So he did not tell the charity that he had broken his leg while working legally as a railroad porter; instead, he concocted a story about the accident occurring while he worked illegally as a house painter. "I lied to them because if they knew it happened while I was working for the railroad then it was obvious that I was entitled to an industrial injuries benefit." At the Jewish Board of Guardians, a clerk told him someone would investigate his claim.

A social worker who was sent to do the checking never uncovered the true circumstances of the accident. Nonetheless, the board refused to pay anything and instead notified Soros that people at the government compensation office had offered assurances that if Soros registered with them, no embarrassing questions would be asked. Since he was already registered there and was anticipating compensation, this assurance was useless. It also made him angry. He believed that if the charity had checked out his story and had not caught him in his lie it was obligated to help him. Seething, he told his contact at the charity that he would not register because he feared that might endanger his chances of becoming a naturalized citizen.

The anger persisted. He was indignant that he had to walk up the stairs with his crutches. He was angry that he had not gained his objective. He felt humiliated. It was like the outburst of pride that had led him to borrow the hundred pounds from his ophthalmologist relative to go skiing after the man had cavalierly offered him a pound to buy chocolates. In the ear-

lier incident he had been bold and now he acted both boldly and unethi-
cally, but in both cases he saw his actions as righteous, even chivalric.
Smoldering with what he now terms "artificial indignation," he wrote to
the chairman of the Jewish Board of Guardians, saying that despite the
board's ruling, he would not starve; still, it pained him "to see how one Jew
deals with another in need."

This letter worked as effectively as the one his friend had sent to the
nurse. The director wrote back that on reconsideration he would personally transmit regular weekly payments by mail so George would not have
to come to their offices and struggle up the stairs.

"So that was a great success, breaking my leg. It was the making of me
as a student. It solved all my financial problems. First I got the industrial
injuries benefit to cover lost wages as a railroad porter. Then I also got a
permanent disability award of 8 percent, meaning that I was 8 percent
incapacitated because of the two screws in my leg. If your award was less
than 10 percent they paid you cash, so I got nearly two hundred pounds,
which meant that I could study the next year without working. Then, in
addition to that, I was getting the weekly payments from the Jewish Board
of Guardians." Only after his leg had completely healed and he had spent
the spring break hitchhiking in France did he write his benefactor at the
board to tell him he could stop sending the money. For sometime afterward, though, he would receive generous gifts from the board on all the
major Jewish holidays.

During the same period Soros received a small unsolicited gift from a
Quaker group. Vera Ansley, an LSE lecturer who had a reputation for
helping Indian students, realized that George was not receiving any scholarship funds and, without telling him, passed the information to the Quak-
ers. Soros then received a note in the mail asking for a few rudimentary
details, which he provided. By return mail he received a check for fifty
pounds. The contrast between the way this donation arrived and his dealings with the Jewish Board of Guardians left him with strong feelings
about charities and how they should work. "I thought to myself: This is the
way to be philanthropic. You trust people, you don't ask questions and
send social workers to check them out," even if they were deceitful and dis-
sembled about the details. Many years later, when he began to make his
own philanthropic grants, the memories of this episode proved instructive.
The overall mission, he resolved, should not be subordinated to bureaucratic nitpicking. It was better to err on the side of generosity.

In late spring, when his leg had mended but before all the payments
were approved, Soros stopped off at the labor exchange to see what jobs

were available. Someone there told him there was work to be had at Quaglino's, an elegant restaurant. From his source he learned about the socio-ethnic conditions in the dining room. It turned out that the waiters, older professionals, were Italian, while the younger men, mostly busboys, were Greeks who had more recently arrived from Cyprus. With the same cunning with which he had analyzed his romantic advantage in the ortho-pedic ward, he determined that the waiters, while still in command, were probably feeling threatened by the demographic shift brought about by an apparent decline in Italian immigration. At the interview with the Italian headwaiter, George said his mother was Italian and claimed to have worked at a hotel in the south of France. He was immediately hired as a busboy. A few weeks later the headwaiter, a Mr. Luparia, told him that the management of the French hotel had written to say no one there had heard of him. Luparia said this had not astonished him, that he could see George had never worked in a dining room. He added, however, that George was doing well and that the restaurant only needed a reference in order to feel protected should he run off with the silver. Soros told them he was at LSE and gave the name of Miss Ansley. It sufficed, and for a while Soros shut-tled between classes, the library, and Quaglino's, where he worked from eight in the evening to two in the morning. "It was hard work but I moved up," he said. "I started on glasses, and then I was promoted to carry out the trays and was even made demichef, which meant that I actually served the diners. I was being paid as a sub waiter but I was beginning to get a share of the kitty. They pooled the tips and used a point system to divide the money, and years later I introduced something like that at Soros Fund Management."

At one point, Luparia praised Soros for his bearing and told him that with work he might one day rise to become an assistant headwaiter. But then George dropped some food on a customer's shirt and was demoted. About the same time, the compensation money arrived, assuring him funds for the next academic year. He quit and spent the summer hitch-hiking through Italy and reading.

The following school year, Soros devoted all of his time to his studies. He attended class, wrote papers, and read a great many books. "I was quite engaged in what I was doing," he recalled. "I felt things and absorbed ideas intensely, but I was unable to make an impact. I think all young people are like that. They feel, intensely, but they are unable to make an impact. Later on, when I was much more able to make an impact, I would feel things much less intensely."

He could have left after two years with a degree from the University of

London, the LSE parent, but if he stayed on an extra year, doing whatever he wanted, he would be eligible for the more prestigious LSE degree. All he had to do was pay the fees and eventually take exams. That is when he decided to ask Karl Popper to be his mentor.

Popper, one of the LSE stars, had been born in Vienna in 1902, and while he had contact with the members of the Vienna circle who helped formulate and promote logical positivism, he gained a reputation as a maverick and referred to himself as a disciple of Socrates. In his writings he originally emphasized the process by which science seeks and establishes truth. In 1937, just before Nazi Germany absorbed Austria, he left with his wife for New Zealand, where he taught in Christchurch. There, far from the war, he spent much of his time writing *The Open Society and Its Enemies*, in which he applied the critical analysis he had first developed while concentrating on pure science to social and political theories, especially those that paved the way for totalitarian regimes.

At the core of this analysis lay his concept of falsification or "fallibilism." As Ralf Dahrendorf wrote,

> Popper is one of the great minds of the century. Some would say that no one in the history of the L.S.E. surpasses him in intellectual stature. Like other great men he stood for one simple but infinitely fertile idea: In a world of uncertainty, we cannot know the truth, we can only guess. No amount of evidence will prove our guesses right, but often one fact suffices to prove them wrong. We have to try again to make better guesses. Some later mocked the simplicity of this idea, but when first formulated it flew in the face of current assumptions, notably those about induction as the method of science.

As applied to social systems, this essential idea had led Popper to observe that societies that encourage continual arguments, refinements, and revisions about their own rules of governance are much more effective than those based on immutable dogmas. While Popper was in New Zealand, *Open Society* was read by Robbins and Hayek. Highly impressed, the two free-market conservatives urged LSE to hire Popper, and in 1945 he was offered a lectureship in logic and scientific method.

Popper was a prickly man, one who would challenge both the great and the humble if he found their reasoning skewed. He aggressively disputed many of the dominant orthodoxies of his age, among them logical positivism, Marxism, historical determinism, linguistic philosophy, and psychoanalysis, which he branded a pseudoscience. Much later, he would seriously tell Soros that he himself was the only person in the world who had the knowledge necessary to critically review his own work. The most famous example of his confident pugnacity, which has entered the philosophical lore of the twentieth century, concerned his confrontation with Wittgenstein in what came to be known as the poker incident. It took place in October of 1946, when Popper was presenting a paper at a meeting of the Moral Science Club at King's College, Cambridge, in the presence of Britain's philosophical elders. Wittgenstein, the head of the club, who had in turn been wunderkind, enfant terrible, and éminence grise of the Cambridge philosophical establishment, had by this time discarded his mathematically precise approach. Instead he was emphasizing linguistics, contending that all philosophical problems were essentially illusions that reflected the ambiguities of language.

At the meeting, Popper and Wittgenstein sat facing each other. A fire warmed the room, and Wittgenstein was cradling a poker. It was apparent that the two disliked each other. Wittgenstein challenged Popper on his terminology, questioning what he meant by "philosophical puzzles." When Popper identified several problems, Wittgenstein scorned them as "pseudo problems." Popper then raised the issue of moral rules. Wittgenstein, who by some accounts was excited and waving the poker, said there were no valid moral rules and challenged Popper to provide an example. At that point Popper replied, "Not to threaten visiting lecturers with pokers." There was laughter, and Wittgenstein stalked out of the room, charging his adversary with confusing the issues. Bertrand Russell, by then estranged from his former collaborator, called out, "Wittgenstein, you're the one who's causing the confusion."

News of the exchange quickly spread through the intellectual establishment, reflecting, among other things, an era when the arguments of philosophers could attract public attention. It also established Popper as a man confident enough to take on Wittgenstein, the resident "genius," on his home ground. Popper could be just as devastating with much lesser lights. Bernard Levin, the journalist, who studied with Popper at LSE and admired him greatly, would occasionally recall his professor's classes in his column in the *Times* of London. "It was not, I must say, an entirely smooth passage into enlightenment; our guru had a sharp tongue," he wrote in one column. "One day, at a seminar, a fellow student offered an opinion in terms greatly lacking in coherence. The sage turned and said bluntly: 'I don't understand what you are talking about.' My hapless colleague flushed and rephrased his comment. 'Ah,' said Popper. 'Now I understand what you are saying and I think it's nonsense.' "

This was the man whom George Soros chose to be his mentor. He was not put off by the bristly reputation; indeed, he was attracted by it. It also did not matter that he was registered as an economics student and had never taken a course with Popper, or any philosophy course. In his summer as a lifeguard he had read *Philosophy in a New Key*, by Susanne K. Langer, which proclaimed an ongoing resurgence of philosophy. He was excited by the book and read many of the works Langer mentioned. More recently he had read Popper's *Open Society* with great interest and some identification. Once more showing his abundant confidence, Soros at the age of twenty-one wrote to the aloof and critical Popper:

> I have just read *Open Society* and it made a profound impression on me. Although it was my interest in historical generalizations that has led me to read it, I agree with most of your statements. I believe, however, that a theory of historical development need not necessarily be historicist. In fact, I find no argument in your book to contradict this.
>
> I am, however, in no position to argue the subject and that is exactly why I am writing to you. My interest, as I said, lies in the study of human development because I think that the laws of change are the only ones that are universally valid for all forms of society. For my first degree, however, I specialized in international trade and at the moment in lieu of a third year B.Sc. Econ course, I am registered for a part time M.Sc. in Welfare Economics.
>
> It follows that I have to work on my pet subject entirely on my own. Science, as you say, is a social process: it is difficult to make progress without guidance and only too easy to become a dilettante or a crank in the absence of criticism.
>
> Having read your book, I am convinced you could help me greatly by directing my studies. I know that it is a very unrewarding service that I ask of you because although I want to work as a postgraduate, my present knowledge on the subject is that of a fresher.
>
> If you could spare me the time, I would be very much obliged if you could see me one evening after 6 o'clock.

CHAPTER 7

WORK

WHEN GEORGE SOROS first ventured deeply and innovatively into international philanthropy in 1982, he called his first foundation the Open Society Fund, and he named the scholarships he was handing out to East Europeans in honor of Karl Popper, who was still alive. Later, as his charitable undertakings spread around the world, Soros consistently praised and honored Popper at every opportunity. The impression left by such tributes was not only that Soros was grateful to Popper for providing him with his philosophical framework, but that the older man had also been a warm and nurturing adviser, a sort of modern-day Plato to a would-be Aristotle.

Actually, the contact between the two during Soros's final year at LSE was not very close at all. It was, in fact, so remote that when Soros wrote to Popper in the spring of 1982 to inform him of the fund and the scholarships established in his name, the seventy-nine-year-old philosopher wrote back saying he could barely recall Soros.

"Let me first thank you for not having forgotten me," wrote the recently knighted Sir Karl in a firm hand. "I am afraid I forgot you completely; even your name created at first only the most minute resonance. But I made some effort, and now, I think, I just remember you, though I do not think I should recognize you."

The doubt was understandable. Soros himself is not sure how often he met with Popper at Popper's home during his time at LSE, whether there was just one meeting or two. But after receiving Soros's request that he oversee his work in the spring of 1952, Popper responded by urging him to write a paper about the differences between "open" and "closed" societies. Soros submitted such a paper, and he is certain that Popper then invited him to his house to offer criticism. "He was very nice and encouraging, though critical. I was supposed to correct the essay based on our discussion, but instead, I wrote him another essay about historical dynamics." This second paper contained the first kernel of Soros's ideas about reflexivity, or the dynamic relationship between reality and attempts to perceive it, which was to become a favored theme he would later apply to finance. Popper was disappointed that he had not revised his first paper, but Soros is not sure whether this displeasure was conveyed in writing or at another meeting. In any case, his contacts with Popper were then suspended: "So that was that with Popper, until much later."

Short as the relationship had been, it marked a profound turning point in Soros's life, one that shaped his most valuable ideas. It is clear that involvement provided Soros with the only peg upon which he could hang his lofty ambitions and messianic dreams during his London years. He did not shine as a student. When he finally obtained his bachelor's degree after taking competitive exams, it was only an undistinguished lower second. Emotionally, he had found nothing in England that could even remotely compete with his ties to his family, particularly to Tivadar. Nor had he experienced anything like the risks and excitements of war and the Communist takeover that followed in Hungary. As for the inspiring richness of British postwar intellectual life, he sensed it only at a distance, as a humbled outsider. George may well have been conceited and arrogant, but he was not deluded; he has always been coldly self-critical. His time in England, he concluded, was not triumphant or even promising. The only bright spots were the dealings with Popper, who, however briefly, engaged him seriously and offered him his thoughts to build on.

Yet those dreams of becoming an original and influential philosopher were so powerful that they have persisted as unfulfilled yearnings ever since, enduring despite all of Soros's remarkable achievements as financier, philanthropist, and stateless statesman. In 1995, he candidly confessed to his desire in a remarkable public speech entitled "A Failed Philosopher Tries Again," which he delivered at the Institute of Human Sciences in Vienna. In it he spoke of his lifelong and mostly solitary effort to establish human fallibility as a principle as, or even more, useful than *"cogito ergo sum."* "I cannot prove it, the way Descartes claimed to prove his own existence. God knows I've tried and sometimes have come quite close, but in the end I always get caught in a web of my own weaving."

In the talk, Soros further declared: "In my case, the belief in my own fallibility has guided me both in making money and giving it away. But there is more to my existence than money. I focused on it in my career mainly because I recognized that there is a tendency in our society to exaggerate the importance of money. We appraise artists by how much their creations fetch. We appraise politicians by the amount of money that they can raise; often they appraise themselves by the amount of money they can make on the side. Having recognized the importance of making money, I may yet come to be recognized as a great philosopher—which would give me more satisfaction than the fortune I have made." Soros's eyes may have twinkled in recognition that his audience might not fully believe his claim, but people very close to Soros, among them his oldest son, Robert, are certain he has never given up the dreams of philosophical greatness and glory.

As for his attraction to Popper's particular teachings, Soros found much in them that echoed his own experiences and interests. What he had seen of Nazis and Communists led him to cherish the philosopher's anti-dogmatic and anti-totalitarian thrust. His father's stress on the inevitability of unforeseen consequences seemed to mesh with Popper's emphasis on fallibility. Moreover, from childhood, Tivadar had tutored his son to welcome criticism, regarding it not as a humiliation but as an indispensable tool for learning and growth. This agreed with Popper's advocacy of learning through trial and error, a constant labor of testing hypotheses, finding flaws, refining ideas, and again testing them to find more flaws.

After graduating from the LSE, Soros's dreams of philosophic breakthroughs and grand, socially beneficial accomplishment persisted although, or perhaps because, real life was providing very little in the way of excitement. Dutifully he wrote perfunctory letters to his parents, who then sent copies to Paul, who was by then living in New York. They also sent George copies of Paul's letters. Paul had escaped from Budapest the year after George left. He spent a year in a displaced persons camp in Austria and arrived in New York with $17. He worked as a tennis pro and attended Brooklyn Polytechnic, where he soon graduated with a degree in engineering. Soon after he arrived he met and married Daisy, a fellow Hungarian, who had also spent part of the war in hiding.

From his parents' letters George learned that Erzebet had taken lessons in pastry-making from the confectioner at Gerbeaud's, the city's historic café. She and Tivadar had tested the limits of Communist tolerance for free enterprise by selling coffee and petit fours at the house on Lupa. Tivadar was giving Russian lessons to Hungarians and Hungarian lessons to industrial managers from Moscow, preferring not to work in a legal collective as all lawyers were forced to do. In addition to the Lupa coffee-house, which operated in warm weather, Erzebet started a nursery school in the apartment on Kossuth Place.

Paul, married and with a job, seemed to be striding forward. When they were boys Paul had always beaten George in sports and at times had beaten him physically. The sense of competitiveness that had bound the two in games and sports spilled over into other realms. George's letters, unlike Paul's, were not very focused. They pointedly avoided any mention of the gap between his expectations and his prospects. His acquisition of a degree from the LSE had brought no great changes in his life. He was living in the same apartment at 23 Dunster Gardens, letting out several rooms to students so that effectively he paid no rent. He had acquaintances and friends and there were frequent parties. He had girlfriends, but in this area, as in school, the successes were modest.

He had not given much thought to making a living, but in that last year at the LSE, as he was working on his papers for Popper, he often spent time with an evening student named Simon Kester, who was eight years older. Kester was studying psychology but harbored ambitions to sing Gilbert and Sullivan; he would later have a career as a television show host. The two friends would go off for hikes in the countryside and talk late into the night. Kester was at night school because he had a full-time job as the general manager of a firm that distributed what were known as fancy goods: leather handbags, souvenirs, and cheap jewelry. Kester introduced George to Freddie Silverman, the son of the owner, and Silverman, who was charmed by Soros, offered him a position.

"The company was one of the leading firms in an industry which didn't have any leading firms," jokes Soros. "Freddie, the son, befriended me. He took an interest in me as a nice slob, and he was very decent. We remained friends forever after. But in terms of a career, or training, it was no good. They had no idea of how to train a management trainee, so they put me through various departments where I worked, building handbags, selling this and that."

The company, L. S. Mayer, employed several hundred people and had a relatively modern factory in London's Islington section where one floor was devoted to fabricating leather handbags and another to plastic bags. There was a showroom and a jewelry department that stocked imports. Much of the business involved importing leather goods from Germany.

The work was, in Soros's words, "boring, demeaning, and meaningless." After he had been routed to all the various departments he was assigned to sales. "Effectively, I became the assistant to a traveling salesman. And I felt I was going in the wrong direction."

He was there for several years before he decided to quit, making a career move into an environment that soon made L. S. Mayer seem elegant. He became a salesman for a wholesaler who sold souvenirs and knickknacks to tobacconists. The man was a jobber who bought some of his materials from the Mayer firm, distributing his goods in several territories. He supplied Soros with a Ford Anglia car and assigned him to work the London area. "He was a very crude man, a really low-class character," said Soros. "The job proved to be impossible because all the London tobacconists were associated with wholesaling cooperatives that supplied all their stuff. So I spent my days driving around, calling on shops, unable to make any sales and often not able to find any place to park."

Having failed in London, Soros was given the North Wales territory, and was once even allowed to go to Blackpool, the seaside amusement park resort that was the hottest market for geegaws, doohickeys, and knickknacks. "I was aware I had sunk even lower. Having realized I had gone in the wrong direction with Mayer, I had taken a further step in the wrong. I remember I was also courting a girl and that didn't go well either. I was becoming depressed. It was similar to the feeling I had had when I had sat in the Lyons Corner house and realized I had reached bottom. This girl I was involved with had just gone up to Cambridge. She abandoned me because I was not in her league. She couldn't quite cope with a traveling salesman taking her out in an Anglia and screwing her. It didn't fit into her life, so she broke up with me and I was very keen on her. This was another low point."

In his despair his thoughts turned to his parents. "I felt they would be disappointed. This was very strong in me. I had the feeling that considering the stable I had come from, I was not the kind of horse I ought to be. This sort of homing instinct, or the standards I brought with me, was very strong in stopping me from sinking into something that was really not me. And I said to myself, I have to make a radical break with this. That's when I decided to try to get into the City, into a merchant bank."

His approach was logical but unusual for the time. He took the stock exchange yearbook and wrote to the managing directors of merchant banks asking for job interviews. He hired a typist whom he found through an advertisement in *The New Statesman* to type the letters. She was a sympathetic woman, and among the interviews that Soros obtained was one she had secured through a contact with a partner at Lazard Freres. Though that meeting did not lead to a job, George found it memorable and highly instructive.

"The man was very nice and he tried to dissuade me from going into the City. He explained that it was a club. I remember that he told me: 'We practice intelligent nepotism,' which he then explained. 'You see, every managing director has a number of nephews. One of them is bound to be intelligent, and so he's the one who is going to be the next managing director.' Then he said, 'Look, if you went to the same college as the current director, you might have a chance, or if you went to the same university, but you're not even from the same country.' "

Soros appreciated the man's candor. It would soon be confirmed when Soros was hired by the firm of Singer & Friedlander, whose principals, two brothers named Hock, had originally come from Hungary and spoke Hungarian; there, at least, Soros was from the same country. He had gotten that interview through his ophthalmologist relative, who maintained an account there.

At the outset of his new employment Soros did not think he had achieved a very significant reversal of fortunes. The position, which paid seven pounds a week, was another vague trainee position in which he rotated through different postings doing humdrum work that he performed rather poorly. In one of these assignments he had to keep running tabulations, by hand, in two ledgers accounting for foreign currency transactions. At the end of the day the two tallies, one a credit, the other a debit, were supposed to cancel each other out, but they never did. In his family he had always had a reputation for carelessness, losing pens, notebooks, and, later, raincoats. Not surprisingly, he was a dud as a bookkeeper, and his bosses regularly had to undo his errors.

For a while he was assigned to help a legendary figure called Captain Pugasch trade gold shares between markets in Johannesburg, Brussels, Paris, and London. Pugasch was meticulous and kept his pencils sharpened to very fine points. Soros did not. Soros's work habits did not endear him to Pugasch, who had his new apprentice transferred as soon as he could. The next stop was an assignment as a clerk—a factotum, he calls it—in the arbitrage trading department. Here his desk was close to the firm's research department, and for the first time he became intrigued by what he heard. One of the three analysts on the research team, another Hungarian named John Ranyi, befriended the newcomer and explained what he was doing and thinking. Soros soon began trading on his own, using a stake of a few hundred pounds that the ophthalmologist put up with the understanding that the two would share profits. Soros remembers his first investment: a special class of stock for the English Hoover vacuum cleaner company that he had learned about from the research people. It paid off.

Technically, his position was that of an arbitragist, albeit junior grade. In those days, arbitrage meant buying in one market and selling in another, seeking to take advantage of generally small variations in price. As Soros explains it, the idea was to spot a trend and position yourself. "Let's say you noticed that Brussels was accumulating one particular gold stock in South Africa, so you would try to buy it in South Africa and then sell it in Brussels later in the day, that sort of thing." It was a highly technical and professional activity involving a good deal of risk and the need to make speedy decisions. Soros was still learning his way when one weekend he had to fly to Paris to see Paul and Daisy, who were at the end of a sad European visit.

Paul and his wife had come from America mourning the death of their infant son, who had been struck and killed by a playground swing near their home. The couple stayed with George in London before moving on to visit with Daisy's parents in Vienna. Now, as they were about to return to New York, George flew to Paris to spend a final weekend with them. But on the Monday when he was to return, the Paris airport was fogged in and he did not get back to London until Tuesday. When he did, his reception was frosty and he was ordered to see the senior partner.

The man wanted to know what had happened and went on to tell Soros that the management had been less than thrilled with his performance. "He told me that if I was waiting for them to find a place for me, I would wait in vain. He said they had no place for me and that wherever I had worked I was a fifth wheel. The partner said that if I could generate business, that would be fine, but if I was looking for a sinecure, well they didn't have any." Soros thought quickly, knowing that in those days even a junior clerk needed his employer's permission to look for a new job. He asked whether the firm would have any objection to his looking for work elsewhere. The partner replied, "No, you can go with our blessing."

Soros came out of the meeting slightly chastened and a little anxious, but within hours what had seemed to be a setback turned into another lucky, life-changing break. He had gone to lunch with another of the firm's trainees, a young American named Robert Mayer, whose father had a small brokerage firm on Wall Street, F. M. Mayer. Soros told his colleague what had happened that morning, and Mayer then told him that his father was looking for an arbitrage trader in New York and that he had meant to offer the post to George but had not done so because of the prevailing etiquette that discouraged luring away another firm's employee. "So missing a day's work and being chastised was what brought me to the United States," recalled Soros.

In fact, his relocation was to take several months. There was a problem

in obtaining a U.S. visa under the quota system. His application was
rejected on the grounds that at twenty-five he was too young to qualify as
a specialist whose services were urgently required in the United States. In
New York, F. M. Mayer consulted a man named Franz Pick, the publisher
of the *Black Market Yearbook*, which kept tabs on black market rates of currencies around the world. Pick submitted an affidavit in support of Soros,
saying that the position of arbitragist was very taxing and that the risks that
such people constantly assumed took a dreadful toll on their health and
nerves and consequently they tended to die young. Pick wrote that they
had to be hired young because by the time they were older they were
either dead or dying. Though there was hyperbole in this declaration, it
contained an element of actuarial truth: a high percentage of arbitragists
did suffer heart attacks. In any case, Pick's affidavit proved persuasive when
it was submitted with Soros's reapplication.

The additional months of waiting had also proven advantageous.
Through the late spring and summer, Soros hit a hot streak at Singer &
Friedlander. The Ford Motor Company had gone public through an international distribution of shares. George realized that the demand for the
shares in America would be higher than in Europe. At his urging the firm
bought up Ford shares in London and sold them in New York, scoring a
significant success.

"After I got the job in America, I became more active," Soros remembers. "My salary was practically doubled. I got twelve pounds a week. I was
a bit more successful inside the firm because I began to trade and I had
some ideas that the firm actually followed. I was beginning to find my way.
The Ford transaction was a big thing."

By the time the visa arrived, Soros's confidence was high. He was heading to New York, where a job and his brother were waiting. He also had
his share of the earnings he had accumulated by investing his second
cousin's money, about $5,000. He booked passage on the liner *America*,
and in September of 1956, George Soros left Europe behind.

PART II

MAKING MONEY

CHAPTER 8

AMERICA

WHEN A twenty-six-year-old George Soros crossed the Atlantic in 1956, he had a concrete plan in mind. He would work hard on Wall Street for precisely five years, which he calculated would be enough time for him to save $500,000. With that stake he would return to England and pursue philosophical studies as an independent scholar. "It was my five-year plan," he recalled. "At the time I did not particularly care for the United States. I had acquired some basic British prejudices; you know, the States were, well, commercial, crass, and so on. I also had some of my father's prejudices. He had visited America before the war and I remember how he used to say that he never wanted to exchange his collective misery in Europe for individual misery in America."

Like so many others, Soros was coming to the United States solely for the economic opportunities the country provided. He moved in with his brother in Queens and started work almost immediately for F. M. Mayer. Soon he found a two-room apartment on Riverside Drive in Manhattan, near the tomb of Ulysses S. Grant. Columbia University was a few blocks to the south and Harlem lay immediately to the east. Each morning Soros took the train to Wall Street from 125th Street, the colorful main thoroughfare of the most famous urban black community in the United States.

F. M. Mayer was not a member of the New York Stock Exchange. It functioned as an over-the-counter trader, and Soros's job was to handle arbitrage in foreign securities, basically trading the same gold shares and oil shares as he had in England. It was not a big part of the firm's business. But barely a month after his arrival, Soros again found luck when the Suez crisis erupted into violence. Earlier that summer, Egypt's president Gamal Abdel Nasser had nationalized the canal, seizing control from the internationally owned private stock company that ran it. In August Nasser expelled British oil officials from Egypt. Then in late October, Israeli forces launched a lightning attack and seized the Gaza Strip and almost all of the Sinai. Taking advantage of Egypt's losses, Britain and France attacked Egyptian positions by air and established their own control over the canal zone until pressure from the United States forced their withdrawal and led to the creation of a U.N. peacekeeping force.

Even after diplomacy forced the European invaders to pull back, scuttled ships and damaged locks left the waterway impassable and forced shipping companies to set their tankers on longer and costlier courses to transport their oil. Given the upheavals, the market in oil shares became very active, and Soros, using connections he had established in England, rushed in. He would look for opportunities in Europe, obtain commitments, and publish his offerings on the so-called pink sheets that were distributed to brokerages as a sort of mimeographed and quite primitive antecedent of NASDAQ. Brokerages would call on behalf of their customers while prices often fluctuated minute to minute. Professionally, it turned out to be a productive time for the newcomer, and except for walking to and from the subway he had no time to explore his new environment.

But in that tempestuous autumn, the Suez was not the only international crisis that gripped his attention. On October 23 the citizenry of Budapest rose up against Communist rule. With bullets, rocks, and Molotov cocktails they drove Russian troops and tanks out of the city and their national leaders seemed on the verge of taking Hungary out of the Soviet bloc. Then by early November the Soviet army rolled back with a vengeance. Street fighting persisted, but the uprising, which Hungarians would later upgrade to a revolution, was ultimately crushed. Hundreds would be hanged, tens of thousands were arrested, and several hundreds of thousands took flight, leaving their apartments with only the documents and keepsakes they could carry and rushing to the Austrian border in hopes of getting across before the escape route was slammed shut. In the stream of fleeing and despairing Hungarians were Erzebet and Tivadar. She was fifty-two and he was sixty-two.

For the second time in their lives the two of them locked up the apartment on Kossuth Place in a flight from tyranny, this time taking a train to Mosonmagyarovar in the northwest. They hired a guide and walked for a long time before a Russian soldier stopped them at a railroad trestle. They were marched back and put aboard a train to Budapest. The following day they set out again for another station in the border area. As Erzebet described it, they walked through muddy fields in the rain, accompanying a fleeing street fighter they had met on the train, his pregnant wife, and their four-year-old child. At one point a peasant gave them eggs and sheltered them in his hut until a Russian patrol passed. Erzebet remembered the anxiety and the mud: "With each step my boots were so full of mud. I must have had at least four or five pounds of mud hanging from each shoe. The walk was very tiresome and the freedom fighter was setting a fast tempo. Tivadar put the little boy on his shoulders and helped the pregnant wife and I was walking behind them and you could hear the church bells ahead where the Austrians were ringing them to point the way for the people who were escaping. Finally we arrived at a highway and we met an Austrian patrol and they told us, 'You are already in Austria.' "

In New York, George, who had long ago reconciled himself to never again seeing his beloved parents, was aroused by the events. He did not know whether his parents were among those leaving, but he thought they might be. From the outburst in October to the revolution's suppression in November, hopes rose and plummeted, and yet Soros does not remember the joys or strains that the news from Hungary inspired. "What I remember are the events. I remember President Eisenhower's speech when he effectively sold the Hungarians down the river. And the Suez crisis with its financial implications. Then you had the beginning of the refugee flow." By early November, his parents had arrived in Vienna and he heard their voices over the telephone. Soon after, George befriended three Hungarian freedom fighters, among the first of the refugees to arrive in New York. They were living at International House, a student residence financed by the Rockefellers that was just two blocks from his apartment. He would join them after work and they became among the first friends he made in New York apart from his fellow workers at F. M. Mayer.

Soros obviously took the Hungarian revolution and its suppression to heart, but he was also able to compartmentalize his anxieties and thoughts about family and homeland, not allowing them to distract him from his work. This ability to keep competing interests distinct is a trait his associates have noted throughout his career. They have described, for example, how he would abruptly turn away from some pending multimillion-dollar venture to address complex problems in his philanthropic foundations and then switch back to the money matters, shifting gears without dropping a beat, a decimal place, or any hint of emotion.

Indeed, when his parents finally arrived on a ship with many other

Hungarian refugees on January 17, 1957, Soros, who had not seen them for almost ten years, was too busy to meet them at the pier—Paul did— from which they were taken to an emergency refugee processing center at Camp Kilmer in New Jersey. Then, as Erzebet recalled it, after three days it was Paul again who picked them up and drove them to his apartment. "George was busy in his office so we just waited for him," Erzebet said, adding that he finally came and took them to live with him on Riverside Drive. "We lived with George for three years; he moved over to the living room couch and we stayed in the bedroom."

Unquestionably, the family reunion was profoundly moving for George. Just three months earlier, he had come to America certain that the Iron Curtain would continue to divide the family. Then, unexpectedly and miraculously, the four Soroses, who had been separated under Nazi occupation and then split by Communism, were together in the same city. George happily welcomed his parents and regarded the idea of sharing his home with them as a blessing.

"For me their arrival was very positive, very joyous. In America children had a great desire to strike out on their own and leave their parents behind. But I had done that. I had been without them for ten years. So for me, it was a source of joy. I had no fear of having to subordinate myself to my parents' wishes. I'd established myself as an independent person and I loved to have them there, especially since I didn't have such a brilliant social life. It was very nice to have parents to come home to and have your mother cook for you."

And yet he had not gone to see them when their boat landed. "I was busy. I was trading, I couldn't miss a day. I could not miss a day, no."

In fact, because of the time difference between New York and Europe, he could not miss a night and had been working pretty much around the clock. "I would get these coded cables that came in a certain sequence of five digits in order to save money on cable costs." The numbers revealed the name of the stock, the volume, and the price. They would arrive via RCA or the French cable company, whose operators would call him at home. "I would be wakened at 4:30, which is 9:30 in London, and then maybe every hour. I'd be asleep, pick up the phone, listen to the numbers and decide to make a bid or not. I might cable back a bid and go back to sleep. Sometimes I would then dream that the stock I had just bought went up and there were times when I'd wake up and have a little difficulty figuring out what I had done and what I had dreamed." Then as the New York business day began he would offer his overnight acquisitions to buyers.

Eventually the Middle East tensions eased and the feverish trading in oil shares subsided. At that point, with the help of Paul Cohn, an older man at the Mayer firm, Soros devised a new market. As he recalls, his first such venture involved a Canadian company, Northspan Uranium, that was seeking capital to develop a new mine. Their bonds had warrants attached to them. After a specified period the warrants could be used to acquire shares. Soros came up with a scheme for trading the bonds and the shares independently. "We employed due bills," he explained. "Let's say you sold the bonds to a reputable broker. The broker would give you back a due bill declaring that they would deliver the shares when they became detachable. And then you made a market in the due bills."

Soros had found an inconsistency in the market and was exploiting price differences between the already matured shares and the due bills, which were like embryonic shares. He called it internal arbitrage "because we were trading one related share against another, as opposed to trading the same unit in different markets as in international arbitrage."

One of the people he met in this period was Alan C. Greenberg, now the chief executive officer of Bear Stearns, who likes people to call him Ace. In 1957, when Greenberg was a twenty-eight-year-old hard charger heading the arbitrage department at Bear Stearns, Soros would regularly call him on the direct phone line that linked the small Mayer firm to Bear Stearns. "George was always full of ideas. He would discuss them and if I liked them we would buy them together with George's firm," said Greenberg.

"I remember one very clearly. Sperry Rand was coming out with a bond issue with warrants. Warrants were a nasty thing in those days. George said that if we sell the bonds we can create the warrants and they're going to be valuable. Nobody had ever done this. So we bought these bonds and we sold them. And the people who bought the bonds from us were strictly bond people; they didn't know stocks and they certainly didn't know warrants, and they couldn't wait to get out of the warrants, which they were happy to let us have for chicken crap. And then we bought the warrants, and they became very valuable and we started trading due bills for them and it worked out fantastically."

Greenberg said that after this he would regularly discuss things with Soros, mostly by phone or over an occasional lunch. "He was always working and I knew right away that he was a different kind of cat. He had all these incredible ideas. Back then there was no such thing as a researcher or an analyst; we called these guys statisticians—at Bear Stearns we had just one—and the research they generated was stuff that came mostly from the newspapers. George would share his ideas with me because for a young man I had a considerable amount of buying power and I don't think F. M. Mayer let him have too much of a line. After Sperry Rand he came up with another warrant deal on Trans-Canada Pipeline. That turned out to be huge."

Greenberg said that in those days, Soros did not have the assets to involve himself in risk arbitrage, where the goal is to speculate in securities whose price might benefit from future corporate mergers. "Back then, his ideas never involved mergers, where things can fall through. He was discovering anomalies, and in his ideas there was no risk of the deal falling through. It was just right or wrong. When he came to me with the Trans-Canada Pipeline, I'm not sure I knew anything about Canada, but you didn't need to know."

As Soros remembers this period, after Northspan he focused on warrants and due bills for other uranium issues and applied the approach to natural gas companies, which for a while became the core of his business. "As I said, it was not exactly my idea. Paul Cohn deserves the credit, the due bill was his invention, but he was too old to trade, so to speak; he didn't have the stomach for it. So I traded." In addition to laying off warrants and due bills with Bear Stearns, Soros found a particularly big buyer for the Trans-Canada due bills in S. G. Warburg in London, where he had a connection.

"I was flourishing," said Soros. "I developed relationships with very reputable houses. Morgan Stanley became an established client. They gave me first crack. I had called on them and they made some complimentary noises about how useful I was to them, and so on. I felt that I had penetrated the inner workings of Wall Street rather quickly. I knew all the telephone numbers of all the brokerage houses by heart, maybe twenty or thirty."

Soros grew more and more confident. In London he had felt a failure when he could not sell fancy goods to cigar stores; now he felt he had put the small Mayer firm on the map by making deals with giants such as Morgan Stanley, Kuhn Loeb, and Warburg. His salary was tied to his performance and though he cannot remember what it was he recalls that he was running well ahead of his five-year plan. "I felt very comfortable; for the first time in my life, I was successful."

He was successful, but he was also lonely. He would visit the Hungarian friends he made at International House and travel to New Canaan, Connecticut, where Paul had moved. He spent his first summer vacation in Quogue, Long Island, where International House had a holiday retreat. He did not socialize much with his business contacts, a pattern he would follow through much of his career. "From the beginning I didn't like to mix business and social life. I realized that if you did, you had to watch your step, you had to be careful of what you said. If you fraternize with clients, then you have to suck up to them and that is hardly relaxing, and so I did not build friendships. I was something of a loner." Greenberg says that he and Soros liked each other but they never socialized.

Meanwhile, Tivadar, who had always been a godfather figure, providing help to others, was finding his own dependency in New York hard to accept. Though George and Paul were happy to take care of their parents, Tivadar found the new situation humiliating. This led him to a quixotic entrepreneurial idea of his own: He and Erzebet would open an espresso bar. She would make cakes, petit fours, and sandwiches and he would act as host. He met a man Paul Soros remembers as a shadowy figure in a white suit who helped Tivadar find what he believed to be a perfect location. It was in Far Rockaway, an isolated beachfront community with few tourists and an aging population. Obviously, his idea was to replicate the success he and Erzebet had when they turned their house on Lupa Island into an espresso bar. But Far Rockaway was not Lupa. In 1957, no one there seemed interested in good coffee or Erzebet's homemade cakes and sweets. In their desire to earn their own way, the elder Soroses fixed up the rented space, put in tables and chairs, and waited for customers who never came. By the end of the summer they conceded failure. The fact that people preferred Coca-Cola to coffee and hot dogs to Sacher torte or pastries simply confirmed Tivadar's misgivings about America, although he remained a great admirer of ketchup, which he had first tasted in Chicago before the war.

Defeated in Far Rockaway, he and Erzebet returned to Riverside Drive, and Tivadar, despite his age, applied for office jobs. George remembers that on one occasion, when an interviewer asked Tivadar what he wanted to do, he had answered, "Well, I'd like to start at the top and work my way down." In the prevailing ethos of corporate conformity, such replies did not go over well. It was hard to be a *lebenkunstler* in the America of the late fifties, and for some time Tivadar thought of going back to Europe, perhaps to live in Vienna.

But in the immediate wake of the coffee house debacle, he drew on past experience. "My father reverted to a lifestyle which he learned as a prisoner of war—to make the days pass quickly while spending the least money possible. I had done something similar when I came to London. He would go to Times Square where before two o'clock he could see a movie for forty cents, then he would have a hot dog for a quarter. He worked it out that he could live on eight dollars a week." In a sense, Tivadar was making a game of his difficulties, but for a while the atmosphere in the Riverside Drive apartment must have been very peculiar. George was getting coded phone calls and making as much money as he could while his father headed for the movies to see how little he could spend.

By his third summer in New York George was renting his own beach place in the Hamptons. He bought a used Pontiac and would go out to the house on weekends with his girlfriend, Annaliese Witschak, whom he would soon marry. During the weekdays his parents used it. Annaliese was an attractive and elegant woman with an interest in art and music who had emigrated to America from her native Germany. She was an orphan who had also survived the deprivations of war and the dislocations of peace near Hamburg. With few family ties holding her to Germany, she came to New York, where she was working for an insurance company entering data on punch cards. George met Annaliese at an outdoor concert at Tanglewood in the Berkshires, one of his early exploratory outings in America. Both shared high-brow preferences for classical music. They visited art museums reflecting eclectic tastes that embraced old masters as well as works of contemporary and avant-garde artists. When they went to the theater, it was likely to be to an off-Broadway performance, and many of the movies they saw were foreign imports. George had always been fond of the ballet, and under Annaliese's tutelage he became increasingly enthusiastic about modern dance. He enjoyed jazz but beyond that he was not attracted to American pop culture. He rarely watched television and would have trouble identifying even the most popular serials or situation comedies of the last forty years. Family members say they doubt whether George has ever seen a baseball or a football game.

But he maintained his interest in participatory sport and quickly found his way to the tennis courts in Central Park and to indoor swimming pools. He continued skiing and once, when he took Annaliese with him, she broke her leg. He brought her home to his apartment, where Erzebet and Tivadar looked after her. The elder Soroses quickly grew very close to Annaliese and she to them. In 1959 George left the two rooms on Riverside Drive to his parents and moved into Annaliese's Christopher Street apartment in Greenwich Village and soon after he married her.

As for Tivadar, in time he found projects. Along with Erzebet he served as a baby-sitter looking after neighbors' children. Tivadar also taught English to other Hungarian newcomers. At one point he bought himself a Greyhound bus ticket good for unlimited travel and used it to explore the country. Though he never felt as comfortable in America as he had been in

Europe, he became a naturalized citizen and acquired some admiration for certain aspects of American life beyond ketchup. He found a circle of bridge players and met some Esperantists. He also tended to the family's old real estate interests in Europe. What was left of his Budapest holdings had been confiscated by the Communists, but the buildings in Vienna and Berlin had survived the war with relatively minor damage. The Austrians had recognized the family's claims and restored the property. In Germany, where the huge apartment building was a valuable asset, the issue of ownership took longer to establish. But eventually Tivadar received title as well as compensation for its seizure by the Nazis. Before his death, he sold the property, using the payment and the compensation, a total of about $600,000, to establish a family foundation in Switzerland.

"My father had this peculiar attitude toward this money," explained George. "He regarded it as the family estate, so he didn't use it at all. His idea was to conserve the capital which led to the Swiss foundation." That nest egg would later multiply, after Tivadar entrusted it to a hedge fund established by George. Ultimately it provided the basis for the first of George Soros's major philanthropies.

Erzebet found acclimation easier than her husband. Though Tivadar's command of English was better, her accent proved less impenetrable. She found it rewarding to work with children as she had in Budapest and made a number of friends, including some who shared her growing interest in Christian narratives and imagery as well as spiritualism. She visited museums, met emigré artists, and eventually enrolled at Fordham University, taking courses in art, psychology, and religion.

George continued to see a great deal of his parents even after he moved in with Annaliese. He also spent some time reading and writing philosophical tracts that he never showed anyone, but mostly he was trading. After three years at the Mayer firm, where he was considerably outperforming the targets of his five-year plan, he was getting restless and had vague thoughts of moving on. These crystallized rather suddenly when F. M. Mayer called him in to question a business decision. "He wasn't harsh but he was asking me, Why do we have this position in Shell? And I felt that this was none of his business, because, you know, I had felt I was in charge. I had built up a record and I resented it. I resented it so much that I decided I was going to leave."

He had no trouble landing a new position with Wertheim & Co., a company larger and richer than F. M. Mayer. It had been founded in 1917, and, unlike Mayer, it was a member of the New York Stock Exchange, which meant that George no longer had to go through outside brokers to trade. He felt he was moving in the right direction. At the age of twenty-nine he would be the assistant to the head of the foreign trading department. The European Coal and Steel Community had been formed seven years earlier and notions of a United States of Europe were in the air. However wispy and premature such ideas proved to be, they were then generating a growing interest in European securities that went beyond the international markers of oil and gold shares. This gave George another opportunity, and he seized it. He was no longer simply a trader: his business card now bore the designation "analyst," a move that in his eyes was definitely a step up. "It was more interesting. I would become an expert in European securities."

"What I was doing," says Soros, "was looking at European companies and trying to establish their values." Throughout Europe, companies were under no obligation to disclose the kind of information that under law companies had to make available in the United States. "It was all very opaque. You had to use your imagination to guess what the true value of a company might be." Sometimes he would work backwards from tax returns to establish that a company had far more assets than were being cited in perfunctory annual reports. He also began to visit the companies, a practice that was then unusual. "I was often the first one to interview the management." He spoke good German and good French, and while Hungarian is hardly an international language, those who do speak it feel an almost conspiratorial solidarity with each other and therefore are more prone to share information or gossip.

One of the first bargains he spotted involved Dresdner Bank. He learned that the bank had a huge portfolio of German industrial shares. "What I showed was that the value of this portfolio far exceeded the market value of Dresdner stock. These were hidden values because nobody paid attention to them. You could, of course, buy shares in, say, Siemens or Bayer and various other companies, but you could buy a large portfolio of Siemens and Bayer and these other companies at a discount if you bought Dresdner."

This represented a major coup. He followed it up in 1960 by investigating German insurance companies and discovering an even greater hoard of camouflaged assets. Soros calculated that the shares in the portfolio of a company like Allianz were worth three times the market price of Allianz's own stock. In fact, only some 30 percent of the stock was floating, because, as Soros also learned, the rest was reserved for an interlocking group of German companies. "The banks owned 30 percent of the insurance companies and the insurance companies owned 30 percent of the banks, and some insurance companies had shares in other insurance companies; it was all pretty incestuous."

With his report on Allianz and the other insurance companies, Soros scored yet another triumph. As with Dresdner Bank, he had not simply written up his findings; he had also taken them to powerful clients to get their orders. He was spreading his wings and working simultaneously as analyst, salesman, and trader. Within a year of coming to Wertheim he had gained access to very large amounts of money and very important players; Morgan Guaranty and Dreyfus were his two biggest clients. Making such contacts had not turned out to be very difficult. The reports he presented, based on his travels, were well-researched, well-written, and impressive, at least by the standards of the time, though years later Soros would look back on them as primitive. Still he claims to have been one of perhaps three people in America who were systematically analyzing European securities; like the one-eyed man in the country of the blind, he says, he was something of a king.

Shortly before Christmas of 1961 he went to see Jack Cath, a Dutchman who was an important figure at Morgan. Soros admits to having been impressed by Cath's debonair style in business as well as his flamboyantly sybaritic private life. In the summer he had visited Cath at his beach home in Southampton, a retreat he called the Cathhouse. Cath's wife was a model, and Soros remembers that there were always many strikingly beautiful women around. But that winter, when he dropped in on Cath, he was preparing a report about the Aachen-Munchen group, a German insurance company that was another repository of intricately enmeshed holdings. He told Cath he had already determined that the stocks sold at a small fraction of the group's total worth and added that he would complete the analysis when he returned from a Christmas holiday. Cath said: "Why should we wait until you do the study? Why don't we just buy it?"

The response delighted Soros. "He bought it, effectively blind. He bought it on my say-so. That was, in a way, the pinnacle of my power up to that time, that just on my say-so I had an unlimited order to buy. I was moving markets with houses like Morgan Guaranty behind me. You know for a young guy this can go to your head, and I certainly thought of myself as the cat's whiskers."

He was adding to an unbroken string of successes that had begun four years earlier with his arrival in America. Each spike in the streak compounded his confidence and projected him further along on an upward spiral. "What I was doing was to some extent intuitive. I would look at the figures and I would feel things. I never actually learned to analyze a company. I mean I did not have the analytical skills that a normal analyst has. In fact there came a point when they introduced a certificate for security analysts, a sort of professional qualification. After avoiding it for a while I sat for the exam and I failed in every conceivable topic. At that point I told my assistant that he had to take it and pass it. As I understood it, the importance of the certificate would not start to matter for another six or seven years and by that time I would either be so far ahead that I wouldn't need it, or I would be a failure, in which case, I also wouldn't need it."

His failure on the exam did not dent his self-esteem. "There was this European boom and I was right out front. I was the first to discover Dresdner Bank, the first to find Allianz. I discovered some pharmaceutical companies. I was a pathbreaker. I was a brash young man and I had a sense of my own powers."

But there came at least one moment when his brassy aplomb failed him. He had been asked to go to Pittsburgh to make a presentation about European securities to a group of people invited by the Mellon Bank. When he was led into the conference room, his host told him that there was $8 billion represented around the table. "That impressed me. In fact I became speechless. I said, 'Look, I'm sorry I really can't talk. You'll have to ask me questions.' I just wasn't able to make a presentation."

Nineteen sixty-one marked the end of Soros's five-year plan, the point at which he had once hoped to have $500,000 and thereafter devote himself solely to philosophy. He had surpassed his expectations, but his aspirations had shifted. Philosophy as an ambition had not vanished, but it seemed less pressing. He and Annaliese moved to an apartment on Sheridan Square. They lived comfortably but well within their means.

The biggest change in lifestyle in this period came when, after renting summer homes for several seasons, they built their own place on a three-acre lot in Southampton that George bought for $15,000. The contemporary house they commissioned cost another $28,000. Francis Booth, an architect, began a long friendship with George and Annaliese in those years. He recalled that while the house was comfortable and attractive the most striking thing about it was the design of the grounds by the noted but publicity-shy landscape architect A. E. Bye, whom George had hired. Booth was impressed that George and Annaliese, who could easily have afforded to put in a swimming pool, preferred to pay for what he describes as an extraordinary work of sculptured landscape by a master.

After the birth of the Soroses' first child, Robert, the beach house took on a significance not unlike the house on Lupa. But George's social life remained unexciting both in comparison to what he was doing at work and to the lives his parents had led in prewar Budapest. While Tivadar had concentrated on being an artist of life and had drastically limited his hours of work, George worked all the time. He did, however, join a newly formed tennis club in Easthampton. He tried to play tennis regularly; later he would say that one of the biggest impacts his riches had on his life was that with more money he could attract better players to compete against. He also joined the New York Athletic Club, where he could swim.

As for friends, few struck him as particularly stimulating. "I would have liked to have met more interesting people; actually, I felt somewhat deprived socially."

CHAPTER 9

FALLIBILITY

GAMES HAVE ALWAYS been very important for Soros, going back to his days on Lupa Island. Competitiveness formed an essential part of Tivadar's pedagogical theories, and he had instilled a desire in both his sons to test themselves through sports and contests, from boxing to chess to Kapital. In George's case the will to triumph was further sharpened through his rivalries with Paul, who had regularly trounced him at tennis, ski races, and swimming.

For more than twenty years Ron Glickman has taken the measure of George's competitive nature on tennis courts. A former tennis pro who as a young man was paid to play with George, Glickman is now a financial consultant and remains one of the dozen or so players who serve as either partners or opponents in matches that Soros's secretaries schedule for him two or three times a week. Now Glickman plays Soros purely for the fun of it. The game is always doubles, which, though slightly less physically demanding, is, according to Glickman, much more intellectually challenging than singles. Glickman, who is twenty-two years younger than Soros, says that George is one of the most competitive people he knows. George, he claims, values competition almost as a physical need, like food and sleep. But, he says, Soros's desire to win, while powerful, is less important to him than his need to improve. "He very much wants to win and he does not like losing, but he knows how to lose. After every match, but particularly after a loss, he goes over his play, thinking about what he might have done differently. He's an absolute sportsman and always plays completely within the rules. I have never heard him complain about a call and he would never try to unbalance an opponent with a comment or a gesture."

Soros's respect for competition goes so far that he would not tinker with it, even for the love of a child. Robert Soros, George's oldest son, who works for Soros Fund Management and who has young children of his own, recalls that his father seldom played games with him when he was young but that when he did, he would make no allowances for age. "You know how you sometimes let your children win," he observed. "Well, my father never did that with us, he would never rig the game to let us win." Robert assumes his father's inability to throw a game of checkers or Chutes and Ladders stemmed from a reluctance to patronize him and to convey the basic lessons of his own experience. "For as long as I can remember he was teaching us about the importance of survival," says Robert, who believes that George's emphasis on enduring harked back to his Budapest experiences in 1944. Apparently, George Soros felt that letting his children beat him at games would only mislead them in sizing up their chances against future adversaries who were bigger, stronger, smarter, more experienced, and possibly even deadly. He also believed that tainted victories would diminish the pleasure his children felt when they finally beat him on their own.

As his work consumed more time and grew more intense, there was less time available for games, and it was the business of making money that provided the major outlet for George's competitive nature. As in tennis, boxing, or swimming, he was establishing his own pace and rhythm. Having started in arbitrage with limited funds, he had been conditioned to operate quickly and seek immediate advantages. In years to come he would sometimes be compared with Warren Buffett, mostly for the huge amounts of money both men made during roughly the same time period. In fact, the two were entirely different in their basic approaches. Buffett has looked for undervalued companies and stayed with them over decades, steering them to prosperous growth. Soros has no interest in running companies or staying the course. He agreed with Lord Keynes's observation that in the long run, we'll all be dead. He moved in and out of markets abruptly, forming no sentimental attachments to companies, neither loving the stocks that brought him gains nor hating those that cost him. And he adapted a dynamic sense of time. "Invest first and investigate later," he would tell his protégés years later, urging them not to hesitate but rather to act quickly when preliminary research pointed to some potential advantage. A decision that was right at ten o'clock in the morning could well be less right fifteen minutes later and quite wrong within an hour. Operating within such a framework encouraged both decisiveness and constant self-criticism. As in tennis he would review the play after the fact, trying to identify his errors. The idea was to find his mistakes early and correct them quickly so as to keep the losses as low as possible. Many years later, when Soros was asked what accounted for his extraordinary record, he would claim that self-criticism was the decisive factor. "I've probably made as many mistakes as any investor," he said, "but I have tended to discover them quicker and was usually able to correct them before they caused too much harm."

Another similarity between moneymaking and games is the precision with which one can keep score. That, too, appealed to Soros. Just as he could mark off a rally on the court by strokes and games and sets, he could tell how he was doing in the markets hour by hour, sometimes even minute by minute. He could come home knowing exactly what he had made or lost since breakfast, how much he was ahead or behind.

And yet, during the sixties, when Soros was concentrating so intently on business, he was not totally committed to becoming rich. Despite his impressive and escalating earnings and the long hours he was devoting to finance, despite the euphoria and competitive zeal he felt with each success, Soros was not willing to admit to himself that he had found his true calling. He acknowledged that he had been drawn in beyond the half-million-dollar mark he had originally set for himself, but he insisted that this was only a temporary detour, a reasonable digression allowing him to ride a hot streak and raise the jackpot. He had shelved his philosophical ambitions but he had not forsaken them. As he saw it, making money was indeed a game. Games, by definition, are not serious. Life is serious. Signifying in life and history was extremely serious, and he still intended to make his name beyond Wall Street through philosophy. He assured himself and Annaliese that when the time was right, he would be able to walk away from the "game," giving up his hunt for profits in order to commit himself to the search for universal truths.

In fact, even in the midst of his market campaigns he kept dabbling in philosophy and nurturing his fantasy. He would carry on interior dialogues with himself about the ways perception and reality affected each other. He read and reread books by philosophers and social scientists and sometimes kept notes. After dinner and on weekends he would withdraw to his desk and write. When Robert began nursery school and was asked what his father did, he replied seriously, "He types."

It was a solitary activity, very different from his life on Wall Street or, for that matter, the games and tennis. In philosophy the rules were quite complex and often contested as various schools argued over what was meaningless, what was admissible, and what was not. Also, philosophy offered little gratification and feedback, no simple way of keeping score. On Wall Street he was earning both money and praise, while his philosophical pursuits remained unknown and thus unvalued. Except for a few mildly encouraging words from Popper during his last year at the LSE, no one had commented on his work; no one even knew of it. Once he had made a tentative effort to discuss his ideas with an expert and got someone to introduce him to Arthur Danto, the chairman of the philosophy department at Columbia. But nothing came of it. "I really didn't connect," says Soros.

On several occasions, he hired graduate students in philosophy to come by and tutor him or talk with him about his ideas. He would pay by the hour the way he paid for tennis coaching. All but one of the tutors vanished after a lesson or two. The single exception was Marco Poggio, an immigrant from Italy who was to become a very close friend.

Soros, who was so bold, even arrogant, in business, was shy about the work he was doing in philosophy, but remarkably he kept at it. He would come home from work and sit at his desk trying to extend Popper's work to establish the role of fallibility and criticism as the engine of change in history.

"I had that kind of bashfulness, the secretiveness of unsuccessful authors. There was this element that you can find in Ibsen's *The Wild Duck*, where the photographer is working on an invention and the children are not allowed to disturb him because he's working on something very important."

He was certainly compartmentalizing his interests, and at times his philosopher alter ego may have ventured beyond the brink of fantasy. Still, in the midst of his ethereal imaginings, he kept working, investing the money he had been saving since he arrived in the United States.

In 1962, he hit rough water. He had put a sizable portion of his savings into Studebaker shares. The Indiana carmaker, which once produced the covered wagons used by western settlers, was then desperately trying to survive in competition with the big three auto companies, Ford, General Motors, and Chrysler. The year before, Studebaker had introduced a sporty model called the Avanti. The company was also quietly trying to diversify beyond cars and trucks.

In addition to normal Studebaker stock, the company was issuing so-called "A" shares, which would not be activated as full shares until a specified date a year or so in the future. These securities, which were available at a discount from the regularly traded Studebaker stock, were similar to the due bills Soros had traded so successfully while at Mayer. There was a discrepancy between the value of the two stocks, and Soros worked out a strategy in which he was accumulating the "A" shares while shorting the regular Studebaker stock. Selling short entails the sale of stocks or other investments by someone who doesn't own them. The process involves borrowing stocks or other assets from a brokerage house and selling them; then buying the same amount back at a later date and returning it to the lender. If in the interim the value of the stock has fallen, the short seller registers a profit: the difference between what the borrowed stock was sold for and what was paid to buy it back. If the stock has risen in this period, the speculator still has to buy it at a loss. The risks inherent in the practice are succinctly summed up in an old bit of Wall Street folk wisdom: "He who sells what isn't hizzen, must pay the price or go to prison."

There was an elegance to the Studebaker deal that may have appealed to Soros: going long and short in two different types of stock issued by the same parent company over somewhat different periods of time in hopes of making money at both ends. The key to the scheme was timing, the premise being that Studebaker stock would initially drop, allowing George to cash in on his short position, and then as the company's fortunes rallied, the "A" shares would increase, adding to Soros's gains.

That was the theory. But as events unfolded, it appeared that Soros had been too smart by half: "Studebaker went through the roof. I had to put up additional margin on my short, and the spread also widened," Soros said referring to the gap between his long and short positions. "I had borrowed money from my brother and I was in danger of being entirely wiped out."

It was his first debacle, the worst experience he had had in any market until that time. As disaster loomed, he chastised himself particularly for putting his brother's money at risk. Paul was then launching his own engineering company, specializing in the design of systems to transport huge cargoes of coal and other substances over land and sea routes. That would have been seriously threatened if George had lost Paul's money.

After a prolonged period during which matters remained touch and go, Soros recouped his money, but the emotional impact of the ordeal was long lasting. "Psychologically it was very important."

The experience had made him realize "that I was not as detached as I thought." Self-critically he was forced to admit his own pretenses and conceits. "I was suddenly aware that I was more connected to this money than I ever admitted." During the unsettled period he had suffered from spells of dizziness and had had some trouble with his balance. "The earth had been turning over and the horizon was no longer straight because the market was shaky. After it was over I could not ignore the psychosomatic symptoms I had. That's when I realized that I'd gotten hooked and that this thing actually matters to me. Before that I had this illusion that I am apart from it, that I'm simply playing this game, like playing Monopoly. You want to win, but it's not the real thing."

As a result of the shock, Soros reevaluated his compartmentalized identities. No longer could he quite so cavalierly disdain the money-making activities he was so good at, subordinating them, at least in his mind, to his philosophical aspirations. "After the Studebaker episode I lost some of my moral superiority." During the next year Soros shelved his more abstract concerns and withdrew into his work at Wertheim, looking for worthwhile investments in new foreign markets.

During this period, late in 1962, he met another setback. At Wertheim, he had taken on a big position in a Japanese insurance company, Tokyo Marine. He had a number of customers committed to buy millions of dollars' worth of the company's shares, when word leaked from Washington that President Kennedy was planning to impose a tax on foreign securities. There was an immediate impact on Wall Street, but, more important for Soros, it became questionable whether the potential buyers would stand by their commitments and whether Wertheim would be stuck with all the Japanese shares Soros had acquired.

Soros did not experience the same degree of disorientation he had felt as a result of the Studebaker venture, but tensions soared. Worst of all, Soros's immediate superior, a partner in charge of the international trading department, denied that he had ever approved Soros's venture or that he even knew about it. Soros was infuriated by the claim, which he saw as unconscionable cowardice. "Of course he knew about it and authorized it."

After several weeks, the disaster evaporated and all the trades Soros had arranged cleared. But Soros felt he had been injured. "My name at the firm was besmirched. All the partners had been informed that I had conducted unauthorized trading. So I went around and talked to all the partners and explained to them that this was not so, but I realized I could not dispel the cloud. It was my word against the partner. I knew that I would never be made a partner, and though by then I did not want to be a partner I knew it was time to leave. Toward the end of 1962 I left Wertheim."

Soros was soon contacted by Stephen M. Kellen, the director of Arnhold & S. Bleichroeder. Kellen recalls the interview with pleasure: "I always had this view that a good way to find good people was to ask good people for their recommendations, and one of our sources told me that if I was really interested in a great analyst in the international field I should meet George Soros." The tall and dignified banker, whose most casual comments have the measured cadences of diplomatic declarations, observed that his first meeting with Soros went very well. A member of a German Jewish banking family, Kellen said he was greatly impressed by Soros. "He was obviously exceptional. It was not just his mind; he had real personality." By the end of the meeting he offered Soros a position.

"When George replied that he would consider my offer and let me know, I said, no, that would not suffice. I had to have an answer immediately, yes or no. I had never done something like that before but I did not want to risk losing him."

Arnhold & S. Bleichroeder was an old-world sort of place. Kellen, along with Henry Arnhold, the co-director and the cousin of Kellen's wife, spoke with German accents and were self-consciously aware of ancestors who had long looked after the fortunes and interests of Europe's richest and most powerful individuals and families. On the walls of the firm's offices hang portraits of earlier Arnholds, and despite the modern furnishings, the place reeks of tradition. The Bleichroeder side of the firm's letterhead traces back to the banker who was the financial adviser to Otto von Bismarck, Germany's Iron Chancellor in the latter part of the nineteenth century. Though the Bleichroeder name provided an impressive patina, leadership had long since passed to the Arnholds. Their fortunes originated in Dresden, where in 1864 the Arnhold Brothers bank was founded. By 1912 its headquarters had moved to Berlin, and after World War I branches were established in London, Zurich, and New York. In 1931, as Hitler was rising to power and denouncing "Jew financiers," Arnhold Brothers acquired S. Bleichroeder, whose founder had also been a Jew. Then in 1937, with the Nazis stepping up their torment of German Jews and the confiscation of their property, the firm managed to relocate to New York.

By the time Soros was hired, it was serving as a broker and asset management firm, with emphasis on global research and trading. Soros, who was thirty-two years old when he agreed to join, saw the move as another step up, but he did not rush in. He told Kellen that he wanted a few months between jobs and would take up his new position in the late spring of 1963.

In the interim, he returned to philosophy. He had assembled many pages and many chapters of a work he titled "The Burden of Consciousness: A Study of the Relationship between Thinking and Society." He had spent many weekends and many nights over the previous years working on it. Now he planned to collate the previous versions and put together a manuscript of several hundred pages. Moreover, emboldened after leaving Wertheim, he reached out once more to Popper, whom he had not heard from since leaving London seven years earlier. Just before he started his new job, during a European holiday in the spring of 1963, he stopped off to see Popper and was elated when the philosopher said he would look at his work. He dropped off some of his writings for his old mentor, but retrieved his major work a few days later in an apparent case of stage fright, after leaving a short note.

"Our meeting gave me much food for thought," he wrote.

> I have not had much time for philosophy recently because I was too busy with business, but I hope to settle down to it in about a month's time. In the meantime I should like to ask you to read my critique of Freud. My purpose has been to give an illustration of a dogmatic thought system on the one hand and to show the need for a convention of incomplete determinism on the other. This is the first time that I attempted to deal with someone else's ideas rather than my own and I am very interested to hear what you think of my approach because I shall have to do more of this as I go along.
>
> On my way through London I rifled your room and picked up the copy of my "Burden" which I left there. I shall return it in due course.

He signed the note "George Soros, the not-so-cultured Hungarian."

Soros was very happy on this trip. Not only was he emerging a bit from the closeted world of the fantasist philosopher but before he had his reunion with Popper he had also scored another triumph of financial wizardry, establishing himself at Arnhold & S. Bleichroeder even before he moved into his new office.

While he was spending a few days in Greece during his European sojourn, someone had mentioned to him that the Olivetti family in Italy was desperately and quietly trying to sell off a large block of shares in the giant office machine company. The information was sufficiently intriguing for Soros to alter his tourist itinerary and travel to Milan. "It was the first time I got involved with Italy," he says. "What I found out was that there was a crisis not so much involving the company as the family. Several million shares were being made available and had been deposited in a Swiss bank and they could be purchased at par," by which he meant the book value of Olivetti shares. The market price of those shares had dropped recently but they were still selling above that level.

He spent a day meeting with the company executives. He also met with the Italian broker Alberto Foglia, who would later become a long-term and prominent investor in Soros's hedge funds. Everyone told him essentially the same story of the family needing funds to cope with a succession of domestic crises. "I remember how I remarked to the company treasurer that the story was so dramatic that it was like a play by Shakespeare and the man said, 'No, it's like Balzac because it's about money and family,' and I thought to myself you don't usually find treasurers who are that well-read.

"But everything checked out and I quickly put together a group to buy the shares." The group included people from German insurance companies, some Swiss banks, and Bernard Cornfeld, the flamboyant American whose Investors Overseas Services and Fund of Funds were then still soaring under the direction of the literal high flier who jetted pop stars to his French castle as he attracted publicity for his dealings. Like the others Soros contacted, Cornfeld was happy to share in the Olivetti bonanza.

So before he officially started his new job, Soros had pulled off another coup. "I remember that I sent a cable to Henry Arnhold saying that on that date the firm bought however many million shares in Olivetti from so-and-so and that it had sold that same X million shares at a higher price to so-and-so."

Nearly four decades after he sent that cable Soros is still amused at the thought of how his message must have been received at Arnhold, which he describes as an extremely conservative firm. "I'm sure they never had a trade like that one. Some guy, who is going to join in a few weeks, sends you a cable that you have bought and sold something. They must have asked themselves, Is this man for real? Is the deal real? Is it bona fide? I'm sure they lost sleep over it. But the trade cleared and I arrived in style."

As things turned out, the Olivetti deal was not quite an augury of things to come. Within a few months of Soros's arrival, the pace of business tapered off sharply, not only at Arnhold but for everyone selling foreign securities in the United States. The boom in foreign investments that Soros had ridden virtually since his arrival in America screeched to a halt. On July 18, 1963, confirming the rumors that had threatened Soros's sales of Tokyo Marine shares, President Kennedy asked Congress to impose a tax on foreign securities, in order to slow the flow of U.S. capital abroad and to improve America's balance-of-payments position. Congress acted, and the foreign investment equalization tax empowered the government to collect a 15 percent surcharge on any foreign security traded during the next two years, after which the legislation would expire. Instantly a gap was created between the European price and the American price of such stock. In the previous three years American holdings of private investment abroad had grown by more than a third. But now Americans would be discouraged from buying foreign shares. Quite abruptly Soros's main activity became one of finding buyers abroad for many of the European shares he had originally recommended to American customers as lucrative investments. "Basically, this was a closing down," he says. "I was sitting with Arnhold & S. Bleichroeder in a time of diminishing business. I had less and less to do. I had a nice position in a firm that was not used to tremendous activity. They were quite happy to have me there. And of course I pulled my weight with the Olivetti deal and with some others, especially selling large positions of Ericsson back to the company in Sweden and selling Allianz stock back to the Germans. So I had a quite secure job that was really a sinecure.

"That's when I really switched my attention to philosophy. This was my chance to do what I always wanted to do and that became my main project for three years."

CHAPTER 10

PHILOSOPHIZING

W HAT DOES George Soros's philosophy amount to? How seriously
should it be considered? Obviously, for Soros himself, the role
of philosopher has been fundamentally important, predating and then
co-existing with the other two identities that were to bring him prominence and fame: financier and philanthropist. But while these other per-
sonae revealed themselves through public activities, Soros the philosopher
worked in isolation and stashed his thoughts and theories in private spaces.
Even during the years that he spent polishing "The Burden of Consciousness," neither Stephen Kellen nor Henry Arnhold, his bosses, both of
whom were close to him, had any idea of that part of his life.

Once Soros became known as a very rich man, anyone spotting his
name on *Forbes* magazine's listings of the world's highest earners was free
to form an opinion of him. It was easy enough to compare him with others
who had achieved great wealth and influence through finance. Similarly,
once the Open Society charities began sponsoring ambitious and provocative projects, their founder's actions and motivations became subjects of
public fascination, discussion, and gossip.

But what could anyone make of Soros's work as a self-taught philosopher? How were people supposed to take the epistemological and moralistic rationalizing that Soros repeatedly referred to but which itself was not
available? When in the 1980s profiles of Soros began appearing in journals
around the world, their authors glossed over the philosophy like skaters
circumventing thin ice. The very first profile, "The World's Greatest

Money Manager," a 1981 cover story in the magazine *Institutional Investor*, never mentioned Popper and simply quoted Soros in its last paragraph as saying, "I would have liked to have been a philosopher."

Sixteen years later, in a cover article on Soros in *Time*, William Shaw-cross did note that Soros had fallen "under the spell" of Popper, and then tightly compressed the consequences of this enchantment:

> It was from Popper that Soros gained his personal philoso-phy of reflexivity. It boils down to the sensible if not entirely original idea that people always act on the basis of imperfect knowledge or understanding; that while they may seek the truth—in the financial markets, law or everyday life—they'll never quite reach it, because the very act of looking distorts the picture. He says he has used this theory "to turn the disparate elements of my existence into a coherent whole."

A lengthy *New Yorker* profile in 1995 by Connie Bruck contained this concentrated sentence: "He always thought of himself as a philosopher and he labored over drafts of theoretical treatises for many years." Bruck wrote that in his first decade in America, Soros was "writing—and end-lessly rewriting—a philosophical essay entitled 'The Burden of Con-sciousness' that dealt with open and closed societies." What he wrote and rewrote, how and why he did it for so long, was not seriously addressed.

Such journalistic evasions are quite understandable in light of the material with which Soros was wrestling. How were journalists, writing for a general public, supposed to absorb and convey decades of abstract think-ing that seemingly yielded no bottom line? When Soros wrote or spoke about finance, economics, foreign policy, Communism, social policies, drugs, death, or philanthropy, his thoughts readily provoked debate, criti-cism, applause, or denunciation. When his subject was philosophy, the reaction, predictably enough, was to move on to some other subject. And yet, according to his own repeated assertions, the philosophy was at the center of everything else.

For decades philosophy as a discipline has been steadily losing its reso-nance with the public. In the fifties and sixties philosophers and philoso-phies still had some impact even on middle-brow culture. Existentialism went beyond opaque texts like Sartre's *Being and Nothingness* to resonate in the writings of Albert Camus, Samuel Beckett, Simone de Beauvoir, the films of Ingmar Bergman, and even the joking asides of Woody Allen. On college campuses, the names of Martin Heidegger, Karl Jaspers, Martin Buber, and Thomas Merton were recognized beyond philosophy departments, even if their works were not necessarily read. A Bertrand Russell could use the fame and authority he gained as an inaccessible mathematical philosopher to address a wide public on issues of war and peace and morality. There were also the Marxists and the counter-Marxists whose arguments sifted down from academic heights. But by the time Soros gained prominence, philosophy had retreated to remote ground, and it was hard to find any practitioners who commanded attention beyond their fellow philosophers.

Soros himself would sometimes scornfully dismiss his philosophical work as an escape into fantasy and describe himself as a "failed philosopher." But should Soros's ventures into philosophy be considered as simply the quirky hobby of a singular man, like Albert Einstein playing the violin badly?

The fact is that for Soros philosophy has never been an affectation or a diversion. It has remained the never fully surrendered first ambition, dating back to his adolescent insights that the idea of God was created in man's image and that the price of consciousness was the fear of death. Much of his ego has been invested in the pursuit, and his self-professed failure in his favored field has certainly influenced—even determined—his successes in his other important endeavors.

In his dismissive mode, Soros has said that he was obliged to write an entire book, *The Alchemy of Finance*, to explain his idea of reflexivity, "when I could have probably done it in five sentences." But in another context he has emphasized the significance such thoughts have had on his life: "I considered the ideas that people now call banal as something precious. It was a great insight to me and I didn't want to let it go. And now I can accept it as banal, but at the time it was a great insight, extremely precious. It was the core of my being."

And so it seems plain enough that while the philosophy with which Soros struggled may not explain the way the world works, it goes a long way to explain the way he functions. A painstaking, sometimes bizarre undertaking, his philosophical strivings represented an extended effort by a successful financier who instead of concentrating on the conventionally hedonistic activities of the flourishing rich sat alone in his apartment and agonized over how historic change occurs. In the process, he digressively took up dozens of themes, among them the limits of knowledge, the development of modern art, the flaws of classical economics, the value of fallibility, and even the prospects of fundamental reforms in the Soviet Union.

One example of his ruminative style could be seen in the critique of Freud he sent to Popper in 1963. The paper's overt aim was to illustrate "the dogmatic mode of thinking," and Soros hoped it could serve as an appendix to what he envisioned as his magnum opus, "The Burden of Consciousness."

"This is not intended as a thoroughgoing critique of Freudian theories," wrote the thirty-three-year-old Soros. "My purpose here is merely to use the specific example of Freud in support of arguments which had been stated in general terms in the main text."

After politely praising Freud for his pioneering explorations of the subconscious mind, he launched into a sustained attack. He contended that by claiming that psychoanalysis could in due course explain all human behavior, Freud had "set himself up as a kind of God," and added that his own aim was "to cut him down to size." He wrote, "Science cannot take the place of religion, unless it deteriorates into religion, as in the case of Marxism and psychoanalysis."

Further, he contended that Freudian methodology violated the very standards of the scientific method it had speciously affirmed. Freud, he said, "leaves no doubt that psychoanalysis is the only truly scientific method of exploring the unconscious. This gives him a monopoly over truth. Critics can be dismissed on account of their hidden motives." Such precepts, he continued, enabled believers to brush aside any skepticism "as a sign that a defense mechanism is in operation, probably covering up a hidden neurosis."

He claimed that psychoanalysis had two of the three salient features of a dogmatic ideology, comprehensiveness and rigidity. "The only element that is missing for psychoanalysis to be turned into a full-fledged dogma is the physical force that would be necessary to enforce its supremacy over actual or potential alternatives."

Writing at his bedroom desk, Soros assailed some bedrock assumptions of psychoanalytic theory, among them Freud's "idealized picture of childhood." According to his summary of Freud's thinking, early childhood lacked the tensions whose later appearance underlay the conflicts that plague man's existence. For Freud, he wrote, "the suckling infant does not know the difference between the mother's breast and his own body. The pleasure principle rules supreme and in his late history man will always look back with yearning on this idyllic beginning. The argument applies to society as well as to the individual: Freud often refers to the Golden Age when instincts were not yet repressed by civilization."

Soros took issue with this, contending that "there is no evidence that the newborn babe is happier than the grown man." As for primitive tribes, "their situation is certainly not an enviable one, quite apart from their lack of protection against outside dangers, their instinctual gratifications are more severely circumscribed by taboos than at any later stage of history." Soros also weighed in with a moralistic objection. "Freudian theory," he wrote, "lends substance to the fantasy of a Garden of Eden to an extent which is not only unjustified but also dangerous. In so far as psycho-analysis has ambitions to compete with religion, the salvation it offers is a return to childhood. This is a pernicious creed. Its avowed aim is a removal of instinctual repressions; the result would be an abandonment of consciousness."

Soros then returned to his basic criticism of Freud's "exaggerated" view of science. "Freudian theory presupposes not only that there is a reality outside the human mind, but also that if only thinking were fully rational that reality could be fully understood." Soros concurs with the first premise but cannot accept the second. Freud, along with his scientific contemporaries, he insisted, was wrong in believing that science could and ought to provide a complete explanation of all phenomena.

"Despite Freud's insistence that he relied on 'facts found in painstaking researches,' his theory of the personality and even more of civilization is not a collection of clinical evidence but an interpretation—and a rather far-fetched one at that—based on the principle that the task of science is to provide a complete and deterministic explanation of human behavior."

Freud had overreached and strayed into hubris. What was needed to temper his methods was the convention of incomplete determinism that Soros declared "maintains that we must proceed on the assumption that a pre-determined pattern of human behavior, even if it existed, would be beyond our ability to comprehend."

Despite its aggressive tone, the essay was duly self-critical, making it clear that its author's own views were also subject to the convention he proposed, and were, like all others, flawed, incomplete, and unavoidably biased. Such emphasis at times reached dizzying levels, echoing the so-called Liar's Paradox that has fascinated Soros since his days in gymna-sium. This formulation, originally expressed by Epimenides the Cretan, sets forth the proposition that "Cretans always lie," and is an example of a self-referential statement that undermines the truth it alleges. There are frequent echoes of it in Soros's writings, passages where he seems to pin his credibility to acknowledgments of inadequacy or incompleteness.

However, in regard to Freud, Soros's most open-minded and characteristically self-critical response was to come seventeen years after he wrote his critique. At that point, spurred by a severe crisis of spirit, identity, and ambition, he pragmatically turned to psychoanalysis for help. His own arguments had not ossified into dogma that would prevent him from recognizing the utility of therapy in that moment. Truth, after all, was a moving target, and just as in finance, what was unacceptable in one instance could become attractive, or even necessary, in another. "It was with a Freudian analyst," he said of the therapy, "but more talking, much more give-and-take than the usual Freudian approach. It was very good. It cleared my mind in many ways."

There is no record of how Popper reacted to "The Critique of Freud." But at the very least it reveals its author as a well-read, curious, and critically observant man, whose eclectic intellectual pursuits would have been unusual not just on Wall Street but in many universities.

Even more striking was the paradoxical mixture of boldness and timidity that its writer demonstrated. The attack on Freud and his followers may not now seem particularly provocative, but in the early sixties, when Freudian orthodoxy was riding high within influential intellectual circles, particularly in New York, it was audacious, and might have been provocative if those intellectual circles had been made aware of it.

Here was an unknown writer, fully aware of having no legitimizing credentials, launching into a full-scale assault on one of the bona fide geniuses of the modern age. But at the same time he was hiding his light. He never published the paper or sought out people, other than Popper, with whom he might discuss it. He was brave enough to put his thoughts on paper but not brave enough to send them out into the world.

The same quality applies to "The Burden of Consciousness" as a whole. By any measure, this was a serious, ambitious, and also quixotic effort. Unlike so much contemporary philosophy it shunned inductive reasoning and framed a deductive argument through nearly two hundred pages of numbered paragraphs, the very first of which declared: "I have very definite ideas about the relationship between my mind and the outside world. I realize that there is a world of which I am part. That world has existed before I became part of it and will continue to exist after I have ceased to exist. I can influence the outside world through my actions and of course the outside world impinges on my existence in an infinity of ways." That was his first premise; the second one asserted "that there is a reality outside my mind, and that my understanding of it is imperfect."

From this point of departure, he built an edifice that he hoped might be a monument. He maintained that over the previous three centuries, much of the success of science as a methodology had resulted from a practice in which scientists "pretended to look at the world as if they were not part of it." That, wrote Soros, was the basis of objectivity. He called it "a useful pretense."

But there were many questions that eluded scientific inquiry, among them "what is reality?" "what is God?" and "who am I?" In fact, he contended, science had limited applicability to human problems. Man's understanding of reality was perceived not directly but through abstractions, signs, and symbols, and thus was inherently imperfect. This was true even in natural science, but in this sphere a methodology of critical peer review, prediction and the testing of hypotheses, and the "pretense" of objectivity all served to identify errors and thus to incrementally purify thinking.

But when it was society that was the subject of thought, Soros wrote, the thinkers were inescapably part of the world and members of the societies they studied. Here mechanisms such as the convention of objectivity proved less useful and affirmations of imperfect understanding were all the more important. Imperfect knowledge, he noted, might sound like a negative quality, but in fact it had a highly positive aspect: what is imperfect can be improved. As Soros wrote: "The resources of the human mind can never be regarded as fully exhausted: it remains a permanent source of new possibilities."

Soros raised the threshold to explore the historical process. Many students of society, he noted, had sought to imitate natural science by making predictions of human destiny, and all had failed. Nowhere had such failures been more dismal or led to more confusion than theorizing about history. But having said this, Soros boldly proclaimed that he would devote much of his work to what he hoped would be a positive attempt to study history.

No man or group, he contended, can control the course of history. "They cannot even comprehend the events in which they participate in all their complexity, let alone anticipate the consequences of their actions." Furthermore, "if history is not determined by man's ideas, it is just as surely not determined by any 'objective' forces beyond man's influence." So what was the relationship between man's thinking and historical events? "The two are influenced by each other but neither is determined by the other." This abstract notion, among others, would soon find its way into

Soros's views of financial markets and become a cornerstone of his investment strategy.

At his typewriter he was aiming for more universal wisdom. In a chapter called "Thinking and Change," Soros identified a tendency in the human mind that wished to "eliminate change from the world." He cited recurring attempts to impose a permanent social order and observed that with the exception of St. Augustine, classical philosophers tried to exclude time from theories they represented as eternally valid. Reflecting the dynamic sense of fluctuations that had served him well as an arbitrager, Soros wrote, "instead of disregarding change we must face up to it and make it a focal point of our analysis."

He conjectured that at some point, perhaps as a result of earthquakes or flood, men who had been living in changeless societies must have become aware of the possibility of change. He hypothesized that subsequently the human mind "may well have abstracted, simplified, and polarized two opposite possible conditions, one an extremely changeless society, and the other a society of extreme changeability." In the absence of change, he observed, the mind had to deal with only one set of circumstances, that which existed at the moment. "What has gone before and what will come in the future is identical with what exists now. Things are as they are because they could not be any other way." As for a changing world, he concluded, "Man must learn to think not only of things as they are but also as they have been and as they could be."

Through such reasoning, he arrived at several categorical constructs. Conditions of changelessness are conducive to what he termed "traditional" modes of thinking and the establishment of "organic" societies. In these the individual is prone to accept the existing order of things without questioning. At the other end of the spectrum, where conditions of extreme changeability prevail, it is the "critical" mode of thinking that is most suitable to assist humans in choosing among many alternatives. In such conditions "open" societies have evolved.

The work meandered, sometimes repetitiously. Soros was aware of this and at one point even noted, "I have tried to be concise but occasionally I have slipped into verbosity—especially where I did not have anything original to say." Eventually, he conceded that he has not found a pattern of history. The best he could do, he said, was to develop a framework that might usefully analyze social development by focusing on how humans react to the idea of change.

Then, about two-thirds of the way through the work, his tone turned more personal. For one thing he speculated that he may have been prodded to develop his ideas about thinking and change by the specific historical situation in which he was living.

> There have been other occasions when the critical mode of thinking prevailed, at least among the higher classes; there has been a period when the rate of economic change was even faster than it is now; but at no time has man been given wider opportunities for making conscious choices. The principles of market mechanisms have become paramount, the natural and traditional aspects of existence have become superseded by manmade or man-chosen forms, and after the discovery of the atom bomb the very survival of civilization is in our own hands. Concurrently we have witnessed the establishment of collectivist societies which at times seemed as definitive and comprehensive as the Middle Ages. In short, we are in the unique position of having experienced something approaching both Open and Closed society as a fact and not only as an ideal.

Such analysis would ultimately inspire Soros's philanthropic initiatives.

In another consideration of the contemporary world, Soros focused on the closed society that then existed in the Soviet Union, ten years after Stalin's death.

> Stalin maintained authority irrespective of the cost in human terms. His successors are unable or, what is probably more to the point, unwilling to do so. Authority is no longer undisputed: there are different factions within Russia and there is a division between the Russian and Chinese hierarchy which extends to the satellite countries as well. The emergence of conflicting views does not necessarily lead to the weakening and eventual downfall of the Russian powerblock; but it does inevitably change the complexion of the regime. Unless one faction reasserts undisputed authority, the entire mode of thinking prevailing in Russia will undergo a radical transformation. Contending points of view will engage in argument and the deficiencies of established dogma will become increasingly apparent. Alternative sources of knowledge will be discovered both in Russia's past and in the outside world and critical processes will be set into motion.

These insights were written two decades before Gorbachev ushered in the new thinking of glasnost and perestroika, widening the cracks in the monolith just as Soros had predicted.

Another striking change in tone occurred toward the end of the work when Soros declared he was ending his own embargo on value judgments. Abruptly the treatise turned into a personal document revealing its author as a somewhat brooding figure. He expounded considerably on the idea of death, describing it as "a private horror which every individual must deal with as best he can." One avenue, he said, was to ignore it, which was what "the large faceless masses of society, who are not very much aware of their own individual existence, are doing." Another way was "to identify oneself with a larger unity which will survive the individual and through which one can transcend one's own finite experience." That, he continued, "is what those who have trained themselves to accept death as the inevitable sequel of life have done, including myself."

And while generally speaking Soros favored the possibilities that open societies provided, he bleakly noted that they tended to encourage an erosion of permanent personal relationships. In traditional societies, he said, such relationships were based on honor, family, sexual attraction, or emotional involvement. "Such ties are inappropriate to a perfectly changeable society and would be replaced by relationships which are subject to change at the slightest tilting in the scale of preferences or opportunities. Friends, neighbors, husbands, and wives would become, if not interchangeable, at least readily replaceable; they would be subject to choice under competitive conditions." He found it unfortunate that people would be inclined to replace old friends and associates with others who struck them as marginally more advantageous, but he saw it as an aspect of open society and the times we live in.

This passage, too, would become relevant to the way Soros's personal and business life was to develop. Many who have worked with him have commented on his preference for tactical alliances and his distaste for permanent bonds. Byron Wien, the chief strategist of Morgan Stanley Dean Witter, who is a close friend, has said, "George has transactional relationships: people get something from him, he from them." Soros hires and fires quickly, and prefers the short run over the long term. He has ordered his top associates to pull back from business contacts who he felt were getting "too close." Was his deploring reference to the fluid associations that open societies encourage also obliquely self-critical, or was it a guideline he may have used, perhaps unconsciously, in his desire to become a man of his time?

The mounting pessimism of the final section no doubt reflected the difficulties Soros was having as he tried to bring all his arguments to some persuasive conclusion. One need not be a Freudian to see a not-so-hidden meaning in one of the final passages, where Soros was once again ostensibly appealing for the avoidance of perfection as a standard. In what reads like a stop-me-before-I-think-again message, he wrote:

> Nietzsche went mad; Wittgenstein hovered on the borderline; Kafka died without finishing a single one of his masterpieces. I do not wish to follow their example and want to advise everyone against it. Those were great men whose creations even in their imperfect form made a greater contribution to our culture than the polished gems of lesser minds. But would they not have been even greater if they had known when not to press further? Would not their masterpieces have been more complete and they less unhappy?

One morning, he read a section he had written the day before and found he could not understand it, and he decided to abandon the project.

Considering the lack of reinforcement he had received through the years of writing, it is remarkable that he persisted as long as he did. The only responses he had had came from Popper, and those quickly dwindled after the first message, in the fall of 1963, which had delighted Soros:

> My first impression has been very good—in spite of the fact that I am strongly prejudiced against anybody who even terminologically makes concessions to Existentialism as you do in your prospectus. You certainly can write well, which is rare nowadays.

No further responses appear to have survived, but declining enthusiasm may be inferred from the abject tone of Soros's own letters to the philosopher. At the end of December 1964, Soros wrote: "I have abided by your request not to trouble you unnecessarily. I revised my work again and again until I reached a point where I am no longer sure that the new version is better than the old one. At this point I need your help."

In August 1965 Soros sent Popper another revision of his work and in an accompanying letter wrote, "Remembering my promise not to disturb you unnecessarily I have not written you earlier. I now enclose my latest version of Chapter I and am very anxious to have your opinion on it.

I believe I may be saying something with my theory of 'reflexivity' which is both significant and original but I do not dare to rely on my own judgment."

The fact that some seventeen years later Popper would admit to having completely forgotten Soros may indicate the deteriorations of age, but perhaps he had found Soros's work less than memorable.

Soros says that since turning his attentions to business, philanthropy, world politics, global economics, and public affairs, he has not read the manuscript, nor has he shown it to any philosophers.

At times, he suggests that for him philosophy is pretty much a closed chapter. At other times, he is more equivocal. He devoted a large part of his first book, *The Alchemy of Finance*, to describing "reflexivity." He has also established contacts with working philosophers. One of these, William Newton-Smith of Oxford, has become a close friend and a leading member of various Soros philanthropic boards. Philosophers whom he has consulted on other matters include Alan Ryan of Princeton, T. M. Scanlon of Harvard, and Bernard Williams of Oxford.

In November 1996, Soros invited seven academic philosophers to spend a long weekend at his Bedford, New York, estate reviewing and critiquing his ideas. He did not show his manuscript or even mention it to the participants, but it was apparent from the discussion that far from having rejected his old ideas as "banal," as he had claimed in various interviews, Soros was still revising them. According to the notes of the meeting, he asked his guests to concentrate on much the same subjects that had gripped him in his mid-thirties: fallibility, imperfection, reflexivity, open society, and the value of criticism.

The philosophers found the weekend memorable, and though no one menaced anyone with a poker, the guests did not shy away from biting the hand that was feeding them. One contended that Soros was wrong in basing reflexivity on the theory of truth rather than causation, while another felt that Popper's ideas about trial and error in science ought not to be extended to social policy. Some felt that Soros would have done better in following the liberal philosophy of John Stuart Mill rather than Popper.

Among the critics was Daniel Hausman, a professor from the University of Wisconsin, who remembered how twenty years earlier, while a graduate student at Columbia, he had been one of those who tutored Soros. He had visited him at his apartment and earned $25, his first pay as a professional philosopher. Hausman said he was probably more willing to bluntly criticize Soros's ideas as a graduate student than as a guest at the estate, though he had problems with them on both occasions.

Jonathan Wolff, from University College, London, remembers the weekend as the only time he has been flown anywhere in business class to discuss philosophy. There were gaps, he said, in Soros's knowledge. "He had apparently read no philosophy since the fifties and had made clear that he did not think that much of significance has occurred in the field since then." Wolff added that "he did not think any of us really understood his ideas. He had some of the typical features of the autodidact—an impatience with anyone who mentioned a text he had not read, and a tendency to change the track of discussion when things got hard—but I should repeat that I came away much more impressed with him than I expected. These were interesting ideas and arguments and very much worth discussing. I had assumed that it was to be an exercise in vanity, but in fact the discussions were of good quality and he was a full participant. Also a very good host."

CHAPTER II

GETTING BACK
TO BUSINESS

In 1965, when Soros reached a dead end with "The Burden of Consciousness," he decisively shifted gears. Kennedy's foreign investment tax would soon lapse and it was again becoming possible to think of a market for foreign investments in the United States.

Soros, however, did not want to pick up where he had left off. Instead, as he emerged restless from his philosophical cocoon, he saw an opportunity to master something new. He felt he had never known enough about American securities and so he devised a system by which he could profitably learn. Arnhold remembers how George came to him with a suggestion that he set up a model stock account with $100,000 of the firm's money. In light of George's track record and intelligence, he and Kellen readily agreed to the project. Soros also obtained $100,000 for the kitty from Alberto Foglia, the broker from Milan whom he had first met when he stumbled onto the Olivetti deal.

He then drew up sixteen slots, each to be filled by a stock he considered promising, and used the stake to acquire a portfolio. "I tried to develop a new business, reorient myself, teach myself how to invest," he says. The slots introduced a control mechanism with which he could compare risk, growth, and returns in various areas, and thus discipline himself to maximize his efforts.

"I established a vehicle for maintaining contact with brokers, which is very important because it gives you a feedback on your ideas." At that point, so soon after his ivory tower period, feedback and dialogue of any kind were particularly important. "When I was concentrating on philosophy I was very isolated. This business of being isolated is a recurrent theme in my life. It had happened a decade earlier in England."

Inspired by his new project, Soros became more and more enthusiastic. He kept notes on his evolving thoughts and filed away memos to himself explaining reasons for every investment decision. He then wrote monthly reports tracking the venture; these he circulated to old clients, restoring old connections. At one point he became interested in the trucking industry and filled four of his slots with trucking firms; in a short time he became known as one of the leading experts on trucking stocks. "New people started to call. I started to get more feedback. People asked questions and forced me to test and improve my ideas. Considering that I was coming from the outside, it was proving quite successful."

The model account was profitable enough that in 1967, Arnhold & S. Bleichroeder established it as the First Eagle Fund, open to the firm's clients. Soros served as manager. The fund started with $3 million in capital, and among its original investors was the Swiss trust that Tivadar had established with the money he received from Germany. George also placed his own money in the fund, initiating the practice he would henceforth continue of investing for others the same way he invested for himself.

The fund grew robustly and in 1969, while still at Arnhold & S. Bleichroeder, Soros set up a second fund called Double Eagle, which started with $4 million. Unlike First Eagle, which was a mutual fund, this was a hedge fund, which meant that Soros would be able to avail himself of a much wider range of investment options and strategies.

Hedge funds had existed since 1949 when A. W. Jones, an economic journalist turned financier, founded one. The approach he pioneered was to assume offsetting long and short positions on shares of companies within a given industry. The basic rationale was that by going short as well as long, his A. W. Jones Group would be able to hedge against industry-wide macroeconomic factors while benefiting from the specific performances of individual companies that were thought to be bucking the tide. Jones determined that having both short and long positions in a portfolio could increase returns while at the same time reducing market exposure. Because of this risk-reducing aspect the nickname "hedge fund" was adopted and stuck.

But, beyond the feature that gave the funds their name, Jones's brainchild pointed the way for vastly expanded autonomy on the part of fund managers, and it was this aspect that would account for the growing popularity of hedge funds, particularly in the soaring markets of the eighties and nineties when greed proved a more powerful stimulus than prudence.

Most important, since hedge funds were constituted as private partnerships, they were exempt from government restrictions and oversight.

While the managers of mutual funds were constrained by government regulations to merely seek out shares they believed would rise in value, the operators of hedge funds could engage in more complex trades, going short as well as long, and moving beyond stocks to speculate in commodities, currencies, bonds, and other assets. Without government oversight or limitations, hedge funds were able to borrow large amounts of capital, enabling them to make huge deals on the basis of relatively small commitments. This in turn enabled them to make more deals.

Basically, hedge funds as they developed were obliged to operate by no other rules than those established by their founders. In exempting them from federal regulations that applied to other funds, the government was assuming that hedge fund investors were rich and sophisticated enough to obtain the kind of expert financial advice that rendered federal protection unnecessary.

In the mid-sixties these funds were still fairly esoteric. There were relatively few of them, and the assets they commanded were estimated at less than $2 billion. Indeed, at first the term "hedge fund" was not understood by all Wall Street professionals. Twenty-five years later they numbered in the thousands and their aggregate investments were said to be worth between $200 billion and $300 billion. Even a casual reader of the financial pages could identify the most prominent hedge funds and their managers.

Soros had been familiar with the concept for many years. He had had some dealings with the A. W. Jones Group when he worked at Wertheim, and he found the autonomy involved in directing a hedge fund to be very enticing. As Leon Levy, the chairman of the board of Oppenheimer Funds and himself a founder of a successful hedge fund, would note in a 1998 interview in the *New York Review of Books*, "perhaps the most important thing about hedge funds is that they take the responsibility away from the investor for choosing what market to put money in and place it entirely in the hands of the money manager. He or she can be in any market at any time." To manage a fund where one was free to ignore both the views of investors and the regulations of government and simply do whatever seemed best—how appealing that must have been for someone like Soros who, though emerging from his meditative solitude, had never fully abandoned the idea of being a philosopher king.

"There were no limitations," said Soros, still echoing a thirty-year-old enthusiasm. "There was no limit to what you could do. You could sell short, you could buy, you could leverage. So there were no holds barred; it was a case of everything goes." To further augment the fund's autonomy, Double Eagle and First Eagle were organized as offshore funds with participation limited only to what its charter listed as "non-American persons" who had tax-free status in the United States.

As Double Eagle got off to a quick start, Soros's energy level and confidence also soared. It was in this period that he began to build an intellectual bridge linking his earlier philosophical theorizing to his strategic views of financial markets. "This is when I started elaborating my concept of boom and bust reflexivity. This is when the philosophy took on a practical application. It was a very stimulating and dynamic period," he says.

There was no sudden breakthrough like that of Archimedes in the bathtub shouting "Eureka"; instead the connection dawned slowly while the Double Eagle Fund was growing. As Soros recalled in *The Alchemy of Finance:* "I did not develop my ideas on reflexivity in connection with my activities in the stock market. The theory of reflexivity started out as abstract philosophical speculation and only gradually did I discover its relevance to the behavior of stock prices."

Back when he was writing "The Burden," he had been fixated by the idea that since the human mind was an active participant in the world it sought to comprehend, it had to be intrinsically biased. He had also been preoccupied with the less-than-perfect correlation between perceptions and the events that had provoked them. He had focused on the impact of events upon perceptions and vice versa. A given perception, he realized, could be a response to a given event, but it also helped to inspire and shape subsequent events, taking its place in a ricocheting chain of causality. Moreover, as he pursued his abstract thinking, he had concentrated on the concept of change itself, examining critical moments in history when one mode of thinking superseded another.

In the end, the "world" and "human history" had proved too inchoate to fit his theories neatly. Financial markets, however, provided a more confined laboratory. And in this sphere he was able to derive the functional counterparts of his earlier big ideas. For example, it now appeared to him that it was the market that, like human minds, was intrinsically biased. Far from being "always right," as classical economists and market participants had long insisted, Soros saw the market as a persistently flawed reflection of economic activity. Then, in another adaptation of his earlier idea, he concluded that something like the reverberating dynamics he had described in his explorations of human experience was operating in terms of stock prices. Or, as he would explain in *The Alchemy of Finance:* "Stock prices are not merely passive reflections; they are active ingredients in a process in which both stock prices and the fortunes of the companies whose stocks are traded are determined. In other words, I regard changes in stock prices as part of a historical process and I focus on the discrepancy between the participants' expectations and the actual course of events as a causal factor in the process."

Another important idea translated from his philosophizing into market analysis derived from his fascination with critical moments of change. Earlier he had hypothesized that one form of thinking gave way to another when conventional wisdom, or a collective bias, finally collapsed under the weight of cumulative errors exposed by critical thinking and testing. He realized that the same sort of shifts took place in markets, and it was obviously profitable to spot them early.

Taken together, such elements drawn from his earlier thinking formed the basis of Soros's reflexive analysis of the boom-and-bust cycle. In a style that paralleled some of the passages of "The Burden of Consciousness," Soros came up with several maxims, such as "markets are always biased in one way or another" and "markets can influence the events that they anticipate." He isolated three interrelated variables. There was the "underlying trend," which he defined as a trend influencing or causing the movement of stock prices. Such a movement might be spotted and understood, but it also operated if undetected. He further postulated a "prevailing bias" that was revealed in the rise or fall of stock prices. The third variable was the stock price itself, which, he pointed out, was determined by the other two factors, but at the same time also influenced the underlying trend and the prevailing bias.

Each of the three elements was in dynamic tension with the others, all constantly changing their values as they interacted. In certain conditions they might reinforce each other, first powerfully in one direction and then in the other. This was the pattern of boom and bust which provided great opportunities for those quick to recognize it.

This theory was not always easy to follow. At times it seemed deceptively simple and obvious, as banal as the recognition that bubbles eventually burst. At other times it grew dense and paradoxical. Like an Escher print or a Bach fugue, the thinking turned in on itself, and certain categories mutated into others, a consequence in one series becoming a provocation in another. In *The Alchemy of Finance*, Soros readily acknowledged that many investors had long been aware of the boom-bust sequence. But from almost self-evident observations, his thinking became steadily more intricate and original, as when he noted that many sophisticated investors had been diverted by "an ingrained and false attitude" that stock prices were merely reflections of some underlying reality rather than being active agents. Stock prices were both responses and stimuli in a historical process. By ignoring this, investors were missing valuable cues, responding much later than those who understood his "rudimentary model" of the process. "That is what has given me my edge," he said.

The first time he systematically put his theory into practice in a major way was when he applied it to the conglomerate boom of the late 1960s. "It enabled me to make money on the way up and on the way down."

As he later explained it, the boom phase got underway when several companies learned how to use acquisitions to generate growth in per-share earnings. He concluded that this "underlying trend" had germinated when a number of high-technology defense contractors realized that their historic growth rates, fueled by Cold War budgets, could not be sustained indefinitely. They hedged by acquiring other companies, and when in defiance of expectations these initial expansions produced high growth and rising earnings, the trend accelerated with more companies following suit.

The market responded energetically, rewarding the acquiring companies, and per-share earnings came to be disproportionately valued by investors. This became the "prevailing bias." It was reinforcing the underlying trend, and both of these impulses were reinforcing the stock prices of the conglomerates, which in turn further bolstered the bias and the trend, and so on.

According to Soros's description of this particular cycle, once the acquisition by leading companies of more mundane companies led to an expansion of per-share earnings, the imitative behavior intensified, leading some lackluster companies to go on acquisition sprees. Soros wrote that "investors responded like Indians to firewater," and gradually, "instead of judging each company on its own merit, conglomerates became recognized as a group." Soros said that the prevailing bias was further reinforced by developments such as new accounting techniques with which companies enhanced the impact of acquisitions and the emergence of "so-called go-go fund managers or gunslingers who developed a special affinity with the managements of conglomerates."

For Soros, none of this was surprising. "Events," he wrote, "followed the sequence described in my model. More and more people realized the misconception on which the boom rested even as they continued to play the same game. Acquisitions had to get larger and larger in order to maintain the momentum, and in the end they ran into the limits of size." Eventually, the process reversed itself. The dominance of per-share earnings diminished and the conglomerate boom gave way to bust.

Explaining what happened years after the fact is neither difficult nor financially profitable. But Soros saw it at the time. As he examined charts of the stocks involved, he recognized how similar the curves were to the one in his "rudimentary model." At a very early point, he saw what was happening and where things were going on a broad horizon. He took advantage of the opportunities, riding the wave as acquisitions grew and then selling short as prices approached their crest. Following his model paid off very handsomely. It would not be the last time.

By 1967 he and his funds were riding high. He had shed the cloak of the introverted scholar and was becoming more socially active as he pursued a widening circle of contacts that might benefit his business. For example, he found people who had specialized knowledge about the trucking industry, and after he had tripled his money on a big stake he had taken in Sony, he made his first fact-finding visit to Japan, where he met a great many sources in business, journalism, and academia. When he returned, he wrote a lengthy report that offered, among other observations, a sexual interpretation of Japan's economic boom.

"I was struck by the preoccupation of the Japanese with the size of their male organs," he says. "They have a tremendous sense of inferiority, and there were all kinds of remarks made at the dinners I attended, like 'The Japanese mushroom looks like a penis, the Japanese mushroom is very small.' That kind of remark. So I realized that the Japanese may be compensating. They have to work hard, extremely hard. To me this seemed a driving force and I mentioned it in the preface." As he recalled his analysis, the ironic inflections of his voice suggested an ambivalent appreciation of the outrageous boldness he had shown when he was thirty-eight years old.

Among his new acquaintances from that time was Byron Wien, who was on his way to becoming the chief strategist for Morgan Stanley Dean Witter. Wien called on Soros because he had been told that he was very well informed about Japan. Wien was impressed not only by Soros's thoughts on Japan, but by his general knowledge and his casual allusions to social sciences, politics, and literature. He continued to visit Soros and during the next twenty-five years Wien became a close enough friend that Soros chose him to be his chief interrogator for a book of transcribed questions and answers that was published in 1995 under the title *Soros on Soros.* Even so, he is still mindful of Soros's aloofness, saying, "The frank and honest truth is, I probably know as much as anybody about him, but I'm astonished at how little I know." He also cites Soros's "tactical" friendships.

In the late sixties Jack Cath introduced Soros to Edgar Astaire, a London stockbroker with expertise on Hong Kong companies. Astaire remembers that in the early days of his association with Soros, "he didn't really seem to know anyone in London and I sort of took him around." In fact Soros knew quite a number of people in London from his days at the LSE, people like Andrew Herskovitz, the Hungarian hustler he had met at the Esperanto stand at Hyde Park, or Simon Kester, the fellow LSE student who got him his trainee position with the handbag company, and Freddie Silverman, his old boss. These were sentimental friends; he kept them distinct from people befriended with an eye to business, people he talked to primarily about money.

It's not that he did not like these newer acquaintances. Indeed, he grew quite fond of people like Astaire, whom he would later appoint as one of the first directors of the Quantum Fund and whose firm later became the chief broker for all of Soros's hedge funds. It's just that he was not inclined to reveal himself or his past, or share thoughts and judgments about history, philosophy, or other topics close to his heart with most of his business associates.

Few people have ever had more day-to-day contact with Soros than Gary Gladstein, who joined Soros Fund Management in 1985. As the managing director he administered the fund's operations during a period in which the staff grew from 24 people to the 220 who were working there as the twentieth century ended. Soros trusted Gladstein enormously, giving him vast authority over staff and his own personal checkbook. Gladstein compiled and submitted Soros's tax returns, which required a sheaf of paper as thick as the Manhattan phone book. And yet, Gladstein says, "George is never very open to me as to what his inner thoughts are." Similarly, Stanley Druckenmiller, who in 1987 was chosen by Soros to succeed him as the fund's chief trader and strategist, observed, "Although I know about his activities, it's remarkable how little I know. He is of course arrogant but he's also shy. He's definitely shy."

His diffidence, like so much else about him, is paradoxical. On one hand he has been extremely forthcoming with strangers and journalists, often revealing an assertive candor, as when he pointed out that his grandfather was a schizophrenic or described his mother as "a typical Jewish anti-Semite." Some of his introspective comments are blatantly confessional and seem like admissions of vulnerability, or testimony to his faith in the dominance of fallibility. But far from inviting intimacy, as one might suppose, these tidbits of self-deprecation are mostly defensive. They are asserted as factual and self-critical observations, offered in the spirit of, "I have nothing to hide" or "Make of this what you want," or, as the French might say, "*Je m'en fou.*"

In fact, calibrating and maintaining what he considers to be the appropriate emotional distance is Soros's foremost mechanism of control. Gladstein noted, "George only allows people to get so close to him, and then pushes them off. He doesn't allow anyone to get very, very close." In the fifteen years he worked closely with Soros, Gladstein said he never heard him shout or curse. "When he is displeased he turns cold and icy," said Gladstein. "Or he'll be very abrupt; he'll walk out of rooms when he is annoyed."

It was not unusual for Soros to pass orders to Gladstein like a captain commanding his helmsman. "He'll tell me, I want to sever this relationship or I want to distance myself from that one. There are some situations where we've had very close relationships, and he will say, I want to normalize that relationship. There have been people he has been close with, some that he discovered and made stars, who just about worshipped George, and they can't understand it when it happens. They ask, What did I do wrong? What did I do to harm the relationship?"

Through much of his life George has shown the greatest loyalty to his parents and his brother, and much of that bond was forged in his fourteenth year when all their lives literally depended on it. His loyalty to his wives and children, while demonstrably strong, seems a bit less demanding than the obligations to those who were with him when he escaped the most dramatic and profound dangers of his life.

Certainly, for Robert Soros, George's wartime memories and the emphasis he laid on survival became unavoidable and bewildering aspects of his own childhood. "He talked all the time about survival, the importance of it, and how he survived the war," Robert recalled. "It was a constant theme in his dialogue with his children and it also, as he got richer, created a lot of problems for him and a lot of problems for his kids. I mean it got to a point in his life where it was obvious that day-to-day survival was not an issue. And yet he was still fighting the issues of his youth. There was always this strong sort of lecture or dialogue about how we have to understand how to survive; you know, it looks good now, but it may not be that great tomorrow. It was pretty confusing considering the way we were living."

But as Soros was shedding his philosopher's cloak and becoming less reclusive, he did not confine himself solely to business friends. He and Annaliese were making new friends who would occupy more intimate spaces than those that George reserved for his more transactional alliances. They had moved to a spacious apartment overlooking Central Park with their two young children. Robert had been born in 1963 and Andrea two years later. A third child, Jonathan, would be born in 1970. Soros almost never brought any of his business associates home. Instead, he and Annaliese would entertain people like Francis Booth, the architect, and his wife, Patricia, a therapist. The two couples, who had children of similar ages, met at a dinner given by a mutual friend in the Bronx. They went out to dinner regularly, and in the summers the Booths were often guests at the Soros beach house. Francis says he cannot remember any talk about business, and adds that for many years he did not know what George did for a living. "George and Annaliese were both very worldly," Booth recalled. "We would talk about books and ideas and cultural things, and, of course, the children, anything but business."

Another friend from this period was Bill Maynes. Annaliese had met his wife, Gretchen, at the nursery school where both families sent their children and George found common interests with Bill, who was then a foreign policy specialist working for the Carnegie Endowment for International Peace. Maynes later would became an undersecretary of state in the Carter Administration, and he served for many years as the editor of *Foreign Policy* magazine before becoming the head of the Eurasia Foundation. He too only learned of George's occupation and wealth some time after they became friends. Maynes remembers, "We'd go for walks and talk about news events, or we'd visit George and Annaliese on Long Island and George would ask about the political situation in far-off places like Indonesia or Nigeria." Soros remembers Maynes as the first American with whom he discussed foreign affairs without focusing on finance.

Maynes said that when he first met Soros, he was "wealthy rather than rich." But even after the transition, he added, many things stayed the same. "Before or after, he did not like any of his guests to ask about where to put one's money. On one occasion, Maynes recalled, a man asked Soros for investment advice. The atmosphere changed. George, turning icy, asked his guest, "How much money do you have?" The guest, left uncomfortable by the question, tried to parry by bouncing it back to Soros: "How much money do *you* have?"

And as the other guests looked on, George shot back, "Well, that's my business, but I never asked you what I should do with it." Maynes said the man was never asked back.

Maynes recalled another incident in his friendship with George that took place after Soros had grown seriously rich. Having been invited numerous times to Southampton, Maynes and his wife felt they needed to reciprocate and invited George to stay at their home in Virginia during one of his trips to Washington. "Gretchen made one of her great meals and George was genuinely pleased and complimentary," said Maynes. But before Soros left, he told his friend: "Now I've seen the way you live and you've seen the way I live so from now on why don't you just stay with us." Maynes says this made sense to him and that ever since he and his wife have abided by George's suggestion.

Soros also maintained close ties with Marco Poggio, his philosophy tutor. The two men would take walks together and in the course of their rambling conversations Soros learned a great deal about his friend. Poggio had had a painful childhood in Italy, where his father was an ardent fascist and his mother a domineering figure. He had come to America to further his studies in philosophy and to escape his family. It was not working, and Poggio often wrestled with depression. At one point, he called George from Montreal in obvious despair. Soros flew up and brought his friend back to New York where he placed him in a psychiatric clinic. He remembers visiting Poggio there and urging him to concentrate on joyful memories from childhood or adolescence. "I have none," his friend told him. Sometime after his release, Poggio walked one night to a children's playground in Central Park, not very far from where Soros lived, and shot himself to death. It had been a close friendship, but when Soros speaks of the man and his death, he talks with clinical detachment, keeping sentiment in check.

Through Poggio Soros met Herbert Vilakazi, a Zulu who had fled the apartheid of his native South Africa and was studying and teaching history in New York. "I was very interested in South Africa and I wanted to know what it was like to live under apartheid. I did not know any Africans and I felt I should know some," says Soros. After he was introduced to Vilakazi, the two visited each other. George read the books that Vilakazi recommended and listened as his friend described the workings of the totally closed society that he had left behind and which he dreamed would change.

Tivadar, meanwhile, was ailing. In 1966 he was found to have abdominal cancer, and there ensued a depressing period of tests and surgery. Again, George drew on his powers of compartmentalization, concentrating on business while he blocked out a good deal of what his father endured in the months before he finally died on February 22, 1968, at the age of seventy-six. Years later George acknowledged that he had handled his father's decline badly, leaving matters largely to doctors and other

health professionals. This awareness would lead him to behave very differently when twenty-three years later he helped his mother face death, making sure that when it came she was in familiar surroundings in the presence
of those she loved most. Eventually, the differences in the way his parents
died would inspire him to establish a multimillion-dollar "Death in America" project to stimulate and promote discussion and dialogue on the taboo
subject of dying.

It was as his father weakened and died that Soros, concentrating increasingly on work, entered into an initially profitable but ultimately tur-
bulent business partnership with Jim Rogers. Soros says he cannot
remember how exactly he first became aware of Rogers while Soros was
managing the First Eagle and Double Eagle Funds. As for Rogers, he
backs away from any discussion of Soros, refusing interviews on the subject; Rogers never mentions Soros in his autobiographical travel book,
Investment Biker, which appeared in 1994. Yet, before the partnership rup-
tured in 1979, the two spent twelve years together operating as a team and
compiling a record that has become a Wall Street legend.

Soros brought Rogers aboard in 1968. It was Soros's first significant
hire, and it revealed an enduring tendency to speculate on unlikely candidates, looking for potential divas in the chorus line. There were many at
Arnhold & S. Bleichroeder who found the twenty-six-year-old Rogers
particularly abrasive. Soros, twelve years older, thought Rogers was just
what he needed. The two men shared some basic characteristics. Both
were extremely ambitious, very hard working, intellectually gifted, and
widely read. More to the point, both were contrarian mavericks who disdained the conventional wisdom of Wall Street and scorned those
investors they regarded as herd followers. But there were also differences,
some subtle and some glaring. While both men were quite confident that
they were smarter than most people, Soros was more self-contained and
quietly self-assured; he found it unnecessary to proclaim superiority quite
as flagrantly as Rogers did. Rogers never let people forget that he was the
country boy from Demopolis, Alabama, who had already come far by way
of Yale and a graduate scholarship at Oxford. He flaunted a pugnacious
nature he would later reveal more widely as a market analyst on cable television. The chip on his shoulder was as unmistakable as the bow tie he
habitually wore. If Soros was a gentleman aspiring to grace, then Rogers
was more of an ascendant upstart, who like Flem Snopes, William
Faulkner's great fictional character, needed not only to rise but also to
avenge old humiliations.

In any case Soros ignored the views of those who thought Rogers a bit too swaggering for such an old-line firm, or who raised questions about character. A man who was said to seek transactional friends was hardly likely to adopt a chivalrous standard when it came to business associates. In 1968 Soros felt that Rogers was definitely a "doer," that vital Sorosian category for those who can accomplish missions and attain goals.

From the start of their collaboration, Soros was the captain, the senior partner, the man who made the choices, handled the trades, and, in his words, "pulled the trigger." Rogers was the analyst, reading dozens of obscure magazines, finding and pursuing leads. The two got off to a quick start.

Two years later, in 1970, Soros spotted another burgeoning chain of events he sensed might conform to his boom-bust paradigm. This time he carefully wrote down his predictions as he invested in real estate investment trusts (REITs), which were stock-issuing funds originally designed to allow small investors to compete with large investors in the real estate market. He envisioned the unfolding events as a drama in four acts. At the early stage in which he was writing, act one, these mortgage trusts were being offered as a relatively new form of investment. To Soros they looked promising because there existed a long-pent-up demand for housing and because high interest rates were likely to discipline the market, limiting construction to projects that were economically justified. He observed that investor recognition of the mortgage trust concept had progressed far enough to permit the formation of new trusts and the rapid expansion of existing ones. Once again, he recognized that a self-reinforcing process was underway.

In act two he foresaw a housing boom. Mortgage trusts would show a rapid rise in size and per-share earnings. Since entry into the field was unrestricted, the number of mortgage trusts would increase. This, he wrote, would lead to act three. In this period, trusts would capture a significant part of the construction loan market. Construction activity would become more speculative and bad loans would increase. The housing boom would abate and housing surpluses would appear in various parts of the country. Some mortgage trusts would find a large number of delinquent loans in their portfolios. Finally, act four would begin. In Soros's view the disappointment of investors in the troubled trusts would carry over to reduce the valuation of the entire group. The self-reinforcing mechanism would reverse direction with lower premiums and slower growth reducing per-share earnings.

Things worked out in just this way, and Soros, following his own script, again made a good deal of money for his funds as the market first waxed and then waned. Actually, as he wrote in *Alchemy*, after closely following matters through acts one and two, he became preoccupied with other concerns during what amounted to an intermission, and only refocused on REITs when he casually picked up his original report and found himself persuaded by his own prediction. "I decided to sell the group short more or less indiscriminately," he wrote. The results were excellent.

Soros's success with the REIT was a major coup. But it also illuminated a growing conflict of interest that would soon lead him to leave Arnhold & S. Bleichroeder. He had made a good deal of money for Double Eagle and its investors by acting on his analysis of the REITs. But the broker's report he had written and adhered to had also been distributed by the firm to its clients. It had been so widely read that Soros once received a call from a bank in Cleveland asking for a new copy because the original had been photocopied so often that it was no longer legible.

Recommending a course of action as an analyst and following that same course as a fund manager seemed to be in conflict with the spirit of Securities and Exchange Commission (SEC) safeguards. There were rules against buying in advance of publication, which were intended to keep unscrupulous manipulators from hyping and artificially inflating the value of their acquisitions. Soros realized he was approaching an impasse, and he came to the conclusion that "this combination of being a broker and analyst and adviser and running a fund had to stop."

"I had the option of what to do next, and I decided, very reluctantly, to go out on my own. I was very happy at Arnhold & S. Bleichroeder. They were pleasant people, they looked after me." He was certain that he could have become a partner—and both Kellen and Arnhold agree that had he wanted to stay he would have become the first partner from outside the family. Soros also realized that by managing the funds within the firm he and Rogers were receiving only a percentage of the management fees instead of the 100 percent they could get on their own. He remembered his introduction to finance as a fifteen-year-old in Budapest, when he had received only a standard broker's commission after obtaining a better-than-expected rate while changing money for the father of a friend. Back then he had argued unsuccessfully that he should have received compensation tied to his performance. Now, twenty-four years later, his fees would be more directly linked to his success. It was a factor in his decision, but he insists it played a relatively small role. After all, in its first five years Double Eagle had grown from $4 million to $17 million, and even with a reduced cut of the profits, Soros was growing quite rich quite quickly and he was very happy in his work.

"It just became impossible to continue running a hedge fund in a brokerage house," he says. "And I realized that I was more interested in running the hedge fund than in being a broker. So in 1973 I went out on my own, in a very amicable way." Indeed, from that time on Soros has always kept Arnhold & S. Bleichroeder as the chief clearing broker for his funds.

"So Jim Rogers and I, with two secretaries, went off on our own. We set up Soros Fund Management, and by that time I recognized that I was entirely on the line; my ego was well and truly engaged."

CHAPTER 12

A QUANTUM LEAP

With Rogers at his side, Soros opened a two-room office on Columbus Circle in Manhattan in what in the early seventies seemed to be a very unlikely location for an investment company, being far from any brokerage houses, bank headquarters, or insurance companies. Soros claims that the choice was dictated mostly by convenience, since he lived two blocks away at 25 Central Park West. He played tennis in Central Park and swam at the nearby New York Athletic Club. Moreover, after the death of her husband, Erzebet had moved to a two-room apartment on 58th Street, where George often stopped by for lunch or coffee. His children were in private schools in the area and, physically, Soros's life was quite comfortably confined, so he lost little time moving around.

But some of Soros's associates see a deeper meaning in his selection of office space. They point out that the location and the unadorned look of the place telegraphed the team's idiosyncratic orientation and its disdain for the culture of the financial district. Soros and Rogers were not interested in public relations or projecting an image. Their principal objective, as the fund's charter declared, was simply to maximize capital appreciation.

In the amicable departure from Arnhold & S. Bleichroeder the shareholders in the Double Eagle Fund had been given their choice of either keeping their assets in the old fund or transferring them to the new venture. At the point of divergence, Double Eagle had grown to around $20 million, and some $13 million of it followed Soros. A few new investors also joined the new fund, so that within a year of the launch date the Soros Fund, as it was then called, stood at just over $18 million.

Those who elected to leave their money where it was and have kept it there since have not done badly, since Double Eagle soon invested half its assets in the Soros Fund while keeping the remainder in stable investments with fixed returns. But those investors who continued to allow Soros to manage their money directly did even better. Those who opted for Soros saw every $100,000 of their original 1969 investment grow to more than $353 million by the end of 1997 if they left their original stake in his fund and allowed their earnings to compound. By 1998, the overall value of the Quantum Fund stood at around $6 billion.

Such expansion was beyond anyone's imagination when the Soros Fund, Quantum's predecessor, was established in August 1973. The original investors were mostly wealthy Europeans who had been dealing with Soros for many years. Finding investors had never been a problem for Soros, or much of a concern. "I never looked for shareholders and, in fact, we did not really issue a lot of shares. As I had envisioned, the growth was internal, just cumulative. If you compound at around 40 percent you grow rather quickly."

The number of subscribers has fluctuated slightly over the years, with some leaving and others buying into the fund, often at a premium. But the total has remained quite limited. Gary Gladstein, the managing director of Soros Fund Management, said the number of shareholders in Quantum and the five other funds that Soros later established probably never exceeded one thousand. They are very rich individuals rather than institutions, and many have interests in several or even all of the Soros funds. Under the laws of Curaçao, where the fund is legally chartered, it is illegal for any of its directors or representatives to identify any shareholder by name, even to the people at Soros Fund Management, the New York part of the operation that determines and carries out investment decisions as the fund's adviser. While some investors have made themselves known to the management firm in New York, many others are simply designated by coded Swiss bank accounts or by financial advisers serving as their nominees. It is quite likely that Soros does not know or, for that matter, care to know all of his shareholders.

But they all know him. From the start Soros loomed as the central, and seemingly aloof, figure in a somewhat Byzantine money-making operation he had brought into being. In addition to the Curaçao-based corporation, there was also Quantum Partners, a sort of holding corporation chartered in the Cayman Islands, and Soros Fund Management in New York. For those who worked within the network, it was not only Soros's ideas and his thinking that were paramount, it was also his money. Executives and employees of the fund have often claimed that everyone at the fund understands their primary obligation to be the profitable investment of Soros's fortune, which represents the largest share of the fund. "From the beginning we've always maintained that George and the rest of us were basically investing his own money and that the shareholders were going along for the ride," said Gladstein.

Until he withdrew as the dominant force in 1989, turning over ultimate responsibility to Druckenmiller, it was Soros who set the strategies, found most of the opportunities, and pulled the trigger on thousands of deals. In the beginning and then throughout the years, when it was basically just Soros and Rogers who were involved, the fund bore Soros's name. But as its wealth grew and as the partnership with Rogers approached the breaking point, Soros decided in 1979 to change this. He did it precisely to deflect publicity, exposure, and self-advertisement. He was not interested in attracting more investors. He did not want to flaunt his wealth or crash society, and he definitely did not want to be besieged by charities seeking his donations. Moreover, he was mindful of his father's instructive fables of incarceration in a Siberian prison camp, specifically Tivadar's account of how a man who accepted the post of prisoner's representative ended up being executed. Prominence, he knew, could attract misfortune.

As for the fund's new name, the one Soros chose to replace his own had deep meaning. "Quantum" was markedly different from either First Eagle or Double Eagle, both of which evoked imperial heraldry—and are names suitable for Central European beer halls. "Quantum" was drawn from the body of physics developed in the early twentieth century by such scientists as Max Planck, Albert Einstein, and Niels Bohr. More specifically, Soros was alluding to the work of Werner Heisenberg, whose principle of indeterminacy, advanced in 1927, declared that because of limitations inherent in nature, it is impossible to determine both the position and velocity of any atomic particle. By this contribution to quantum mechanics Heisenberg had established the impossibility of accurately charting the future movements of any given particle and had thus undermined the concept of causality in physics. Soros's choice was both an ironic wink and a gesture of homage to notions of fallibility, reflexivity, and his own convention of incomplete determinism. On another level, the name also conveyed the idea of a huge and sudden increase in values, as suggested by the phrase "quantum leap."

If the ideas and metaphors that swirled through the small office in the 1970s evoked an academic environment, the tempo of activity there was more like that of a sweatshop. For Soros, those first years, when he and Rogers collaborated so energetically, remain vivid:

> It was a very, very productive partnership, and we did a lot of interesting things. We were very innovative. Basically, Rogers understood my sort of dynamic concepts. So we talked a short-hand language.
>
> I worked very hard. I was really totally absorbed in this. It was extremely preoccupying and very strenuous, and sometimes extremely painful. Particularly with the short selling and so on, with ups and downs in the market, the stress was enormous. And it's always inversely related to success. If you are successful, no problem; if you are unsuccessful, it's very bad. I mean, it was something that played with my primeval instincts of fear and greed. I sensed things. The fund took on a life, as a sort of parasite of my body. I felt it, I had my nerve endings in the fund. On good days I was euphoric and on bad days despondent. And I could sense things going bad before they actually went bad. I had these backache problems when my back was giving me signals of some impending doom. It was like having an organism live off you.

In 1974, the first year on its own, the fund registered 17.5 percent growth, while the Dow Jones industrial average dropped by almost 24 percent. The next year the fund grew by 27.6 percent, and a year later, 1976, it registered a leap of 61.9 percent, outperforming the 23 percent increase by the Dow. By 1978 its value jumped beyond $100 million.

Amid all the positive growth, 1978 also brought Soros some distress: he was charged with stock manipulation by the Securities and Exchange Commission. The SEC had contended that on October 11, 1977, Soros had aggressively sold off shares in a company called Computer Sciences, driving the price down on the day before a public offering of the stock, which he then acquired at what was alleged to be an artificially reduced price. The charge formed the basis of one of 267 cases brought by the SEC in 1978. Like the vast majority of SEC cases in any year, it ended in the signing of a consent decree, which essentially meant Soros neither admitted nor denied the charges, while agreeing not to act in such a way in the future.

The case had little measurable impact on the fund's fortunes: in 1979 it recorded another extraordinary rise of 59 percent, which was followed in 1980 by a soaring increase of 102 percent, dwarfing the Dow's rise of 22 percent. Up to that time it had never experienced a losing year.

In Jack D. Schwager's *Market Wizards: Interviews with Top Traders*, Rogers sketchily outlined the firm's modus operandi. "We invested in stocks, bonds, currencies, commodities, everything—long and short—all over the world." He told Schwager that in trading currencies and commodities they made full use of credit margins. "We were always leveraged to the hilt when we bought something and [when we] ran out of money, we would look at the portfolio and push out whatever appeared to be the least attractive item at that point. For example, if you wanted to buy corn and ran out of money, you either had to stop buying corn or sell something else."

For the most part, Soros concentrated on macroeconomic thinking while Rogers focused on less cosmic trends and opportunities, studying specific industries and companies. "It was very clear," Soros jokingly recalled. "He was the man who did the work and I was the one who was pulling the trigger and executing. I was the chief executive and he was the chief of research. I was the captain and doing the trading and he was doing the analytical work. He would come up with ideas and would check on the companies we owned."

In fact, the division of labor was not quite so simple or categorical. Both men were scanning wide horizons in search of provocative and original ideas. Rogers was more likely to pore through the fifty-odd trade magazines that cluttered the office while Soros spent more time in consultations with an ever expanding number of sources around the world. He developed ideas that, while original, were often simple observations that pointed to great opportunities. One of the earliest examples of such a lucrative conceptualization took form when Soros recognized that the nature of banks and bankers was about to undergo a dramatic change.

In 1972 First National City Bank hosted a dinner in New York for security analysts. Soros was not considered important enough to be invited; perhaps spurred by that rejection, he undertook his own investigation of the banking sector. In this study, Soros concluded that banking was emerging from a long sleep. It had been "a dull business" that attracted "dull people." There had been little movement or innovation in the industry and bank stocks were ignored. But, as Soros understood, all this was about to change. He noted that a new breed of bankers was emerging from business schools and that it was much more focused on profits. In his report he recommended a bouquet of bank stocks and within a year his fund earned about 50 percent on these shares. An even greater benefit of the study was that it left Soros well positioned to explore and then exploit the intricacies of international currency markets when the old system of fixed exchange rates gave way to floating parities a year later. As he would later note, his study on "growth banks" represented a key transition point in developing and sharpening his interest in macroeconomic processes.

Rogers was also casting his nets in a wide arc. With the help of his research, the fund presciently invested in fertilizer producers just before poor harvests were reported. Its backing of companies that serviced oil drilling paid off very well as oil prices rose. Even more productively, Rogers was one of the first analysts to foresee a great surge in defense stocks in the mid-seventies. Since the end of the Vietnam War, such stocks had been fairly inert, but Rogers predicted this would change as a result of the Yom Kippur War of 1973. Though the Israelis ultimately repulsed the Egyptian and Syrian forces who invaded their country in October, they lost many more tanks and planes than they had in any previous conflict. Though the predominant view of news analysts attributed the losses to the surprise attack that caught Israel offguard, Rogers considered another hypothesis and raised it with Soros: What if the military equipment supplied to the Arab forces by the Soviet Union had improved? What if the gap had been narrowed between Russian weapons and those the United States had provided to Israel? If that was the case, or even if enough Pentagon analysts thought this might be the case, American defense spending would be certain to increase significantly.

After investigating and confirming this premise, Rogers pinpointed a number of defense companies whose prospects were likely to improve on the strength of contracts about to be renewed. Among them were such then lumbering giants as Northrup, Grumman, and Lockheed. He also discovered such little-known companies as E Systems and Sanders Associates. Such companies proved to be something of a threshold to the emerging field of electronic technology, which Soros and Rogers also fruitfully analyzed.

In the mid-seventies Soros shunned newspaper interviews, was rarely cited in the financial press, and was never profiled. Still, among Wall Street insiders his record of success was attracting interest and fascination.

Questions that began to be asked at that time have echoed and intensified over the next two decades as investors and ordinary citizens have sought to discover what accounted for Soros's remarkable record. Did the key lie in the information he was able to glean, in his analytical skills, in the level of his desire—or was it hard work and an uncanny streak of good luck? What were his most valuable attributes? Some who observed him even wondered whether he was a genius, one of those prodigiously talented people such as Mozart or Michael Jordan, whose achievements defy simple explanations.

Being analytical and extremely self-critical, Soros, too, has reviewed his past looking for explanations for his success. At various times he has cited his father's tutelage, the experience of wartime risk, the postwar black market, and, of course, the transference of abstract philosophical concepts to financial markets. In his books, notably *The Alchemy of Finance*, he has documented money-making ventures as "real-time experiments," recording each step as if it was a laboratory procedure. But when his closest associates—those who have watched him operate for the longest time and from the closest vantage points—describe his special abilities, they stress that what sets him apart is not science so much as art—not pure rationality, but hard-to-grasp qualities of intuition. Robert Soros once observed:

> My father will sit down and give you theories to explain why he does this or that. But I remember seeing it as a kid and thinking, Jesus Christ, at least half of this is bullshit. I mean, you know the reason he changes his position on the market or whatever is because his back starts killing him. It has nothing to do with reason. He literally goes into a spasm, and it's this early warning sign.
>
> If you're around him a long time, you realize that to a large extent he is driven by temperament. But he is always trying to rationalize what are basically his emotions. And he is living in a constant state of not exactly denial, but rationalization of his emotional state. And it's very funny.

Byron Wien's assessment of his friend's methodology and motivation also stresses emotional factors. "Back when he started Quantum, I think he was interested in making a lot of money. He was interested in proving himself as a money manager; that was the first thing. Then the second step was to prove that he was making this money because he had a method, a philosophical insight that nobody else had; you know, that the rest of us who were managing did okay but we didn't have reflexivity so we would never do as well as he did." Wien believes that along the way a shift occurred, and the validation of the theory became the primary motive. "It became a case of, you know, I went down the wrong road when I didn't become a

George Soros, five years old, in Budapest, 1935

Skating with his mother, Erzebet, 1934

George's parents, Erzebet and ‌adar Soros, outside their summer ‌ome on Lupa Island shortly before World War II

(Above left) Soros in 1955 punting in Cambridge, England, with his brother, Paul, and his sister-in-law, Daisy; (above right) George Soros at thirty-two, a specialist in foreign securities for Wertheim & Co.

(Right) George married
Susan Weber, his second
wife, on June 19, 1983.
From left: Soros's daughter,
Andrea; his brother, Paul;
the bride and groom; and
George Soros's sons, Jonathan
and Robert

(Below) Susan and George
at a Waldorf Astoria
reception in 1995

(Opposite page) After Soviet troops
crushed the Hungarian uprising of
1956, George's parents fled Hungary
and were reunited with George, whom
they had not seen for ten years. Shortly
after their arrival they posed with Beno
and Lily Aczel (second and fourth from
left), old friends from Budapest, while
George stood with his girlfriend,
Annaliese Witschak, whom he would
later marry.

(Left) Soros on Nantucket with three of
his sons, Alexander (wearing hat),
Gregory, and Jonathan

Philosopher Karl Popper was Soros's mentor at the London School of Economics in the early 1950s. Forty years later Soros invited him to a ceremony in Prague at which he bestowed scholarships named for Popper, who had first led him to think about open societies.

(Right) Soros with Boris Yeltsin in Moscow

(Opposite page) Meeting John Paul at Castel Gandolfo in 1985

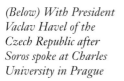

(Below) With President Vaclav Havel of the Czech Republic after Soros spoke at Charles University in Prague

Soros wore a flak jacket when he came to a besieged Sarajevo in November 1993 to inspect a water purification plant that Fred Cuny (left), the self-styled "Master of Disaster," installed within the tunnel in the background while on assignment for the Open Society Foundation. © Beka Vuco

Soros inspecting a nursery in Kiev, Ukraine, a part of his controversial $100 million Step-by-Step project to reform early childhood education in some thirty countries

As a fifteen-year-old boy in Budapest at war's end, Soros was at times forced to turn over his wristwatches to Russian soldiers. In 1999 he quite happily presented a watch to the Russian admiral who welcomed him to a once-secret naval base in Kaliningrad, where the admiral expressed his appreciation for a Soros program that trained midlevel officers to become private entrepreneurs.

Soros with Aryeh Neier, the president of his Open Society Institute (right) and Sonia Licht, the head of his Yugoslav operation, in Belgrade in June 1996. At the time, Slobodan Milošević was threatening to expel the foundation. © Beka Vuco

Soros with Iren[e] Vesaite, the hea[d] of the Soros Foundation in Lithuania, one of the many women whom Soros has eleva[ted] to prominence within OSI
© Beka Vuco

Soros in Moscow with Ekaterina Genieva. After a number of people had failed to provide effective leadership for the Russian foundation, this former librarian established tight control and won Soros's ultimate accolade: he called her "a doer."

philosopher, but now I've become a speculator and the only reason I'm successful at it proves that I really could have become a philosopher."

Wien recognizes that such reasoning has given Soros a focal point and real advantages. "To some extent his view is right, though probably not as right as he thinks. But I honestly don't think he would have made it as a philosopher, because while he likes to think of himself as a pure rationalist, he is very intuitive. And a lot of his written work, including the least satisfactory written work that he's done, was an attempt to provide a rational link for what was essentially an intuitive conclusion."

Gladstein, who has worked closely with Soros for fifteen years, describes his boss as operating in almost mystical terms, tying Soros's expertise to his ability to visualize the entire world's money and credit flows. Gladstein pointed out that historically the firm has made most of its money on the macro front, meaning currency and bond trading. "He has this macro vision of the entire world. He consumes all this information, digests it all, and from there he can come out with his opinion as to how this is all going to be sorted out. What the impact will be on the dollar or other currencies, the interest rate markets. He'll look at charts, but most of the information he's processing is verbal, not statistical."

No one has studied Soros's financial moves more closely than Stanley Druckenmiller. For more than a decade, Soros had been searching for someone to take over so that he could devote more time to his philanthropic foundations. Many were chosen, but none lasted. When Druckenmiller, who is twenty-two years younger than Soros, was sounded out for the job, he was intimidated by Soros's record of hiring many and firing quickly. Nor was he reassured when, after taking the job, he was introduced to Robert Soros, who told him that he was "number nine, my father's ninth successor."

But Druckenmiller, who accepted the position because he wanted to learn from the man he calls "the standard," endured. He is so committed to tracking markets that he rises each morning at 5 and is asleep by 9 p.m. Before he left in the spring of 2000 he had spent more than a decade walking in Soros's shoes as the fund's chief trader and macroeconomic strategist, occupying a rare position from which to observe and evaluate his mentor's role in the world of high finance.

"How remarkable is he? Well, basically, he is the standard," says Druckenmiller. "He developed the hedge fund model and he [managed a fund] longer and more successfully than anyone so far. It's one thing to do this for five or ten years. But to have the stamina to have done it really full-time from 1969 to 1989 is incredible. There's constant intense pressure."

Druckenmiller pointed out many traits that gave Soros a competitive advantage: the ability to compartmentalize, intelligence, coolness under pressure, insight, a critical and analytical mind. But repeatedly he kept returning to Soros's brilliance in "pulling the trigger." This, Druckenmiller said, provided the critical difference. Soros himself uses the term, saying it was what primarily distinguished him from Rogers while they worked together. "Pulling the trigger," said Druckenmiller, "is not about analysis; it's not about predicting trends—it's really about a sort of courage. It's hard to describe. You know, the ugly way to describe it would be 'balls.' To be willing at the right moment in time to put it all on the line. That is not something, in my opinion, that can be learned. It is totally intuitive, and it is an art, not in any way a science."

Druckenmiller, who with Soros's backing pulled the trigger in the fund's most famous speculation—a bet against the British pound that in 1992 earned more than a billion dollars—claims this capacity to maximize stakes and payoffs is very hard to find. "There are thousands of people who are good at analysis and hundreds who are good at predicting trends, but when you get down to using that information, pulling the trigger, putting it on the line to make what you are supposed to make, you are down to less than a handful."

In 1992 Druckenmiller calculated that, despite public assurances to the contrary, the Bank of England would not be able to avoid devaluating the pound. He called Soros to discuss his thinking. "I told him why I thought the pound could collapse and the reasons I had and I told him the amount I was going to do. I did not get a scolding, but I got something close to a scolding, which was, well, if you believe all that, why are you betting only two or three billion." With Soros's encouragement, Druckenmiller more than tripled his original stake.

Another example Druckenmiller cited involved Soros's response in 1985 to the Plaza Accord, when finance ministers meeting in New York signaled to the world that the dollar was overvalued and that it needed to come down. Prior to the announcement, the Soros fund had been accumulating yen, anticipating that the Japanese currency would rise in value. Once the announcement was made, the yen, of course, soared against the dollar. "The normal reaction, what most people would have," explained Druckenmiller, "would be to sell it and take your profit and go home and think how smart you are. My God, you just had one of the biggest hits ever, the yen is up 8 percent. And in fact some of Quantum's traders started to sell yen. George heard about it and ordered them to stop immediately and instead to buy a lot of yen. The normal human emotion is to take a profit, but George was looking ahead and realized the yen was going to go much, much higher and just because he had a big hit, the real hit was yet to come, and he ended up just plowing huge amounts of money." That year, aided significantly by this move, the fund achieved its highest annual growth ever, a staggering 122.2 percent.

"When you talk about leverage, and going for the jugular, I'm not even in his league," said Druckenmiller.

As yet another example of Soros's ability to act decisively in extreme situations, Druckenmiller cited his response in the stock market crash of October 1987. Soros was hurt badly. "When the crash occurred here the thing went to hell," said Druckenmiller, referring to the United States. In Japan as well, Soros's investments plummeted. "His long positions in the U.S. market were going down and his short positions in Japan were not going down because the Japanese authorities intervened to rig things. He was on leverage and the very existence of the fund was threatened. He found a trader in London and he sold out their entire portfolio off the exchange at well below market prices. When he put in that order, he told the trader, 'I'm going to walk out of here, they're not going to carry me out.'

"I was still working at the Dreyfus Fund then," continued Druckenmiller, "but I'll never forget how that Sunday, *Barron's Weekly* wrote this big piece on what an idiot he had been, how he'd sold out at the bottom. But they didn't understand the true dynamics. Here was a guy who had made money for eighteen years. He knows he's good. He knows all he has to do is stay in the game and his talents will come back. And for the threat of looking silly, he's not going to sit there and jeopardize the fund.

"And just about every manager I knew who was caught in that crash became almost comatose afterwards. They became nonfunctional, and I mean legendary names in our business. George took a bigger hit than any of them. And then within two weeks, he put on a massive leveraged dollar position. He had the wits to get right back up. In a week or two he shorted the dollar, and the fund ended up nearly 15 percent on the year despite the crash."

Druckenmiller said that no one in his business endures loss well. The pain, he said, can be unbearable. "A lot of people won't take a loss when they should. Their ego just cannot deal with it. George is a magnificent loss taker. He just gets rid of it and doesn't worry about his ego or what the world is going to say." Gladstein too said he has been with Soros on days when the fund, and he personally, lost hundreds of millions of dollars and yet nothing in Soros's behavior revealed either sorrow or rage. "He is always in control."

One of Soros's tennis partners, Yves-Andres Israel, had long marveled at Soros's ability to keep his emotions in check no matter how tense the game was. He asked Soros how he managed to remain so calm. Soros replied, "Why let your opponent know you're upset?"

Where did such qualities come from? Druckenmiller said that while he was not a psychiatrist he felt that his mentor's childhood experiences in war must have been significant. "Clearly, when you're facing life and death experiences, I think it's probably a great training ground for the kind of battles I'm talking about. They involve a lot of money and a lot of ego, but they're insignificant compared to what he went through as a young teenager."

Among the traits his associates have cited as extraordinary, none has mentioned administrative skills. All who have worked with him said he was not very good at spotting character or putting together a smoothly functioning organization. Soros agrees that he lacks this talent. Early on, when he and Rogers were registering rapid successes as a partnership, the issue of bureaucratic growth was not important. They could handle everything between them with two secretaries. But as the assets grew, running the operation like a candy store was becoming less feasible. Soros, the senior partner, did not want to be bothered with staff matters, and he delegated the hiring and training of staff to Rogers. The problem was that Rogers was not particularly interested in broadening the partnership. So despite Soros's desire to have the office grow, it was not growing. What was increasing along with the profits was the burden of work and the tensions between the two partners.

All of this, Soros claimed, came to a head around 1978 when the fund reached $100 million. "It became apparent that the more successful we were, the more work there was, the more you needed to do, the more you needed to know, the more ideas you had to find. It turned into a labor of Sisyphus."

For years before that, Soros had pressured Rogers to find people who could share the load, but somehow the expansion never took place. "Rogers seemed to have a kind of fixation on me. I was a sort of father figure for him. For him, our operation was an exclusive relationship and no one else could be admitted."

Periodically, said Soros, Rogers would oversee the training of traders, most of whom were women with no Wall Street experience. "We made a point of not taking anybody from Wall Street because we were against conventional investing." All these efforts collapsed. "Rogers liked being in charge of the training because he liked to be dominating. But when the people reached a certain point where they could actually contradict him, or differ with him, he couldn't take it and would set out to destroy them. So there were some really unpleasant dynamics developing. People were around for a couple of years, and just when they began to be productive, then he would turn on them."

It is Soros's view that underlying the problems with staffing were the opposing visions he and Rogers had about the future and about pulling the trigger. "He wanted us to be smaller. He would have been happier if we reached a certain point and then just distributed the money we earned and went back and did it all over again. You know, just the two of us against the world because we are cleverer than all of them put together." As for himself, he found the burdens onerous but he enjoyed confronting new challenges. How long could he register such high yields? The greater the fund, the more ingenuity was needed to sustain such a record. Perhaps one day his fund might reach a billion dollars in equity. No hedge fund had ever grown that rich.

Through the seventies the tensions kept mounting. The staff never grew beyond eight people, and few of them stayed very long. On the other hand, as Soros contended, Rogers was doing remarkable work that he said would have taken six men to equal. Soros realized that something had to give. In 1978, while he and Rogers were attending an electronics association meeting in Monterey, California, at which they picked a number of highly promising companies, Soros informed Rogers of his plan to resolve the problems they were having because the fund was growing while the management was not. "I said to him, We'll try to solve it together, then we'll try to solve it without you, and if that doesn't work, we'll try to solve it without me."

Phase one came to an end in 1979, when Rogers agreed to leave with the millions he had earned. The prelude to the separation, Soros recalls, was amicable, but when the actual parting occurred in 1980, Rogers became "extremely hostile." "There was no legal action, but he absolutely turned against me and he has spread rumors. He was looking for me to fall on my face without him. He was sure that I can't live without him. I got him a job at Morgan Stanley, but he didn't last there. And then he went out on his own, managing his own money and going on a motorcycle trip around the world and writing a book about it. But he's had it in for me ever since. Once I called him for some material I wanted for a book I was writing and he refused to give it to me. There's been that sort of thing."

The breakup with Rogers was clearly a matter of significance. In the twelve years they were together they achieved many victories and came to be perceived as a legendary team by their competitors. For Soros this marked the longest continuing period with one business concern up to that point in his professional life. He had been with Rogers longer than he had been at the LSE, or at F. M. Mayer, or Wertheim, or Arnhold.

The fragmentation of the partnership was clearly significant, but it was hardly the only stormy occurrence of this period, nor was it even the most unsettling. As he approached fifty, Soros increasingly asked himself disturbing questions about where his happiness might lie. As he tried to manage the fund on his own, his twenty-year marriage to Annaliese was crumbling.

CHAPTER 13

MIDLIFE

Always analytical and self-critical, Soros at the age of forty-eight had grown miserably aware of a looming contradiction in his life: he was rich and successful, but he was not at all content and he was far from happy. "Here I was," he says, "extremely successful, but I made a point of denying my success. I worked like a dog. I felt that it would endanger my success if I abandoned my sense of insecurity. And what was my reward? More money, more responsibility, more work, and more pain. The fund reached $100 million, my personal wealth must have been around $25 million, and I was close to the breaking point. It did not make sense."

To make matters more absurd, Soros, at least on one level, appeared to disdain the money he was making. He recalled how Tivadar had always stressed that money should be considered only as a tool, a means to achieve certain ends and not an end in itself. It was not meant to be taken terribly seriously. George had absorbed this lesson from his father and even passed it on to his children. He believed it. Yet in his own case, what was the end?

Soros had none of the passions that so many other rich men seem to develop to keep pace with their growing wealth. He was not a collector. He did not need to amass paintings, or stamps, or antiques, or showgirls. He did not like to gamble. He did not love cars or gadgets. He was not religious and he did not have a craving to see his name carved into stone as a benefactor. He did not want to be well-known for what he possessed, nor did he wish to buy his way into the company of those as rich as or richer than himself. He was really not a materialist.

Once, at a dinner party, Mary Breasted, a novelist, who was sitting next to Soros, asked him when he had first decided that he liked making money. "I don't like it," he told her. "I'm just good at it."

Byron Wien also pointed out that "George is really not interested in money." Soros would dispute that. "I had to be interested in money. I could not do what I did for so many years if I were not interested in money. I was interested in money in the same way that a sculptor must be interested in clay or bronze. It was the material in which I worked." But, as Wien implied, his interest in money was less tied to luxurious living than that of most plutocrats.

Which did not mean that George and Annaliese were living humbly. The apartment with a view of Central Park had four bedrooms and was well-appointed. There were original paintings on the wall, a number by Hungarian artists, but none by anyone who was immediately recognizable. Robert and Andrea were going to expensive boarding schools. Jonathan was at a private day school. The Soroses could have had a chauffeur but they did not need one. They did have a maid, but Annaliese liked to cook and was very good at it. For his part, George loved to eat, enjoying all sorts of food, French, Italian, and all the Asian cuisines. The only dishes he has never liked are cream soups. On his travels to remote places he finishes off even plain food with gusto, maintaining a good appetite. He always liked wine and has in recent years filled the cellar that came with his Bedford property with a wide and valuable collection. Bill Maynes said that the bottles Soros provides for his guests are impressive. "It was not Petrus, and it didn't have to be, but it was always very good." Maynes said the same principle applies to other expenditures. "Annaliese was a very elegant woman and always dressed well, but I don't think she bought her clothes from designers."

Here was a paradox fit for an absurdist playwright. A man who is brilliant at making money belittles the money he makes and disparages the personal costs involved in making it. At the same time his ego and his competitive nature are so fully engaged in the process that he cannot simply stop. He goes on accumulating money, a commodity that everyone wants, while realizing that he already has more than he can figure out how to meaningfully use. Because of various experiences in his youth, he disdains charity as a misguided ego trip and contributes very little. And in order to keep making money, he continues to cultivate the punishing feelings of insecurity that he believes are the essential goads that make him earn even more.

It might seem funny, not credible, said for effect—but the pain was real. In the end it drove Soros to embark on what Robert Soros regards as the latest in a succession of dramatic reconstructions. "Basically, his whole life has been a series of recreations of himself, in various forms," said Robert. "After hiding under an assumed identity during the war he left home at seventeen and, alone in London, created a new life as a student and a philosopher. He came here and recreated himself as a financial wizard. He progressed and grew, and then when he separated from my mother he did it again, this time setting out to create himself as a more public figure."

According to Robert, the separation and ultimate divorce were in large measure triggered by his father's desire for a more public life and what Robert termed a "grander persona." Annaliese had always treasured her privacy. George, on the other hand, while struggling with his outlander's shyness and fear of publicity, had long hungered for more intellectual friendships and a more engaged social life. Robert, who was at Choate when the marriage dissolved, remembers having heard his parents talking about these differences. "They had reached a point in their relationship at which my father wanted to go one way, and she didn't want to go that way. He wanted to have a bigger, grander life and they were inherently conflicted about that."

That such differences contributed to the breakup seems likely, but there were more immediate tensions, many involving the children. Soros has openly conceded his failures as a father. He was, he says, more distant from his children and haughtier than his parents had been with him, and this aloofness caused problems. Soon after the separation he confided to an old friend that some months earlier he had irreparably damaged the marriage by refusing Annaliese's plea that he search for his daughter when she did not come home as expected.

He had other traits that undermined domestic tranquillity and challenged the tolerance of his adolescent children. He could be as maddeningly mercurial at home as he was in business, reevaluating, altering, and even completely reversing his views as he continuously weighed new evidence. He never shouted at the children, but when angry he would confront them with the same iciness and silence he used with his associates. He sought to control by withdrawing his interest and affection. And most painful of all for his children was his constant criticism. After all, critical evaluation was a principal tenet of his philosophy and he applied it everywhere. In fact, he was critical of everyone, but his children found his judgments particularly hard to endure. It provided scant comfort for them to know that his assessments were lovingly meant or that he was much harsher on himself than on them or anyone else.

Soros could be remarkably blunt, demonstrating an assertive honesty that could land with the impact of a slap. Basically, he said what he meant without equivocation or diplomatic modulation. Several of his business associates described seeing him in this mode, looking down at his shoes and firing someone by simply telling them they were not good at their job. He did not enjoy the exercise and kept it as short as possible. He has also terminated job interviews by telling applicants that there was no sense continuing because someone whom he would name had told him they were not competent. In later years, he would demonstrate such direct and even confessional candor not only by telling interviewers about his paranoid schizophrenic grandfather but also disclosing in an op-ed piece his children's experimentation with marijuana, or saying that he himself was over the hill as an investor.

It is debatable whether being too forthcoming is a defect or a virtue, but it clearly can cause resentment and embarrassment. Robert remembers a time when he was applying to prep schools. His cousin, Paul's son Jeffrey, was going to St. George's in Rhode Island and Robert wanted to go there as well. At one point father and son took part in a required joint interview on the campus, during which a school official casually asked whether they had any questions.

Robert remembers his shock as he heard his father ask about the school drug policy while revealing his own permissive views toward youthful indiscretions. "He wanted to know did they kick out kids the first time or did they give them a second chance. I can't remember if I had tried pot at that time or if we had discussed it, but I guess he was just pursuing his own thoughts. Meanwhile I could just see my chances of admission go out the window." While George had meant his questions and the discussion they generated to be a free exchange of ideas, Robert was convinced his father had unthinkingly and inadvertently fingered him as a potential drug problem. He was not admitted and ended up at Choate instead.

The family conflicts of this period have subsided, but the time leading up to and following the separation were difficult for all the children. When the separation occurred, Robert was fifteen, Andrea was thirteen, and Jonathan was nine. Byron Wien remembers that when George had him serve as his interlocutor for *Soros on Soros*, in 1995, he delved into family relationships and George's responses were included in the original draft. Wien said that George then deleted the passages after his children read the manuscript and told him they did not want to "relive their experiences in the book." Wien said he strongly disagreed with George's decision to "sanitize" the book out of respect for their feelings but could not talk him out of it. Soros is still unwilling to discuss these things.

Robert says that while all three children were marked by the tensions of that time, "the divorce itself was amicable; they didn't haul each other into court." Indeed, Soros was so impressed by the intelligence and grace shown by William Zabel, Annaliese's lawyer, that once the divorce was settled, he retained him as his own personal lawyer. By all accounts the settlement was generous and Soros has remained on good terms with his former wife, seeing her often and always referring to her with fondness and admiration. He has also grown closer to the three children. Jonathan worked for the Open Society Foundation and then went to Harvard, where he simultaneously obtained a law degree and a master's from the Kennedy School of Public Administration before joining the Soros Fund. Andrea founded the Trace Foundation, which supports Tibetan causes. Robert, of course, works at Soros Fund Management.

It was in the late summer of 1978 that Soros left the family. He rented a small furnished apartment a few blocks away on Central Park South, and when he departed, he went by cab, taking with him only a few suitcases of clothes and some books. He did not own a car. A few hours before he took his things to his new place, he went to play tennis at a court on Columbus Avenue near 97th Street. Playing on an adjacent court was Susan Weber, a twenty-three-year-old woman whom he had met once before. The two recognized each other and waved.

Within an hour, heavy rains interrupted play and George and Susan chatted in the clubhouse. She had graduated from Barnard as an art historian, and after spending a year in Europe she was working with a woman named Courtney Sale, making films about New York painters such as Mark Rothko and Willem de Kooning. Earlier that summer, while she was working late, she had received a phone call from Jacques Leviant, a businessman friend of Sale's, who said he had wanted to ask Sale to dinner so that she could tell him and a friend of his about the documentaries. Soros was the friend and it was an unusual sort of thing for him to tag along, but he was at loose ends and he did have a recurrent interest in art. Sale was out of town so Leviant asked Susan if she would join them. They met at an East Side restaurant and Susan remembers that she had a long conversation with George about his daughter. "He kept asking me questions to better understand his daughter." The girl, Susan later learned, was undergoing an adolescent crisis.

Now, some three weeks later, as the two chatted during the rainstorm, George asked if Susan wanted to come have lunch with him. In the cab he asked, "How old are you anyway?" She looked younger than her age. A few weeks earlier George had turned forty-eight. Over lunch he told her that he had just separated from his wife and that he was going to move his bags that afternoon. He asked if she would come and help him. She said no. "I was scared," says Susan. "I ran off. I said I had to go somewhere." But she agreed to see him for dinner the following night.

She remembers that on this occasion he told her that he'd been very successful on Wall Street and had made a great deal of money in the stock market. "I thought, this man's definitely a phony, he must not have two nickels to rub together," she says, "because the way I was raised, we were taught that no one talks about money, and if you have it, then you certainly don't talk about it." She had been brought up in a well-to-do but hardly patrician family. Her father, Murray Weber, owned factories that produced shoe-related items such as polish, shoe trees, and leather dyes. His father had emigrated from Russia and had started the business. Her mother, Iris, who died soon after Susan graduated from Barnard, had been a housewife who had passed on her fondness and appreciation of decorative art to Susan. The family was Jewish but was not observant. "We were cultural Jews," says Susan, who attended an Episcopalian private high school in Brooklyn. "My sister Robin says that I'm a WASH, a White Anglo-Saxon Hebrew."

In retrospect, she thinks it was insecurity and nervousness that led George to talk about his money on that first date and not an attempt to impress her. But at the time she thought it vulgar. When she returned to work after the weekend she mentioned her dinner with George to Courtney Sale. Her friend and mentor had dated older men and would soon marry one. In 1982 Sale became the last wife of Steve Ross, the flamboyantly buoyant tycoon who rose from presiding over parking garages and funeral homes to orchestrate the first of the huge media mergers and head the Warner Brothers empire until his death. A year after Sale's marriage, Susan married George Soros.

But in the late summer of 1978, Susan found the idea of going out with older men amusing. "I used to tease Courtney, asking her if she was going out with some grandfather, and she would always say to me, 'Wait until you date an older man and you won't say that.' So when I got back to work that Monday I told her I had met an older man." Sale had never heard of Soros but when she called Leviant to inquire, she learned that George was indeed very successful.

Susan and George continued to see each other, going to galleries and, as she remembers, talking a great deal about art. "I felt he had worked very hard," says Susan. "He obviously wanted a new life. He was very open to everything. I mean, it was probably male menopause. He moved into that tiny furnished apartment and he wanted to own nothing. He didn't want to be bothered by possessions, he wanted a totally new life. He's in the tackiest apartment you can imagine, with sort of cheap plastic furniture, and he doesn't care."

Susan quickly began to play an important role in George's period of transition and transformation, but the relationship was not exclusive. Over the next few years they saw each other often, but they both dated other people as well. George enjoyed the company of women and had no difficulty attracting the interest of many, among them more than a few fortune hunters. But the women with whom he had his longest relationships in this period were intelligent and discreet as well as attractive. Notable among them were a journalist who wrote about Third World economics and another woman who was actively involved in human rights issues and had contacts with Eastern European dissidents.

At the time Soros was quite clearly stripping down, divesting himself of emotional and business ties. He had jettisoned his family and Rogers. He was still tending to business, though reducing his hours and intensity. "I was trying to loosen the reins," he says. He also began to see a psychoanalyst two or three times a week. He did not lie on a couch, but instead sat while he talked, seeking to make sense of his life. Despite his earlier strong criticism of Freud and psychoanalysis, he would later claim that this period of therapy had enabled him to successfully integrate disparate elements of his life into a less tormented personality. More specifically, he believes that his conversations with the psychoanalyst had enabled him to identify and confront long latent sources of his insecurity. As Soros came to understand himself, he had been burdened for most of his adulthood with an "oversized" sense of shame. There had been, he said, "a kind of guilty secret of some sort." He realized that in order to compensate for that shame, he had resorted to illusions of grandeur, presenting himself as wonderful when he knew he was not so wonderful.

Evidently, his façade of self-satisfaction had something to do with his success as a moneymaker, but he had also felt superior when he was almost penniless in London. Essentially, it was tied to his survival skills and the notion that, like his father before him, he could do whatever was necessary. But the countervailing doubt—that he was not really wonderful—was also deeply rooted. His only success, he realized, had been in making money, a lesser pursuit than his dormant but never eradicated dreams of formulating a philosophy that would last for centuries. By the standards of his secret aspirations, his financial achievements were puny.

His sense of shame, he later confided, had spurred him both to financial success as well as to the philosophical quest he had secretly pursued like Hjalmar Ekdal, that photographer in Ibsen's *Wild Duck*. As for the basis of that shame, he said that after several years of therapy, he was able to understand that "it had partly to do with my Jewishness and partly with sex." In regard to the Jewishness, he grew aware that he had not in fact emerged from the war quite as unscathed as he had believed. "I realized the impact of the attacks on my identity that occurred when I had to deny my Jewishness and live under false pretenses. For a fourteen-year-old boy it could not have been easy." The experience, he came to understand, had left him with an ambivalence that had condensed into shame. He had always known he was Jewish and he knew that he could well have been killed because of it. But outwardly, such awareness rarely concerned him. He was, after all, not religious. He was an atheist. Annaliese was not Jewish, and Robert said he grew up without any religious identity. At the same time, Soros had developed a contempt for tribal sectarianism of all kinds and found much of the zeal of pro-Israeli Zionists to be unappealingly chauvinistic.

He had seen corpses of those killed only because of their Jewishness. But what did Jewishness mean, particularly if one stripped away religious belief and rejected solidarity with those building a Jewish state? Some of his relatives who shared the same experiences and similar views had simply stopped being Jewish. Erzebet had always treated her Jewishness ambiguously and at times even contemptuously. George was aware of that with his reference to her as "a typical Jewish anti-Semite." Under Tivadar's influence she had remained nominally Jewish, but after his death she drew away from the tradition into which she was born; like other members of the family, she attended Christian services. Susan Soros explained that one reason George had avoided publicity for so long was in part to protect the privacy of those relatives who had changed their religion. "Some became Protestants," she said.

But George did not convert. What sense would conversion make for someone who was an atheist? Therefore it was not apostasy that was the source of his guilt. Instead, the "secret shame" seemed to originate in his having minimized an identity that had quite literally been a life-and-death issue. Concealing who and what he was at fourteen had implanted an ambivalent duality. Not finding any way to affirm that identity afterward might well have been seen as a breach of solidarity with the millions who had died. From a psychological point of view, one could surmise how even an indifference to this particular identity, stopping well short of self-hatred, might suggest some unintended acquiescence to Hitler's attempt to rid the world of Jews. In light of those very real Hitlerian efforts, which the young George had witnessed and escaped as Sandor Kiss, the adult George may well have felt nagging obligations to affirm a Jewishness that had been so central to his own life story. But as an atheist and an anti-nationalist, how exactly was he to do it?

In *Underwriting Democracy*, a book he wrote in 1990 as an expansion of an earlier British version, *Opening the Soviet System*, Soros noted that despite his success in the United States, he had never fully become an American and his Jewishness "did not express itself in a sense of tribal loyalty that would have led me to support Israel." On the contrary, he wrote, "I took pride in being in the minority, an outsider who was capable of seeing the other point of view. Only the ability to think critically, and to rise above a particular point of view, could make up for the dangers and indignities that being a Hungarian Jew had inflicted on me."

Elsewhere in the same book, Soros commented further on the schizoid pattern established in adolescence. "I have lived with a double personality all my life. It started at age fourteen in Hungary when I assumed a false identity to escape persecution as a Jew. It continued in England, where I was a refugee and had to work in various menial jobs in order to maintain myself and had to pretend I was not very different from the people around me in order to get by." Soros, who wrote that the duality continued during his years on Wall Street, had clearly spent much time in therapy dealing with the impact that his temporary, necessary, and pragmatic denial of Jewishness at the age of fourteen had had on the development of his personality.

The other area he confronted and explored under analysis was his attitude and behavior toward women. "There had always been this ambivalence in me towards women, where I was kind of afraid of women. I was afraid of intimacy, because it's too penetrating, too violating. So I protected myself against women and also appeased them. I acted well, but I was also very distant."

At the heart of this conduct, he discovered, lay his parents' relationship to each other and particularly his own complicated ties to his mother. "I had internalized the conflict between my mother and father. I had been very close to her and at the same time I knew my father looked down on her in some ways. It was a very complex situation." His brother had been able to distance himself from Erzebet at an early age, leaving George as her principal ally. He was the child she would turn to for solace and protection against the humiliations of a husband she worshipped and adored. In those months in 1944 at Lake Balaton, when he posed as her godson, George was her protector. "In analysis I came to understand how she had gotten inside me, how she had violated my space. She was very intrusive."

It was in this period, as he approached fifty, that "I separated myself from my mother." Twenty years later he still admired her enormously, describing her as "a wonderful woman," whom he believes he greatly resembles in personality. "I never really turned against my mother, but I managed to recognize that because of her relationship with me I had protected myself against women. So I think that having worked her out of myself I had a very good relationship with her, and she also learned to be very much more independent. She grew a lot."

Soros feels that psychoanalysis served to dispel his secret shame in regard to both Jewishness and women. The more deeply he looked into his life the more he realized "that there was nothing to feel ashamed of." As he understood the origins of his feelings and fears, they vanished. Once, he remembered, he had suffered great pain when a stone had formed in his salivary gland. He had an operation for it and when the surgeon gave him the stone as a souvenir, it soon dried and crumbled. In the same way, he said, his fears and shame dissolved when they were brought to the surface.

Soros credits analysis with at least one further meaningful insight. It helped him to understand that his cyclical mood swings—from the extended periods of introverted behavior to those of increasing social engagement—also grew out his internalization of the conflict between his mother and father. "I could see how I kept going from one parent to the other. My father was gregarious, practical, and had great judgment and so on. My mother was involved with abstract ideas and was in some ways a loser. And in my life there had been this repetitive pattern of three or four years of extroverted activity followed by a period of withdrawal." He said that here, too, recognition of a pattern helped him to alter it. "I felt I had put something together. It brought on a big change in my personality and I've been much more comfortable with myself ever since."

The psychological breakthroughs occurred from 1979 to 1981. During that time, Soros kept looking for someone who could take over the management of the fund and relieve him of some of the burdens. "I made the decision that I [had] to get off the treadmill." He negotiated with a number of people but found none who fully satisfied him. Meanwhile, he was forcing himself to pull back from the fund. He still followed the markets, still called the shots, and still pulled the trigger, but he traveled more, read books, dated a number of women, and pursued other interests. "I relaxed my control. I didn't involve myself in every detail, and the immediate result was that the fund had its greatest growth." In 1978 Quantum grew by 55 percent, bringing its assets to $103 million. The following year, the growth was 59 percent and assets increased to $178 million. In 1980, bolstered by huge gains Soros had registered in trading British Government bonds, the so-called gilts, the fund more than doubled its worth, growing by a staggering 102 percent to attain a level of $381 million.

Soros's own wealth was growing at an even faster rate. Under its contract with the fund, Soros Fund Management was entitled to 20 percent of the yearly profits as a performance fee plus 1 percent of all assets under management. Since most of these fees then went to Soros, this meant that, counting only such remuneration, his personal wealth swelled by something like $60 million in the three years. But since his wealth was fully invested in his fund's shares, his fortune was compounding at the same rate as the fund, growing robustly. If his stake in the fund had been $25 million in 1977, that alone would have been worth some $120 million by the end of 1980.

He had been rich for quite a while; now he was becoming very rich. But he was still living in the furnished apartment that Susan Weber found tacky. And his reputation for success had not extended very far beyond the financial elite. He had virtually no public identity. In 1975 the *Wall Street Journal* ran a front-page article on the fund, noting the high earnings it had gained for its foreign shareholders. Three years later, Soros had a letter published in the *New York Review of Books*, contending that a writer in a previous issue had misunderstood and undervalued the thinking of Karl Popper. Soros would not appear in *Who's Who* until 1994. He had no public relations consultants, and his instinct had always led him to shy away from journalists who wanted to write about him. But with his growing desire to experiment and broaden his life, that resolve weakened, and in the spring of 1981 he agreed, with some reluctance, to meet with a journalist, Anise Wallace. As a result the June issue of *Institutional Investor* carried that six-page cover story about Soros under the headline, "The World's Greatest Money Manager."

The admiration expressed by the title was carried forward by the opening paragraph: "When the name George Soros is mentioned to professional money managers, their responses tend to echo the remark once made by Ilie Nastase about Bjorn Borg: 'We're playing tennis and he's playing something else.' As Borg is to tennis, Jack Nicklaus is to golf and Fred Astaire is to tap dancing, so is George Soros to money management."

Wallace backed this up with accolades from financiers and with statistics. She also depicted Soros as something of a mystery man, a loner who never telegraphs his moves, who keeps even his associates at a distance. "As for fame," she wrote, "it's widely agreed that he can happily do without it. 'He doesn't like publicity or need it,' says a Paris based money manager. 'I don't think he wants recognition.' "

Wallace continued: "Indeed in a rare interview for this article, which he had long ducked, Soros said in his thickly accented voice, 'You're dealing with a market. You should be anonymous.' "

Soros evaded some of Wallace's questions about the market and about investment decisions, but he was typically revealing and self-critical about himself. At one point after describing his conflict with Jim Rogers and his failure to find a suitable partner, he declared: "I am, in fact, somewhat burned out, in my view, in the sense that I no longer enjoy doing the same thing that I have been doing for the last twelve years over and over again. I don't do it as well as I used to because I don't enjoy it."

He spoke of his hope of finding a successor to take over, or, ideally, three people who could assume the burden. "I really want to kick myself upstairs," he said, though he added that even in that case he "would always be there and I'd always pitch in when something is on fire."

Within three months of the article's appearance, Soros, still alone at the helm, had a four-alarm blaze on his hands. He had brought on the crisis by trying to find and hire replacements for himself while continuing to make investment decisions. He was overtaxed, and for the first time since he started his hedge fund, it was down. As September approached, the fund's value had dipped by 26 percent since the year began. As word circulated that he was in some sort of crisis, Soros took a very unusual step: he sent a letter to each shareholder saying that it was "inadvisable to rely upon one man to take sole responsibility for every investment decision." The letter noted that while Soros would continue to set strategy, other managers would be hired or portions of the fund might be farmed out to outside specialists. As George remembers his intent, he was advising his shareholders to consider their options carefully.

As he expected, there were defections. Gary Gladstein had not yet joined the fund at the time, but one of the largest and oldest shareholders, Alberto Foglia, later confided how he wrestled with his decision. Foglia's heart told him to stay, because he felt great loyalty to Soros for his past achievement. His head, however, suggested that George was losing his concentration. Ultimately, he listened to his heart, but as he told Gladstein, his brother decided to pull his money out. According to Gladstein, Foglia's punchline was that as a result of all this he has become worth much more than his brother.

In fact, so many investors withdrew their money that the small number of American shareholders sanctioned by the SEC—basically Soros himself and other managers—was coming close to exceeding the specified percentage of American participants, which in turn would have meant a loss of highly valuable tax benefits. In the end the defections stopped short of this figure, but for a while the value of the fund hovered at $200 million, down from $400 million.

For Soros, it was a painful time, but looking back he regards the episode as a triumph, a moment of maturation when he tamed his demons and was able to separate from the fund as he had separated from his mother. As he would tell Wien in *Soros on Soros*, he had been waging an internal conflict with his fund and had come out on top. "I refused to remain the slave of my business. I established that I am the master and not the slave. It was a big change in many ways, because I began to accept myself as someone who is successful; I overcame fear of the misfortune that might befall me if I admitted my success."

Before the year ended Soros was able to reduce the losses for 1981 to 22 percent. In 1982, the fund registered a gain of 57 percent, beginning another remarkable streak of gains that was to last for fourteen years.

PART III

GIVING IT AWAY

CHAPTER 14

INTO PHILANTHROPY

E MERGING FROM HIS midlife transformation Soros could finally
admit his success to himself. But he was still a long way from either
extending his accomplishments beyond moneymaking or having his deeds
widely recognized. At fifty, he had become a man of considerable wealth
who had demonstrated prodigious investing skills and become the envy of
other money managers. He had, however, failed to make any mark as a
philosopher, his first and still lingering ambition. His marriage had ended,
and neither he nor his children would have given him high marks as a
father. His only publicly accessible writing was that short letter to the *New
York Review of Books.* By his own lights, he had certainly not redeemed his
father's failed promise, as he had once felt obliged to do. Had his life ended
at that point, his obituaries would have been modest, necessarily concentrating on the growth of his fund and the fortunes he made for foreign
investors and himself. Even in terms of wealth he had not yet broken into
the ranks of the truly superrich. As for his views about world affairs,
human rights, open societies, justice, altruism, or charity, there would have
been no reason for the obituaries to mention them.

Yet within the next two decades Soros would become a significant
player in many parts of the globe, regularly meeting with world and
national leaders and offering policy initiatives as well as financial aid. He
would be nominated and seriously mentioned as a candidate for the Nobel
Peace Prize. Indeed, if a fully involved life was to be measured by its mixture of ideas and action, then Soros arguably would become the most
broadly and deeply engaged private citizen in the entire world as the cen-

tury turned. There were obviously others—presidents, foreign ministers, heads of international agencies—whose fields of interest and activity were expansive, but their objectives were much more narrowly focused, shaped by institutional, national, or regional interests and limited by bureaucratic and diplomatic practice. Moreover, the influence of such people lay in their offices and it evaporated once they stepped down. By contrast, Soros, who sometimes called himself "a stateless statesman," served entirely at his own pleasure and depended exclusively on his own resources of mind, character, and pocket. In his ventures into world affairs he reveled in the same autonomy that had so appealed to him as a hedge-fund operator.

Rich men have often engaged in public or political life. America in the twentieth century has had its Lehmans, Harrimans, Rockefellers, and Kennedys in public office. Beyond that, from at least the time of the Medicis, merchant princes or bankers have served as advisers to leaders both monarchial and democratic. Through the 1930s and 1940s, Bernard Baruch, a self-described stock speculator, was regularly portrayed as an adviser and confidant of American presidents. But unlike Soros, Baruch had confined his counsel solely to the leaders of his own country. For his part, Soros has offered advice and engaged in dialogue with the leaders of dozens of nations, large and small. He has skirmished with more than a few, castigating them for what he took to be their failures, weaknesses, and sins with the same bluntness he showed when firing incompetent traders.

On his own he floated ambitious schemes for economic reform and organized rescue missions for countries like Russia as they foundered in post-Communist transition. He reached into his pocket to tide governments over short-term crises. He energetically backed international peace initiatives in the Balkans and elsewhere, acting virtually like a sovereign power, though one without armed forces. He pointed out economic hazards to leaders such as Boris Yeltsin, Nelson Mandela, and South Korea's Kim Dae Jung. In Poland and the Czech Republic, he related warmly to powerful politicians he had first come to know and support when they were persecuted dissidents. The leaders of most countries returned his phone calls quickly. He established ties to Kofi Annan, the secretary general of the United Nations, Secretary of State Madeleine Albright, and James Wolfensohn, the head of the World Bank, and testified before the United States Congress on the need to reform and extend the international economic institutions that came into being at the end of World War II.

As his prominence grew, he dramatically excoriated Malaysia's autocratic strongman, Mohamed Mahathir, at a World Bank meeting. Openly and quite undiplomatically, he feuded with leaders he regarded as anti-democratic opponents of open societies, men such as Aleksandr Lukashenka of Belarus, Slobodan Milošević of Serbia, the late Franjo Tudjman of Croatia, and Vladimir Meciar of Slovakia. In Macedonia, Ukraine, and Bosnia he turned away from leaders who once impressed him, cutting off his personal involvement and reducing his generosity as promised reforms failed to materialize, and attacking them in op-ed pieces.

Such activities led Morton Abramowitz, a former American ambassador and the director of the Carnegie Endowment for International Peace, to offer that characterization of Soros as "the only man in the United States who has his own foreign policy and can implement it." In a similar vein, Byron Wien claims that his friend had come to wield "more influence in the world than anyone who has never held high elective or appointive office."

This extraordinary example of a private citizen achieving so much influence in so many countries is unprecedented in modern times. There have been private figures who gained considerable power in specific regions; for example, the African imperialist adventurer Cecil Rhodes, or Calouste Gulbenkian, whose influence in Central Asia and the Middle East gained him precious oil leases, or Armand Hammer, the American oilman who cultivated close ties to Soviet leaders. But in comparison to Soros, the spheres of interest and the objectives of such men were modest. They simply wanted to further enrich themselves. As for Soros, though some critics have at times doubted his altruism, it seems he genuinely wanted to change and improve the world. As a child, he imagined the world as a peaceful barnyard. In his philosophical quests, he hoped to chart and, implicitly, to harness history. Such dreams lay dormant as he made money, but they gained force with what his second wife referred to as his midlife crisis. He linked the money to his older ambitions.

His ruling sin was no longer greed but hubris. With his emphasis on open societies and with his philanthropic commitments in so many parts of the world, Soros revealed perspectives that lay far beyond national politics or economic self-interest. In the modern era it has been writers, philosophers, and revolutionaries who, from positions beyond conventional politics, have acted on world-changing impulses—men like Lord Byron, Mikhail Bakunin, Victor Hugo, Mahatma Gandhi, Albert Schweitzer, André Malraux, Martin Luther King, Jr., Malcolm X, and Che Guevara. By the 1990s Soros had joined their ranks, in the startling capacity of a globally engaged billionaire and a revolutionary plutocrat who was often welcomed and sometimes feared in many corridors of power.

How did he do it? How did he find his way into those well-guarded vestibules?

Soros openly acknowledges that he had long aspired to such influence. In his dismal student years in London, he felt blocked off from the people of high intelligence and importance with whom he identified. Taking refuge in what he has termed "messianic" fantasies, he read about Keynes and dreamed of leading a similar life of meaningful impact. In England he never enjoyed the company of people like the Apostles of Cambridge, and later, in America, he endured what he thought was a pedestrian social life while he pursued profits through finance.

Within a decade or so of his midlife makeover, he would attain the access for which he yearned. In the end, the formula proved rather simple. His legendary wealth and his open-handed generosity, coupled with his imagination, eventually gained him the worldly stature and the international contacts. In the process, he redefined philanthropy. In 1996, in his book *Inside American Philanthropy*,* Waldemar A. Nielsen, an American scholar of philanthropy, would write of Soros:

> By the scope of his vision, the scale of his commitments, and the courage of his initiatives, Soros already ranks with the greatest American philanthropists ever. His international efforts constitute a heroic chapter in the history of philanthropy—in terms of creativity, courage, timeliness, and the scale of commitment. Not since [John D.] Rockefeller and Carnegie has such a force been seen in the field of donorship.

No doubt, Rockefeller had provided something of a precedent for Soros by committing himself to philanthropy with the same energy he had earlier devoted to making his fortune. He established extraordinary institutions, and his donations reflected his devotion to his religious ideals as he contributed to higher education, racial justice, and medical science. But Rockefeller was much less personally involved than Soros in the day-to-day choices that his giving entailed, nor was his vision ever as global.

The similarities between Soros and Carnegie, a Scottish immigrant, were greater. Not at all religious, Carnegie had a secular philosophy of his own that served as an ideological framework for his philanthropy. Like Soros, Carnegie wrote reasonably well and sought to convey his philosophy in articles and books such as *The Gospel of Wealth*. Less abstract than

---

*University of Oklahoma Press, 1996.

concepts of fallibility and open society, his basic view was that men of wealth should serve as trustees for their poorer brethren by providing educational and cultural institutions. Carnegie's sponsorship of more than three thousand libraries in English-speaking countries was rooted in a belief that people should be encouraged to help themselves, a view that Soros has shared. Carnegie also had internationalist visions that were unusual for his time. He contributed to the establishment of the International Court in The Hague and the Pan-American Union. He also established the Carnegie Endowment for International Peace, to study the causes of war and promote international law.

There was, however, a striking difference between Soros and both Rockefeller and Carnegie. The philanthropic pioneers of the nineteenth century came from tithing traditions and contributed to charities for all of their adult lives. The concept of alms and Christian charity had shaped their outlooks from childhood. They believed in philanthropy. Soros did not. He had contributed virtually nothing since he brought his piggy bank savings to that Hungarian newspaper editor to help the Finns in their 1940 resistance to Soviet forces. Indeed, he openly disparaged philanthropy, and as he continued to examine and expand his life in the late seventies it did not seem to offer him a particularly fruitful option. "I had a very negative view of philanthropy," he recalled.

As late as 1981, when the cover article about Soros appeared in *Institutional Investor*, his charitable efforts merited only a single sentence, which claimed he had supported dance companies and backed efforts to improve New York's Central Park while also contributing to Amnesty International.

In those days, the only solicitations he regularly received came from Jewish organizations. "I absolutely did not respond to them," he said, acknowledging that his general contempt for philanthropies was even more pronounced in the case of Jewish organizations. He traces this antipathy to that day in Hungary when as a fourteen-year-old messenger for the Budapest Jewish community organization he had delivered messages, drafted under Nazis pressure, ordering Jewish lawyers to present themselves for deportation. His disregard for sectarian groups in general and Jewish charities in particular was further heightened by the memory of his own treatment by that Jewish charity in London.

So his first ventures as a donor, carried out while he was still living with Annaliese and their children, were quite ordinary. He and his wife liked modern dance and often went to performances. He contributed to several companies, principally to that of Alwin Nikolais and his partner, Murray

Lewis. Soros cannot remember how much he gave but he thinks he was a major donor. "I was on the board but I didn't bring in too many people, because, frankly, I didn't know many people. I was pretty much a loner.

"I liked the company and I thought the arts would be an area that might be fun to support. And in fact, I think it's a very legitimate and rather wonderful thing to support the art you like. But I never followed up on it." Years later, when Soros's national foundations began to support contemporary art in the thirty countries where they were established, he specifically kept his preferences to himself and allowed experts to choose recipients.

In this later period Soros once puckishly demonstrated such hands-off deference when he visited Vilnius in 1995 to take part in the fifth anniversary of Lithuania's Open Society Foundation. The festivities included the opening of an exhibition of paintings and sculpture by artists who had been supported by the foundation. After Soros examined the works, a Lithuanian official of the foundation asked him what he thought about them.

Soros responded, speaking for several minutes as a sizable crowd of luminaries listened politely to the famous benefactor and patron. None, however, could understand what he was saying and it was generally assumed that for some reason Soros had decided to speak in Hungarian. At the dinner that followed, Irena Veisaite, a survivor of war and Communism who has led the Lithuanian foundation since its inception, asked Soros what it was that he had said in Hungarian.

"Oh, that wasn't Hungarian," he replied. He explained that he had answered in a nonsense language of his childhood called Halandsza, a patter of transposed syllables similar to the pig Latin used by English-speaking children. He said he really didn't understand much of the art he had just seen but felt he should keep his views to himself lest they carry more weight than they deserved. "The idea came to me that it was appropriate to speak Halandsza so I did."

Soros's interest in Central Park as a possible object of his earliest philanthropic initiatives was provoked by several visits he made to Budapest, beginning with his first return to the city in the late sixties. He was repeatedly struck by the attractiveness of Margaret Island, a popular recreational area in the Danube, with swimming pools, spas, restaurants, and theaters. Soros thought it absurd that a park maintained under Communism could be more inviting than Central Park, which was increasingly avoided by citizens who felt it had grown shabby and unsafe.

After one Hungarian trip in the late seventies he had some meetings with city officials and eventually, along with Richard Gilder, a stockbroker, he established a committee called the Central Park Community Fund to raise private contributions to restore the park. Meetings were held and members were being recruited when in 1979 another group with similar goals arose under the leadership of Elizabeth Barlow Rogers.

Slightly more than a decade later, in September 1990, Soros recalled his Central Park initiative in remarks he made at the first meeting of representatives of all his European foundations. Speaking in the Czech spa town of Karlovy Vary, Soros told the delegates about what happened with his Central Park Community Fund.

"I don't like foundations," he said. "I think foundations corrupt the impulse that led to their formation. That is because foundations become institutions and institutions take on a life of their own. A lot of people feel good when they have created an institution, but I feel bad. There is only one thing that can excuse the crime: if the foundations do something really worthwhile; otherwise they have no business existing.

"Before I started the Open Society Fund, I got involved in a very small local project in New York to help renovate Central Park. There was another organization—the Central Park Conservancy—which turned out to be more successful. We were on the verge of attacking what the other foundation was doing because it wasn't us doing it. Fortunately at that point I killed the foundation, and I am more proud of that than I am of having created it."

Gilder joined the other group and eventually donated $17 million to improve the park. Many years later Soros would also contribute $1 million for the park. By that time he had found many other projects.

In the early 1980s, he was still concentrating very intensely on his business but he was reaching out in many directions. For one thing, through his friend Bill Maynes, he contacted the Brookings Institution in Washington and commissioned the think tank to provide an analysis of Britain's economic future. Through the Open Society Fund Soros paid $100,000 for the study that was presented at a conference held at Ditchley, Winston Churchill's wartime country residence near Oxford. At the time Soros considered the meeting to have been a complete bust, a banal exercise in which platitudes dominated. However, as it turned out, at Ditchley he met people from the British Treasury who would soon prove useful to him when Margaret Thatcher came to power. The conversations he had at Ditchley helped Soros to realize just how serious Thatcher was in her commitment to privatize the economy and balance the budget. When she moved to raise the interest rate, Soros concluded that the British securities would rise in value and rushed in to establish a big speculative position in gilts.

"At that time there was a particular method of distributing gilts which meant marking down the price at time of issue," said Soros. "There was in effect a club in which brokers received the shares at a reduced price and distributed them as the gilt market recovered. Although I was not a broker I joined the club and I kept subscribing to gilt issues and distributing the shares between issues. And eventually I took up between 5 and 10 percent of every issue, which was a very big position for an outsider who was not a broker to take. This turned out to be a very profitable business, and I got rewarded in an unexpected way for my philanthropic effort at Ditchley."

Soros was broadening his horizon. At about the same time he dealt with Brookings, he began to involve himself in his first purely philanthropic venture overseas. His earlier interest in South Africa had grown. Soros, who had long been repelled by apartheid, had been hearing about developments in the country from his friend Herbert Vilakazi. Events there were quickening. In 1976, the Soweto riots flared when police fired at black schoolchildren protesting against mandatory classes in the Afrikaans language. A year later the death of Steve Biko while in police custody aroused more protests that challenged the defenders of white rule. By 1979, Vilakazi felt he needed to return to his native land; he took a teaching position in Zululand. Soros decided to visit him.

It proved to be an exciting trip. With his friend as his guide, he traveled to places that most tourists and, for that matter, most white South Africans had never seen. He spent time in Soweto, the sprawling black township near Johannesburg, and went to Zululand, where Vilakazi's father was a respected elder and poet. He also visited Transkei and went to schools, clinics, and shebeens, the shanty bars of the black townships. He met people who had been imprisoned with Nelson Mandela, and who would years later rise to political prominence once apartheid lost its grip. He also met with white opponents of racism, including the novelist Nadine Gordimer and the women of the Black Sash movement, whose silent vigils challenged the government and the system of separation it administered.

By this time he had established the Open Society Fund, though his plans for it were modest, vague, and unrealized. The fund was set up in 1979 as a charitable lead trust. With customary candor, Soros describes the motives for creating the foundation as basically selfish: "A charitable lead trust is a very interesting tax gimmick. The idea is that you commit your assets to a trust and you put a certain amount of money into charity every year. And then after you have given the money for however many years, the principal that remains can be left [to one's heirs] without estate or gift tax. So this was the way I set up the trust for my children." At the outset, his idea was that he would contribute up to $3 million a year for twenty years.

In South Africa, he recognized a promising challenge. "I felt that here was a great place to start with the Open Society, precisely because it was a closed society offering some small possibilities of change."

On that initial trip, he visited the University of Capetown, which under its vice chancellor, Stuart Saunders, had accepted a small group of black students. "I met with Saunders and I thought that here was an institution that believes in multiracial education, an open society. I thought that to support this institution to bring in more black students would be a very efficient way to go about things. Actually, the state was paying most of the costs of the students. My thinking was that I would pay their lodgings, their supplemental costs. In this way I would be using the mechanism of a generally oppressive state to subvert it, to widen and expand a small area of interracial activity. At the same time I would be helping to build a black elite, and I still think that the creation of elites among persecuted people is the most effective way to overcome prejudice."

He thought through the idea and came up with a program to provide stipends of $2,500 each for eighty students. He gave the money to the university to administer the program.

After a year he returned to South Africa, this time with Susan and his children. He discovered that his intervention had been a failure. The number of black students had increased, but by far less than the number of scholarships he was providing. He realized that his money, instead of being used to supplement the state's contribution, was being used to replace part of the government's original commitment to black higher education. "Instead of me subverting them, they were subverting me," he says. Soros found that though the vice chancellor continued to endorse the project, much of the faculty and administration were opposed to enlarging black enrollment and were sabotaging the program. He met with the black students and found them very upset and angry. "They felt discriminated against," says Soros. He abandoned the project after the first year, but he learned from the experience.

His South African travels provided yet another instructive encounter. At one point he asked Gordimer to bring together a group of important and well-meaning figures engaged in the struggle for a democratic South Africa that was not divided on racial lines. "Well, these people showed up and they were a very good group, white and black, many of whom I later worked with," says Soros. "But at that time I had this image: I was a pot of gold in the middle of the room and all around people were trying to take spoonfuls for themselves." It made him feel uncomfortable. As an opportunity to explore and exchange strategies and ideas, the meeting was a failure. He vowed that in the future he would make his contacts differently, seeking people out one or two at a time.

"The point was that I was experimenting, I was exploring ways to use my money."

CHAPTER 15

HUMAN RIGHTS

F OR MUCH OF HIS time in America, Soros's knowledge of world affairs had been equal to that of a reasonably careful reader of the *New York Times* and the *New York Review of Books*. But toward the end of the 1970s his expertise in this area began to rise sharply and steadily as cracks appeared in the Iron Curtain. Once again Soros's instincts anticipated the extraordinary changes that were soon to come, not in any market but in the way the world was organized politically.

Though then widely unrecognized, a new era was taking shape that would soon replace the bipolar structure that had emerged from World War II. As the seventies drew to a close, the notion that Communist power and the Cold War might soon disappear lay beyond serious contemplation, somewhere between wishful thinking and outright delirium. There were, however, a handful of people who had glimpsed the faint prospect of significant geopolitical change. For them the triggering mechanism had been the passage on August 1, 1975, of a long-negotiated agreement on security and cooperation in Europe, which came to be known as the Helsinki Final Act.

For the first time, an understanding between states had recognized that the treatment of human rights was one of the major principles determining international relations. The Soviets and their East European allies were eager to sign the Helsinki agreement because it froze and recognized postwar borders, including those of East Germany. To secure this, they were willing to trade away their earlier insistence that questions from abroad about the denial or abuse of human rights constituted an unacceptable interference in the internal affairs of a sovereign state.

It was a departure, but at the time of the signing no one saw how deep and wide a wedge human rights would eventually drive into the Iron Curtain. In the West, there were critics, mostly right-wing, who objected to trading something as hard-edged as border guarantees for something as soft and mushy as human rights. The critics assumed that the language covering issues like freedom of the press and free expression and movement were merely window dressing and would have minimal impact on political realities. Yet very soon after the signatures dried on the final act, those human rights clauses galvanized people in many countries to act. Ordinary citizens, ranging from innocent amateurs to cunning Machiavellians, risked ostracism, isolation, and persecution to confront the totalitarian bureaucracies maintained by the Soviet superpower. Within months of the ratification, brave but highly marginal figures formed a Helsinki Watch group in Moscow, in an effort to hold the Soviets to their promises. The following year, KOR, or the Committee to Defend Workers, was founded in Poland where it was to become a precursor of the Solidarity free labor movement. And a year later, in 1977, the playwright Václav Havel and a handful of his dissident colleagues established Czechoslovakia's Charta 77.

Soros could not fail to take such developments personally. His escape from Communism had, after all, formed an essential part of his own legend. His parents had lived under the system and Soros had a deep practical awareness of what was at stake. Moreover, as early as 1962, as we've seen, as a disciple of Popper and a proponent of open societies, he had written that Communist dogma forcibly maintained by Moscow would someday erode in the face of critical thinking. With the signing of the Helsinki agreement, it seemed that the critical method was gaining a vital if precarious foothold.

The Helsinki process, as it unfolded, provided Soros with an opportunity to test his philosophical analysis. He had used his theories quite successfully in financial markets. Now he wondered whether he could make use of them to chart and anticipate truly historic changes, the challenge that had first inspired his philosophical speculation. Was it possible that under the terms of his logic, the extension of human rights beyond sovereign control was establishing a fruitful "underlying trend"? Could the work of activists and dissidents in the East, supported by their allies in the West, help build a "prevailing bias" that viewed Moscow-led Communism as neither immutable nor impregnable? And, as was the case with market booms, might underlying trends and prevailing biases reinforce each other to ignite an explosive surge leading to freedom and democracy?

By 1980 Soros had only vaguely intuited such possibilities, but the concepts involved were powerfully attractive. He began to seek out individuals and groups who were pinning their hopes on the Helsinki Final Act. One of his earliest influences in this regard was Svetlana Kostic Stone, one of the women he dated after his separation from Annaliese. She was an assistant to the director of the New York Academy of Sciences who had been following human rights issues in Eastern Europe and Russia for several years. Stone's life had its own personal links to totalitarianism and the rule of law. She was born in Yugoslavia, where, after the war, her mother had met and married an American soldier, the son of Harlan Fiske Stone, the Chief Justice of the United States Supreme Court in the forties. An attractive woman, whom some of Soros's friends referred to as the "Balkan Bombshell," Stone introduced Soros to the human rights community in New York. Through her he met people like Ed Kline, the head of a company that owned twenty-four department stores in the Midwest, who since the early sixties had befriended Soviet dissidents. Kline had set up Chekhov Press, which published books in Russian by writers banned in the Soviet Union, among them Joseph Brodsky and Nadezhda Mandelstam. Some copies of those books found their way across Soviet borders. Kline had become the principal contact in the west for Andrei Sakharov, the Russian physicist and human rights campaigner confined in internal exile in the city of Gorky.

Stone also introduced Soros to Aryeh Neier, who had been director of the American Civil Liberties Union for much of the sixties and seventies and had become the founder and executive director of the Helsinki Watch group in the United States. Stone began taking George to Wednesday morning meetings that Neier conducted in which human rights issues around the world were discussed. Neier's organization arose when it became obvious to some influential Americans, among them U.N. Ambassador Arthur Goldberg and McGeorge Bundy, president of the Ford Foundation, that in the absence of press attention, Moscow was successfully ignoring charges raised under the human rights provisions of the Helsinki treaty. With a $400,000 Ford grant, Helsinki Watch in the United States was established as a citizens group that would monitor and call attention to the state of human rights within the Helsinki framework. It would provide information to the media and lobby political figures for strict compliance with the agreement. Its chairman was Robert Bernstein, the CEO of Random House, who had previously headed a publishers' group that crusaded against censorship in the Communist sphere. The dominant force, however, was Neier, a man whose phlegmatic demeanor and bureaucratic skills sometimes unintentionally camouflaged his passionate commitment to justice and the rule of law.

Neier had been deeply involved in America's social crusades of the sixties including civil rights, the anti-war movement, the struggle for legal abortion, and the fight for prisoners' rights. But unlike more flamboyant and better-known activists, he shunned television appearances and disdained barricade tactics of personal aggrandizement. His ego was sustained more by achievements than exposure. Born in Berlin in 1937, he had fled Nazi Germany as a young child, arriving with his family in London. Soon after, a bomb destroyed the room where his family had found refuge. Together with other blitz victims, the Neiers were relocated to the countryside, where patriotic Britons took them in. After the war, Neier's older sister met and married an American GI. The family soon followed her to New York, where Aryeh attended public schools before going off to college at Cornell. Like Soros, his dedication to liberty and tolerance had roots in childhood. In his adult life, he came to have two heroes, whose portraits he would prominently display. His office is dominated by a painting of Hannah Arendt, the scholarly yet passionate critic of totalitarianism; at his home, there is one of Norman Thomas, the American socialist and frequent presidential candidate, for whom he had worked as a young man.

Soros was impressed by Neier's noncharismatic leadership. He recognized him as someone like himself, a doer, a man who achieved things, while keeping out of headlines. Informally, he enlisted Neier as his chief guide into the world of human rights and international affairs. Years later, he would name Neier as the senior manager of his philanthropic empire, a sort of secretary of state figure to Soros, the executive stateless statesman. In that role Neier would administer budgets of close to $500 million a year, spent in more than thirty countries.

All this, of course, was impossible to imagine when Soros regularly began attending the Wednesday morning meetings at Helsinki Watch. The meetings began at eight o'clock, and George would listen carefully as staff members detailed developments in the countries they monitored. He spoke little; he was not yet a good public speaker and was often ill at ease at a podium. They reported on specific allegations of Helsinki violations, including censorship, torture, and mysterious killings. Sometimes visitors would be invited to talk about issues such as imprisonment, mental illness, election fraud, surveillance, and government blackmail, often from their personal experience. A Pole might describe methods of police interrogation; a Czech intellectual would tell of being forced to work as a bathroom attendant, while a Romanian might explain how the Ceauşescu regime was imprisoning women for practicing birth control.

Stone was also suggesting books for Soros to read and introducing him to scholars and experts. In September 1982, Soros and Stone traveled to an international conference at the Bellagio castle near Lake Como, where representatives from twenty-two countries gathered to take up an appeal that Sakharov had issued from Gorky. The Russian physicist felt that unless the small Helsinki groups in the East were bolstered by their Western counterparts, they would soon be crushed by Communist states. From his confinement Sakharov had urged "the creation of a unified international committee to defend all Helsinki Watch group members." As the meeting began, with Neier serving as chairman, dramatic news arrived: The original Helsinki watchdog group in Moscow was being forced to shut down. All but four of its members had been placed under arrest; the four still at liberty were quite old and ailing. The delegates then responded to set up a federation of national Helsinki groups that would aid the vulnerable groups behind the Iron Curtain. Soros, who was there as an observer, provided funds to help the federation set up its offices in Vienna.

According to Neier, the meeting significantly highlighted the potential of civil society. At Lake Como, Soros witnessed how a group of unelected citizens—some well-connected and others quite powerless— came together to defend their moral principles in the context of tough global politics. As every freshman taking political science knows, governments are guided by their own interests. Was it possible for people like these concerned and informed citizens of several lands to act persuasively on even higher values? Was it possible to turn the sort of airy-fairy grassroots universalism that had once appealed to Soros's father in the form of Esperanto into a concrete and pragmatic instrument of foreign policy? For Soros, such questions were very seductive.

He was once again learning by doing, this time in philanthropy. He contributed to Amnesty International, which in 1977 had won the Nobel Peace Prize, and he increased his contributions to Helsinki Watch. He made contact with Frantisek Janouch, a Czech nuclear scientist living in Stockholm, who had established a foundation in Sweden to support Charta 77. Through Janouch, Soros became the foremost financial supporter of the Czechoslovak dissidents around Havel. In 1977 he had made his first trip to the Soviet Union as part of a delegation of American businessmen. In Moscow he broke away from his watchers long enough to call on Vladimir Furman, a "refusenik" whose name he had been given by Amnesty International in New York. Over the next several years he would send, through a Swedish airline stewardess, about $100,000 in cash to Furman's network. He thought of the enterprise as "an adventure" and never received any accounting for the funds. Once, however, he received a postcard postmarked in Gorky. It bore no signature and had no message but the picture was a reproduction of Michelangelo's fresco *Creation of Man*, focusing on its divine and mortal forefingers nearly touching. He took it as an expression of gratitude and as confirmation that his money was serving some useful purpose.

Other causes beckoned. By 1981, there were 85,000 Soviet troops in Afghanistan fighting bands of anti-Communist *mujahadin*. The Soviets, who had invaded two years earlier, were suffering heavy casualties and heading for a humiliating defeat. As the war continued, Soros would often meet with Vladimir Bukovsky, a pugnacious Russian emigré who had spent many years in Soviet prisons and mental hospitals for his refusal to accept the limitations of Communism.

Over lunch Bukovsky would tell Soros that he should send money directly to the Afghan fighters. Soros, who had vivid memories of clandestine life, siege, and survival in wartime Budapest, was tempted. He was routing money to Russia, without knowing how it was being used, and he hoped that the money he was providing to Charta 77 was being used to undermine the power of the Czechoslovak leadership.

What were the moral limits involved? Did Bukovsky have a point when he claimed that Soros had an obligation to support people whose commitment to overthrowing the Soviet system was so strong that they were willing to die? "I had some heart-searching times," says Soros, "asking what's right, what's wrong. It was pushing the borderline, you know, engaging in an armed struggle." Ultimately he rejected Bukovsky's arguments. "I felt that as an outsider, I mustn't do that." He limited himself to supporting humanitarian assistance mostly through Aide Médicale Internationale, a French group that was sending doctors into war-torn regions of Afghanistan.

"When I got into this business of philanthropy it was definitely a process of trial and error. From '79 to '84 was a period of painful experimentation. I didn't know what the hell I was doing, and I made some wrong steps. I felt very embarrassed at times. I would break into a sweat. I was playing a certain role and it didn't quite fit me."

He found it hard to accommodate his various selves: the practical man of money, the philosopher, the highly self-aware critic, and the idealistic and messianic fantasist. "Of course I had grandiose ideas and false conceptions, many pipe dreams which never came to pass. But I managed not to reveal them too much so that I didn't get written off as a hopeless dreamer. And at the same time there was a dream, some kind of fairly grand conception that I came closer and closer to actually implementing. And I really do think that I have a certain understanding of historical dynamics—this reflexivity thing that I have kept trying to present in an abstract way in my books, which maybe doesn't quite come through. But I actually practice it, you know."

He persisted, trying to come up with his own approach to philanthropy, often drawing on his experiences in business. He kept questioning his contributions just as he had critically evaluated his investments, asking himself whether his money might accomplish more elsewhere. He kept checking back to see what effect his donations were having, eager for the sort of feedback he had learned to rely on in business. He was as impatient as a donor as he had been as an investor, looking for quick impact. In both capacities he trusted his instincts. He could grasp the heart of promising ideas without having to pore over voluminous materials. Often, the better the idea, the more simply it could be conveyed. In both business and philanthropy he shied away from permanent entanglements. Just as he had never wanted to control or build companies, he favored projects of limited duration but great potential impact. He was uninterested in pyramid building or monuments to glorify the Soros name. As with financial markets, he liked undertakings where he could go in, get out, and have something substantial to show for his trouble.

Another common thread involved publicity. "I was opposed to it. In business I felt that publicity was the kiss of death, and that view was confirmed when the fund had its first losing year right after the *Institutional Investor* piece had called me the world's greatest money manager. My feeling was more than just a superstition. With publicity you become wedded to your words. They become more difficult to retract. There's also the problem of believing in your own magic. So I knew that publicity can be very harmful to performance and I shunned it. I wanted to be anonymous, basically."

For quite a while he succeeded in keeping himself and his activities in the background. For example, during 1985, when he had already set up his pioneering foundation in Hungary, his name was mentioned only once in the *New York Times* and that was in a story that had to do with investing. It was the same in 1986. He disdained public relations advisers, and once refused to meet with a high-paid public relations consultant for Soros Fund Management who said he needed to spend time with George to learn how his mind worked. "I don't want him to know how my mind works," he told his associates as he refused the request. And when his foundations got around to hiring their own public relations people, they tended to be young and inexperienced. Soros pointedly let them know the limitations of their jobs. "Look," he told Michael Vachon, one of those hired, "I am sixty-five years old and I never want to be handled."

Despite the challenges, Soros was enjoying himself. His social life was becoming much more varied and satisfying than it had ever been. While he was not yet meeting powerful luminaries or world-famous figures, he was coming into contact with interesting people doing interesting things. He met emigré writers and through them was introduced to the poet Allen Ginsberg, who was to become a life-long friend. Ginsberg told Soros about his theory that the drug problem in the United States originated when prohibition was repealed, claiming that those bureaucrats who had been concerned with intercepting alcohol built up the threat of marijuana and other narcotics in order to stave off their own obsolescence and pending unemployment. In addition to Neier's human rights meetings, Soros attended informal gatherings where speakers such as Susan Sontag and Joseph Brodsky discussed cultural developments behind the Iron Curtain. Such people provoked and challenged Soros's thinking. He found them much more congenial than his business associates, and he was more willing to socialize with them, meeting them at restaurants or sometimes having a group at his apartment for conversation and games of chess.

There was another difference between these politically engaged acquaintances and the older friends that he and Annaliese had entertained. With the newer acquaintances, he did not at all discourage talk of money—not about investments, of course, but about projects such as the one he had launched in South Africa. When it came to philanthropy he was quite willing to mix friendship and patronage.

Years later, as noted earlier, he would reveal this tendency so often that employees would claim only half-jokingly that if Soros sat next to an articulate person for more than an hour, he was very likely to offer a job heading one of his foundations—especially if the person was a woman and if she had the gumption to disagree with him. (They would add that he inevitably dismissed such hires a few months later.)

That is essentially what happened with Svetlana Stone, whom Soros named as the first president of the Open Society Fund. She resigned in 1982 when Soros's intentions toward Susan Weber became what Victorians would have described as serious and honorable. When Susan and George were married in 1983, Soros invited Stone to the reception. She reportedly wrote back expressing her best wishes but archly informing George that she would pass up his wedding, though she might consider attending "your next one."

Philanthropic activities were clearly growing more important for Soros. He was, however, still devoting the bulk of his time to the fund. "The fact is that despite the philanthropic experimentation, I remained very committed to the fund. The business was my major business." As he said he would do after his losing year in 1981, he farmed out some of the fund's portfolios to managers brought in from the outside. In 1982 he nominally placed more responsibility in the hands of Jim Marquez, a thirty-three-year-old fund manager, but in fact he continued to remain fully engaged, leaving Marquez often feeling second-guessed.

The fund recovered from the debacle of 1981, registering 56.9 percent growth in 1982 and 24.9 percent in 1983. Soros kept insisting to his associates and to himself that business would always be his prime concern, that his philanthropic pursuits were merely a preoccupation. He spoke of philanthropy as an "ego trap" he would certainly avoid. And yet his involvement in this area kept growing.

He obviously liked and admired many of the people he was meeting through his new activities. He liked the discussions he was having, many of them late-night speculations about which of the Soviet satellite states were most likely to challenge Moscow's authority in the future, or how private foreign capital could best be used to build and strengthen independent elites in totalitarian states. He particularly liked the idea that at least some of the people he was meeting respected his thoughts even before they learned of his wealth. But as he made new friends, he also had occasion to draw on some very old ones.

Gyorgy Litvan was one of Soros's childhood friends from Lupa Island, one of the group who had greeted each other with shouts of "Paaapuuuaa!" He had survived the war and lost track of Soros after he left Budapest. Litvan stayed behind and became a high school history teacher. When the Hungarian rebellion erupted in 1956, Litvan joined the uprising as a supporter of Imre Nagy. He was arrested and spent three years in prison. By the late seventies he was allowed to travel, and on his first visit to New York, he found Soros and spent a good deal of time with him.

Soros asked whether there were any Hungarian thinkers or writers whom he should support. Litvan named several, including Istvan Eorsi, a playwright and the same man whose baby teeth Soros had knocked out in a Budapest sandbox.

George began corresponding with Eorsi, who had also been imprisoned for his role in the uprising. After a four-year term, he wrote plays that, while banned in Hungary, were produced and praised in West Germany. A confrontational bohemian who shaved his head and dressed habitually in black, he bore witness to the spirit of revolutionary solidarity that had blossomed in October 1956 only to be crushed by Russian tanks and prison terms. He wrote a memoir of that time entitled *Ah, the Good Old Days*.

By 1979 Eorsi was one of a number of "unofficial" cultural figures from the East who was attracting some attention in the West. Most important, he had gained the friendship and respect of Annette Laborey. In a divided Europe, Laborey, then thirty-two years old and based in Paris, had become one of the busiest and most effective links between East and West. The daughter of a German botanist, Laborey had come to Paris from Munich to study history and political science at the Sorbonne, hoping to become a diplomat. Instead she married a Frenchman and in the early seventies began working for the Foundation for European Intellectual Cooperation, which had originally been created in 1950 as part of the Congress for Cultural Freedom. This umbrella organization, established by intellectuals from many countries to challenge Communist influence and propaganda, had capsized in 1966, when newspaper articles in the West disclosed it had received secret CIA funding through private foundations. While the revelations doomed some of the congress's most prestigious projects, like the influential publication *Encounter*, the Foundation for European Intellectual Cooperation endured. By the time Laborey arrived there, it was a modest, low-profile organization supported largely by the Ford Foundation.

Laborey had methodically visited the countries of the eastern bloc, setting up informal networks of independent-minded men and women whose judgment she came to trust. She wanted to find exceptional people who had never been outside of the Communist World and have them spend up to six months in the West. Her sources recommended young people, for whom she arranged such stays. They could study if they chose, but Laborey urged them to avoid highly structured programs, suggesting that they spend their time serendipitously, making friends, discussing issues, relaxing and reflecting. By the time the foundation closed in 1990 she had given three thousand intellectuals their first glimpses of the West, its freedoms and its possibilities.

Though not all her choices were dissidents, many of the beneficiaries were highly independent thinkers deeply distrusted by ruling parties and security forces. For example, Laborey was able to provide Adam Michnik, the Polish dissident, with his first trip beyond Communist society. Michnik, who was to become one of the driving forces of the Solidarity revolution, was already well known to Polish authorities as a troublemaker when Laborey tried to bring him to Paris. He had by then been imprisoned for leading a student protest in 1968, had been expelled from university and forced to work in a light bulb factory, and was officially labeled as an antisocialist force. And yet Laborey was able to persuade Polish authorities to let him travel by shrewdly arranging for Jean-Paul Sartre to issue the invitation. She rightly calculated that the left-leaning philosopher would have sufficient clout in Communist Poland to enable Michnik to get his passport.

In addition, she introduced dissidents from different countries to each other, and as travel restrictions eased, her offices at 38 Boulevard Beaumarchais became a clearinghouse and a meeting ground for activists from the Baltic to the Balkans. It was Laborey who introduced Michnik to a persecuted Romanian dissident named Andrei Plesu, who, ten years later, would become his country's foreign minister.

In 1980 Laborey secured a scholarship for Istvan Eorsi to teach the history of drama for one semester at the Case Institute in Cleveland. Eorsi was excited about coming to America but was not thrilled by the prospect of spending time in what he considered the provincial Midwest. He came to New York instead, spending several weeks with his childhood friend, Soros.

Eorsi remembers the visit as a wild time, spent mostly with Soros and Ginsberg, whom he had earlier met in Europe. Before Eorsi set off for California in a secondhand car he had bought from one of Soros's girlfriends, he told George about Laborey—and he wrote Laborey about his rich friend. She was sufficiently intrigued to ask her contacts at the Ford Foundation about Soros; she remembers that no one there knew anything about him. Eventually a meeting was arranged. Laborey recalls that toward the end of the lunch George asked whether she might help him find older and more distinguished candidates from Eastern Europe for the Karl Popper fellowships he was establishing at Columbia University and at New York University's Institute of Humanities, where Neier was teaching and serving as director.

He asked her how much she would need to start looking for such people. "I didn't know what to say," Laborey recalled. "Nobody had ever asked me how much money I needed or wanted. I had no idea how much money he had or how large a program he was thinking about. But he pressed me and I said, Well, maybe $20,000."

Laborey laughed at the memory. "He looked at me with his amused eyes and said, Well, actually, I was thinking of something considerably more ambitious."

That program began quickly. From Hungary alone, Laborey recommended people like Elemer Hankiss, an eminent economist; Gyorgy Bence, a philosopher who had been unemployable since he wrote a critical analysis of Marx; and Miklos Vasarhelyi, a historian who had been secretary to Nagy in 1956. While they worked at Columbia, they often visited with Soros, discussing political developments in their homeland and throughout the Communist world.

Soros's thinking was further shaped by events in Poland. There on December 13, 1981, General Wojciech Jaruzelski declared martial law. That morning tanks went into the streets and troops arrested thousands of men and women who in the previous year had challenged the Communists' monopoly of power by striking under the banners and slogans of the Solidarity movement. Long before the government crackdown, Soros had been captivated by what was happening in Poland, reading news accounts about the events in Gdansk in French, German, and English. Spurred by the shipyard strikes, increasing numbers of common citizens were organizing themselves into social and cultural groups independent of either the government or the ruling party. Slender shoots of civil society appeared to be sprouting on previously arid ground.

Soros had sought out Polish emigrés like Czeslaw Milosz, the Nobel Prize–winning poet, and Leszek Kolakowski, a philosopher who in the 1950s had inspired many of those who grew up to lead the emerging opposition. But nothing much came of these meetings, and Soros was still exploring ways of helping when Jaruzelski ordered his troops to crush the union and put an end to the social movement it had aroused.

As Soros read of union offices being padlocked and activists being led off to prison, he asked himself, as he had in the case of the Afghans, how far he should go in supporting the Poles in their resistance to tyranny. Through his friend Ed Kline he had learned about a young woman, Irena Lasota, who was teaching political science at Fordham University in New York. Born in Poland, she had been arrested in Warsaw during the anti-Semitic campaign that followed student protests in 1968. In New York thirteen years later, on the day after martial law was declared, she established the Committee in Support of Solidarity and immediately went off to wave a banner with the distinctive Solidarity logo outside the Polish consulate.

Soros had lunch with Lasota and told her that he wanted to help Solidarity. Unlike the Afghans, "Solidarnosc" had consistently stressed nonviolent tactics. Those of its leaders who had avoided the government dragnet were about to embark on imaginative tactics of passive defiance that would create an underground culture of illicitly produced newspapers, magazines, art shows, theatrical productions, and lectures, all free of government and Communist party supervision.

Soros was very direct in his first meeting with Lasota. "He told me that he wanted to be sure that his money would help the union inside Poland," she says. "He did not want it spent on fundraising or administration, or public relations. He wanted it to help the underground." By the time their coffee arrived, Soros had agreed to give Lasota an initial $20,000.

Over the next few years Soros would continue funneling funds to the Polish opposition movement, through Lasota as well as through other channels. He supported an ambitious book-printing and smuggling operation based in Paris, and he provided backing for what eventually became an even more ambitious nationwide network of illicit publishing ventures inside Poland.

Lasota remembers that unlike some other benefactors who tried to discover details of various escapades they may have financed, Soros suppressed his curiosity and showed the tactful discretion of an experienced conspirator. "He always sensed what I could say and what I could not say," observed Lasota, who was then using a variety of conduits to get money and other support to Poland. When she did provide him with an accounting, he paid little attention to it. "I even wished he would ask more about certain expenditures, so that I could hear him say 'Wow!' when I explained it, but it was all professional and there were no 'Wows.' "

What he wanted from her was less bookkeeping and more ideas. Without a staff and with no one to be accountable to, Soros realized he had a great advantage over traditional foundations in the speed with which he could respond to crises. As an investor he was accustomed to committing enormous amounts of capital on very short reflection. Now he was doing the same as a philanthropist, reacting quickly to dynamic events such as those in Poland and backing ideas he believed in. It was another form of pulling the trigger.

At one of their meetings, Lasota told Soros about her idea for a specific kind of scholarship program. "I told him to imagine a physically unattractive woman in her thirties from a provincial Polish town who needed two months to complete her master's dissertation but couldn't seem to find the time because she spent every night after work at her dreary official job editing and typing materials for the underground press." Though she appreciated the scholarships that Soros and Laborey were providing for recognized intellectuals, she felt that the sort of people she had in mind would not qualify for them, and yet it was precisely those people who would constitute a primary source of civil society once Communism collapsed.

Soros liked the idea as soon as he heard it. He said he would back it if Lasota agreed to administer the program, and he asked her to outline the project on a single sheet of paper. Within days Lasota called upon her own wide array of contacts in Poland to come up with candidates, and as the rigors of martial law subsided, 1,130 people, attractive as well as plain, were sent for two-month stays in Paris and London at Soros's expense.

Soros has never been a naïve bleeding heart. At that point, he had persevered and prospered in the most competitive of environments. He was hardly sentimental. He was famous for getting rid of stocks that had made him millions at the first whiff of rot, with no regrets. He could fire those who did not match his expectations. That was business. He tried to maintain the same toughness in philanthropy, but he was discovering a great difference.

Financial speculation, he had always known, was an amoral pursuit, where choices were validated and vindicated only by the bottom line. As in a tennis match, one needed simply to stay within manmade rules and there was no point in worrying about the social consequences. But thinking about the real world and acting on those thoughts to make things better involved very different criteria. What was at stake went beyond the ratios of supply and demand and profit and loss to murkier issues of right and wrong and good and evil. Here, the moral dimension was unavoidable.

For Soros, with his childhood musings about the peacemaking efforts of a donkey named Peaceful and with his unfulfilled dreams of philosophical achievement, such values were appealing. Even as he kept insisting that philanthropy would never be more than a sideline or that he was only practicing charity to limit the tax liability on his estate, he was also indulging long-dormant fantasies of changing the world. And in the process he found that his new life was becoming seductively exciting. He was enthralled by such relatively unknown but passionately committed figures as Laborey, Kline, Bukovsky, and Lasota; he was pleased that they and others like them felt free to call him at home or at his office. He was also trying to meet even more powerful figures, and he was eager to extend himself into new areas.

One of these was writing. Soros had essentially abandoned writing when he put aside "The Burdens of Consciousness" in the late 1960s. Since then he had confined himself to occasional brokers' reports that focused on the prospects and pitfalls of specific economic sectors such as the Japanese economy or real estate investment trusts. However, in 1983 he prepared a twenty-three-page report entitled "The International Debt Problem, Diagnosis and Prognosis" that revealed a new tone and voice.

The report, published and circulated by Morgan Stanley, offered no specific moneymaking suggestions. Instead it contended that the problems of international debt, far from having been solved by a rescue mission of international bankers in 1982, would continue to threaten economic growth and political stability around the world. In its boldness, Soros's article resembled his earlier Popperian attack on Freud or some of the more provocative passages of "Burden," but this time he was not timidly writing in his bedroom. He was ready to have his ideas published, read, and discussed.

Soros described how a decade earlier the poorest of debtor nations had been victimized when banks eager to recycle petrodollar deposits aggressively offered them loans. Unrestricted by regulations, the epidemic of lending expanded credit to a point that jeopardized the liquidity of the international banking system. Then the international monetary institutions stepped in to shore up the system with rescue packages. In the process, the flow of credit to the most indebted nations was choked off, leaving them and their populations to face years of suffering and underdevelopment. While Soros lauded the international cooperation involved in easing the crisis of 1982, he was among the first to claim that the banks should acknowledge responsibility for the flood of indiscriminate loans that had precipitated the crisis. He also called for new international efforts to provide credit to the debt-beleaguered countries, saying that without it "we are liable to hover on the brink of disaster for an extended period."

In the writing, moral commentary was interlaced with economic observations. "It is unfair that the debts were contracted when dollars were cheap and have to be repaid when dollars are expensive. It is unjust that the United States should prosper while Latin America wallows in depression." And as a practical matter, Soros contended that "what makes the moral argument relevant is that it has far-reaching political implications.

Depressed economic conditions in Latin America are fostering political turmoil. The Soviet Union and its allies can easily exploit the situation and events can be interpreted in geopolitical terms."

Soros continued to study the debt problem for several years. By 1984 he went so far as to appeal for the establishment of a new international institution he called the International Lending Agency, which would help indebted countries deal with balance-of-payment problems when banks, reversing earlier patterns of generosity, tightened or withheld credit. In presenting this view at a Washington economic conference, he said there was little chance his ideas would bear fruit, acknowledging that the entire scheme "may be viewed as somewhat utopian." But even so, in publicly addressing the issue he sounded much more like his hero Keynes than the world's most successful hedge-fund operator or Ibsen's shrinking-violet photographer.

CHAPTER 16

HUNGARY

O NE SUNDAY AFTERNOON in the late fall of 1983 Alajos Dornbach, a lawyer, returned to his Budapest home where his wife informed him that he had received a call while he was out. A man speaking fluent but stilted Hungarian, she reported, said that he would drop by later that night to obtain some legal advice. He would be coming late, after the opera, and since he would not have had a chance to eat, he wondered whether Mrs. Dornbach might prepare some snacks for him. He said his name was George Soros.

It took Dornbach a while to place the name. Then he remembered that some of his dissident friends who provided him with most of his legal work had told him about a rich American of Hungarian origin who lived in New York and was providing scholarships for academics. He told his wife that Soros was the benefactor of the novelist George Konrad, and had been a childhood friend of Gyorgy Litvan, whom the couple knew well.

Around midnight Soros arrived, alone. After he politely declined the caviar he was offered, Mrs. Dornbach said that the only other food she had on hand was *disznosajt*, a peasant concoction of intestines baked in a pig's stomach, resembling the Scottish haggis. Soros was delighted and told the Dornbachs how his father had sometimes received this delicacy from his legal clients. Soros ate the dish with gusto.

Now he explained what he wanted. He was interested in establishing a foundation in Hungary that would support culture and education.

This information aroused little enthusiasm in the lawyer. He knew there was no legislation in Hungary that would permit the establishment of anything like a real foundation. A few years earlier Dornbach had helped set up a quasi-foundation for Katinka Andrassy Karolyi, sometimes called the Red Countess. This aristocratic grande dame was the daughter of an Austro-Hungarian foreign minister, and even more impressively, she was also the widow of Mihaly Karolyi, the princely heir of old Hungary's largest landowning family, who had served as president in the short-lived Communist regime established in 1918. For decades she had joined her husband in exile on the French Riviera but returned to Budapest after his death to command a salon of Communists and fellow travelers from East and West. Despite the privileges extended to her by the ruling regime, it had been extremely complicated and time-consuming for Dornbach to create her "foundation," a modest venture that did little more than publish the leftist writings of her husband. Dornbach had to assume that creating a foundation for an American millionaire and speculator, a capitalist who had fled Communism, would be much harder. At that first meeting Soros also mentioned that he wanted his foundation to be fully independent of government and party control; that struck Dornbach as impossible.

But he hid his skepticism and asked how much money Soros was ready to commit to such a project. He knew that Countess Karolyi's endowment was providing 60,000 florints a year, the equivalent of $1,000. He thought that Soros probably had more in mind, but the answer staggered him.

"A million dollars," said Soros.

This got Dornbach's attention. "I was suddenly energized," he recalled. In the Hungary of 1983 a million dollars was an extraordinary amount of money, and Dornbach assumed that the figure represented the total capital, and that as in the case of the countess's operation, Soros was planning to finance actual programs with the interest this contribution would earn. He took out his pen and began calculating how much might be generated annually.

Soros interrupted him. "No, I mean a million dollars a year," he said. "When you use it up I will give you another million and then if things work out we could raise that to three million."

Dornbach is a cool and laconic man who habitually plays things close to the vest. With his white hair, blue eyes, and energetic vitality, he looks a bit like the actor Paul Newman. For an instant he wondered whether Soros was rational. He had been a lawyer for more than two decades and prided himself on judging character. He looked carefully at his visitor—who was finishing up the pork belly—and concluded that Soros was serious. Dornbach said he would investigate the political possibilities and would remain in touch. Then Soros took out a small pad on which he had names of some thirty people. One by one, he asked Dornbach about them, about their reliability, their background, their independence. In some cases, he would question Dornbach's assessment, saying that someone else had ventured another opinion. Dornbach understood that Soros was looking for staff and for allies. From the names Soros was asking about, he determined that his visitor had done his homework well.

In fact, Soros had been developing the idea of a Hungarian foundation through discussions with people like Vasarhelyi and Bence in New York and with scholars and dissidents on his visits to Budapest. He would tell himself and others that Hungary was not really closer to his heart than any of the other satellites. He was not a nationalist, nor was he drawn to the place by nostalgia. Susan, his new wife, did not like it at all, finding the intellectual pretensions and hauteur of many Hungarian intellectuals hard to take. He also recognized that what was happening in Poland with Solidarity was more meaningful and promising than any developments in Hungary. And yet it was in Hungary where he made his first big gamble to confront Communist power and to implant and extend open society. Years later he would say that the main reason for his choice was "the damned language." The intricate and bizarre Magyar tongue, so bewildering to outsiders, bound him to other Hungarians. Because of it, he could enter more deeply into the consciousness and hopes of Hungarians, and he could tell more easily who was trustworthy and who was less so.

Still, even with the help of excellent advisers, the idea of setting up a foundation in any Communist country was daunting. In Poland, as Communist authorities sought to contend with a populace aroused by Solidarity, Josef Cardinal Glemp, the primate of the powerful Roman Catholic Church, had for years been trying to establish a foundation through which Western assistance could be funneled to Poland's private farmers. It was a good idea that could bring in much-needed capital and increase the nation's food supply. The church had enormous clout in Poland. The Pope supported the plan, as did the United States government. Even important elements within the state and the party saw value in the concept. And yet nothing came of it. Could Soros do better in Hungary?

As he pursued his idea, Soros was quite aware of how difficult the struggle would be, but he also knew he possessed some tactical advantages in addition to his money. Within the eastern bloc, Hungary prided itself on having the most innovative and liberal economy. It was the period of "Goulash Communism," when, under party leader Janos Kadar, the old dogmatism of a planned economy was giving way to permit and even embrace some private initiative. As some key party figures looked nervously at what was happening in Poland, they seemed willing to move down the road of economic liberalization, believing this could placate public opinion while retaining for themselves control over social, cultural, and political life. As the prominent sociologist Elemer Hankiss said of the transformation under way in 1983: "It's very cunning and clever, and very Hungarian; everything has been changing but no one realizes it." A second economy of small private businesses was springing to life, with the mute consent of the seventy-two-year-old Kadar. International tourism was being encouraged, and the government was counting on expanding trade with the West to sustain a standard of living that was already the highest in the eastern bloc.

Meanwhile, in Moscow, Yuri Andropov died in 1983 without having implemented any of the economic reforms he was planning. His replacement, Konstantin Chernenko, was presumed to be less committed to reform, but the directions from the Kremlin were ambiguous. How far could Hungary go with the purely economic reform that some of its leadership seemed to favor? How much of a green light did it have from Moscow?

From Vasarhelyi, then at Columbia University, and from other proponents of change whom he met in Hungary, including Hankiss, sociologist János Kenedi, the economist Marton Tardos and Ivan Berendt, an economic historian, Soros learned that the pro-reform wing of the party would be tantalized by establishing links with a very rich American. Its members would view his Wall Street connections less as an ideological impurity than as a business opportunity to be energetically exploited. For them, Soros's foundation was worth talking about because it would demonstrate to the West Hungary's commitment to reform and help the country gain development loans and credits to build foreign trade. Arrayed against this group were the hardliners, including the security apparatus, who feared that economic reforms would necessarily lead to political and social changes that would endanger the system and their own positions.

To Dornbach's surprise, when he began making inquiries with contacts at the Ministry of Justice he found considerable receptivity. Indeed, he encountered more resistance from some members of the democratic opposition who felt that any attempts to negotiate with the party leadership would inevitably end in disaster. They imagined that Soros was an innocent do-gooder whose money would be used by party figures to reward their own catspaws and marionettes. On Soros's instruction, Dornbach kept negotiating, mostly with Ferenc Bartha, a deputy minister with responsibility for foreign trade. From November 1983 into spring 1984,

Dornbach kept Soros informed about negotiations while Bartha's reports went to the Central Committee. During this period Soros would often travel to Budapest, and several times, when the talks stalled, he threatened to pull out entirely. During one vital meeting, he went so far as to leave the table and place his hand on the doorknob.

The basic problem was how the foundation was to be constituted within Hungary, and there was the related question of how independent it would be. Soros realized that these questions were similar to those he had faced in South Africa, where he had failed. He knew he would have to associate himself and the foundation with some existing institution, as he had done with the University of Capetown, but he was determined that this time it would be the ideas of open society that would ultimately co-opt those associated with the repressive party and state, rather than the other way around.

The first scheme suggested to Dornbach was to have the foundation run out of the Department of International Cultural Affairs. Like most informed Hungarians, Dornbach was well aware that this bureaucracy was dominated by the secret police. When the idea was presented, Dornbach cleverly replied that he was afraid this would be impossible, "because I do not believe I will be able to convince Mr. Soros that the institution does not belong to the Ministry of Interior." At this point, the director of the department, who was present, reddened, picked up his papers, and stormed out of the room. "It was quite comical," the lawyer recalled.

The authorities then put forth a number of similar concepts, which were also rejected. But from the weakening responses of his counterparts, Dornbach could see that the basic idea of establishing a foundation was gaining support at the very highest levels. It seemed to Dornbach that those who were willing to actively support or passively tolerate the foundation now outnumbered those who despised the idea.

At this juncture Dornbach suggested that Soros take the initiative and propose a governing board of seven people, of which he would be chairman. The board would approve or reject the grants of applicants who presented themselves. Seizing upon this notion the political authorities suggested a body with two co-chairmen, proposing that Kalman Kulcsar, a sociologist and party member who was the secretary general of the Academy of Science, serve alongside Soros. The government side further suggested that both Soros and Kulcsar would have veto power. Under this formula, the foundation would be anchored within the Academy of Sciences, the highest organ of intellectual life under Communism. Soros accepted this arrangement and even conceded on the name of the organization, realizing that "Open Society" was too provocative for the authorities. The new body would simply be called "The Hungarian Academy of Science/George Soros Foundation."

A breakthrough had been achieved but negotiations dragged on over bylaws and guarantees of independence. Soros insisted on his right to withdraw all his money and cancel his entire commitment if a pattern of political interference emerged in the selection of grantees. Even in the absence of such a broad pattern, he insisted on his right to privately back any applicant he felt was being turned down because of political discrimination. After much discussion, the government accepted both points in a gentleman's agreement.

Then the security apparatus dug in its heels, insisting that the administration of the foundation, the people who would process the applications, provide support and equipment, send out the grants, and keep track of the projects, be recruited from their cadres. This was obviously meant to provide a way around the decision-making board, and it was unacceptable to Soros, who understood that such a provision would undermine the credibility of the foundation from the start. Frustrated, Soros called on Gyorgy Aczel, the Central Committee's cultural kingpin and a man very close to Kadar. Soros told him he could not accept a less-than-independent administration and that he was leaving. At the very end of the meeting, Aczel asked, "What do you really need to make the foundation work?" Soros answered, "An independent executive director." Aczel replied, "Let me see what I can do."

Within a week, a bizarre compromise was worked out. Just as there were two co-chairmen of the board, so there would now be two executive directors supervising the day-to-day work, and all decisions would require both their signatures. Soros chose as his representative Laszlo Kardos, a sociologist who had been thrown out of the university for his nonconformist thoughts and was now a much persecuted dissident. Soros had been sufficiently impressed by Kardos, a hard drinker and smoker, to insist on him when Aczel complained that the man "had spots" on his record.

As for the other executive director, the party designated Janos Quittner, who for seventeen years had been an apparatchik seconded to the Academy of Sciences by the Department of International Cultural Affairs. He says it is unfair to call him a policeman but acknowledges that he spent his time dealing with those who traveled to other socialist countries. "It was very formal, even worse," he said somewhat cryptically. Quittner had found his sinecure within the party, filing reports. In 1984 he was asked by his superiors to take the job at the foundation. "Two other people had been asked and they refused," says Quittner. "I guess they thought it was too risky. I thought that I am at the end of my career, why not take a chance. Maybe something can happen."

From the start, his job at the Soros Foundation was delicate. "Inside the office it was me on one side and everybody else on the other, but I understood that. I shared an office with Kardos, and when he was talking to his friends, I would step out." Gradually, Quittner won over many of those who doubted him. Perhaps because he could see which way the wind was blowing or perhaps because of a more genuine change of heart, Quittner became one of the earliest converts to new possibilities, asserting himself within limits after a lifetime of humiliations, including deportation to German factories with his family during World War II. In 1989, when Communism collapsed in Hungary as elsewhere, Quittner was asked to stay on at the foundation and continued to work alongside Kardos. He is more proud of his work in the foundation than of anything else he has done, and he openly admires Soros.

The final and most important member of the foundation leadership was Miklós Vasarhelyi, whom Soros named as his personal representative, his surrogate. In this capacity the then sixty-seven-year-old Vasarhelyi chaired the board meetings and charted strategy. While Soros carefully filled most of the board with people from the liberal mainstream who were unlikely to provoke strong antagonism within ruling circles, with Vasarhelyi, as with Kardos, he was pushing the limits. Vasarhelyi had been press secretary to Imre Nagy in 1956. After Russian troops suppressed the revolution, he was tried and spent four years in prison. Released from prison he could find no job other than that of a menial clerk in a housing cooperative. Later he obtained a position in the Institute of Literature. All the while he kept appealing for a full account of what had happened in 1956, and he called upon Hungary's leadership to reveal where Nagy and the others executed after the uprising were buried.

On May 28, 1984, Soros signed a formal agreement setting up the foundation. According to Dornbach, that act in itself marked a hugely significant step in the decline of Communist power in Hungary and around the world. "It marked the first time that Communist authorities anywhere had met with people from the private sector and negotiated on matters of social and cultural significance. They offered guarantees of independence and accepted the participation of so-called forbidden people. It was simply unprecedented."

There was no great rush of publicity when the agreement was signed. The international press ignored the event, while Hungary's party-controlled media provided only a cursory mention of the agreement. But even without media exposure, the foundation soon made its mark in Hungary. Vasarhelyi quickly planned the first project, showing his superb tactical sense. Quittner would later say of him, "He always knew exactly where the authorities had drawn the line, and then he would cross over just a little bit. In this way he kept climbing, step by step." Vasarhelyi asked the directors of Hungarian educational institutions and libraries which books they wanted from abroad. He assembled a list and gained the assurance of the government that none of the books would be confiscated. Meanwhile, in New York, Soros established a support staff for the Hungarian foundation, hiring two people who were given a corner of his Quantum Fund offices. One of these was Liz Lorant, a woman who had studied business administration. She spoke Hungarian, having come to America from Budapest as a teenager in 1956. "My first job for Soros was to get the books," she recalled. "I called three hundred university presses and other publishers trying to get big discounts on all sorts of books—economics, sociology, politics, but also works by Solzhenitsyn that were banned in Hungary. Altogether we sent fifty thousand books."

As the project unfolded, Soros innovatively required the various libraries and academies to pay for the books they ordered, but in florints. He laid out the dollars to purchase the texts in the United States and Britain, and the foundation in Budapest then collected payment in Hungarian currency that could be used for future projects. The books, many of which had been banned and were inaccessible in any form, were openly displayed and news of their availability spread by word of mouth, along with the name of the foundation that brought them in. The success of this program led Soros and Vasarhelyi to conceive an even more dramatic idea: the importation of Xerox copiers.

Vasarhelyi knew firsthand how great a challenge it was to copy anything in Hungary. In the three years he spent at Columbia he had been astounded at how easy it was to find copying machines. In Hungary the preoccupation with security sharply limited access to copiers, which were kept locked within professional institutes. "In Budapest, at the Institute of Literature, where I worked," said Vasarhelyi, "if I needed to have something copied I would have to fill out an application listing the specific material, from a particular line on a specific page to another line on another page. Then it went to some office where the material was inspected. It might be approved or it might be rejected. Each application might take weeks."

Hungary was not quite as bad as its neighbor Romania, where every typewriter had to be registered with the police, who kept samples of writing on file like fingerprints, but copiers were regarded with great suspicion. Soros realized that in Hungary copiers stood as a clear metaphor for the entire concept of an open society. They not only reflected the idea of unfettered access to information; they also signified citizen involvement, in finding data and passing it on. What better way was there to advance critical habits and reverse dogmatic thinking? Soros told Lorant to find two hundred copiers with three-year service contracts and send them to the institutions Vasarhelyi had lined up. He had little trouble finding takers willing to agree to keep the machines in open, easily accessible places where they would be used freely. The machines were state-of-the-art examples of Western high technology, which itself carried a cachet of modernity. Lorant sent the first batch and then two hundred more, with similar shipments continuing for several years. Once more the users paid in florints, which went to pay for other foundation programs.

The program was an even greater success than the book project. Quite suddenly, without any announcement, people in intellectual or university environments were able to copy whatever they wanted—research papers, love letters, financial records, political and religious tracts, and, no doubt, censored materials. One of the prime laws of life under totalitarianism was being amended, namely that everything that was not specifically permitted was forbidden.

The Xerox project became one of Soros's earliest philanthropic triumphs; he would point to it as a model for many years. It was the kind of effort that changed perceptions and behavior. It was immediately understood, and it had the additional virtue of requiring finite amounts of money and time. Years later, Soros would replicate the idea in different forms, sometimes by beaming educational radio programs to Mongol nomads or, much more ambitiously, by spending close to $100 million to connect every regional university in Russia to the Internet.

But in 1984, the greatest benefit of the copier program was the positive momentum it generated for the Hungarian foundation. Support for projects and travel stipends were not unknown in Hungary, but in the past they were awarded mostly on the basis of political patronage. Now, in a revolutionary departure, ads appeared in academic journals and leaflets were distributed at university dormitories inviting broad participation in open competitions based on merit. Anyone could submit outlines for projects that would be considered by the board. Scholarship applications for study abroad were welcome, as were requests for support of ongoing research in Hungary. Soros's name was not yet widely recognizable, but a fuzzy myth was growing about a fabulously rich American who was providing books and copiers and seemed ready to subsidize research and travel.

Neither Kulcsar nor Vasarhelyi ever used their vetos. On two occasions when Kulcsar asked that a vote on a project be delayed so he could seek instructions, Soros was informed and immediately backed the projects involved through his Open Society Fund in New York, which he was then using to finance people and groups in Poland, South Africa, and elsewhere.

As the workload in Budapest increased, the staff grew larger. Kardos and Quittner worked out their modus vivendi. A third batch of applicants were selected by the board, with some fifty scholars chosen. As stipulated in the bylaws, a press release was prepared and sent to the newspapers. Soros had insisted on such publicity in the long months of negotiations, and the government had agreed it would disclose the winners. For Soros, this was not a matter of vanity; it arose from his desire to promote transparency in public life. People should know about the foundation and should be made aware that they, too, could approach it with their own ideas. When earlier sets of winners were announced, the papers lived up to the agreement and published the winners' names and projects. This time there was no such publication.

From friendly editors at *HVG*, an economic weekly, Vasarhelyi learned that a ukase had gone out from the highest circles banning publication of the recipients' names. Hungary is a relatively small country, and it did not take long for the foundation to discover that it was Kadar himself who had issued the order. He had come upon the list of approved grants and noticed that one of them was for a biography of Matyas Rakosi, the Communist leader of postwar Hungary. Kadar, not an admirer of Rakosi, was indignant that money from an American millionaire capitalist was being used to finance writing about one of his predecessors. In Kadar's view only the highest and most trusted figures in the ruling party had the power to decide how the lives of Communist leaders were to be treated, who would write about them, what was to be included, and what had to be avoided. Presumably, he wondered whether one day some non-Communist or even anti-Communist might decide to look into and write about his own life.

When advised of this, Soros moved quickly in cold fury. Dornbach remembers how Soros called him late at night to say that he would appear that weekend on *168 Hours*, Hungary's foremost weekly radio show, and that he planned to deliver a stern ultimatum: Either the government withdrew its objection to publicizing the grants his foundation had awarded or he would shut down all his projects in the country. For the first time Dornbach totally disagreed with George's strategic thinking. He felt that since Kadar himself was involved, it would be impossible for the decision to be reversed. Dornbach pleaded with Soros not to go on the air.

Sixteen years later, in recalling the episode, he said, "Thank God I did not succeed." On the radio, Soros issued the challenge. There was no immediate reaction from the government, but three days later an editor from *HVG* called to say the paper had been informed it could print the entire list of the chosen applicants and summaries of all their projects. The myth of Soros and his foundation continued to grow in Hungary: not only had he brought books and Xerox machines, he had stared down Kadar, and Kadar had blinked.

From this point on, the Hungarian foundation grew stronger and stronger. Hundreds of projects were sponsored, including many on taboo subjects like the treatment of Jews and Roma, or gypsies, in different historical epochs, ecological policies, and Western economic thinking that was decidedly non-Marxist. Among the thousands of young people whom the foundation sent to study abroad were scores who would hold influential posts once Communism had faded, including Prime Minister Viktor Orban. Even the best-known enemies of the state were aided. Foreign specialists were brought in to lecture on all sorts of subjects but most notably on practical aspects of economics and management. Exchanges were sponsored between economic reformers in Hungary and China. Soros's original commitment of $1 million a year expanded within two years to $3 million; later, after the fall of Communism, it would peak one year at $22 million. By then programs had proliferated to include health issues, early childhood education, law, journalism training, media monitoring, Roma rights, local government, and civil society.

As it expanded in the post-Communist period, shedding its link to the Academy of Science, the rechristened Soros Foundation–Hungary moved into impressive new quarters. Over time, as Communism lapsed and crumbled, Soros developed mixed feelings about the Hungarian foundation, which had made his name as well-known as any other in his native land. At the turn of the century he felt detached from its more recent achievements and thought that like some of his other foundations it had grown increasingly bureaucratic, more bloated, more smug, and more conventional as Hungary became a more normal country. He knew the foundation still promoted useful, if not revolutionary programs, but he was nostalgic for the revolutionary moment. Hungary was in line to join NATO, and it was unquestionably a modern and European state. But if success was comfortable, it could also be boring.

Even after spending billions around the world, Soros prizes the memories of his Hungarian triumph above his other philanthropic successes. "The Hungarian thing, that was the most fun of all," he says. "Because our advisers were much more reliable and clever than the people we were dealing with on the other side, we were able to run circles around them. We had virtually no corruption, we published the information about the grants so that was a social control. The Xerox machines, that was beautiful. We had a few employees, but all our supportive committees were volunteers. Our grantees got equipment or trips abroad, but whatever [the advisers] were doing they did for free because they wanted to do it. It was amazing, with just $3 million we were having a bigger influence on the cultural life of Hungary than the Ministry of Culture."

CHAPTER 17

DOMESTIC REFORMS

On June 19, 1983, several months before Soros met Dornbach and set his Hungarian foundation in motion, he married Susan Weber. During the civil ceremony, when the officiating judge asked the groom to utter the conventional vow about "sharing his worldly goods," George called out to William Zabel, his lawyer, and deadpanned, "You never told me about that." It was a joke, but some of the guests were not sure. After the afternoon reception George went off to play tennis. Susan was annoyed that the *New York Times* refused to carry the wedding announcement. "We were nobodies," she says. "According to the *New York Times*, we were nobodies."

There were more serious tensions as well. Paul came to his brother's wedding, but his wife, Daisy, stayed away. Erzebet attended the ceremony but she was quite cool, even hostile, to the choice George was making. On the surface, what seemed to touch off the antagonism of the Soros women was the age difference between bride and groom. George was two months short of fifty-three and Susan was twenty-eight. They had dated off and on for five years and Susan liked to say that George had been waiting for her to grow up.

But it was not merely Susan's youth that accounted for the cool reception. Two years after the wedding, as Erzebet, then eighty-two years old, began dictating her oral history she said: "I have three daughters-in-law. The older two are very good friends but Susan doesn't want to have anything to do with Daisy. They clashed before George and Susan got married so it's more comfortable for the boys just to meet alone."

The tensions rose and subsided but they never fully vanished. Almost two decades after the wedding, when a reporter for the *Times* asked Daisy how her husband differed from his better-known brother, she archly remarked, "The biggest difference is that George's wife is thirty years younger than I am."

But the most painful conflict was between Susan and Erzebet: George, caught between them, was pained by their skirmishes. Susan claims that Erzebet took a dislike to her from the time she first entered George's life. "I think she had the idea that she was going to be the woman in his life, once he became separated from his wife. And then I arrive on the scene, and she's not happy. She's not happy that I'm openly Jewish, she's not happy with my ideas, she's just not happy with me. Whatever I do is wrong. And I tell him how horrible his mother is being to me and he says it's my imagination. He can't believe that his splendid mother could be so terrible to me. Because she is a wonderful woman, I can see that. All the dissidents that come to visit us, she brings them into her house. She helps them. She has an amazingly generous spirit to everyone but me. And the house is a battlefield."

Soros largely agrees with his wife's view. "It was a classical case of a possessive mother-in-law," says Soros. "My mother considered Susan to be a big spender, a conspicuous consumer, where she lived very frugally. Susan was too Jewish and materialistic for her liking. I can remember several occasions where my mother really surprised me with the vehemence of her attacks."

It is paradoxical that religion played a role in the conflict. Both women were born Jewish, but while Susan was fully confident and accepting of her Jewishness, Erzebet was not. While Tivadar was alive he had humored her mysticism with its New Testament focus while cautioning her against conversion. He wondered why anyone who had not converted in Nazi-ruled Hungary would do so in America. But several years after her husband died, Erzebet formally left the religion into which she was born, converting to Catholicism at a Hungarian church in Florida. "She had also very much liked Annaliese, who was not Jewish, and all of this contributed to her resentment of Susan," says Soros. "It was quite complicated and painful."

At the time of the marriage, Susan was doing graduate work in decorative arts at the Cooper-Hewitt Museum, completing her thesis on James McNeill Whistler as an interior designer. She was also publishing *Source: Notes in the History of Art*, a scholarly journal with a circulation of about a thousand, which was still in existence twenty years later. For some time before the wedding she had actively joined George in his education on philanthropy and human rights, accompanying him on trips to South Africa and Europe and attending Aryeh Neier's Wednesday meetings—which she referred to as the "torture sessions."

Susan was attractive but hardly stunning, an energetic blonde who often peered at the world with an unconscious squint. Despite the antipathy she aroused in some members of the family, none of her critics could dismiss George's choice as a conventional matter of glandular determinism, or explain it as the prototypical trophy second marriage of a competitive alpha male. She was hardly a gold digger or a Jezebel. She was not apt to serve as a living advertisement for George, nor to stand demurely in his shadow.

Her willingness to express strong opinions and to disagree with her elders—including George—may have alienated her mother-in-law and Daisy Soros, but it was a high virtue in her husband's eyes. So, too, was her ability to remain unintimidated by huge pots of money, people of power, or close proximity to real brilliance, genius, or swaggering arrogance. Susan noted that at the time she married George "he was definitely not comfortable in his own skin." From the beginning, George thought her extraordinarily comfortable in hers. She prided herself on detecting and scorning pretense. She says of herself, "I have always had very little tolerance for bullshit."

For George, who thrived on criticism, such bluntness was endearing. He admired her for looking past appearances, ignoring snobbish categories, and wanting to keep working in her field. For him she was quintessentially and charmingly American in her sense of belonging, an innate democrat who could say whatever she meant to anyone without worrying about the consequences. In contrast to himself, she had no hang-ups about marginality, no conflicts of suppressed identity or torments over her Jewishness or any scarring experiences of exclusion more serious than the *Times* rejection of her wedding announcement.

Her Americanness clearly gave her distinctiveness within the family though it further antagonized her enemies. Erzebet had remained profoundly European and specifically Hungarian. Annaliese had been an orphan of war and an emigrant who settled modestly, even timidly, within the alien optimism of the new world. Daisy had been shaped by her own painful European years. George and Paul spoke with accents and also reflected the ambiguities of tempestuous European experiences. George has often said that he never felt himself fully American. By contrast Susan had been born into the American faith of welcoming one's own good luck without apology. And she flaunted it with no hesitation.

For someone like George, who at the time of his second marriage was quite consciously trying to reorder his old life and expunge all traces of the brooding negativism he had come to associate with his mother, Susan's abundant American self-assurance was an elixir. But for Erzebet and Daisy, who remained close and sympathetic to Annaliese, Susan's behavior and outlook could seem confrontational and annoying.

There was, for example, her less than admiring attitude toward many aspects of Hungarian life. She did not hide her contempt for many of the Hungarians with whom George was spending more and more time. "I didn't like the chauvinist aspect of the society," says Susan. "It was very much male. I didn't like the bravado. You know, everything Hungarian is best. That used to offend me, this feeling that America is a provincial place and that Hungary is the capital of the world."

Three years before the marriage, Soros bought a very large old house near the ocean on Old Town Road in Southampton. The property included a guest house that Soros turned over to his mother. There Erzebet spent summers with her own friends, people like Elsa Brandeisz, the dancer who hid her during the war and became her best friend.

Around the time of her wedding, Susan began redecorating the main house, an effort that led to one of her earliest fights with her mother-in-law. "I am redoing the old house, really sinking major money into it," says Susan. "I blast the house, pull the marble out. I redo every inch because it's the only way we are going to be happy in this house, and his mother is incensed. I paint the living room pink and she calls him up screaming, 'My son, everyone is going to think you are a homosexual.' Later the bulldozers come to clear, to put in the patios, and she's literally standing in front of them. We have to call George to move her out of the way. She thinks it is so nouveau riche to do what I was doing."

There were some truces over the years, particularly after Susan gave birth to her sons, but still Susan claims, "It was a battlefield until the day she died." It was shortly before Soros's marriage that he had discovered through psychoanalysis how he had internalized the conflict between his carefree and practical father and his more fearful and spiritual mother. Now he found himself once more caught in the crossfire between hostile forces, both of whom he loved. It cost him a great deal of emotion, but he kept the lines of communication open and he tried to love all the people who loved him even if they had trouble loving each other.

One way that George and Susan dealt with the running mother-in-law conflict was to turn it into a private running joke. He would say, "My mother is very beautiful," and she would respond, "No, she is ugly."

Guests at the summerhouse would sometimes be shocked by such exchanges. Long after Erzebet died, at a mammoth New Year's party to mark the new millennium, George obliquely referred to this repartee in his midnight toast. He was dressed as Columbus, the figure of the previous thousand years he most admired, and Susan as Queen Isabella. George told his guests that Isabella was said to have been a very ugly woman and added that he had always been very fond of ugly women and thought them beautiful. With a nod at Susan, he drank his champagne as a number of guests looked puzzled.

In the early years of his marriage Soros was contending with more than family dynamics. He was being forced to alter old and comfortable patterns of behavior and to confront the challenges of a new lifestyle that, like the beach house, was also being redesigned by his wife.

During his bachelor years he had not paid great attention to his housing. Until he bought a large cooperative on Central Park West, he had lived comfortably in several rented quarters that ranged from functional to elegant but that hardly reflected his growing wealth. Except for some paintings by little-known Hungarian artists, he had no major art. Once a Swiss art dealer had loaned him a painting by Paul Klee. He loved it, but sent it back saying he could not separate the painting from the figure on its price tag. He clearly felt there were limits to luxury, even for the exceedingly rich. Susan believes that this was his mother's doing, that she had "instilled in him the belief that it was common to live in a bourgeois manner." And indeed, Erzebet did spurn her sons' offer of a larger apartment, servants, and a chauffeur, preferring to spend the rest of her life in the modest two-room apartment with mismatched furniture. Now, as George's artistic new wife sought a suitable place, he was feeling conflicted.

Susan began looking on Manhattan's West Side, but expanded the search to the East Side after nothing suitable had turned up. Soros had spent his entire life in New York on the West Side, mostly on Central Park West. The differences between the West Side and East Side are largely matters of style. Viewed in very broad strokes, the East Side, which has the largest concentration of luxury apartments, is generally regarded as more Protestant, more old money, more Republican, and less reliant on public transportation. The West Side is widely perceived as more bohemian, more multiracial and multicultural, more Democratic, and more anarchic in its street life. While there is believed to be more wealth on the East Side, there are far more panhandlers on the West Side, presumably because the beggars believe the West Siders to be more generous. With such stereotypes in mind, Soros's move across Central Park was an irritating displacement, though hardly as psychologically wrenching as either his flight from Hungary or his departure from London for America.

"He sent me out to look for apartments," said Susan. "Every apartment I show him he turns down. It's too expensive, he says, or it's too big. He says he doesn't want to live that way, don't show him anything on Park Avenue. He wants to stay on the West Side." In the end, with his ambivalent concurrence, Susan bought an apartment on Fifth Avenue. "He had a real problem with living even on Fifth Avenue," said Susan, who had no such reservations and found his hang-ups amusing. He told Susan to decorate the apartment as she chose, adding that he did not want to see it until they moved in.

"When I was finished, I called him at the office and told him to go to the new place after work. It was full of paintings and antiques, just the way it is now. He walks around and he is reeling. He holds his head in his hands and asks, 'What have you done to me?' " He was particularly worried about what his social-reforming confederates and his dissident friends might think in such a museum-like setting.

Susan comforted him: "Look, we are not different, we are the same people."

But George was changing. That, after all, was the point of his midlife transformation. He had wanted to change. That was why he had undergone analysis, left one wife and married another, and sought to limit his involvement in business. So, despite the pull of his past, despite his regard for his mother's feelings and despite his own disdain for arriviste extravagance, George followed Susan's lead, and not merely to the East Side. He sensed it was precisely the optimistic boldness his wife had in such abundance that he needed to fully transform his life, to make it larger, more engaged. How, after all, was he to break out and gain significance in the world if he couldn't even venture beyond the West Side?

Eventually, Soros accepted and then even came to like his new surroundings. Some time after the move, the couple traveled to Czechoslovakia and visited United States Ambassador William Luers and his wife Wendy. He was impressed by the furnishings in the Prague palace that served as the ambassador's residence. It turned out that the place had been decorated in the same style and by the same people Susan had hired for their apartment. "That's when I became more comfortable," says Soros. "I realized that our place wasn't just a home, it was also a residence." Even confirmed East Village bohemians like Allen Ginsberg and George Konrad felt comfortable, as did Susan's fellow students from Cooper-Hewitt. Under his divorce settlement, George had joint custody of his children, and Robert, Andrea, and Jonathan often spent time there. The tempo of life quickened. By George and Susan's first wedding anniversary in 1984, the Hungarian foundation was getting into full swing, and George was involved with dozens of other philanthropic projects. He kept studying the problems of deeply indebted countries, paying visits to Brazil and Mexico. He was working very hard, but, needing relatively little sleep, he often read for pleasure late into the night. He could also read in a moving car, and he liked to listen to classical music as he read, both at home and on the highway. He favored Mozart, Schubert, Bach, Brahms, and Beethoven, and he liked listening to opera singers, though when he did he set aside his reading material. He rarely watched television.

Meanwhile, he was once more fully in command of Quantum. By late 1984, in response to appeals from some of his older shareholders, he had reclaimed the pilot's seat from Jim Marquez. He also took back some of the portfolios he had farmed out to outside managers. Within a few months he hired Gary Gladstein to oversee the staff, leaving himself free to focus on markets and questions of what used to be called political economy. As Soros told his associates, he was expecting colossal movements, even "the storm of the century."

His instincts remained sharp. He reasoned that Margaret Thatcher had so much riding on her privatization policies that she would ensure that initial stock offerings of formerly nationalized British industries would be undervalued. He bought large amounts of Jaguar and British Telecom and did well with them. Similarly, he was quick to sense how the emergence of fax technology would choke the business of Western Union, and sold that stock short, realizing a big profit.

As for the storm he kept looking for, he felt it would appear first in tempestuous currency fluctuations. Through his theoretical musings on reflexivity, he had identified a pattern he called "Reagan's Imperial Circle." From the start of the Reagan presidency in 1981, America had supported a strong dollar, a strong economy, growing budget deficits, high defense spending, a growing trade deficit, and high interest rates. All of these pursuits reinforced each other to establish what Soros recognized as the boom phase of a boom-bust sequence. For five years America's economic growth kept pace with the rising value of the dollar, but Soros knew this situation was unsustainable. Eventually strong dollars and high real interest rates would weaken the American economy, even with the stimulating effect of the budget deficit. He knew Reagan wanted to keep the dollar high, but Soros believed the president had more compelling reasons to bring its value down.

In August of 1985, Soros began keeping an investment diary, recording the ruminations that preceded his business decisions. Once again, motivated by intellectual pride, he was eager to prove the validity of his theories of change and reflexivity. Right or wrong, he would lay his thinking on the line in what he termed a real-time experiment.

As those notes showed, by early September Soros was convinced that the yen and the mark would have to rise against the dollar. He was so certain that he assumed long positions in both currencies that amounted to $100 million more than the entire value of the Quantum Fund. Early that month he extended that leverage by another $100 million even though the yen and mark were still declining.

Within three weeks, the finance ministers of the Western industrialized powers and their central bankers met at the Plaza Hotel in New York and announced a new system to replace the older free-floating rates of exchange with limits that forced the dollar to fall; the yen and the mark rose, just as he had anticipated. It was then that Soros showed his virtuosity, urging his giddy troops to stop taking profits by selling yen and to hang on for its continuing upward flight. On September 28, 1985, he wrote in his notes that he had experienced "the killing of a lifetime." By November, the entire value of the Quantum Fund had grown to $850 million. On December 8, when he returned from his office to the Fifth Avenue apartment, he wrote, "I have about as firm a conviction about the shape of things to come as I shall ever have, as witnessed by the level of exposure I am willing to assume." At that point the fund's leveraged positions stood at $4 billion, more than four times the value of its holdings.

His confidence proved justified, and the year ended on a soaring note. During the previous twelve months, the total value of the Quantum Fund had risen a staggering 122.2 percent to reach just over a billion dollars, thus becoming the first hedge fund to break that barrier. Pegged to the fund, his personal fortune zoomed proportionately. The magazine *Financial World* wrote that in 1985, Soros had been the second highest paid money manager in America, claiming he had earned $93.5 million.

Soros had more than money on his mind in 1985. On October 27, Susan gave birth to their first child, Alexander. Soros was consulting regularly with Vasarhelyi in Budapest about the foundation there and was particularly excited about the importation of the Xerox machines. With the vindication of his thoughts on the "imperial cycle," he decided to expand his experimental notes into his first real book, *The Alchemy of Finance: Reading the Mind of the Market.* He wrote it in longhand, much of it late at night.

The breadth of Soros's accomplishments in 1985 was staggering, but in line with old habits of self-criticism he wondered how he might do more. When his book was published in 1987, it included this obviously humorous, tender, but also revealing dedication: "To Susan, without whom this book would have been ready much sooner."

Susan recalls the period as one of frenzied but purposeful activity. "The growth of the fund, the success rate, it was like a whirlwind. And George needs a high level of challenges. This is a man whose idea of relaxing is playing eight hours of chess or highly competitive tennis. That's the way he winds down."

Soros has always apportioned his time rigorously. He is punctual and programs his days well in advance. He tries to take advantage of every sudden or unexpected opening on his calendar. Antonia Bouis, a translator of Russian who worked closely with Soros on his Russian foundation, recalls how George had impressed her during a trip to Washington with his practice of maximizing the use of his time. Calculating that the two of them had fifteen minutes to spare before an appointment, Soros directed his driver to stop at the National Gallery just long enough for him to dash in, look at a Vermeer and then continue, right on schedule, to the appointment.

Susan became a vital link in allocating his time. She kept track of his schedule, arranged for his tennis matches, and coordinated his movements with his two secretaries. She also assumed the duties of an aide de camp, packing George's clothes for trips, buying many of his clothes, and replacing the pens and raincoats that he regularly left behind. Another obligation she undertook at this time and has continued to carry out ever since was arranging the summer weekends at Southampton. By spring she blocked out each weekend, sending off invitations to interesting people, both old friends and newer acquaintances, to come on specific dates. The idea was to assemble eclectic mixes of a dozen or so people who would generate interesting discourse while amusing each other and enjoying themselves. Those invited transcended cliques or classes. Susan brought together penniless dissidents recently freed from foreign jails, artists, scholars, writers, and, on occasion, even a few magnates who might qualify as "doers." Guests at a typical weekend might include Fritz Stern, the Columbia University historian; Jacques D'Amboise, the dancer and choreographer; John Whitehead, a former diplomat; Vera Mayer, a childhood friend of George's from Lupa Island who works for NBC News. There might be an occasional banker, someone like William McDonough, the president of the Federal Reserve Bank of New York, but there might also be tennis players or foreign students from Bard College or antique specialists and quite likely a number of Soros Foundation employees or grantees. The Southampton weekends provided George with the kind of interaction he had yearned for since reading about Keynes's association with the Cambridge Apostles and the Bloomsbury group. But in contrast to Keynes, who kept in constant close touch with his friends, George was more remote, not seeing some of his guests from one summer to the next.

As his fortune increased and as he settled into his second marriage, he found it easier to spend money, even on things his mother would have scorned as bourgeois or parvenu acquisitions. He may have been alarmed at the sight of the antiques and art in the Fifth Avenue apartment, but he never gave his wife a budget or set limits. Though Susan had known a comfortable existence as a child and as a young woman, her life with George was at an entirely different level. "It was a quantum leap," she said. "I live in a very unreal world. I buy whatever I want. George is very generous. When the bills come I just pass them on to somebody at his office and that is that. At home we never discuss money. He is bored by it."

For himself, Soros continued to shun conspicuous spending. For many years he flew mostly in business class, and he has never owned a private plane. In cities, he preferred to use public transportation. But sometimes, particularly when it concerned Susan, he enjoyed flaunting his wealth.

Once, before they were to attend a ball, he told Susan to buy herself some jewelry. She picked out what she thought were very beautiful pieces and took him to the store to approve her selection. "These are not good enough," she remembers him saying. "He then buys me the most expensive necklace in the entire store. It's the one we call the Giant Wurlitzer, because it's a super thing; it's really too much."

When money was discussed at home, it was usually in connection with philanthropy. Susan remembers when she and George both read *The Golden Donors*, a book by Waldemar Nielsen. George was very impressed by the case Nielsen made in claiming that living donors tended to be much more creative and inventive in the way they dispensed charity than boards of directors managing the legacies of dead benefactors. Nielsen noted that the burden of fiduciary responsibility on directors is so great that they will generally avoid risky or dramatic options in favor of conservative ventures with predictable, if modest, outcomes. In contrast, people like Carnegie, who make the money themselves, feel free to spend it more imaginatively.

Philanthropy was then still an avocation for George, but he was beginning to think more systematically about it. He and Susan noticed that
there seemed to be a group of people who appeared to be philanthropic
apparatchiks. The couple particularly noticed the differences between the
enthusiastic amateurs, unpaid or minimally paid, who were so dynamically
leading the Hungarian foundation, and the seemingly slow-moving and
less productive philanthropic professionals they encountered in the West.
George and Susan had their own word for those they felt were living off
philanthropy as bureaucrats: "philanthropoids."

Fearful of such tendencies on the part of his own employees, George
dismissed some of the New York staff he had hired to provide support for
his foreign projects in Hungary and elsewhere. Soon after Alexander was
born, George asked his wife to take over the foundation in New York as
president. Working mostly at home, she handled the paperwork, maintained the accounts, oversaw transfers, and coordinated the work that went
into a growing number of programs, including those in Eastern Europe,
South Africa, the Philippines, and Chile.

The six years she spent on the job provided Susan with many insights
into her husband's management style. They also put a strain on the marriage.

"There began to be tension between us," she says. "I felt I was doing a
reasonably good job. I made decisions and then he countermanded them
without even telling me. We had some pretty huge blowups. He is incred-
ibly impulsive. He would do things that seemed right to him without even
including me in the discussion. And I got rather angry and thought, Here
I am running these things very professionally and there's this person, and,
yes, it is his money, but, yet, if I am running them, he should at least hear
my point of view.

"I was also at a point where I was getting jealous over the projects. It
was no fun anymore just funding them. I wanted a project of my own. So I
knew it was time to get out. I told him he had to replace me, because it was
neither good for our marriage nor good for the foundations. At the end of
the day I was not a foundations person."

Nonetheless, Susan maintained her role as president of the Open Society Fund even after she gave birth to her second son, Gregory, on April 29,
1989. She formally relinquished the position three years later.

During this period, as Soros's foundations were growing and encroaching on the available desk space in the fund offices, Gary Gladstein was
looking for larger quarters. At one point he received an offer from Donald
Trump, who was so eager to have Soros as a tenant in his newest, most

ornate office building that he was willing to make the rent competitive with another bid Gladstein was considering in a less trendy skyscraper at 888 Seventh Avenue. Gladstein informed Soros, who immediately rejected Trump's offer in favor of the other building. "How could I expect people from my foundations to feel comfortable when they visited me in a building like that," said the man whose hedge fund was then hovering somewhere above a billion dollars.

CHAPTER 18

CHINA

Among the books George Soros read in 1984 was *Son of the Revolution*,* in which Liang Heng, a forty-year-old Chinese scholar then at Columbia University, described his rise to adulthood in feverish times. The son of a newspaper reporter, Liang had been raised to worship Mao Tse-tung as an avatar of wisdom and goodness. Even when Liang's mother was denounced as a rightist and forced to leave the family, his faith remained unshaken. When China's Cultural Revolution erupted in 1957, Liang's father was purged from the newspaper he had helped found, branded as an intellectual elitist. Liang, however, became a twelve-year-old Red Guard, traveling through the country with troops of slogan-shouting youths. As old, once-respected teachers mopped toilets, he chanted passages at them he had memorized from Mao's *Little Red Book*.

Meanwhile, his father was writing endless pages of self-criticism in a reeducation camp. Liang was eventually reunited with his father and the two were sent to a remote collectivized village where their neighbors regarded the newcomers merely as two more mouths to feed. Liang's revolutionary ardor was slowly subsiding.

Despite periodic hunger, Liang grew to a height of six feet, one inch, quite rare in southern China. While playing basketball for a factory team and working for an oil company, he dreamed of studying literature. In 1976 Mao died. The Gang of Four was toppled and arrested. In the spasm

---

*New York: Alfred A. Knopf, 1983.

of liberalization that followed, competitive examinations for university admission were restored. Liang took the test and in 1978 was accepted by the Chinese language and literature department at Hunan Teachers College. There he met Judith Shapiro, an American anthropologist and Chinese scholar, who was one of the first Americans allowed to teach and study in China after Mao. They fell in love and married in 1980. Later that year Liang and his wife came to America, where, with her help, he wrote *Son of the Revolution*.

Since his early days as an investor it had been Soros's custom to reach out to people he believed had specialized information, and he used the same technique in his philanthropic pursuits. He would call someone out of the blue and set up a meeting. In early 1985 he called Liang.

"I got a call from him," recalled Liang, who at the time was about to complete work on his master's thesis at Columbia. "I never heard of George Soros. I did not know anything about him, but I went to meet him at a French restaurant. We stayed three hours. He was so excited. He wanted to know everything about China."

Soros said he wanted to do something for China. He summarized what he had done in Budapest and said he knew that the Chinese economic reformers were interested in Hungary's "goulash socialism." He wondered if an exchange could be worked out to send Chinese economists to Budapest for short periods.

At the time, Liang was about to launch a Chinese-language magazine, *The Chinese Intellectual*, which he would soon distribute outside China. He had been away from China for five years and was planning to go back for an extended journey of rediscovery. Soros was drawn to Liang at that first meeting. Soros likes to portray himself as an unsentimental figure and he is in fact rationally detached and disdainful of conventional pieties. But it is easy to see why Liang's story appealed to George's emotions. Here was the saga of another small boy ensnared in a chaotic and deadly maelstrom. George told Liang he would help him with his magazine, and he asked Liang to investigate whether it would be possible to set up a foundation in China.

Liang spent three months traveling in China. He met a number of intellectuals and told them about Soros's ideas. Among them was a liberal economist named Chen Yizi, who served as economic adviser to Premier Zhao Ziyang. Zhao, who at the time ranked just behind Deng Xiaoping in the far-from-transparent Chinese power structure, was a forceful proponent of economic liberalization. He had assembled bright young economists who were exploring such recently taboo subjects as free labor markets, public opinion polling, and even possible structures for a stock exchange. In 1984 Zhao established the Research Institute for the Reform of the Economic Structure (RIRES), a think tank for the young economists. Chen Yizi was its director.

By the time Liang met Chen, RIRES was already a significant engine of modernity. Its seventy-five staff members were extremely enthusiastic and passionately engaged in charting reforms that would increase China's gross national product, convinced that once that happened political reforms would follow. They were privileged and protected, enjoying the patronage of Premier Zhao. On a regular basis, they dealt with Zhao's right-hand man, a fifty-three-year-old rising star of reform named Bao Tong, who was even more openly supportive of broad economic reforms than the premier.

It was Deng Xiaoping himself who had appointed Bao Tong to be Zhao's personal secretary. Bao Tong had passed on to Zhao some of the papers and proposals produced by the RIRES economists. On occasion, the economists would get their papers back with the premier's comments, and sometimes their ideas were incorporated into policy.

Chen and Bao liked what they heard about Soros from Liang. They quickly agreed that Soros could finance the trip of eleven RIRES economists to the Karl Marx Economic University in Budapest, an institution that, despite its name, Soros was then helping to transform into an American-style business school. Soros flew to Budapest to meet the visitors, and he held talks with Chen.

The meetings left Soros excited. He sensed that within the extraordinary turbulence of Chinese society, he had luckily found the right people. They were clearly intelligent, and while strongly committed to market reforms and some democratic innovations, they were not marginal dissidents but a part of the Chinese establishment.

Chen listened as Soros explained his idea for a foundation that would be run "for Chinese, by Chinese." He would put up the money, but the programs would be submitted in open competition for grants, to be chosen by a panel of unaffiliated experts. Chen seemed to be sympathetic to Soros's insistence that the foundation would have to be an independent organization, free of party or government control.

Soros envisioned the Chinese fund as an adaptation of the Hungarian model. Instead of the Academy of Science he would take RIRES as his local partner. As in Hungary, there would be two co-chairmen; he would be one and Chen would be the other, with both men having the right to veto any program. As the Chinese counterpart to Vasarhelyi he would name Liang, the son of the revolution, to be his personal representative.

In October 1986, George and Susan traveled to Beijing, where Soros presented his concept. Remarkably, Bao accepted it virtually on the spot, and signed the registration papers of the Fund for the Reform and Opening of China, with guarantees of independence.

It was an astonishing and unprecedented development. Andrew J. Nathan, a leading Chinese scholar at Columbia's East Asian Institute, says that at the time the fund was established there was probably not a single institution in China that had this kind of autonomy—not a school, a religious institution, or a social club. For decades Chinese Communist leaders had been openly suspicious of the concept of civil society. The notion of a foundation financed by a capitalist citizen of the long-reviled United States operating without direct oversight of the party was an extraordinary reversal that, according to Nathan, emerged from Zhao's general policy of sponsoring many liberal innovations in the hope that some would take root. Nathan also suspects that despite the assurances of independence, the authorities must have counted on maintaining indirect control of the fund through secret surveillance and infiltration.

Nonetheless, in the fall of 1986 Soros had an agreement that on the face of it would enable him to bring in and constructively distribute money to recipients of his choice, ostensibly with no government interference or party oversight, in one of the world's most rigidly controlled countries. In the custom of the Chinese press, newspapers tersely reported the establishment of the fund along with other official communiques, without underscoring just how unusual an event it was.

For Soros it was another triumphal moment. As he visited the Great Wall and exchanged toasts with his banquet hosts, his hopes soared. He had succeeded in establishing an unprecedented beachhead of civil society and openness. Would that fund be able to open up Chinese society, which had been closed for so long? It was a thrilling challenge, the sort of prospect that could easily feed latent messianic dreams.

But, ever critical, Soros reined in his euphoria. In Budapest he had well-informed confidants who knew what was going on within the innermost circles of power. In China he was relying primarily on Liang, never an insider, who had spent the last five years outside the country and who was dividing his time between Beijing and New York. Soros himself was hardly an innocent, having had experience with both schemers and sharks. He repeatedly cautioned Liang to be vigilant and alert to subversion. And yet, despite such wariness, the fund would soon become entangled in complex and, for the most part, undetected intrigues.

Soros wanted Liang to begin cautiously. "He told me to start slow, not to do too much," says Liang. A small office was rented and only four staff members were hired. An advisory board of professors, economists, and editors was put together to review grant applications. Unlike Hungary, there were no public advertisements for projects, but news spread by word of mouth. In that first year, 1986–87, there were two hundred applications, of which forty were approved for grants.

A number of these were small but groundbreaking efforts. An art historian came to the offices one day saying he wanted to gather examples of folk art, which during the Cultural Revolution had been powerfully repressed. Old crafts had been forbidden and ceramics, weavings, wood carvings, and baskets were destroyed as plastic representations of Mao replaced older icons. With the foundation's help, the art historian sent out teams of scholars who collected and catalogued thousands of examples of traditional items that had all but vanished.

By the late eighties, "The authorities were emphasizing slogans about looking forward not backward," said Liang. No one, however, interfered when the advisory board supported a project to gather oral histories of people uprooted in the turmoil. The fund also sponsored a project to rediscover traditional music, which had also virtually disappeared after being banned in the sixties. With a grant of a few thousand dollars, a musicologist was able to find old people who were able to hum, sing, or whistle enough forbidden melodies and provide enough lyrics to produce a set of five tape cassettes. During one of Soros's periodic trips to China, the musicologist presented the tapes to George and emotionally told him that whether he knew it or not, he had played a critical role in rescuing from almost certain extinction music that had been played and sung for hundreds of years.

Many of the programs proved similarly fruitful. By 1988, the number of annual applications had grown to more than two thousand, of which 209 were approved. These included travel grants to study in America, notably at Columbia, Harvard, and Princeton. There were grants in all the academic disciplines, though the emphasis was on economics and the social sciences. A well-known Chinese journalist, Dai Qing, received a grant to conduct what turned out to be a robust investigation of the ecological and social consequences of building a massive dam that would flood a large area at the Three Rivers Gorge. Her study was critical of the government-sponsored project.

A large share of the grants involved people associated with RIRES. This troubled Soros, who repeatedly urged Liang to challenge Chen, who he believed was trying to monopolize Soros Fund resources for his own favorites and protégés. Soros cautioned Liang to broaden the applicant pool, to make the fund available to as many Chinese as possible.

What Soros did not comprehend was that the fund was becoming deeply embroiled in China's intensifying factional politics. Because it was brought into being by Bao, with the obvious support of Zhao, the fund was seen from the start as a subsidiary of the pro-reform group, both by members of the group and by their rivals. This was certainly not what Soros wanted. He, of course, sympathized with the reformers, but he wanted his foundation to be above national politics. Within China's dialectical and polarized factions, this proved impossible.

The hardliners emphasized stability and order and feared that economic reforms would necessarily lead to social disruption and chaos. They looked with dread at what was happening with Solidarity in Poland. The reformers favored free markets and greater democracy. The leaders of the two groups struggled for the blessings of Deng Xiaoping, whose advancing age raised the political tension as China wondered whom he would choose as his successor.

It was in this context that Soros and his fund became matters of high political concern—and Soros began to lose interest in China. The great expectations had not been attained. The projects had been modest, and the budget for China never went beyond a relatively skimpy million dollars. Moreover, he was becoming tantalized and preoccupied with his newest foundation, the one he was establishing in Russia.

At this point, in 1987, in a dossier circulated by the Chinese hardliners Soros was identified as an agent of the CIA. The report, prepared by security agents of the Public Security Bureau, contended that Soros was seeking to undermine Communism with his foundation. The charges coincided with a political attack on students and bourgeois elements, which clearly included the reformers. The RIRES economists were being derided as "Zhao Ziyang's Storm Troopers" or his "little feet."

That campaign ultimately failed. As for the specific attack on Soros, Bao answered it by distributing his own reports about Soros's other foundations. He noted in one meeting that Andrei Gromyko, the veteran Soviet Communist, had just given Soros's newest enterprise in Moscow his own seal of approval. Presumably, old Communists would understand that a canny survivor like Gromyko would not publicly endorse anyone who he thought might be tied to the CIA.

At one point a high party council ruled that the fund should be closed. Zhao, who was by then the party chairman, intervened personally and signed an order overriding the decision. Soros only learned a few details of the attack on himself and the foundation after it had been repulsed.

Soon after these allegations were squelched, Bao suggested that Chen step down as the Chinese co-chairman of the fund and that RIRES withdraw as Soros's Chinese partner. It would be replaced by the Chinese International Cultural Exchange Center, which Soros thought was a fine idea. As he would write in his second book, *Underwriting Democracy*,* "I had not been satisfied with the way the foundation was operating and had given poor Chen Yizi a hard time for keeping too much money for his own institute, so I was naïve enough to be pleased when he relinquished control."

Further intrigue followed, and steadily the atmosphere at the Beijing office worsened. Fewer intellectuals were showing up to chat and socialize; fewer were willing to discuss ideas. Late in 1988, Soros paid a short visit to Beijing and saw for himself how things were deteriorating. He was taken to see a mobile library operated by the Young Pioneers; the event was totally staged, with the people ostensibly borrowing books delivering obviously rehearsed lines and simulating delight and gratitude. Soros noticed that through it all Zheng Xiao-mei, the fund's secretary, had tears in her eyes.

Soros's hope for a foundation run "by Chinese for Chinese," independent of party or government, was proving impossible. Then, early in 1989, Soros learned that the state security operatives were knee-deep in the operation of the fund. The news was conveyed in a letter from Dai Qing that Liang translated for Soros as the two men walked in Central Park on a bitterly cold day.

"George was very upset," recalled Liang. "He said that's the end of the foundation."

Liang tried to hire an independent co-executive secretary, but failed. The work of the fund slowed to a standstill. The China Fund was shut down in the spring of 1989.

In retrospect, Liang believes the challenge was simply too great. "The fund was trying to be the only independent institution in all China. There was no tradition of critical thinking, no real concept of independence. We wanted to work with independent intellectuals, but before 1989 there were

---

*New York: Free Press, 1990.

almost none. We were struggling against too much, the politics, the economics, the culture, and the mentality."

Within a month of the closing, the student-led democracy campaign erupted. As Tiananmen Square became a throbbing arena of debate and protest, the latent conflicts between reformers and hardliners burst into the open. Zhao and Bao, showing sympathy for the students, came under direct attack.

As Soros read of the developments, he may well have wondered whether his fund, had it still existed, might have played some useful role in what appeared to be a revolutionary moment. If he entertained any such regrets, they surely vanished as crisis quickly turned to tragedy. Among the upper echelon Zhao Ziyang and Bao Tong were the only ones to face charges in the wake of the massacre and in both cases their involvement with Soros formed a significant part of the government's accusations.

Soros was appalled. He was worried about the consequences that his activities in China might have on the lives of Zhao and Bao, and anxious that those who had worked with the fund or received grants from it might also face difficulties. At that point Soros wrote a letter to Deng Xiaoping refuting the allegations against him and the fund and said he would be willing to come to China to discuss the matters further. He wrote in part, "Having benefited greatly from an economic system that is capable of generating considerable wealth, I am eager to assist the Chinese government in reforming its economy to produce wealth for the whole country."

He received no answer but learned the letter was reprinted without commentary in a publication circulated to senior party and government officials. It is hard to tell whether Soros's intervention, with its hint of willingness to someday resume assistance, had any impact on the treatment of Zhao and Bao. Zhao was sentenced to house arrest; ten years later he was still confined to his spacious house in Beijing, able to receive only visitors authorized by security forces. Bao spent seven years in prison and two years under house arrest. Andrew Nathan claims the penalties against Zhao and Bao were lenient, particularly in comparison to the death sentences given to the Gang of Four. "Their real crimes were that they had lost the power struggle and everyone understood that," said the professor. Chen Yizi fled China soon after the Tiananmen massacre, along with many of the RIRES economists, and now lives in New York. Soros and Liang know of no one who has suffered for having received grants.

The entire involvement had been both frightening and educational. Soros had become embroiled in a situation beyond his full understanding or control. In *Underwriting Democracy* he wrote: "It became clear to me in retrospect that I had made a mistake in setting up a foundation in China. China was not ready for it because there were no independent or dissident intelligentsia. The people on whom I based the foundation were members of a party faction. They could not be totally open and honest with me because they were beholden to their faction."

A decade later, Soros regarded his Chinese intervention as less than a total debacle. "The foundation did a lot that was very good. We supported a correspondence school that brought education to a great many people, [we funded] the exploration of the Yangtze, the recovery of handicrafts, and we helped create pockets of critical thought that survived. A lot of people in today's regime benefited from the foundation."

Liang agrees. His magazine, *Chinese Intellectual*, which Soros subsidized, has folded, and he now serves as a correspondent for Chinese periodicals. He lives in suburban New York and often visits with George, to whom he feels very close. "You know there were two people who changed my life, who made me believe I could do very important things: one was Mao Tse-tung when I was a boy and the other was George Soros."

CHAPTER 19

RUSSIA

O N DECEMBER 15, 1986, a team of workmen arrived unexpectedly at the Gorky apartment of Andrei Sakharov to put in a special phone line. The next day Mikhail Gorbachev called from the Kremlin to tell the persecuted scientist that he could come back to Moscow where he should resume his "work for the public good."

Gorbachev had been talking of new thinking and reform, but until his call to Sakharov Soros had remained skeptical about the Soviet leader's commitment to real change. When he read of this in New York, his doubts subsided. He was amazed and delighted not only that Sakharov's confinement in the Urals was ending, but that Gorbachev was inviting him to the Soviet capital with carte blanche to organize and agitate for democracy. Several of Gorbachev's predecessors had sent troublemaking dissidents abroad, most notably Aleksandr Solzhenitsyn and Joseph Brodsky.

Soros believed that Sakharov's return might have as profound a catalytic impact on the Soviet Union as Lenin's return from his years in Switzerland had had on imperial Russia seventy years earlier. Then it had been German officers who secreted Lenin in a sealed boxcar in the hope he would foment a revolution and compel a preoccupied Russia to withdraw from World War I. Now it was a Russian leader who was summoning the Soviet Union's most assertive and persuasive proponent of democratic reform.

Recognizing the moment, Soros immediately set off for Moscow. He was intent on exploring the possibility of setting up a Soviet foundation and hoped he could persuade Sakharov to run it. As he waited for the physicist to see him, he visited political contacts and spent days in smoky apartments listening to bestirred intellectuals exchange and debate news, gossip, and ideas. Eventually he met Sakharov, who rejected his offer and warned that if Soros persisted in his plan to deal with Soviet officials, he and his foundation would be fleeced. "You will end up lining the coffers of the KGB," Sakharov said. Soros tried to assure the scientist that he had not made his fortune by being gullible and that he was much more of a cunning Hungarian than a naïve American.

That was the origin of Soros's involvement in the Soviet Union. Within a year he had his foundation, this one called the Soviet American Foundation Cultural Initiative. It was to become the centerpiece of his worldwide philanthropic operation, consuming hundreds of millions of his dollars, implementing imaginative ideas while also serving as a target for con men and self-serving operators and security agents.

In February 2000, Ekaterina Genieva, an iron-willed and imperious literary critic and librarian who took over as chairman of the foundation in 1996 and finally stabilized it, offered a pithy statistical profile of the organization. "Right now we are administering forty-seven big programs. We have 1,010 employees. We have offices in 156 Russian cities and towns and we calculate that at any given time there are five million people who are directly benefiting from our programs and grants."

Indeed, since involving himself in Russia, Soros has financed extraordinary achievements unmatched by any group or foreign government. He spent more than $100 million to maintain Soviet scientists when the state had no money to pay them. He spent close to another $100 million to free the teaching of humanities and social sciences, such as history, economics, sociology, law, and psychology, from their forced adherence to Marxism-Leninism. He paid for millions of textbooks. He directed additional scores of millions to award and motivate elementary and secondary school teachers and to maintain libraries, and eventually made it possible for all thirty-three regional universities in Russia to establish links to the Internet. Large amounts were spent to promote independent media and to retrain midlevel military officers for new lives as private entrepreneurs. In another huge project, millions of dollars were spent to study and combat a virulent strain of drug-resistant tuberculosis that was advancing in Russia, notably in its prisons. All this was in addition to tens of thousands of smaller grants and projects.

Soros became as well-known in Russia as any foreigner. Virtually every professor, editor, scientist, and school administrator at least knew someone who had received help from the foundation. Many prominent Russians, including Gorbachev, have recommended him for the Nobel Peace Prize. Soros's name has entered the Russian language in many ways. One scientist named a star he had discovered for him, while another used the name Soros to designate a newly identified microbe. A teacher in a village in Kyrgyzstan named his daughter Sorosgul, or Soros flower, in honor of the man whose generosity had reached his remote region. More commonly, Russians have turned his name into a verb, "Sorosovat," which has come to mean seeking grants from any quarter, in the same way "Xeroxing" is now universally used to mean copying with any kind of machine.

Compared to his earlier efforts in Hungary and China, Soros's Moscow foundation represented a great leap not unlike the one he had made when he left the Double Eagle Fund to establish the Quantum Fund. He had been contributing a total of between $3 million and $5 million a year to philanthropy. After the opening of the Moscow office, his contributions soon grew to more than $350 million a year. But unlike Quantum, where each year brought soaring growth and cumulative success, the Moscow initiative got off to a very precarious start and for many years remained mired in inefficiency, mismanagement, and smoldering scandals.

When on October 7, 1997, the foundation celebrated its tenth anniversary at a gala reception in Moscow, Soros delivered a speech that did not overlook the painful failures of those early years:

> My hope was that the foundation would spearhead the transition from a closed to an open society. As it happened, the foundation itself got caught up in the process of transition, and instead of leading the process, we went through the same difficulties as the rest of society. We started out as a Soviet organization. The people working in the foundation could not shed their Soviet upbringing. The result was that the foundation functioned as a closed society for the promotion of open society. To break this pattern I had to organize a putsch. Unfortunately, the man who organized our own putsch turned out worse than the people he replaced and disobeyed my instructions. So I had to organize another putsch to get rid of him, but in the meantime the historic opportunity was lost.
>
> Even then our troubles were not over. The next crisis was a reflection of the next phase of development in Russian society. Everything was for sale and money was scarce. The temptation was too great and we discovered that the foundation kept a large deposit in a less than reliable bank. We didn't lose any money and there was no actual crime involved but we have had to have

another reorganization. Finally we have a good organization. As you can see, my involvement in Russia can hardly be considered a chain of easy decisions and success stories.

In the speech Soros glossed over important details and minimized what must have been his own feelings of betrayal. The record of what happened in the early years of the foundation remains incomplete. At least two audits were ordered by Soros, but neither was seen through to completion or made public. Many people were dismissed or encouraged to leave, but no criminal charges were ever brought; it appears that Soros decided to absorb his losses as quietly as possible rather then expose any misdeeds to publicity that might have endangered the continuation of the effort. Rather than seek justice or restitution, he swallowed these defeats stoically and, in the spirit of Popperian methodology, refined his approach.

In marking the foundation's tenth anniversary, Genieva commissioned Leonid Nikitinski, a Russian journalist, to write a history of the Soros Foundation. Entitled *"Trudno Delat Dobro,"* or "It Is Hard to Do Good," the booklet is a discursive work that concentrates largely on the waves of personnel changes and conflicts. It also includes a short afterword in which Soros wrote that while he disagrees with a number of points, notably the psychological motives that Nikitinski ascribes to him, he saw no reason to stand in the way of its publication.

Nikitinski points out that from the outset Soros selected associates from two antagonistic spheres: the dissidents who had long been marginalized for their anti-Communist beliefs, and members of the *nomenklatura*, the privileged insiders who understood how decisions were made. This was not an accident. Soros had always been drawn to contradictory situations and to strategies that engaged power in the hope of harnessing it. It is what he had done in South Africa, Hungary, and China. In Russia there were two vague concentrations of power; one involving the growing moral authority and energized commitment of the dissident reformers, and the other drawing on the power of connections, access to resources, and personal ambitions. Soros was genuinely fond of the moralistic purists he recruited, but his experience had taught him that those driven by less altruistic, greedier motives could often prove more valuable. They often tended to be the doers he so admired.

Soon after he established Cultural Initiative, Soros envisioned the establishment of specific sectors that would serve as contagious islands of capitalism. He wondered, for example, whether the organization of a processed food industry, dominated by private firms, might demonstrate the advantages of competitive enterprise and set off imitative reverberations.

Soros pursued the idea with international experts and Soviet leaders; it also found resonance within Soros's own Cultural Initiative Foundation. There Soros approved of having one wing, dominated by such *nomenklatura* insiders as a former director of Komsomol, the Communist youth organization, deal with openly commercial ventures. The assumption was that, beyond serving as a pioneering vanguard of a new economic culture, such initiatives would also generate a profit that could be turned over to the charitable programs. In Soros's mind this was a logical extension of the practice he had used in Hungary, where the compensation he received in local currency for the Xerox machines he was supplying to libraries and schools was providing his Budapest foundation with useful funds, particularly since the transfers were calculated at very favorable rates of exchange. Indeed, he himself had worked out a copiers-for-rubles deal with Soviet authorities.

Soros, however, underestimated the buccaneering instincts of his chosen doers. Some of them began using the foundation as a cover for their own international business dealings. While the scope of these undertakings, all carried out without authorization, has never been fully determined, enough details have surfaced to suggest that the scams were broad and imaginative. For example, a fishing fleet operating off Nigeria had been using the foundation's name, credit, and, perhaps, its funds. Another venture involved the purchase of 110 thoroughbred horses and their sale in Italy. Three one-time directors of the foundation ended up establishing a department store. Cars meant for the use of the foundation ended up as private property. Soros's reference to an "unreliable bank" had to do with deposits that, according to Nikitinski, should have generated interest of as much as a million dollars a month that was never credited. Whatever profit may have been earned by the commercial ventures, none was transferred to the charitable departments.

In the wake of tentative audits and mounting suspicions, directors and staff members left, staff turnover grew, and morale declined. Valuable equipment vanished. At one point the foundation's management used secret video cameras and tape recorders in efforts to discover fraud and pilfering—a clearly misdirected approach for an institution that championed openness and transparency.

There were also attempts at infiltration. Nikitinski writes how peculiar it was to have many ideological dissidents being offered jobs at a foundation that was headed by Vladimir Aksyonov, a former Komsomol official, "and most likely chock full of KGB agents." Alexander Yakovlev, who was Gorbachev's closest Politburo colleague in the early years of glasnost and perestroika, remembers high-ranking KGB officials repeatedly bringing him complaints about Soros. Now pursuing his original profession as a historian, Yakovlev, backed by Soros foundation grants, is publishing volumes of documents from the KGB's once-secret archives. As early as 1987 he was given a dossier on Soros by the KGB to pass on to Gorbachev. "It was fifteen or twenty pages and it said that Soros was a CIA agent. It had no facts just such phrases as 'our Hungarian friends tell us,' and so forth. There were similar unspecified allegations from China. It was a very primitive denunciation but the line was clear. They were trying to link Soros to the CIA and then they tried to link Soros to independent intellectuals, our own writers and poets and thinkers who they named and who they were trying to compromise."

Yakovlev said that Vladimir Kryuchkov, the head of the KGB, who had been a senior officer in Hungary at the time of the 1956 uprising, cited more unnamed contacts in Budapest in another report he brought to his and Gorbachev's attention. This one contended that Soros's interest in Soviet science was intended to glean scientific and military secrets for the CIA. Yakovlev said that he and Gorbachev both regarded the allegations as nonsense. On the other hand, while Yakovlev met with Soros, Gorbachev avoided any direct contact with the philanthropist, presumably aware how the KGB might have exploited any such meeting. The wisdom of Gorbachev's caution became apparent when Kryuchkov was identified as a ringleader of the 1991 coup that sought to bring down Gorbachev and his policies.

Yakovlev noted that the unsophisticated allegations tying Soros to the CIA continued to be leaked by the security apparatus. After he left office in 1991, *Sovetskaya Rossia*, a newspaper associated with the old Communists, published a long attack on Soros, drawing heavily upon material that Yakovlev remembered reading in the KGB files.

In light of such challenges and setbacks, why did Soros stay on in Russia? Indeed, why did he steadfastly intensify his commitments to Russia and the other smaller fragments of a disintegrating Soviet Union?

This was his own odd explanation, in his tenth anniversary speech: "Those who are puzzled by [my involvement] and question my motives are right to do so. I am a little puzzled myself and I shall try to analyze my motives for my own enlightenment as much as for the general public. As in most cases where I find myself deeply involved I can discern two levels of involvement, one is abstract and the other is personal."

He explained it was his devotion to the concept of open societies that led him to establish his foundations and devote so much of his resources and energies to Russia. "On a personal level, I had gotten to know Russia through the eyes of my father," he said. He told of the impression left on him by the stories his father recounted at the Budapest swimming pool. He mentioned his own unfavorable adventures with Russian soldiers after the war. "On a more positive note," he added, "I also got to know Russian culture. I read most of the classics of Russian literature."

While such explanations made a certain degree of sense, they seem incomplete and unconvincing. More recently, when asked why he stayed in Russia but withdrew from China, Soros pointed to the many extraordinary people he found in Russia. In addition to the operators and con men, he had come into contact with courageous, brilliant, and independent people who were even more eager than he to transform Russia into something it had never been, an open and democratic society. "If they could devote their energy and lives, I felt I should commit my money," he said.

But even this does not fully account for it. Soros's extraordinary commitment to the Soviet Union and then to Russia seem to have been a product of his monumental confidence and stubbornness. In a very concrete way, Soros's willingness to spend great amounts of money, time, and thought on the various components of the Soviet Union reflected a competitive assertion of his own beliefs in the face of public scorn.

In June 1988 in Potsdam, Soros was to address a meeting on European security that was sponsored by the Institute for East-West Security Studies, a Western-based think tank. The most dramatic aspect of the conference was the unprecedented public appearance in East Germany of West German foreign minister Hans-Dietrich Genscher.

Soros, who was still widely unknown, had been asked to deliver the opening address to some two hundred people. He was surprised by the invitation and suspected that the institute's director, John Mroz, was trying to flatter him into making a donation. In any case he wrote a speech he thought was weighty and important. It pointed to the postwar Marshall Plan as one of the great achievements of the age, an act of imaginative generosity in which the United States helped to convert a ravaged Western Europe into a prosperous and peaceful democratic region. Countries that had flourished under the Marshall Plan, he noted, could compound the benefits they gained by making their own massive investments in the stillpauperized societies of Eastern Europe, which would in turn give a renewed sense of purpose to Western Europe, intensifying unity and increasing security.

When Soros finished speaking, he was greeted by laughter. He remembers looking out and seeing a man named William Waldegrave, a junior secretary in Margaret Thatcher's cabinet, leading the laughter. The next day the German press mentioned the speech but only to point out that it drew laughter.

The incident was obviously painful. Soros has mentioned it repeatedly in his books and articles. Despite his wealth and his achievements, he was still the outsider; the experience rekindled old memories of his student years in London when he felt he had much to say but found no one willing to listen. Considering the events that followed Communism's collapse, his Potsdam speech was hardly off the mark. Soros had foreseen the consequences of the Helsinki process; now he was certain that the deterioration of Communism's closed system, which he had predicted thirty years earlier, was in its final phase. He was as sure as he had been when he anticipated the decline of the yen or the end of the boom in real estate investment trusts, having applied similar reasoning in all cases.

After his Potsdam speech, he attempted to meet world leaders, to impress upon them the opportunities they had to seize the historical moment, to support massive democratic changes throughout Europe. Prime Minister Thatcher and President George Bush declined to see him.

The snubs only fortified his resolve to do what he could on his own, to come up with, in effect, his own Marshall Plan. Such an effort, though remarkably ambitious and generous for any private individual, would obviously fall short of what major governments could do if they had the vision and the will. But it seemed that they did not, and in the quickening politics of the late 1980s he saw an opportunity to test and dramatically prove his thinking about historical change and reflexivity.

If Communism was indeed on the verge of collapse, what sense would it make to withdraw from Russia, no matter what the provocation? Encouraging transitions to free markets and democracy in Hungary, Poland, Czechoslovakia, and the other satellite states was, of course, important and profoundly useful. But Russia was something else. It was the epicenter of the collapsing system, the very heart of the beast. The idea of changing Russia, modernizing her, bringing her into Europe, had challenged and ultimately defied the ambitions of many historical figures. Istvan Rev, a Hungarian historian who is very close to Soros and serves on many of Soros's boards, believes that George was fundamentally attracted to Russia by the same things that had attracted Napoleon: "its vastness, its historical challenge, its backwardness, its perpetually unfulfilled promise." Unlike Napoleon, however, Soros stayed.

By the fall of 1989, when Communism collapsed in Europe, Soros had withdrawn almost completely from his business. Druckenmiller, who had been hired as his replacement a year earlier, says he can remember Soros's exact words when he told him that he was leaving for what he thought would be four or five months to concentrate on his foundations and Euro-pean developments. "You know, possibly I have been in your hair, and that's a problem," said Soros. "While I'm away, we'll find out whether it's been me, or whether you are really inept."

Druckenmiller says that Soros kept his word. "Luckily for me and for him, the Berlin Wall came down. It had enormous economic implications, if you could figure it out in terms of currencies, bonds, and everything else. And I was very lucky. I did figure them out. I made enormous profits. He really kept away for five months. When I finally heard from him, he acknowledged I had done extremely well. He completely let go and we have never had a contentious argument since then."

To permit easier travel to Eastern Europe and Russia, George and Susan moved into a London house they bought and renovated. Through much of 1989 and well into the next year, Soros, the capitalist speculator, resembled a nonviolent version of Mikhail Bakunin, darting from one rev-olution to another just as the Russian anarchist had done in the European miracle year of 1848.

One of the ideas that excited Soros was his concept of "a market-oriented open sector that would be implanted within the centrally planned economy." He pushed it and received enough support from Soviet officials to establish an international task force to draft proposals. At his expense he assembled preeminent scholars such as Wassily Leontief, the Nobel Prize–winning economist from Harvard; Edward Hewitt; and Marton Tardos. The ideas were refined, and Soros was present as they were pre-sented to the economic section of the Central Committee. That was as far as he got. "It was a lesson in the ways of Soviet bureaucracy," he says. "We had a good discussion but we never got the guidance we asked for. I real-ized that our recommendations would not lead to action."

In Poland, he had better luck. General Wojciech Jaruzelski, the coun-try's last Communist leader, agreed to a meeting, during which Soros spent an evening trying to convince the Polish leader that he should enter into negotiations with Solidarity's representatives. He particularly praised the intelligence of Bronislaw Geremek, a medieval historian who was an important adviser to the movement. Soros had been very impressed by Geremek; years later he seriously considered establishing a major European university in Warsaw with Geremek as its rector. By that time Geremek was Poland's foreign minister. Jaruzelski, who struck Soros as a well-meaning and patriotic figure, scorned Geremek as an opportunist, but soon after the meeting he agreed to the round-table talks that led to Poland's final and bloodless retreat from Communism. By then Soros had already established his Stefan Batory Foundation in Poland, named for a Hungarian who became king of Poland, a man Soros would sometimes quote as having said that "you can do much for the Poles but you cannot do much with them."

As Poland made a clean break with the old system, Soros turned his attention to the country's economy. Drawing on his work on debt relief, mostly in Latin America, he drew up a plan that would transfer portions of Poland's staggering foreign debt into equity. Foreign shareholders, he reasoned, would serve to discipline and quickly revitalize Polish industry. The idea, which found favor with Polish leaders, was spurned by Poland's creditors. Soros had a greater impact on Poland's economic transformation when he sponsored the work of Jeffrey Sachs, a Harvard professor who advocated a harsh and brusque conversion to a market economy, a strategy that would end subsidies and hopefully confine belt-tightening sacrifices to a short transitional period when the public, still rejoicing in triumph, would be relatively willing to endure the necessary growing pains. Soros also consulted with the key Polish economists who collaborated in drawing up the highly successful conversion plan of finance minister Leszek Balcerowicz.

In Czechoslovakia, the turnaround was even more sudden. In October of 1989 the small group of dissidents of Charta 77, whom Soros had been supporting for the previous eight years, were isolated and remained publicly shunned as they had always been, but just a month later they were being cheered as the custodians of national honor by half a million ecstatic people thronging Wenceslaus Square. Soros read about the events with delight and maintained close contact with Czechoslovak dissidents he had supported for so long.

But he could not yet leave for Prague. In New York Erzebet was dying. Soros, who had been shuttling between London and Eastern Europe, would periodically return to visit his mother, and when she went into her final decline he stayed by her bedside. He had long been reading about death and dying, and he determined not to turn away from her death as he had from his father's.

As his mother's health and eyesight declined, he spent time with her talking to her in Hungarian and English and reading to her, even from the mystical texts and poetry that she liked and he scorned. Despite her religious beliefs she had joined the Hemlock Society and obtained medication to bring on death if pain became unbearable. Soros said he knew about it, adding, "I would have been willing to help her take it if she had asked me to do it, but she didn't and I was relieved."

When Erzebet died on November 18, she was in her home with her family around her and George holding her hand. "Her way of dying was very positive for the family. She was telling us that she could see the approaching gates of heaven. At one point she said she better let go of my hand because she didn't want to take me with her into death and I assured her that my feet are fully on the ground and that I can take care of myself."

Soros had been separating from his mother throughout much of his life: at thirteen when he left to hide, at seventeen when he went to London, and at fifty when under psychoanalysis he loosened her hold on him. But he did not let go of her hand until the end, and for him her death was less traumatic than some of these earlier passages. He had come to terms with her and with himself. As a result of Erzebet's death, George's emotional ties to his European childhood receded. Susan would no longer have her role and taste challenged, and old tensions vanished. But for Soros the greatest significance of the death turned out to be the way he had experienced it, in contrast to the reactions he had had when Tivadar died.

"When my father was dying, he tried to cling to life, and it seemed he had lost what it was that made me admire him," said Soros. "In a sad way I had written him off even before he died. I ignored the fact that he was dying. When my mother died, I participated more fully." Five years later, as an outgrowth of his experience, he would initiate his Death in America project, which sought to confront the denial of death in contemporary society.

By early December 1989, as huge rallies took place in Prague and Charta metamorphosed into Civic Forum, an embryonic political party, Soros visited Czechoslovakia and set up another foundation, quickly providing the money to finance many of the building blocks of civil society, among them independent media outlets and cultural organizations.

Soros, along with several Charta stalwarts, went to visit Marian Calfa, the acting president. Calfa, a lifelong Communist, told his visitors how his view of the world had been shaken in three weeks. With a remorse that Soros accepted as genuine, Calfa said he had been unaware of his party's vindictive behavior and was ashamed of how Communists had lost touch with reality. Soros joined the others in telling Calfa that it was very important that Václav Havel, the often imprisoned playwright and leader of Charta, become president of the country as soon as possible so as to avoid any opportunity for the old guard to reassert itself. Calfa agreed. He told them the party leaders were opposed to turning over power to Havel, but added, "As acting president I have certain prerogatives and I intend to use them." On December 29 Calfa formally nominated Havel as his successor, saying, "He has won the respect of all." Once again Soros had witnessed revolution from backstage. "It was an unbelievable situation," he said. "The head of the apparatus of repression that just weeks before had routed a student demonstration was voluntarily abdicating in favor of a dissident."

Soros's excitement had kept pace with the events of 1989. He was spending more on his philanthropies, and he was less reluctant to speak out. He had shunned publicity about his activities in Hungary, China, and Russia, both because of his long aversion to press coverage and for what he considered to be tactical reasons. "In order to be able to function with my foundations I thought it best to keep my opinions to myself as an observer. Only since the collapse of the Soviet Empire in Eastern Europe have I been less concerned with the fate of my foundations than with making my views known and influencing Western policy."

He was very excited by the historic shift he saw looming, and he was frustrated that world leaders were lagging far behind him in their appreciation of the challenges and possibilities. Emboldened, he began writing essays and articles for various op-ed pages that revealed his chronic and professionally useful impatience. In June 1989 he wrote an article for the *New York Review of Books*, titled "Gorbachev—Dream and Reality," in which he found the Soviet leader's "new thinking" most deficient in economic matters. But he described the changes in Russia as "nothing short of miraculous." He concluded with an appeal to the West to respond quickly and positively to Gorbachev's initiatives and supply both the resources and know-how needed to replace an economic system that the Russian leader wanted to shed.

For the next five months, Soros was too busy to write anything more than the notes for what would appear a year later as his book *Underwriting Democracy*. But in December, as Communist rule was disintegrating, he felt he desperately needed to convey his thoughts on fading opportunities to President Bush, who was about to hold a summit meeting with Gorbachev off the coast of Malta. He wanted to persuade the president that only the promise of huge Western assistance for the Soviet Union could "prevent a descent into the abyss." Bush would not see him and the best Soros could manage was an interview with Lawrence Eagleburger, the undersecretary of state. And he shared his thoughts with the readers of the *Wall Street Journal* op-ed page. On December 7, as much of Western public opinion was indulging in Cold War victory laps, his plan was published as "Can the Soviet Economy Be Saved?—Not without U.S. Aid."

CHAPTER 20

BLACK WEDNESDAY

O N OCTOBER 24, 1992, George Soros was in London. Some months
earlier he and his family had moved back to New York. Susan had not
liked living in London. She complained that the schools for her sons
seemed too snobbish, that it was hard for her to assert her own identity, that
she missed her friends. Susan had also found herself embroiled in one of
those overblown stories on which much of the Fleet Street press thrives.
She had flown in an American woman chef to supersede and ultimately
replace a British couple who had been working for the Soroses as butler and
cook. After they were dismissed, the couple moved in the courts to obtain
compensation, providing grist for the tabloids, notably the *Daily Mail*,
which paid the butler for his account. Among the details he provided of life
upstairs and downstairs at the Soros home was his conflict with the new
cook over which spoon should be used to serve a soufflé. The dismissed
butler cited the difference in the ages of his employers and said that Susan
had fired the couple while George was away, implying that doing so without consulting the master was a breach of civility or protocol. He also complained that George would not speak with him after the incident. The story
lasted a few days, playing up to stereotypes of ostensibly boorish and parvenu Americans being put in their place by professionally trained British
staff who knew not only how soufflés were served but how households
should be run. For George and especially for Susan, it was an unpleasant
episode that accelerated the family's decision to return to New York.

But they maintained the London house at Onslow Gardens and
George often stayed there, using it as the base for his frequent travels

through Europe to further his philanthropic and reformist goals. So on that Saturday morning in late October, he was leaving to play tennis with some friends. As he opened the front door, he was met by a throbbing scrum of Fleet Street reporters and photographers, all shouting at him.

"Did you really make a million on the pound?"

"Can we have an interview?"

"Just a few questions."

He retreated into the house, thought things through, and telephoned Anatole Kaletsky. Kaletsky was a journalist who at the time was economics editor of the *Times* of London, but he was also a friend. The two men had met in 1983 when Kaletsky was the Washington correspondent of the *Financial Times*. He had read Soros's papers on Latin American debt relief and found them impressive. Over the years of discussing economic issues, the two men became friends.

"When George called me he said he was being besieged by the press and he asked me as a friend what he should do," says Kaletsky. What had drawn the newsmen to Soros's home that morning was another story in the *Daily Mail*. On its front page, the newspaper showed a stock photograph of a smiling Soros holding a drink with a headline proclaiming "I Made a Billion as the Pound Crashed." The alleged killing had taken place more than a month earlier on September 16, a day that by then had become known as Black Wednesday, when the British government succumbed to a 20 percent devaluation of the pound.

By the October morning when Soros found himself trapped by clamoring journalists, everyone in Britain knew that Prime Minister John Major and Chancellor of the Exchequer Norman Lamont had been dealt a humiliating defeat. Since August they had repeatedly maintained that the government would stand up to speculators who were betting that the pound was overvalued. They had spent billions of the government's foreign reserves to buy back pounds and thus shore up the value of sterling in the face of the speculative wave. Those foreign reserves, it turned out, had been squandered in a futile defense of a currency in a time of recession. And, as the press made clear, the paychecks, pensions, and savings of the British people suddenly shrank by 20 percent once they were calculated in terms of American dollars, German marks, or even French francs. Here and there, amid the handwringing and the cries of dismay, a few commentators portrayed the devaluation as a belated triumph of realism that would reverse a troubled economy. For example, on Black Wednesday Kaletsky had written an analysis in the *Times* that was absolutely buoyant.

Millions of Britons woke up this morning to read with horror about the devaluation of sterling, the utter collapse of the government's economic policy, the personal humiliation of the Prime Minister and Chancellor, and generally Britain's relegation to the third league of banana republics. But what will these dreadful events mean to the man in the street? Here are a few suggestions.

By this time next year Britain will have the fastest growing economy in Europe and after Japan probably the strongest in the industrialized world. Interest rates will be down to 6 or 7 percent and unemployment will be rapidly falling.

He went on to say that personal income would be growing by 5 to 6 percent a year and that the balance of payments would improve markedly while inflation would hold at 3 percent or less. The headline on the article was "Happy Days Are Here Again." In time, much of Kaletsky's predictions came to pass, and by the end of the century conventional wisdom had come to regard Black Wednesday as a positive turning point toward British economic recovery. But in October 1992, the nation was still glum, defeated, and bewildered.

For more than a month the British had read about the rounds of speculative betting against the pound, and it was obvious that there were some speculators who had won such bets. But it is not customary for individual speculators to trumpet their victories, and banks do not issue press releases to announce their gains. But that Saturday, the *Mail* put a face on one winner. Soros was not the only one who had benefited, but as of late October 1992, he was the only figure known to have bested the British government. To many Britons the smiling photograph in the *Mail* made Soros seem like a smirking villain.

Soros quickly learned that at the very least he had a public relations problem. After a few phone calls he realized how the *Mail* had fingered him. In accordance with its obligations in the Netherlands Antilles, the Quantum Fund had issued a quarterly statement showing a huge rise in its position in sterling. That tidbit of information made its way from Curaçao to Wall Street, where someone tipped off the *Mail.* The newspaper pulled together just enough details to justify the front-page photograph, the headline, and a short story that did not even specify whether it was a billion pounds or a billion dollars that Soros had gained.

When Soros turned to Kaletsky for advice, the journalist asked if the *Mail*'s story was true. Soros said that the basic facts were correct. Kaletsky remembers that after several calls in a short period of time, Soros said, "I think I should tell the story."

Kaletsky told him that if he wanted to write a first-person account, he could get the *Times* to run it, or Kaletsky himself could do an interview. Soros said he would prefer the interview. Kaletsky said he could not necessarily limit himself to what Soros told him; he might use other sources. Soros said that would be fine. Later that Saturday, Kaletsky walked through the cluster of newsmen into Soros's house.

"I went in and he told me the whole story," says Kaletsky. "Not just what he had done on Black Wednesday, but how a hedge fund works. I knew he was wealthy, but I had never realized that he was one of the world's most successful financiers. To my amazement, he gave me figures. When I asked him what percentage of the fund was his own, he said he didn't want to say exactly but added, 'You could say around 30 percent.' "

Kaletsky wrote up the interview, which ran in the Monday issue of the *Times* across five columns, with a matter-of-fact headline that said "How Mr. Soros Made a Billion by Betting against Sterling." Kaletsky also wrote a shorter piece for the front page in which he referred to Soros as "the man who broke the Bank of England," a phrase that was to become an epigrammatic title. There was also another, newer picture of the financier, this one showing George at his London home with worry lines around his eyes and just a hint of a smile.

The opening paragraph introduced Soros as an "intensely intellectual man" who was also "the world's biggest currency speculator." Kaletsky wrote: "In the two weeks leading to Black Wednesday, Mr. Soros engaged the British government in the highest-stakes game of poker in history."

The articles, which served to introduce Soros to a broad public, were remarkably laconic. There was no mention of Soros's European childhood or his years at LSE. There was only a passing reference to his philanthropies and his interest in Eastern Europe and no reference to the foundations he had by then established in eighteen countries. Kaletsky focused almost exclusively on what Soros and his fund had done to challenge Major and his stated resolve to maintain the exchange rate for sterling within the limits of the Exchange Rate Mechanism (ERM), the so-called snake that since 1979 had linked the value of European currencies to each other, with all of them pegged to the German mark. Within the snake, each member country was committed to maintaining its currencies within predetermined limits. In the case of Britain, the pound was to trade at a level of about 2.95 marks.

In the interview Soros explained why he was ready to stake his entire wealth and more on the eventual failure of policies to which the British government seemed so irrevocably committed. "We did short a lot of sterling and we did make a lot of money, because our funds are so large. We must have been the biggest single factor in the market in the days before the ERM fell apart. Our total position by Black Wednesday had to be worth almost $10 billion." His candid tone in the interview made him sound like an ecstatic chess player recalling successful moves in a critical match.

"We planned to sell more than that," he said. "In fact, when Norman Lamont said that just before the devaluation he would borrow nearly $15 billion to defend sterling we were amused because that was about how much we wanted to sell. But things moved faster than we expected and we didn't manage to build up to the full position. So a billion is about right as an estimate of the profit, though dollars, not pounds."

Later in the interview he explained that he had coupled his bet on the pound with associated ventures taking large long positions in British, German, and French interest rate futures. He also bought heavily into British stocks, and within a week of the British devaluation he sided with the French government, successfully betting that the franc would survive an attack by other speculators. Kaletsky wrote that all of Soros's initiatives in Europe that fall brought profits of $2 billion to his funds, Quantum and three smaller offshoots.

Soros explained that he was so sure of what would happen that he borrowed one and a half times the funds' assets to make his bets. It was Druckenmiller who had charted the strategy. Like many other speculators, he had concluded that the Bundesbank, preoccupied with the challenges and the cost of German reunification, would not commit itself fully to defend the pound and the ERM, either through massive buybacks of sterling or by lowering German interest rates so that capital might flow to London. Druckenmiller calculated that in the crunch, Germany would rather see the ERM collapse than endanger its own post-unification boom. But, it was Soros who, having accepted Druckenmiller's reasoning, goaded his deputy to increase fivefold his proposed bet of $2 billion.

Almost all of the Kaletsky interview concentrated on Soros's business activities, though there were a few comments that suggested Soros was not wholly motivated by economic self-interest. In one passage he was quoted as saying, "Speculation can be very harmful, especially in currency markets. But measures to stop it, such as exchange controls, usually do even more harm. Fixed exchange-rate systems are also flawed, because they eventually fall apart. In fact, any exchange-rate system is flawed and the longer it exists the greater the flaws become. The only escape is to have no exchange rate system at all, but a single currency in Europe, as in the U.S. It would put speculators like me out of business, but I would be delighted to make that sacrifice."

The impact of the interview was enormous. Soros, who despite his foundations, books, and articles had limited name recognition in the West, suddenly became a celebrity. The man whose ideas about the need for a new Marshall Plan had been laughed at in public and whose appeals for audiences with world leaders had been brushed aside, was propelled into worldwide prominence.

Soon after the *Times* article ran, Kaletsky asked Soros what he should tell his journalistic colleagues who were asking how they might contact the now famous financier. George said they should make their requests for interviews through the Soros fund offices in New York. Soros granted several, speaking openly about almost any issue that was raised, from his messianic dreams in childhood to praise for Popper. At one point he jokingly noted that having failed to convince Western governments to massively aid East European states emerging from Communism, he now found himself in a position where he himself could make such a transfer, in effect taking money from the British public to underwrite his efforts in the East.

And rather remarkably, without the benefit of publicists' advice, he gained a measure of tolerance and even admiration. He walked London streets without protection. "The reaction amazed me," said Kaletsky. "Here was this guy who had symbolized a $10 billion loss to British taxpayers and in a very short time the public response was that he was a genius and quite possibly a hero. Nobody said he was a villain." Kaletsky remembers reading some months later a small item in a chatty column in the *Times* that mentioned in passing that Queen Elizabeth's financial advisers had invested some of her money in Quantum, and thus she, too, had profited as the pound deflated. Despite the go-for-the-throat reputation of the British press, there was no follow-up to this report, and while such a lapse might be explained by taboos of lèse-majesté, Kaletsky believes it was not so much editorial timidity that kept the press from inquiring into the queen's investments as the public's growing recognition that those who were smart and bold enough to take advantage of stupid economic policies deserved credit, not contempt, and that this respectful attitude embraced Soros and—if indeed her advisers had been smart enough to put her money in Quantum—the queen as well.

Soros's newly enhanced reputation spread beyond Britain. Pieces about him and interviews soon appeared in hundreds of cities. Quickly he grasped both the irony and the possibilities of this new situation. Originally he had had no intention of ever owning up to his speculating coup. He still feared publicity of this sort and remembered well the rare bad year that followed his interview in the *Institutional Investor.* But the *Mail* had forced the issue. He spoke to Kaletsky essentially to break the newsmen's siege at his doorstep. And the unexpected result was that he was now being taken more seriously than ever before. The influence he had not been able to gain through his ideas, his writings, his philanthropy, and even his great wealth was now unexpectedly coming to him as the Man Who Broke the Bank of England.

That designation gave him the access he had long sought and multiplied his power. He would not be shy in using these assets. Somewhat wistfully, Leonid Nikitinski contends that Russia's fate would have been both different and better had Soros made his historic killing in the pound earlier. "He should have brought the pound down two years before. Should this have happened, Gorbachev, Yeltsin, Bush, Thatcher, and others would have listened to him attentively and hordes of Western investors would have followed his advice. As a matter of fact, the destiny of one-sixth of the earth's inhabitants might have been very different due to the efforts of a single person. However, in 1990, Soros was not yet the person he would grow into in the autumn of 1992."

CHAPTER 21

BRANCHING OUT

BEFORE SUSAN AND GEORGE spent those years in London, they had purchased a house in the small town of Washington, Connecticut. On their return from England, they decided to enlarge the property with the idea that their sons might attend school in the area and that they would use the Connecticut home as their primary residence, shuttling from it to the city and the beach house.

They intended to build a barn and a sports complex with a pool, but when they filed their plans, according to Susan, "Our neighbors and the community rioted against us." Hate mail and anti-Semitic literature began arriving at the house. "We didn't want to live in a town that doesn't want us, so we moved." They found a place in Bedford, New York, a Westchester County hamlet some forty miles from Manhattan. The 100-year-old house they bought had been designed by Charles Adams Platt, a well-known architect and painter, as the first concrete residence in America. It had spacious grounds and stables and a large wine cellar. "We saw the house on Thursday and bought it on Saturday," said Susan. A sports complex was built and drew no complaints. In fact, Susan soon won some local admiration by agreeing to open up the trails that crisscrossed their property. Susan, who as a child wanted to be a veterinarian, kept several dogs and acquired some llamas as pets for her sons. Bedford has now become the family's primary home; they spend the summer months in Southampton, and the Fifth Avenue apartment provides a city base.

While in London, Susan applied for the post of director of the graduate program at Cooper-Hewitt. She was interviewed several times during the next eighteen months but in the end was turned down. There were not many other options in her field. Though 450 American schools offered programs in fine arts, only three specialized in decorative arts, or what Susan describes as "the dishes and rags" of art studies. Certain that there was room for another program, she approached Bard College with the idea of establishing a graduate program focusing on the history of decorative design.

Susan first met Leon Botstein, Bard's president, while serving as president of her husband's foundation. She found the college innovative, and with Botstein she arranged for several dissidents to spend time at Bard's leafy campus above the Hudson River. Botstein appointed her as a college trustee. Botstein is a polymath, an aesthete, and a former wunderkind, something of a throwback to the multitalented figures who impressed Soros during his years at LSE. An accomplished musician, he serves as the director of the American Symphony Orchestra. He was appointed president of Bard in 1975 when he was just twenty-eight years old, and by then he had already spent five years as president of a smaller school, Franconia College. He had written books on educational reform and had generated increases in Bard's student body, faculty, reputation, and endowment. He would become George Soros's associate as well as Susan's.

After her rejection for the Cooper-Hewitt post, Susan, with her husband's encouragement, proposed that Bard establish a graduate center in decorative arts and that she run it. Accompanying the proposal was an offer of $5 million to pay for the program and the building in New York City that was to house it. Botstein agreed, ignoring the criticism that came from some academic circles and gossip columnists suggesting that Soros was using his money to buy an academic position for his wife, who did not then have a doctorate.

The arrangement was another example of Soros's reliance on transactional friendships. From his perspective Bard was providing an appropriate outlet for the unquestionable talents of a woman who happened to be his wife. In exchange, the college president was receiving a valuable asset for his university. Later, after he came to know Botstein, he saw no reason not to ask him to serve on his own philanthropic boards.

By the time Botstein joined the Open Society board, Susan had turned the Bard Graduate Center into a widely acknowledged success. "There were a lot of snide remarks at the beginning," Soros recalls. "There were suggestions that I was acting like a rich man buying an opera house for his wife who likes to sing. But I think Susan has had the last laugh." She had obtained her Ph.D., and her dissertation on E. W. Godwin, a British architect and designer, was published by Yale and won several prizes.

A year after Black Wednesday, Susan was going to work daily at the Bard Graduate Center. George, meanwhile, was intensively engaged in a growing list of pet projects. Even before the triumphant speculation on the pound, the numbers of his charitable foundations had begun to expand as Communism kept crumbling. New foundations were set up in Poland, Romania, Bulgaria, Yugoslavia, and the three Baltic countries. Then, as the Soviet Union dissolved, still more Soros foundations were organized in the newly independent states that emerged from the lapsed superpower: Ukraine, Belarus, Moldova, Georgia, Kazakhstan, Uzbekistan, Kyrgyzstan, and Tajikistan. When Czechoslovakia split in two, the old foundation continued its work in Prague while a new one was formed in Bratislava. Another Soros foundation opened in Albania. And when Yugoslavia began to unravel, foundations came into being in Croatia, Slovenia, Macedonia, and Bosnia.

The New York staff had also grown. By 1992, Soros had concentrated his operations, financial and philanthropic, on two floors of the skyscraper at 57th Street. Upstairs, on the thirty-third floor, more than 150 well-dressed men and women sat in cubicles, their eyes fixed on computer screens as they sought to make more money for George and his funds. Fourteen floors below, others less fashionably attired sat in somewhat sloppier cubicles routing his funds to pay for charitable projects in faraway places.

Soros himself worked out of an office among the moneymakers, though he and his two secretaries spent much of their time on philanthropy and public policy. In contrast to most philanthropists, Soros was not limiting himself to putting up the money. He was fully engaged in selecting and monitoring projects and personnel. Since 1989, when he turned primary responsibility for the fund over to Druckenmiller, his interests had shifted to what he had once called his messianic fantasies. However vainglorious it sounds, since the revolutions of 1989 Soros was preoccupied in trying to make the world a better place. On a daily basis he explored ideas to advance open society and entrench democracy, consulting with a growing Rolodex of advisers around the world. He regularly tracked hundreds of projects launched with his money.

On a routine day, he would be driven down from Bedford by nine o'clock and check on the funds' overnight dealings in foreign markets. The nature of the business was such that its gains and losses were instantly available to Soros and the rest of the staff, allowing them to follow the fluctuations of their fortune as easily as they monitored the Dow. Soros did not concern himself much with the ups and downs unless there was a big shift, though he might speak a few times a day with Druckenmiller. But most of his time was devoted to dispensing money rather than making it.

He would call people in his foundations around the world to check on projects or problems. Often, he wrestled with ideas on broad policy. For example, was the Dayton peace accord for Bosnia likely to gain acceptance and if so, what projects could he finance to encourage its implementation? Was the later proposal to enlarge NATO a good idea or not? On such issues he would waver back and forth, calling people he respected around the globe, trying to reconcile opposing arguments, before deciding that he would support the Dayton process while remaining dubious about the value of bringing Poland, Hungary, and the Czech Republic into NATO.

Often a visitor from a foreign foundation, a once imprisoned dissident or an expert on some area of foreign policy, would be invited to lunch. The food, prepared by a chef, was served in a room where the guest was always seated in a place of honor looking out on an exquisite view of Manhattan with Central Park as its dramatic centerpiece.

Since the days when Soros had first seen the possibilities of the Helsinki accords, he had been drawn to dissidents. He admired their bravery and resolve. But now times had changed and he was broadening his contacts. He realized that dissidents who were indispensable when dogma prevailed could be difficult and obstinate in times that called for compromise. He had had that important dinner with Jaruzelski urging him to reach out to those around Solidarity. He established extremely close ties with Bronislaw Geremek. Soros heard flattering reports about Tatyana Zaslavskaya, a Russian sociologist and one of Gorbachev's early advisers. He wanted her to join the advisory board of his troubled Russian foundation. When he learned that she was one of 170 people on a Russian delegation visiting the United States, he hurriedly invited the entire group to his Fifth Avenue apartment for dinner. He made sure that Zaslavskaya was seated next to him and they had "a wonderful meeting of minds," he recalled.

He corresponded with Havel and Mandela. He called famous economists to discuss ideas and strategies, men like Wassily Leontief; Stanislaw Gomulka, who was steering Poland's transition to a market economy; or Jeffrey Sachs. He sought out Teodor Shanin, a Lithuanian-born Israeli sociologist teaching at University of Manchester, who was the author of a classic study of Russian peasants. Similarly, he established contact with Mark Malloch Brown, a former British journalist and public relations specialist who represented liberal figures and causes. Malloch Brown, who would later become a vice president of the World Bank and then the director of the United Nations Development Program, recalls his first meeting with Soros in 1987: "I was planning to ask for his support for a group of political activists in Chile that I was working with to overthrow General Pinochet." Soros provided some money, but what Malloch Brown remembers best about the meeting was Soros's questioning him about Thailand, where he had administered a Vietnamese refugee camp. "Tell me about the health of the king of Thailand," said Soros, adding, "I happen to own 5 percent of the Thai stock market this week."

In addition to his growing list of outside advisers, Soros was also assembling a smaller circle of confidants within his foundations, people who had gained his particular trust and respect. There was Vasarhelyi in Budapest and Annette Laborey in Paris, who now served as a roving troubleshooter. There were also some newcomers, most of them women, who found their way into Soros's inner circle through the national foundations.

One of these was a Lithuanian, Irena Veisaite. Like George, she had been fourteen when the Nazis came to her country. Endangered as a Jew, she remembers the last time she saw her mother, visiting her in a hospital in Kaunus, from which the Germans refused to discharge her after a routine operation. "The last thing she told me was 'to tell the truth, to live within your means and not to seek revenge.' The next day they sent her away." Irena survived the war on false papers, living in Vilnius with the Gentile family of a woman she calls her second mother. During the occupation Irena worked as a chambermaid at an orphanage. After the arrival of the Red Army, her "second" mother was sentenced to years of exile in Siberia as a class enemy. Irena studied German literature and culture, not a popular subject in the Soviet period, but one she thought would help her understand what had happened in Europe during her early years. She taught for years at a university. She married an Estonian filmmaker and wrote about cultural topics, never considering herself a dissident. She tried to adhere to her mother's final instructions, but she was careful in her classes, dodging provocative questions. At the most she might introduce a student she trusted to writings that were not on the prescribed curriculum. Once glasnost took root, she joined in the national movement that led to Lithuania's independence, and when Soros's aides from New York came looking to hire people for the foundation they were setting up, many recommended her. Eventually, she became the chairman. She visited New York, took part in meetings, and gained widespread admiration for her honesty, good sense, and passion. She particularly supported efforts to aid national minorities and promoted multicultural projects as antidotes to the threats of zealous nationalism. Once, when Soros was asked what it was he thought of when someone mentioned Lithuania, he immediately answered, "The dark eyes of Irena Veisaite."

Another exceptional woman who rose through the foundations was Sonia Licht, from Belgrade, a short, chain-smoking, coffee-loving dynamo. She had been a dissident, though before that she had been a thoroughly patriotic believer in the Yugoslav Communism of Tito. She had proudly worn the red scarf of a Pioneer, and in 1956, as an eighteen-year-old schoolgirl, she was judged reliable enough to be sent to the World Youth Forum, an international gathering in New York sponsored by *Scholastic* magazine. She spent several weeks at Bayside High School in Queens, giving lectures condemning capitalism and Western policies. The experience changed her, and back home she became increasingly critical of political dogma, joining the dissident group Prakxis at the university, where she studied sociology and anthropology. She thought of writing her dissertation about the Hungarian Communist Georg Lukacs, "examining how someone as intelligent as he could subordinate his own ideas to political ideology." She gave up the idea when she figured out that what really concerned her was not Lukacs's self-censorship but her own. She became involved with the Helsinki movement and helped form a feminist group. Her husband, Milan Nikolic, was arrested and sent to prison for two years for his writings. Licht had her passport suspended for seven years. She wrote scores of articles, many warning of the dangers of ethnic politics. Soros, who first met her in 1990 in Dubrovnik, chose her to start his Yugoslav foundation; soon after, as with Irena Veisaite, he included her in his empire's highest consultative councils.

Later he would do the same for Chinara Jakypova of Kyrgyzstan. He first met her in the spring of 1992 when he hosted a reception in New York for the ministers of education from the countries of the former Soviet Union. She was then the youngest member of the Kyrgyz government, but a year and a half later she resigned. In one of her reforms she had introduced a computerized university admission test. This aroused some of her fellow cabinet members, who found they could no longer manipulate exam results for relatives of backers. Leaving government, she began an independent newspaper, which the government soon shut down. "I was in a terrible depression. In the morning there was a call from George Soros, inviting me to New York. There he asked me to become the executive director of the Soros Foundation in Kyrgyzstan. He said, 'Welcome to the family, Chinara.' "

Two years later, in 1996, Soros asked her to serve on the board of the Open Society Institute and she soon accompanied him on one of his inspection tours to the former Soviet Union. At one stop, she approached a member of the local Soros foundation and asked to meet with him for lunch. "As I have an unmistakable Asian appearance and speak Russian with a Moscow accent, which according to the post-Soviet mentality is a minus, the man refused. He told me he prefers speaking with only Western people. It was not the best moment of my life but I said nothing. Somehow George learned about it and from then on he insisted that I sit next to him at every stop."

Jakypova saw a good deal of Soros on such travels and says she came close to figuring him out. "I think it was easier for me to understand Soros than many of my colleagues. In my understanding, he is not a very Western personality. Maybe I understand him because we are both born under the threatening sign of the lion. Sometimes he is a combination of uncombinable things: He is a man of heart and at the same time a cruel pragmatic. He is sensitive and at the same time he protects himself with an armor of logical arguments. He is an absolutely free man and at the same time he is dependent on his obligations and commitments. He adores everything new. His favorite thesis is that any changes are better than no changes. He adores new ideas and new people, but he has a strong emotional attachment to the past."

In Moscow, Soros had of course found Ekaterina Genieva, who at staff meetings in Moscow and at interfoundation meetings, the so-called jamborees, would stand and deliver pronouncements in imperious and didactic tones. Her beliefs are not rooted in any state dogma but in hopes for economic reform, greater democracy, and Christian deliverance. She had been a scholar of English literature, an expert on James Joyce, and the director of the Library of Foreign Literature in Moscow. She was also a devout Christian, the spiritual daughter of Father Aleksandr Men, an Eastern Orthodox priest who preached the gospel of Christ with emphasis on love and personal responsibility. The last time Genieva saw Men was on September 8, 1990, when he came to her library. "He told me he was hungry," she says. But when she offered him food he would not eat. She sees this as a sign that he was aware of what was about to happen. The next day, as he hurried to catch a train to take him to his church, someone smashed his head with an ax. His killer was never captured. Genieva's piety and mysticism contrast sharply with Soros's atheism and empiricism, but the two clearly appreciate each other as indispensable partners, and she candidly claims, "I love George."

Soros has had close and special relationships with all these women and a number of others. Though they can be as pragmatically transactional as his other associations, there is something about his ties to women that is more visibly emotional, less rigorously intellectual than those to his male associates. Certainly, Soros has favored greater gender equality as an aspect of his views on open societies, but his closeness to so many women in his organization goes beyond ideology. It seems to be deeply rooted, perhaps a consequence of watching his mother evolve from a dependent satellite of her husband into a strong personality with her own distinct beliefs. In Susan, he found another woman who chose her own path.

There is yet another possible explanation. Soros may have found that it was easier for women to be honest with him than many men. Smart, vigorous, and competitive men would often find themselves awed in his presence, intimidated by the mixture of money, intelligence, and moral questioning. Some would show off to gain his attention; others retreated into outright sycophancy, and there were some, aware of how he hated sycophants, who would fake confrontational stands simply to ingratiate themselves. Perhaps women who had long experience contending with stridently self-important male achievers saw Soros as less threatening than other alpha males. In any case Soros genuinely likes the company of women and has always sought their views.

Though the number of Soros's confidants and advisers had grown steadily by Black Wednesday, there was no one who worked for him in New York whom he considered part of his brain trust or a soulmate. The Open Society staff on the nineteenth floor had grown to about forty people, but only a handful had more than clerical responsibility. For Soros this philanthropic workforce was the equivalent of a backroom at a brokerage house, people tending to rather mechanical chores. No one on the nineteenth floor had any idea of the full scope of Soros's philanthropic efforts. Only Soros knew about every project, and he saw no reason to share this knowledge with those he felt should simply focus on their own specific duties. There was no annual report and not even a budget. In short, it was not a very open society. Morale was understandably low, and turnover was high.

Soros had never really administered a large staff, and he was not interested in such responsibilities. At Soros Fund Management, the growth in staff took place only after Gladstein was brought in. But in the early nineties, with national foundations sprouting like mushrooms after rain, there was no counterpart to Gladstein to oversee the philanthropic operation. Soros had always hated bureaucracies and feared their growth. He scuttled his first foundation, the one dealing with Central Park, precisely in order to choke off any self-perpetuating impulse. Ever since, he has evoked comparisons to Trotsky or Mao Tse-tung by his eagerness to incite turmoil, if not perpetual revolution, as a stimulus for creativity within his own organization. His preference for chaos over stultifying order was well-known and rooted in both his experience and his personality. Throughout his professional life, he jumped in and out of markets, constantly reassessing, revising, and amending decisions. He has always had a very low threshold of boredom; he scorned stability and cherished his impulses. Beyond that, in his philosophical musings he has always been fascinated by the way that very unstable conditions enhanced prospects of meaningful change.

From the start, his concept for his foundations was that he would provide the money to implement the ideas of people from countries undergoing transition. It would be entirely his money and mostly their ideas. So where was the need for a large group of people in New York? By late 1992, he was not sure the slapdash structure that had evolved was appropriate. Things on the top floor were sedately buoyant and working smoothly under Druckenmiller and Gladstein. Within the philanthropic realm, however, the situation was quite different. While some foundations were achieving excellent results, others were stalled, spending money in ways Soros thought unimaginative. Some were split by factions, and, as the audits in Moscow suggested, inefficiency, patronage, and outright corruption were not uncommon. With so many foundations starting up so quickly, the entire effort seemed to be going off in many different directions. Energy was being diffused, and the core idea of promoting open societies was being swamped. Even with his tolerance for creative tensions, Soros found the situation troublesome and would often discuss questions of structure with people he trusted, among them Sonia Licht.

"I would remind him of what Max Weber had written," says Licht. "I told him he had a choice: he could either be a charismatic leader or he would have to build a bureaucracy. But George couldn't accept either approach. His belief in democracy and open society would not allow him to accept a charismatic role, and on the other hand, he hated bureaucracy."

The situation embodied the kind of paradox that had long fascinated him. Would he be better off with energetic but perhaps selfish rascals dominating his foundations or with punctilious but deadening apparatchiks? Was there a way to strike a balance between the two? More practically, how were open civil societies to take root if the local pioneers were subordinated to the inevitably patronizing oversight of bean counters in New York? Yet how much pilfering, corruption, and mismanagement could Soros write off as unavoidable growing pains?

Licht listened sympathetically. "I felt him suffer. He wanted to solve problems that no one had ever solved. He was still the philosopher. I would tell him that nobody ever figured these things out, not Popper, not Weber. Still, I could see he wanted to do it."

Soros had never shied away from U-turns if he concluded they were appropriate. He began to think of turning over some real responsibility to someone else, just as he had done when he brought Gladstein and Druckenmiller into SFM. He had reached this point by late 1992 when, during one of his regular dinner meetings with Aryeh Neier, Neier mentioned that he was being "worn down" by the fundraising he had to do at Human Rights Watch. Neier remembers that Soros quickly took advantage of the opening to offer him the presidency of the burgeoning philanthropic empire.

"It was an opportune moment," recalls Neier. "George was finding the management of the foundation network more than he could handle. On the one hand he didn't want to give up control, and on the other he needed someone to take responsibility." In the course of the dinner Neier agreed that at an appropriate time he would make the switch. After eight months of familiarizing himself with the operations, Neier took over the day-to-day leadership of the Open Society Fund in the fall of 1993. He was fifty-seven years old, six years younger than George. He was also the very model of the anti-bureaucratic bureaucrat, a man who understood and shared George's fears of unimaginative institutional inertia but also a man who had successfully run large and often controversial organizations, first the American Civil Liberties Union, then Helsinki Watch and Human Rights Watch.

The publisher Andre Schiffrin remembers Neier from the mid-fifties when he was a college student at Cornell. He had succeeded Schiffrin, then at Yale, as leader of the Student League for Industrial Democracy, a fledgling socialist campus organization that fifteen years later would evolve into the Students for a Democratic Society. "He was just as he is now, a bureaucrat," said Schiffrin.

Neier is a deceptively soft-looking man. His round and fleshy face usually betrays little of what he is thinking. He wears dark suits, and moves and speaks with slow precision. He has the slightest trace of the English accent he picked up as a wartime refugee from Germany. His manner is aloof and formal but behind the placid demeanor are strongly held passions for freedom, liberty, justice, due process, and open debate. He prefers small audiences of influential people over the seductions of mass media. Neier is often the man in the room who avoids notice until the discussion becomes hopelessly entangled. Then, methodically, he parses the previous arguments, identifies the various viewpoints, places issues in context, provides perspective, and drives matters forward. Neier guards his private life zealously, retreating to the book-filled Greenwich Village apartment he has lived in for three decades or to his summer home on Nantucket. He is devoted to his family and loves visiting art museums and galleries looking for and at modern sculpture. He is not without ego, but he does not need the spotlight and he seems happy enough in his own skin. Even more than his experience and contacts, this may be his most valuable attribute, the quality that has enabled him to manage the Soros Foundation's single greatest asset: Soros himself.

When Neier moved into his new job, some doubted he would last long. "I was noted for being somewhat headstrong and George was noted for being headstrong," said Neier. A local gossip column predicted the partnership would quickly dissolve. "But I was more confident. I had known George for a long time and I was comfortable working with him."

Neier had been a leader at the ACLU for fifteen years, from the civil rights revolution through the Watergate crisis. He headed the often-embattled organization from 1970 to 1979, leading it into an era of expanded activism that saw its agenda grow to include new causes such as women's and reproductive rights, prisoners' rights and patients' rights, as well as racial justice and anti-war activities. Despite the heat of such subjects, Neier never attracted the public recognition of some of his arguably less effective but more telegenic contemporaries. He was deeply involved in the great sweeping social struggles of the sixties and seventies, but few ordinary Americans would recognize his name or his face. The closest he came to notoriety was in 1978, when the ACLU successfully defended the right of American Nazis to march in Skokie, Illinois, a community with a high percentage of Jewish Holocaust survivors. Critics, including offended

Jewish leaders, questioned why a fellow Jew and a victim of Nazi persecution like Neier was supporting the right of people to openly march under the swastika. Neier answered the attacks with a book, *Defending My Enemy.**

Neier was better known within elite circles of patrician activists and donors. There he had a reputation for steering programs from idea to implementation. He knew everyone who mattered, among them the rich and often aloof people who funded and ran the great American foundations such as Carnegie, Field, Ford, Kaplan, MacArthur, and Rockefeller. He had known many rich people, and while he had been impressed by some of them, he found many strange, particularly when it came to money. He remembered a lunch he had with John D. Rockefeller III at a time when wide ties were in fashion. "I was wearing a wide tie and Rockefeller fingered it and told me he had several like it from the last time they were in fashion. I remember thinking to myself: John D. Rockefeller holds his ties for twenty-five years." He also recalled stopping at a diner for a cup of coffee with a member of the Pratt family, a descendant of one of Rockefeller's Standard Oil partners. The price of coffee had just jumped from ten to fifteen cents a cup, and Neier was surprised when his colleague spent fifteen minutes questioning the diner manager about the higher price. Soros, he found, was remarkably generous for a rich man, though he too had his peculiarities in this area, often carrying no pocket money and asking companions to pay for cabs or coffees.

Over the years Neier had developed a large number of associations that went far beyond the wealthy to include professors, journalists, editors, religious figures, radicals, and ex-cons. At Human Rights Watch, he extended these contacts internationally, coming to know hundreds of human rights campaigners, victims, writers, journalists, and dissidents around the world. His ideals were unabashedly liberal, but his management style was rigorous. Describing Neier, Anthony Lewis, a columnist for the *New York Times*, once wrote that "his substance is left, but his style is right." When Neier took over as executive director of the American Civil Liberties Union in what amounted to a coup of young Turks, he fired much of the staff the first week. Needing only four hours of sleep a night, he drove those around him almost as hard as he drove himself.

As Neier describes it, his arrival at the helm of the Soros foundations was neither smooth nor simple. Soros was finding it difficult to surrender

*New York: E. P. Dutton, 1979.

control while Neier was struggling to figure out what it was that he was supposed to be managing. "By the time I came, there were already some twenty foundations. George was entirely focused on them. He knew the people in them. He had collected these people, and he was the only person who had any comprehensive knowledge of what was going on. To the degree that there was any sense of mission, it wasn't something that the forty people in New York had; they didn't have an overview of what was going on. George was the only person who had that."

Indeed it would take Neier more than a year to figure out the extent of the operations. There was, he recalls, a complex and bewildering legal structure, with tax exemptions established for many different legal entities. One of Neier's first accomplishments was to reorganize the welter of initiatives as the Open Society Institute. "It provided a kind of overarching legal structure that would have the legal right to do all the things, or almost all the things, that we actually wanted to do," says Neier.

As he plodded on, Neier kept discovering new, often surprising things that Soros had done. "It was daunting. I could not see how I was going to figure everything out. I kept being astonished about what the foundation had been doing. In my first year, there was hardly a day that I didn't learn about some significant program that I did not know about previously." Some six months into his job, Neier learned of a project involving Yugoslav students at universities in foreign lands. As the country fragmented, these students found themselves marooned abroad, cut off from their sources of funding. Neier had a particular interest in the Balkans and had followed the conflicts there very closely. Still, neither Soros nor anyone else had bothered to tell him about the foundation's program to support several thousand of these Yugoslav students. It turned out that $13 million was being spent on the marooned students, but Neier only learned about the project accidentally, in a chance conversation. Similarly, he remembers attending meetings at the Council on Foreign Relations and elsewhere at which speakers identified themselves as directors of Soros programs. Not only had he, the man at the helm, never heard of the speakers, but he was also unaware of the programs. "I often despaired that I would never figure everything out."

Of course, in time he did. He hired someone to put together an annual report. A budget was prepared. He introduced regular meetings to pool information.

Before taking the job, he had talked to Soros about extending the scale of operations. Neier had expressed the hope of starting new foundations in countries that had not been touched by Communism. He was particularly interested in India. Soros brushed this suggestion aside, saying that at the time he was the single largest investor in India. "He told me that in order to avoid conflicts he had a rule of no philanthropy where he was an investor and no investing where he was a philanthropist," said Neier. But Soros confided that he was eager to expand his philanthropy elsewhere, to such places as South Africa, Latin America, and the Caribbean. "He told me that he would be spending much more money on more projects," says Neier.

CHAPTER 22

DEEPER POCKETS

A ND SPEND he did. Between 1994 and 2000, Soros's contributions to
his foundations amounted to more than $2.5 billion, growing from
the $300 million in Neier's first year to $574.7 million in 1998 and some
$570 million in 1999. Soros's Open Society Institute was outspending all
other broadly focused foundations. Only England's Wellcome Trust and
the United States Lilly Endowment, both of which concentrated on medical research, had made greater disbursements.

The numbers certainly captured attention, but Soros's charity was distinguished by more than his generosity. To a degree unmatched by any
other foundation, the Open Society Institute was the instrument of its living donor, reflecting his philosophy, his wishes, and his instincts. In contrast to other foundations, it was Soros himself who made all the most
important decisions about how and where his money should be spent. Following the pattern he had established as a speculator, he relied on his own
judgment, shunning trustees who he realized would necessarily be timid in
exercising fiduciary responsibility over someone else's money. None of
Soros's foundations were endowed, and virtually all expenses came out of
his pocket. He listened to his various advisory panels and he delegated a
good deal of discretion over spending to the national foundations he had
created, but when it came to big and new initiatives, it was he who decided
the questions of yes or no and how much, just as he had decided on the size
of his bets on currency movements. In philanthropy as in business, Soros
was pulling the trigger.

The extent to which Soros was involved in seeking out, supporting, and refining ideas and projects was even more unusual than the amounts he was committing. In 1999, when the Microsoft magnate Bill Gates set up his own foundation with a gargantuan initial endowment of $17 billion, Soros was asked if he had any advice for his fellow billionaire, who then regularly headed the *Forbes* list of the richest Americans. Soros replied: "Giving away money is more difficult than making money in one respect. In business, there is a single criterion of success: the bottom line. In philanthropy, the bottom line is a cost item, and the benefits are spread over a wide variety of social effects. You need to have your own set of social values to evaluate the effects."

Soros had been ruminating about social values since he wrote his papers for Popper, or even before, when he had imagined parallel universes as an adolescent. While many were dazzled by the amounts he was spending, other philanthropists tended to be impressed by Soros's thoughtfulness in selecting targets. Ted Turner, the flamboyant communications billionaire, claimed that Soros was the philanthropist he most admired and that it was Soros's approach that had inspired his own decision to donate as much as a billion dollars to support United Nations programs. Turner acknowledged that like most very rich people he had eagerly awaited *Forbes's* annual listings of the top earners, regarding the rankings with competitive zeal. Inspired by Soros's achievements, Turner recommended that a similar list be published annually rating people not in terms of the money they made but by how much they gave away. He said he hoped it would extend competition among donors. In 1992 and 1993 Soros would have placed at the top of such rankings; since then, he has maintained his leading position for annual generosity, even though his ranking for annual earnings among billionaires dropped from first place in 1993 to sixtieth on the *Forbes* list in 1999. He ranked 116 on the magazine's listing of the richest people in the world.

From the outset, "openness" provided the framework for Soros's efforts, establishing criteria for projects and providing an intellectual cohesion for the thousands of initiatives he was sponsoring all over the world. Though Soros would often become fascinated by some more modest and out-of-the-way project such as supporting the pro-democracy movement in Burma or sponsoring school construction in Albania, it was usually the biggest and costliest of programs that most engaged him, the ones that ended up costing as much as $100 million.

The movement toward big projects came as his wealth and notoriety increased. For several years he had been content to focus on his various national foundations, encouraging them to develop and pursue their own agendas. The governing premise was that the people in the foundations knew best what was needed. But as Communism faded, and the exciting ideas churned up in the revolutionary moment gave way to more mundane concepts, Soros began looking more actively for huge projects.

Those he looked into differed widely in their emphasis, but all followed a similar pattern. They were characterized by big ideas that could be reduced to simple, easily grasped language. In seeking out such concepts Soros did not need thick position papers or feasibility studies. What he was looking for were projects with the same self-evident utility as sending Xerox machines into Communist Hungary to undermine censorship.

In due course he found plenty of concepts of this kind that he rendered into pithy imperatives—for example, creating a university to train men and women in the skills needed to democratize and privatize formerly Communist states, or reforming nursery schools in such countries, or introducing long-forbidden social sciences to the former Soviet Union, or saving Russian science from bankruptcy, or providing housing loan guarantees to enable poor South Africans to acquire dwellings in cities where blacks had previously been banned, or vastly expanding the role of after-school centers in the United States.

The first of these involved the university. Soros had dismissed the idea when it was first broached to him in Dubrovnik in April 1989, while Soros was taking part in a workshop involving academics from both sides of the Iron Curtain. In that period of incubating glasnost, the participants were discussing what might be done to introduce and promote social science education in the East. Under Communist rule, instruction in science and technology had been maintained at a high level, but the teaching of social sciences, which would invariably confront and challenge Marxist shibboleths, was ignored or skewed to conform to ideological constraints. William Newton-Smith, the Oxford philosopher and Soros's occasional chess partner, had brought George to the meeting. There, along with others, he urged Soros to consider founding a contemporary equivalent of a medieval university, an island of free inquiry that would bring together scholars from throughout the world.

Soros was not interested in building monuments. Not only did he have contempt for the kind of bureaucracy that a university would require, he did not like real estate. "At that time I opposed the founding of a new institution because I felt the purpose could be better served by informal, non-institutional initiatives," he says. These included the scholarships he was providing to Easterners to allow them to study in the West. "But the fall of the Berlin Wall changed my mind. I recognized the need for an institution to reinforce the idea behind the revolution of 1989; that is to say, the idea of an open, pluralistic, democratic, market-oriented form of social organization."

There are not too many precedents for one man building a university from scratch entirely with his own funds. The greatest such achievement in modern times was probably the creation of the University of Chicago by John D. Rockefeller. In size and riches, the Central European University (CEU) that Soros established in 1991 is not at that level. Nonetheless, it was a formidable achievement. It has a main center in Budapest and smaller outposts in Prague and Warsaw. So far it has trained more than three thousand students from eighty-nine countries while enduring and surviving years of identity crisis. Its deans, faculty, and students have joined Soros and his advisers in ongoing debates over whether it should be an elitist academy or a more utilitarian professional school. Should it be more like the highly academic Cambridge of John Maynard Keynes that Soros had so admired, or more like the LSE, with its five E's and its Fabian tradition of social transformation? So far, there have been stormy patches and three rectors. At times the debates over mission and destiny have spilled beyond campus into parliaments. In Prague, the then prime minister, Václav Klaus, skirmished with Soros, accusing him of being insufficiently respectful of the primacy of markets. Klaus was also feuding with Václav Havel, who served as one of the university's three patrons. Consequently growth of the university in Prague was stunted. In Warsaw, political enemies of Geremek, the second CEU patron, similarly thwarted campus expansion. And in Budapest, right-wing nationalists also attacked Soros and his university, at times resorting to anti-Semitic thrusts. But there Soros was well-entrenched, and with the active support of the CEU's third patron, Hungary's President Arpad Goncz, the university took root and grew in Budapest. Soros acquired several large downtown buildings, one of which had been secret police headquarters under the Communists. He provided a library that would soon house the archives of Radio Free Europe, and added a converted hostel in another neighborhood to serve as a dormitory and conference center.

During its first eight years, most of the students came from the former Warsaw bloc and were supported by full scholarships from Soros. The faculty now includes sixty professors from twenty-six countries. The language of instruction is English, with most students enrolled in a one-year master's program, though a doctoral program is expanding. Areas of specialization include economics, environmental sciences, gender studies, history, legal studies, medieval studies, nationalism, and sociology. A CEU press publishes monographs and textbooks that are widely distributed within the region. Soros himself speaks at commencement exercises, sending off graduates to jobs in diplomacy, government service, international or regional organizations, and private enterprise. Soros has spent about $20 million a year in maintaining the school and its students.

Soros's big projects are often joined by a narrative link: someone Soros meets while pursuing one set of ideas leads him to a new challenge. Newton-Smith, for example, met Soros in London in the early eighties. At the time he thought George was a lonely traveling businessman who wanted to talk about philosophy over dinner. Over time, the British philosopher would receive money from Soros that he turned over to dissident academics in Czechoslovakia. That led to the conference in Dubrovnik and the eventual establishment of the CEU, where Newton-Smith now teaches, commuting between Budapest and Oxford.

A similar chain of happenstance led from the CEU to other big ideas. After Soros had committed himself to the idea of starting a university but before he had spent money on the project, he sought out people who might have suggestions about how to structure a school. Someone told him about a man named J. Frazer Mustard, who had established the Canadian Institute for Advanced Research and who ran something called the Founders' Network. Mustard was a physician and a pathologist with eclectic interests. He was concerned with economics, Third World development, science, technology, communications, and education. Like his countryman Marshall McLuhan, he saw himself as a futurologist, and he had established interdisciplinary ties with people around the world whose research and thinking he admired.

Mustard remembers that in the early nineties a friend suggested a meeting with Soros, whose name then meant nothing to him. "He flew here to Toronto and we had a very interesting day talking about many things. He was thinking about starting a university for Central and Eastern Europeans."

Mustard kept a memo of that meeting, and according to it the two men provoked and confronted each other for several hours. Mustard tried to convince Soros to turn the university into a research and policy institute at the hub of a network of socially engaged programs, involving education, economics, and health. Soros said he was quite willing to provide support for individuals in this area so they could do what they wanted but did not want to get into a situation where he would be seen as endorsing their research. Mustard said he should think of establishing powerful advisory boards with a strong indigenous leader to head the university. In his memo

Mustard wrote that Soros saw any advisory board for the university project as "window dressing," and "seemed apprehensive about the concept of a leader, mentioning he would prefer a bureaucrat." Mustard added, "I presume he runs the show because it is his money." At one point the two men talked about health projects. Soros, Mustard wrote, "wants to see immediate results and is thinking of providing a glass of milk a day for every school child in Hungary. He is willing to invest $5 million in this initiative."

He added, "If I am correct he will put money in but not leave anything with real capability to be permanent. He is too interested in short-term goals to lead to the development of something that would have the capability to create real strength for the future. The short-term outlook may be a reflection of his business personality."

All in all, Mustard's memo leaves the impression that he had little hope that Soros would absorb any of his own ideas. In fact, Mustard had made a strong impression. Over the next several years, Soros would establish his own network of think tanks and policy institutes, which were initially integrated into the CEU but soon became independent and relatively autonomous bodies within the Soros empire. There would be the Institute for Constitutional and Legislative Policy, which monitored the growth of law and due process and stimulated legal education in the post-Communist sphere; an Institute of Local Government and Public Service, which studied how decisions were made and carried out within cities, towns, and villages as new structures and patronage networks replaced Communist Party monopolies; there was an Ecological Center, a center encouraging civic education, and a center supporting independent media. A privatization project gathered and compiled data on the transition to market economies, and Soros also funded the Roma Rights Center, which studied and publicized the persecution of and discrimination against Gypsies.

During their far-ranging talks, Mustard mentioned that if Soros was intent on using education to change the mentality of a people, he would do better to focus on nursery schools than universities. Mustard's studies of brain development had convinced him that early childhood was a key period for extending intelligence, creativity, and health over a lifetime. Soros clearly took this to heart, perhaps because the idea conformed to his own formative experiences with Tivadar, who had introduced him at a very early age to his own life-shaping values of competition, survival, and the weight of unforeseen consequences.

Soros invited Mustard to Southampton, where two men continued their talks. Mustard soon realized that Soros had both heard and understood him at their first meeting. Meanwhile, Soros summoned Liz Lorant and told her to consult with Mustard and draw up a program to support nursery school education. Lorant met with experts who explained how Communist states had used early childhood training to inculcate the hierarchical values of the system. Toddlers were led to accept authority while curbing expressions of curiosity. Conformity was encouraged; individual initiative or divergence from the norm was suspect. Now, though Communism had crumbled, elements of the old mentality remained. Teachers, themselves products of Marxist training, were still promoting vertical views of society.

Lorant spoke with people who had framed the Head Start program, which in the 1970s had reformed early childhood education in the United States. Among other things, it had introduced the teachings of Jean Piaget, who emphasized learning by doing. In the end Lorant drew up a short proposal. "I think it was a half page. I remember I brought it to George while he was on the telephone talking about some business deal. I left it for him and went back in a little while. He said, 'Yes, that's it. I would like to spend around a hundred million on this.' " She says she was surprised by the great size of the figure.

That was the origin of what became known as "Step by Step," the Soros version of Head Start. It would take about eight years for Soros to reach his target expenditure, by which time the program had been introduced in some thirty countries, with some of the national governments incorporating aspects into their educational systems and assuming the costs. Under the program, new curricula were developed, teacher training institutes were established, new teaching materials were translated and printed, and pilot nurseries and kindergartens were established in cities and rural areas.

Given Mustard's original assumption that Soros was interested only in projects with instant results, it may be surprising that the actual impact of Step by Step is still highly debatable. "If you go into a Step by Step classroom, you'll have a big smile on your face," said Neier. "But the amount we have spent per child is very large and several questions arise. Are we succeeding in getting the educational systems in the countries where we have launched the programs to replicate them and make them available generally? And secondly, what kind of lasting impact will they have? Will the form of education provided in subsequent grades continue to support the approach that is embodied in Step by Step, programs that enhance the values of an open society? If that approach is not the same, you effectively lose a lot of the value of those programs. I don't know the answer to those questions. I suspect that in some countries the programs will take hold and they will have a significant impact, but that in the majority of countries they will not take hold and what we will have achieved is a Rolls-Royce early childhood education program for a relatively small number of children."

Neier added, however, that there were many within the foundation who "think it is the greatest thing we have ever done and who swear by it." Though skeptical himself, he realized that there was no way to test the premise, except to launch the full-scale program. Setting up a pilot project in one country and weighing the results there before moving elsewhere would have taken five or six years. "You couldn't do that if you are in a hurry like George. It is of course possible that it might not work, but you can't tell unless you do it. Ultimately George determined that we should try, and it was his $100 million."

Now that the money has been spent, Soros himself is also "unsure" about the project, realizing that its impact might not become fully evident until the toddlers who went through the process reach maturity. He does not, however, regret the expenditure. As Neier says, "It was the kind of risk that only a living donor could take." As for Mustard, who has remained in intermittent contact with Soros over the years, he long ago changed his mind about Soros's unwillingness to listen to suggestions or stay the course. "He has been my very best graduate student," says Mustard.

Another mentor Soros discovered as his philanthropic spending soared was Teodor Shanin, the sociology professor at University of Manchester. He had developed a program to bring young Russian scholars to the West for crash courses in sociology. The project received some funding from Soros and in time the two men met. "I liked him," said Shanin, a tall, bald, powerful figure who had survived World War II in Russia before making his way to fight for an Israeli state in Palestine. "I had the feeling that he was a man who despite his wealth had not quite achieved what he had wanted to achieve. We would meet and speak about Russia. He really wanted to know about the country. One reason I liked him was that he could not be explained by the simple Homo economicus formula since he was plainly doing things that were not maximizing his wealth. I was delighted to meet such a person, particularly since he was a financier. To me he became one of the goodies of the world. I was pleasantly surprised; there are many academics who are goodies, but I do not know of any other financier. Goodies as a group do not include many generals, ministers, or millionaires."

Soros read Shanin's book on Russian peasants, and the two men formed a close association. "There was a period that I was his favorite pair of eyes in Russia," said Shanin, adding that his discussions with Soros were often

quite sharp and argumentative. At some point in 1991, Shanin received a
long fax from Soros, in which Soros said he had come to believe that education in the social sciences and the humanities was one of the weakest
links in Russia's development, and he put forth a proposal to improve the
situation. His idea was to take large numbers of university instructors and
send them for a year's training in the West. To take their place, he suggested that scholars from Russia's research institutes fill in for the teachers
who had gone abroad. In contrast to the United States and Britain, where
teaching and research are interdependent functions, in Russia, as in
France, they are distinct, with teaching limited to the university and
research generally confined to institutes. Shanin vigorously criticized the
plan, saying that it would not work. The Russian teachers would not be
willing to leave their jobs, and, he was certain, even the best of the
researchers would make bad teachers. Soros wrote back that he found
Shanin's arguments powerful, but that he was still setting aside $5 mil-
lion to somehow deal with Russian social science and he wanted Shanin to
join him in talks with Russia's ministers of education and higher education. From those talks developed the Transformation of the Humanities
Program.

Under Shanin's direction competitions were organized in which
authors were encouraged to submit manuscripts for both textbooks and
monographs covering such long-overlooked fields as economics, psychology, anthropology, sociology, social linguistics, history, political science,
and art analysis. Committees were organized to select manuscripts for
publication, introducing previously unknown concepts of peer review;
within two years, four hundred titles were published. At the same time fifty
previously unavailable classics, including works of people like Hayek and
Popper, were translated into Russian, produced in large press runs, and
circulated to schools. According to Shanin these programs did much to
alter and improve Russian education in the transition period. He also contends that the seminar discussions and the strategic committees the project
sponsored helped propagate a culture of give-and-take and tolerance.

He himself caused a stir at one such meeting when a university librarian asked him whether pluralism meant that libraries should include even
Hitler's work. "Personally," answered Shanin, "I would refuse to attend or
work at any university whose library did not include *Mein Kampf.*"

The project blossomed at a time when the rest of the Russian foundation was foundering. An enthused Soros raised the budget from $5 million
to $20 million, and at one point he even recommended spending $100 million, a sum Shanin felt was unnecessary. A short time later, Soros confided

to Shanin that an audit had found serious corruption in the Russian foundation and that he was considering shutting down the entire Moscow operation. Shanin recalls that Soros asked him to take over the leadership and that he declined. In the next months, before Ekaterina Genieva took up the reins of the foundation, the ties between Soros and Shanin grew tense.

At one point Soros wanted the American auditors he had hired to look into Shanin's program. Shanin refused on the grounds that part of the program involved outlays by the Russian ministries, which he felt lay beyond the oversight of American auditors. "We had a row," said Shanin. "I do not react calmly when someone implies I am a thief." One day, while Shanin was leading a meeting of educators, he was called out to take a phone call from Soros. "He told me he was firing me because I had an 'impossible character.' "

Shanin left the project, though after some interruption, he continued to receive Soros funding for the crash courses he had been running in the West to train aspiring sociologists. In time the two men resumed contact and occasionally met. "But it was not the same," said Shanin. "When George wrote his book *Soros on Soros* in 1995 he sent me a copy with the inscription 'to inflexible Teodor.' "

"He lost me," said Shanin, who has since become the founder and rector of the Moscow School of Social and Economic Sciences, a part of Moscow University. "But that does not change my view of his contributions. He did more for Russia than any Russian minister, which is saying a great deal. He moved when there was no movement, and by himself, he was a hundred times better than all the American advisers."

As for Soros, he too looks back on the association with some nostalgia, pointing to it as an example of how his social relationships grew richer as he turned his attentions increasingly from business to philanthropy.

"The fact is that I am a loner, and being a loner can be lonely," says Soros. "When I was focusing on business I would not want to build friendships on moneymaking. I avoided it. I'd rather have Herbert Vilakazi, the South African, as a friend than fund managers. But when it came to the foundations, I thought it was worthwhile to engage. So the big difference between my business life and my foundation life is that in the latter I was genuinely engaged and because of that I had genuine human relations. I mean, though I was willing to discard people or draw the line or whatever, I still have warm human feelings for people like Shanin. At one point, in fact, I fired him, but that doesn't mean that I haven't remained fond of him. The difference with business was one, that on the human level I connected, and two, in terms of the objective, I felt that it was worth putting yourself out. When I was rushing around trying to arrange a loan for my fund in London, I was under such tension that I thought I might have a heart attack on the street. And I remember I said to myself: You know if I drop dead now, I'm really a loser. It wasn't worth it. Whereas, you know, if I got shot doing something in China or Russia, I wouldn't have that feeling."

The desire to change Russia's history and alter its culture has persisted, as he showed in October 1999, when he flew into Russia's westernmost city of Kaliningrad to turn the switch on his Internet project, which brought modern and irreversible communications to thirty-three regional universities. He also flew in seventy-five academics from the participating universities, stretching out from the Caucasus to Siberia.

He was then sixty-eight but he looked quite fit as he landed. His hair, once sandy, had grown whiter and he no longer wore it in a brush cut. His weight has stayed pretty much as it has been for decades. He said he needed more sleep than he once did but not much more. He continued to travel a great deal, although the style of voyages had changed markedly since the days when he could slip into cities as an unknown figure eager to meet dissidents. Now his arrivals were treated as news, and there was always an unavoidable ceremonial aspect.

Soros has grown used to his comforts, but he is an adaptable traveler, and as he showed on that short visit to Kaliningrad, he can readily do without them. Like his guests who had flown in from the far reaches of Russia, he checked into a small, minimally furnished room in the Commodore Hotel at the heart of the now dreary city that as Königsberg had been the capital of East Prussia and the home of Immanuel Kant. Today it is Russia's westernmost outpost, a spoil of war separated from the rest of Russia by portions of Lithuania and Belarus. It is a sad, neglected place that shelters the country's atrophying and largely mothballed Baltic fleet.

At the university there were speeches, and then Soros pushed a button that brought the last two Russian universities into the World Wide Web. It was not the sort of function that Soros enjoys, but he has come to accept such obligations and he dutifully went to Kaliningrad to affirm what had been accomplished there with his money. He flew in and flew out two days later. Watched closely by a seven-foot bodyguard who had been specially brought from Moscow, he took part in some perfunctory sightseeing, stopping at the city's dilapidated Teutonic church and at Kant's grave, which had been disturbed three times, most recently by Nazi scientists who measured the philosopher's skull with calipers to assure themselves of his purely Aryan origins.

Soros also visited a needle-exchange program his Russian foundation had sponsored in the city where the incidence of AIDS was the highest in Russia. In the rain, he spoke with a small group of addicts, who praised the program. He met the governor of Kaliningrad province, a heavyset, mugging, old-school politico named Leonid Gorbenko.

Just before he left, Soros was given a tour of the navy installation aboard a Russian vessel that had been renamed for him, presumably for the length of his visit. The base commander toasted the philanthropist, noting how strange it was that only several years earlier the base was one of those secret Soviet places off-limits to any foreigner and now he was sharing a meal there with an American capitalist. Another officer raised a tumbler of vodka and added that Soros was doing more to prepare people like himself for the future than the government he had served for so long. Soros ate, drank, and smiled but his mind seemed elsewhere. A lieutenant presented him with a scale model of the ship used to tour the harbor and with two Russian naval uniforms in children's sizes. Later Soros discreetly turned over the ship model to his huge bodyguard, but he took the uniforms with him as he rushed back to Bedford, where in two days' time Alexander would celebrate his bar mitzvah. But on the way home, he stopped for a few hours in Helsinki to meet with Martti Ahtisaari, the then president of Finland, and discuss ideas for encouraging regional economic cooperation in the Balkans once the conflicts there ended.

CHAPTER 23

RESCUE MISSIONS

IN THE YEARS when Soros was concentrating solely on accumulating wealth, he would often instruct his associates to "invest first and investigate later." In the nineties he adapted a similar impulsive approach to his philanthropy. This was evident when he committed his funds to the relatively undefined Step by Step program. A number of similarly impetuous interventions followed. None of these would prove larger, more imaginative, and more dramatic than two rescue operations that Soros precipitously decided to lead and finance in two fragmenting regions, the former Soviet Union and a dissolving Yugoslavia. The first of these was his attempt to save Soviet science. In the second Soros set out to save a militarily besieged Sarajevo and to preserve the imperiled notion of a multiethnic society that the city symbolized.

As usual, in both efforts he found extraordinary collaborators, two very different men who were consummate doers. The first of these was Alex Goldfarb, an anti-establishment Russian-born biologist, and the second, Fred Cuny, was a lusty Texan who specialized in disaster relief.

The story of the two triumphant achievements began late in 1992, when Soros became patron to both men, pulling the trigger on huge, daring efforts that lay far beyond the capabilities of other foundations and even of the most powerful governments. More than any of his other initiatives, these two undertakings demonstrate Soros's speculative vision and philanthropic courage.

The two efforts came to life at about the same time, but the science project got off to a quicker start. As in the case of the CEU and other Soros initiatives, it evolved through a refinement of ideas and false starts. Soros first met Goldfarb in 1986. At that point he was actually trying to meet Goldfarb's father, David, an eminent Russian geneticist and a leading "refusenik," who for seven years had fruitlessly sought to emigrate from Moscow. Finally, in October of 1986, Mikhail Gorbachev allowed the ailing elder Goldfarb to leave. He was flown out on the plane of Armand Hammer, the American oil magnate who had long done business with the Soviets, and was taken to Columbia Presbyterian Hospital in New York for treatment of diabetes. In a paralyzing snowstorm, Soros went to the hospital to ask whether the scientist would be willing to serve as chairman of the Russian foundation he was then considering. For his part, Goldfarb said he was too ill and too tired and suggested that Soros talk to his son. Alex Goldfarb was a microbiologist who had been associated with a group of Soviet dissidents before he was allowed to emigrate to Israel in 1975. He had studied there and in Germany and by 1986 he was running his own research project in genetics at Columbia University.

Alex is a stubborn, suspicious, and prickly man. He has scored his most important victories by standing up to bureaucrats, by demanding things, by refusing to compromise, and he has seldom shown gratitude. Few people within the Soros empire have nice things to say about him, and many describe him as "arrogant," "rude," and "cunning." Goldfarb says he is used to being described as impossible, and adds, "Probably I am impossible, but that is because I cannot work with bureaucrats." Soros says that "Alex is the ultimate conspirator and is very devious and difficult to control." With a touch of regret, he notes that it was Alex who had introduced him to Boris Berezovsky, the oligarch whom Soros believes to be Russia's most villainous figure, guilty of great crimes and capable of more. But before coming to this understanding Soros accepted Berezovsky's contribution of more than a million dollars to the Science Foundation, a donation brokered by Goldfarb. Soros offsets his reservations about Goldfarb with praise for him as a real doer, the man most responsible for helping him establish the International Science Foundation, which he considers perhaps his greatest single philanthropic achievement.

Following up on David Goldfarb's suggestion, Soros sought out Alex and continued to meet with him periodically. At one point he provided $60,000 so that Alex could bring three Soviet researchers to work in his lab in New York. After Soros launched his Russian foundation, Goldfarb offered his own criticism, contending that George had made a fundamental mistake by dealing with any Russian government officials. He also learned about financial irregularities at the Moscow foundation from his Russian friends and passed the information to Soros.

Late in 1990, Goldfarb ran into Soros in Moscow. Over a late dinner after the ballet, Goldfarb told Soros about a project he was running in Russia with $150,000 from the United States National Science Foundation. He complained that under the terms of this grant the money could only be used for equipment and supplies to aid research projects but not for salaries to maintain scientists. "At the time the scarcest commodity was cash," Goldfarb recalled. Researchers often went unpaid for five months or more. They maintained their ongoing experiments as best they could, but the pressure was driving many to look for work abroad or in other fields. Government figures would show that 14 percent of all science professionals left the field during 1990. With the government lacking the funds to provide salaries, which for senior scientists amounted to the equivalent of between $20 and $30 a month, the prospect of even greater defections was very likely.

Soros found Goldfarb's comments interesting. He knew that for decades the Soviet Union had produced preeminent scientists and pioneering research. He was also well aware that it was largely within the community of scientists that his own cherished values of openness and fallibility had endured through the years of dominating dogma, kept alive by people like Sakharov and the older Goldfarb.

That night Alex talked about how useful it would be to provide salary supplements to scientists, perhaps as a pilot project. He remembers how Soros responded: "Okay, good idea. Let's do it." Very quickly a program was set up to provide grants of $500 a year to each of some four thousand scientists. Included in the project were researchers at an academic community in Novosibirsk and a group of scientists involved in genetic biology. "It was very successful. People worked and were very happy," said Goldfarb. Overall, Soros was spending around $4 million in support of science in the former Soviet Union, and Goldfarb had no reason to think Soros was intending to do anything more in that vein.

In actuality, Soros was thinking a great deal about the entire question of subsidies and safety nets for Russia. On November 11, 1992, he published an op-ed article in the *Wall Street Journal* that ran under the headline "A Cold Cash Winter Proposal for Russia." In it Soros drew a "cataclysmic" scenario, saying that since the spring he had been envisioning a process of "disintegration without end." Citing the failure of economic reform and the puniness of Western aid, he anticipated a period of hyperinflation followed by an inevitable attempt to reintroduce price controls and the production quotas of the old planned economy. This, he contended, "would be resisted by the regions, leading to civil war."

In his bleak assessment Soros acknowledged a glimmer of hope: "The truth is that the situation could still be turned, but only if Western governments would put their heads together and use a little imagination." Specifically, he urged that Western countries intervene directly to provide social security to the most vulnerable of Russia's people. "They could provide minimum subsistence to the unemployed, the pensioners, and the needy." Soros calculated that these people without income needed no more than $6 a month to buy bread and other essentials at unsubsidized prices. An emergency program of this sort, he argued, would not only get people through the winter, it would ease the transition to a market economy because by avoiding the threat of pauperism, "it would remove the main obstacle to closing inefficient factories." Soros believed that the entire scheme could be put into effect with just $10 billion, and that figure would cover not simply Russia but all the successor states of the old Soviet Union. "This is a pittance," he wrote.

The idea was a logical extension of Soros's earlier ideas for massive Western assistance on the scale of the Marshall Plan to help shape societies emerging from dictatorship and Communism. Four years earlier, when he first proposed the notion, he had been greeted with ridicule. Now Soros was modifying that concept. It would cost less, involve a smaller area, and last a shorter time. But the benefits he envisioned would be extremely positive. First of all, people would not starve or freeze to death, inefficient enterprises could be closed for good, and support for reform policies would rise. Moreover, the rising appeal of the then-resurgent Communists would be curtailed, and the goodwill for the West in Russia generated by such intervention would bear fruit well into the future. Finally, a collective Western effort to get the people of Russia through the winter and over the hump of transition would provide the West with a cohesive sense of mission and strengthen the ideals of Western civilization as the new millennium approached.

Soros's article generated no serious discussion. The worst of the disasters he envisioned, widespread hunger and extensive violence, did not in fact materialize, and Soros would later acknowledge that he had failed to take account of the cushioning impact of Russia's reliance on barter. But Russia continued to face very hard times. Soros was upset that once again his ideas on public policy were being ignored, even though his wealth and his reputation were providing him with greater access. Indeed while Russia was growing markedly poorer, Soros was becoming richer and far better known. His article in the *Wall Street Journal* appeared only eighteen days after the British press had revealed him to be the "man who broke the Bank of England." While he could now address his suggestions to powerful elites, Western political figures still paid little heed to his proposals.

Alex Goldfarb remembers that soon after the *Journal* article appeared, Anthony Richter, one of Soros's aides at the New York foundation, called him. "He said that George wanted to give $100 million to Russian science and that he wanted to announce the program in Washington and could I come? It came completely out of the blue." Goldfarb went to Washington, where the announcement proved to be a dud, drawing virtually no press coverage when it was made at a meeting of low-level bureaucrats at the National Academy of Science. Typically, Soros had relied on inexperienced in-house staff to get the word out rather than hire the well-connected public relations specialists he disdained. Later that day Soros told Goldfarb that he wanted him to figure out how best to distribute the money. "George completely understood the situation. He was focused on the idea and on the tempo. He knew that the value of the dollar was very high, that for X amount of dollars you could get a lot. He understood perfectly that the Russian government was broke and that the sector of science was the only intellectual milieu that was worth saving." Soros left the details to Goldfarb.

Goldfarb had long been distrustful of the financial side of the Russian foundation; he insisted that the rescue mission be organized as its own independent entity. At his insistence the International Science Foundation (ISF) was legally based in New York, fully subject to oversight by Western accountants. By Christmas 1992, a Moscow staff was being recruited. By February an international board of scientific luminaries was assembled under the chairmanship of James Watson, the Nobel laureate who unlocked modern genetics as the co-discoverer of DNA.

Also in February, the ISF announced its first and in some ways most original initiative, the Emergency Grants Program. Its goal was to provide timely and immediate assistance to leading scientists, and it was kept as simple as possible. All scientists in the former Soviet Union who had published at least three articles in any of a long list of leading scientific journals during the previous five years would receive $500, or more than a year's pay. The idea, devised by Goldfarb, was enthusiastically approved by Soros. The money that the scientists were to receive so unexpectedly recalled Soros's own gift of fifty pounds from the Quakers when he had been an impoverished student at LSE. Receiving that check without any fuss or bother had at the time led him to conclude that this was the ideal way for charities to function. Now he was pleased to replicate and enlarge on his own experience.

In all, 20,763 people received such grants, or a number representing 18.5 percent of all researchers in national laboratories and universities in the former Soviet Union. Letters of gratitude flooded back, scientists writing that the unexpected funds had allowed them to sustain seriously imperiled lifelong work, or that they were now able to "live like normal people," or that they no longer needed to look for work as salesmen or mechanics. Semion Musher, a bushy-headed physicist, in 1999 recalled his own reaction eight years earlier upon learning he had received one of the grants. "Very simply I realized I was still a scientist, that I could do my work and feed my family." Musher, an enthusiastic and puckish figure, later received several other Soros grants as he gradually shifted his interests from physics to communications theory and the Internet. In the late nineties he became the executive director of yet another $100 million Soros program, the one that in October 1999 succeeded in connecting regional universities in Russia to the Internet. That project was a far more ambitious and expensive reflection of the old Xerox program, similarly using an irrevocable technology to foster the ideas of openness and free expression.

Soros's willingness to take on the Internet program was another consequence of his happy experiences with the ISF over its three-year lifespan. Once the $500 grants were delivered to the first batch of researchers, additional grants of $1,500 were disbursed to each of a thousand research teams chosen on the basis of the number of citations their work had attracted in scientific journals. Their parent institutions each received another $1,500 for equipment purchases. Long Term Research Grants, a competitive undertaking that among other things introduced Russia to an open system of soliciting proposals and their selection through peer review on the Western model, eventually consumed $80 million. In all there were 16,400 applications, and more than 50,000 specialists from many countries were enlisted to judge the entries. About one-fifth of the applications resulted in grants that ranged from $9,000 to $32,000. The ISF also issued travel grants that allowed scientists from the former Soviet Union to attend international conferences and enabled research facilities to renew thousands of lapsed subscriptions to international scientific journals.

Throughout the ISF's existence there was no scandal. There was, however, rivalry and skirmishing between the ISF and the Moscow foundation, some of whose officials resented Goldfarb's access to Soros and thought he was poaching on their turf. The foundation's work was also frequently misunderstood by Western media, which often wrongly portrayed Soros as being intent on keeping Russian scientists from being lured by rogue states like Iraq or North Korea. This was never a real consideration, but since Soros was hoping that Western nations would follow his lead and increase their own commitments to Russian science, such distortions were at times considered useful and it seemed pointless to challenge them. Much more menacing were the allegations raised from within Russia's political amalgam of former Communists and right-wing nationalists that periodically sought to depict the ISF as a CIA effort intended to gather scientific secrets. According to Alexander Yakovlev, Gorbachev's closest aide, reports from the KGB and its successor, the FSB, had persistently and amateurishly sought to plant and develop such lines. More than a year after the last grant was made, such charges were again raised in the Duma. During the parliamentary hearings that resulted, more than four hundred scientists submitted letters of praise for the ISF, and in the end the government expressed its formal gratitude to Soros while a parliamentary committee urged that the ISF experience be taken as a model in drafting a new law regarding nonprofit organizations. In 1997, Irina Dezhina of Moscow's Institute for the Economy in Transition published a study assessing the role of the ISF. She noted that ISF funding overwhelmed that of any other government or multinational donor and effectively provided greater support for science than did the Russian Foundation for Basic Research, the main conduit for government funds. She specifically credited the ISF with having stemmed the defections of young scientists, improving the morale of all scientists, providing them with international contacts, and establishing procedures for grant review that have persisted.

As for Soros, he remains quite pleased with the record. "I think it was a roaring success, particularly because it came to an end. The ISF did its job. It had clear objectives, transparent operations, and it delivered. You know that there were some thirty-five thousand people who got the money, and in a way I proved what I had been saying about what Western governments could have done with social security subsidies."

Soros's verdict on his Balkan efforts and the Sarajevo project is more ambiguous. "The mere fact that I had to spend $50 million on it is a defeat," he said of his Bosnian intervention. "I consider humanitarian spending as a defeat, in the sense that we failed to prevent disaster, that things deteriorated to the point where spending on humanitarian activities became necessary. I'm opposed to humanitarian spending. Generally, I think there is a time when CNN comes with the pictures, and people

become aroused, and by then it's too late. The Open Society Foundation
has got to be ten years ahead of the curve."

But, Soros acknowledged, there were positive elements in his Sarajevo
involvement. "The redeeming feature was Fred Cuny. Fred did something
fantastic. He really was a genius in disaster relief."

Cuny was an original, a big man in the way that John Wayne and Lyn-
don Johnson were big, both physically looming and emotionally expansive.
By the time Soros first heard of him, Cuny had already established a
worldwide reputation for organizing relief efforts for masses of dislocated
people. Since childhood he had yearned for a military career as a fighter
pilot, but to his shame he had washed out of a marine officer training program by failing to graduate from college on time. He consoled himself
with flying where he could, as a charter pilot and a crop duster. In 1969, he
joined other pilots bringing relief supplies to Biafra, the breakaway region
of Nigeria then fighting a losing war for independence. The airport at
Port Harcourt was a mess and Cuny offered to help the Red Cross organize it. He had a flair for such things and soon the airport was under control. He had found his calling.

Back home in Texas he founded the Intertect Relief and Reconstruction Corporation, specializing in international humanitarian aid. Working
under contracts from international organizations, charities, and governments, he carried out assignments at the scenes of earthquakes, cyclones,
floods, and wars on four continents. He coupled his engineering skills with
a military sense of organization as well as courage, compassion for the dis-
possessed, and a highly communicable Texas can-do confidence. Along the
way he gained the respect of both dovish do-gooders and hawkish generals. In his biography of Cuny, *The Man Who Tried to Save the World*, Scott
Anderson pointed out a number of epithets that Cuny accumulated,
among them "the Lone Ranger of Emergency Assistance" and "the Red
Adair of humanitarian relief," which referred to the globetrotting specialist who doused oil-field fires. But the nickname he liked best was "the Master of Disaster."

Cuny was particularly skilled at breaking through bureaucratic log-
jams, dealing with national bigshots, local satraps, and even brigands when
necessary to bring relief to suffering people. He was very innovative. For
example, at one point he realized that the rectilinear grids on which all
refugee camps were organized, in emulation of military units, were
tremendously dehumanizing. He redesigned the camps, organizing them
into smaller, circular subdivisions that he perceived to be more like villages

and thus more likely to discourage despair and stimulate initiative and energy.

In 1991, at the end of the Gulf War, Cuny was called upon to deal with one of his greatest challenges. About 400,000 Kurdish refugees from Iraq had streamed into the mountains of southern Turkey, fearful of the vengeful recriminations that a vanquished but still untoppled Saddam Hussein might order his Republican Guard to carry out against them. Without shelter, medicine, or much food, the panicked Kurds headed for the sanctuary of high ground in Turkey, where, as in Iraq, they were a historically suspect minority. As desolate roads turned into thronged avenues of escape and steep mountainsides filled with frightened families, Cuny was flown to Turkey to take over the de facto leadership of Operation Provide Comfort, the rescue mission led by the United States military.

Very quickly he realized the dangers. Morton Abramowitz, who was then the American ambassador to Turkey, remembers a meeting in April with Cuny and American military commanders. He did not know Cuny before that but "I certainly knew his reputation." Abramowitz recalled how the large Texan looked him in the eye and declared, "I've got a plan that'll get all the Kurds back home in two months." The ambassador did not hide his disbelief. "That's great, Fred, but you're full of crap. That'll never happen," he told him. Still he listened as Cuny explained his ideas. The people in the mountains had to be lured down quite soon. Their water supply was limited to the snow that was melting quickly, and once it was gone there would be overwhelming health problems. Interim camps should be built in the valleys quickly. At the same time the United States needed to establish and maintain a militarized security zone in northern Iraq; that would assure the frightened Kurds that they could return to their villages without threat. That, too, needed to be done speedily since it was important that the people return to their fields in time to plant for the year's harvest.

Abramowitz was impressed. Listening to Cuny, he thought maybe the man would succeed. He became more impressed as he watched Cuny in the subsequent weeks. In the end, he overshot his estimate of two months but only by two weeks, an incredible achievement that won him praise from political and military leaders. A looming humanitarian disaster had been avoided. The refugees came down from the precarious perches, settling briefly in the tent cities. Then, once Cuny started escorting influential elders to show them villages no longer under Iraqi military control, the exodus reversed itself into a swarm of homecoming.

More than a year later, in the late summer and fall of 1992, a new humanitarian crisis was building in the Balkans. George Soros was following the situation in Bosnia very closely. In New York he would discuss events and their likely consequences with the most prominent members of the Council on Foreign Relations, including its director, Leslie Gelb; Peter G. Peterson, a former commerce secretary in the Nixon Administration; and Henry Kissinger. He discussed Balkan issues, among other matters, with Madeleine Albright when she was United States ambassador to the United Nations and later when she became secretary of state. Richard Holbrooke always returned his calls. But his sources of information and advice were hardly limited to the United States. As Serb forces lay siege to Sarajevo, Soros was in daily touch with Sonia Licht in Belgrade. He would also call people like Geremek in Warsaw or Ernest Gellner, a world-renowned authority on nationalism who shared Soros's admiration for Popper. In 1993 Soros persuaded Gellner to leave his Cambridge University professorship to set up the Center for the Study of Nationalism within the CEU.

Soros also consulted regularly with Neier, who had been monitoring the Balkans for years and had his own network of human rights activists, professors, and journalists. These included people like Vetan Surroi, an editor of Albanian papers in Kosovo; Kostek Gebert, a Polish reporter with great expertise in the Balkans; Fatos Lubonja, an Albanian writer in Tirana who had spent seventeen years in prison under the bizarre rule of Enver Hoxha; and Gordana Jankovic, a Serbian who, with Soros's backing, had been providing support for independent newspapers and radio stations in the Balkans and throughout the entire formerly Communist region. Neier and Soros also had contacts with many of the most knowledgeable English-language writers dealing with contemporary Europe, among them Timothy Garton Ash, Mischa Glenny, Anna Husarska, Anatol Lieven, Noel Malcolm, Laura Silber, and Chuck Sudetic.

Inflamed by the ethnic separatist propaganda of Serbia's strongman Slobodan Milošević, his followers and guns were killing civilians and burning homes in several portions of a dissolving Yugoslavia beyond the borders of Serbia. As the West responded with rhetoric and porous economic sanctions, Serb militias, backed by Belgrade, were openly using policies of ethnic cleansing, terrorizing non-Serbs with pogroms, forcing people to leave land they had earmarked for a Greater Serbia. In areas of the old Yugoslav crazy quilt where other non-Serb nationalities prevailed, the tactics of ethnic cleansing were echoed by Croats, and at times by Bosnians.

Soros, who knew about ghettoes, terror, and deportations from personal experience, fully recognized what was at stake. For the first time since World War II, Europeans were once again using racist rationales to justify murder, rape, and expulsion.

The worst violence was occurring in Bosnia, that mountainous cauldron of nationalism where World War I had been ignited. Its capital, Sarajevo, long an example of multicultural co-existence and sophistication, was being fought over by nationalist sectarians. Soros, who months before had profited spectacularly on the pound, might have preferred to invest in long-term projects to deter such situations, but in a very personal way he felt he had to do something. Sarajevo, after all, lies just 250 miles south of Budapest. Beyond memory and sentiment, Soros was also aware that his foundation had the ability to act more quickly than governments or international agencies.

In December 1992, at about the same time that he was committing $100 million to save Russian science, Soros announced that he was donating $50 million to alleviate the suffering of the civilians in Bosnia. He claims that in addition to generally altruistic motives, he had an immediate and practical goal. "It was a political gesture, meant to bring in U.N. troops to protect the nongovernmental organizations." His thinking was that the money would attract NGOs to Sarajevo to carry out the programs he would finance. Their presence, in turn, would put pressure on Western governments to send U.N. peacekeeping troops to the city to protect the aid workers, thus internationalizing matters on the ground. "But that also didn't work; as a political gesture it was not successful," says Soros. He concedes, however, that as a project to help the people of Sarajevo, "it was a good one."

After announcing his gift, Soros and Neier organized a conference of experts to determine how the money should be spent. Among those invited was Abramowitz, who had retired from the State Department to head the Carnegie Endowment for International Peace. At the time, Abramowitz did not know Soros but would soon become one of his close advisers. At the meeting Abramowitz and Lionel Rosenblatt of Refugees International urged Soros to bring Cuny in on the plan. In January 1993, Cuny made his first visit to Sarajevo and brought back an activist agenda that greatly appealed to Soros. Rosenblatt said that until then the general feeling had been that Soros's money should be spread around to agencies that were already providing relief, such as the Red Cross. Cuny had a very different idea for the city, which then had some 350,000 residents. "To him the whole goal was to make Sarajevo work again," explained Rosenblatt.

"To make it a viable city—not a city of helpless victims, but a city of survivors, and to do that you had to involve the locals. Well, that's exactly the kind of thing that George Soros wanted to hear."

In March 1993, Cuny settled in Sarajevo, renting a house he would call the embassy of Texas. His projects consumed only a portion of the $50 million. With the help of Soros's funds, a daily newspaper kept functioning under mortar barrages and sniper fire. Radio networks were hooked up, movies were made, art exhibits were organized, several journals were produced—among them a highly sophisticated arty magazine called the *Phantom of Liberty*—and textbooks were printed and distributed.

Among this panoply of projects, Cuny's particular efforts stood out. In the years of siege, food was a constant problem. With the help of the International Rescue Committee, Cuny quickly organized a seed distribution scheme in which residents were encouraged to grow victory gardens in backyards and terraces. There was virtually no electricity, and Cuny, overseeing a team of engineers, was able to tap into a functioning grid beyond the city's limits to provide some power for key operations, notably the plasma unit in the hospital that functioned throughout the war, permitting teams of surgeons to operate around the clock.

Cooking and heating also presented problems. Electric stoves were useless without power, and Sarajevo is cold enough to have been the site of the Winter Olympics. There was, however, a pipeline that carried natural gas from Russia down from Hungary and Serbia, which desperate residents were trying to tap into with ineffective and often dangerous contraptions. Cuny had local engineers design a cheap but safe portable cooking and heating stove and found a factory to produce them. Meanwhile, he flew in fifteen miles of reinforced plastic tubing and organized 15,000 residents, many of them on the brink of despair and depression, to work in crews digging trenches for the tubing and running safe gas connections into apartments. It was all done as the city was being shelled. "An unbelievable project," Aryeh Neier called it.

Throughout his stay in Sarajevo, Cuny was highly visible. A gregarious figure, he attracted a following of friends and admirers. He deputized some to argue with local politicians or to charm and bribe Serb customs agents at the airport. He was always looking for those who had experience working on big projects. One of his finds was Faruk Slaki, the son of a Bosnian mother and an Albanian father, who had been born in Sarajevo, but who had worked as a civil engineer in the Middle East and Africa.

Slaki is now the superintendent of construction for the Soros-financed Albanian Educational Development Project, a large-scale effort that uses school construction as a tool for community organizing in Albania, a country where civil society had been virtually eradicated. For two years in the midst of war, he worked closely with Cuny in Sarajevo, and he still grows markedly excited when he talks of that time.

"Fred was exceptional," said Slaki in a Tirana restaurant, the neighbor of another eatery named the Pizzeria Soros, presumably a demonstration of its cosmopolitan hipness. "He had such energy. He knew everybody. He made everybody feel that we were part of something so important, that we were a team. I remember feeling that this was the one time in my life that I could do such things."

What they were doing was constructing a water-purifying facility that would restore the flow of water to the city's dry taps and thus prevent snipers from killing any more people. Since the siege started, Serbian sharpshooters on the high ground overlooking the city had killed scores of residents, mostly women, as they filled cans at several wells. The usually simple act of getting water had become a matter of life and death, and each new incident deeply humiliated the living.

Cuny came up with a plan. In peacetime, Sarajevo received its water from rivers that lay just beyond the city. The Serbs who now controlled these streams had blocked the intake valves that led to the reservoir, which remained within city limits. But there was another river, the Miljacka, that ran through the city proper. Its gently trickling water could theoretically quench the city's thirst if there were only some way to clean it—upstream the Miljacka was being polluted by sewage. Cuny ran tests and concluded that existing water-purification technology could remove the impurities. All he needed to do, he explained, was to bring a large and complex filtration plant into a blockaded city surrounded by hostile gunners, set it up as the enemy looked on, find electricity, pump water through the equipment into the reservoir, and let it flow into the long-unused taps to some 275,000 people.

In March 1993, he brought the idea to Soros. Soros knew quite well what was at stake, not only from the accounts he was hearing but from personal experience. Toward the end of World War II, when he was living with his father and brother in a single room on Vasar Street, his chore had been to fetch pails of water from a working tap in a basement several houses away as the German and Russian armies battled for the city. Soros readily approved the project.

Cuny then commissioned Freeman-Millican, a Dallas firm, to adapt its standard filtration module so that its three units could fit into a C-130 transport. He orchestrated a charm offensive aimed at the Serbian customs officers. He brought in a generator that would be able to pump the water up to the reservoir, and more miles of plastic pipe. He secured a tunnel on a mountain road, where the most critical of the three components would be housed beyond the reach of Serb artillery.

And miraculously it all seemed to be working out. In August 1993, a U.N. cargo plane landed and a waiting flatbed truck took the imported components past the mystified but accommodating customs men. In homage to Soros's commitment to cultural pluralism and to his own veneration of women, Cuny named the components Sanya, Jasnya, and Svetlana—Croat, Muslim, and Serb names, respectively. Over the next four months hundreds of workmen dug trenches to lay pipe. Meanwhile Cuny met and negotiated with representatives of dozens of overlapping bureaucracies, among them neighborhood toughs, Bosnian politicians, Serbian chieftains, United Nations officials, and foreign diplomats and army officers.

By January, the work was completed and the water was ready to flow. But there was still one obstacle. The Bosnian officials were refusing to authorize the operation, raising absurd objections. Cuny believed that much of this resistance stemmed from the corruption of politically influential figures who were running a lucrative business selling cans of water from municipal trucks. Soros had another, even more cynical explanation: "My theory is that they wanted more pictures of people being killed as they went for water. They needed the footage. But the fact is that they didn't allow us to turn it on. I wrote a letter to the authorities saying that unless you give me satisfaction, I'm going to go public."

The threat worked. By August 1994, thanks to Cuny and Soros, water flowed into the kitchens of Sarajevo. During the entire year of 1995 the filtration system provided the major source of water for the city. The project saved some lives and improved many more, but of equal importance, it also gave expression to Sarajevo's will to endure as an outpost of an open civilization.

Soros visited Sarajevo ten months before the water project was completed. "I was not eager to go. But I realized I was expected to; it was appropriate that I go and I didn't resist too much. I knew what it would be like. I've lived through a siege, so I didn't need to have that firsthand experience. But I did go and I was very impressed with what Cuny accomplished. Truly, I think that Fred probably did save Sarajevo. You know, water, gas, the seeds and gardening, running in the electric cable and the blood plasma unit. He really did it, and that, you know, is something."

CHAPTER 24

DEATH OF A HERO

THE SUCCESSES OF the ISF and the Sarajevo project had been flamboyant. International media had paid attention, and within the Soros network, the achievements of Goldfarb and Cuny took on the force of legend. Pride and confidence were bolstered as employees realized that Soros and the Open Society Institute were willing to take on challenges that sovereign states had found daunting. Then, with the inevitability of Greek tragedy, hubris beckoned. Flush with their triumph in Bosnia, Soros and Neier gave Cuny his head as he sought to accomplish more wonders, this time bringing aid to war-ravaged Chechnya. And there, in a remote hamlet, sometime in April 1995, Cuny and three colleagues were killed by Chechen rebels. Their deaths did not become known immediately. Their bodies have still not been found and the motives of the killers and the exact nature of Cuny's last mission remain matters of conjecture. But for years after Cuny and the three others disappeared, the episode kept tearing at the Open Society Institute.

Before the seizure of Cuny's party and their execution, none of Soros's workers had been killed. They had often been exposed to war, violence, and intimidation, but for the most part OSI and Soros had been lucky. In New York, OSI leaders were well aware of the risks to which people were exposed through their associations with the Soros foundations. In many countries workers and grantees had been hounded and harassed by state authorities. Some had lost their jobs, or faced legal actions, or even were forced to leave their homelands for exile. In such instances, Soros would provide help by securing legal representation or aiding in relocation, and arranging for scholarships or employment. When Bao Tong faced persecution, Soros had written to the highest level of China's leadership. But what could he or his foundation do after the heroic Master of Disaster went missing or when, sometime later, it turned out that he had been killed? Bao, after all, had never worked for Soros; he was a politician who took risks on his own. Cuny was in Chechnya for OSI.

Moreover, Cuny had been a bona fide hero both inside and outside the organization, with many influential admirers all over the world. Beyond his tragic disappearance and death, OSI was left with a huge, looming public relations problem. For before Cuny left on his final mission Alex Goldfarb had raised strong objections against it within the organization. He had categorically demanded that Cuny's mission to Chechnya be aborted and accused Cuny of behaving dangerously and provocatively. Those objections had been overridden, certainly by Neier and probably by Soros.

Goldfarb's outburst came after Cuny had been sent to Chechnya early in 1995 to gather ideas about what might be done to alleviate suffering there. Though Soros has repeatedly maintained that humanitarian aid is tantamount to an admission of failure, at that point he and all of OSI were riding high on what Cuny had accomplished in Sarajevo. As an object of Soros's often flighty enthusiasm, Cuny had become much more than a flavor of the month: he was seen as a real miracle worker. OSI quickly signed Cuny's company to eight contracts, including school reconstruction projects in several countries. Of these, it was the work in Chechnya that most intrigued Cuny. At the time, its capital, Grozny, was being shelled into rubble. Many refugees had staggered out while those left behind burrowed into mud cellars. Chechnya's claims to sovereignty were internationally unrecognized, and anyone trying to deliver aid on the ground had to work through or around the conflicting interests of Chechen militias and Russian authorities. The international relief agencies found very few openings to do their work. Soros realized that with Cuny's talents at his disposal he could once again act where others were either unable or fearful to involve themselves. He earmarked an initial $1 million for humanitarian aid in Chechnya.

Cuny spent January and February in the region, darting back and forth across the line of artillery with which Russia had encircled Grozny. He spoke with Russian commanding officers and wandered through the city's network of underground utility tunnels along with three-man rebel patrols that specialized in ambushing Russian armored carriers.

Cuny calculated that in three months of fighting, as many as 15,000 civilians and 5,000 Russian soldiers had been killed. He called Grozny "the worst place in the world." In an article for the *New York Review of Books* that he wrote after this exploratory trip, he contended that Russians were concentrating their firepower on a tiny group of fighters the Chechens had committed to the city while the overwhelming bulk of the Chechen forces were being maintained in the countryside. With their barrages the Russians were having little effect on their enemy while leveling the city and punishing civilians, most of whom happened to be ethnic Russians. He charged the Russians were pursuing "fruitless combat for an objective that is ultimately meaningless."

Cuny wrote that the Russians "continued to pound the rebel-held quarter with thousands of guns, rockets, and bombs day and night, and to waste the lives of their soldiers in capturing a few abandoned, bombed out buildings, so as to advance their lines each day. To put the intensity of firing in perspective, the highest level of firing recorded in Sarajevo was 3,500 heavy detonations per day. In Grozny in early February, a colleague of mine counted 4,000 detonations per hour."

The greatest brunt was being borne by the 30,000 mostly elderly, mostly Russian pensioners. "It is ironic that the Chechen rebels are fighting the Russian army to protect a section of the city full of Russian grandmothers," he wrote. In the middle of February, during a short ceasefire, Cuny drew up a plan to bring the civilians to safety. In a highly imaginative memo to Soros headquarters, he recommended that if the ceasefire could be extended, buses should be brought to the outskirts of Grozny. He emphasized that these should be very big, articulated buses of a Yugoslav type that would be more intimidating than conventional Russian buses and therefore would be more likely to be waved through vital checkpoints. The bus convoy, he wrote, should be accompanied by media representatives. "Outstanding public figures including members of Parliament, retired military officers, human rights groups, soldiers' mothers, and others should ride on the buses." Once in Grozny, the buses could start shuttling the civilians to refugee camps beyond Chechnya's borders. Cuny claimed he had an agreement in principle from Aslan Maskhadov, the Chechen commander in chief, and a similar acceptance from senior Russian officers on the ground.

It was the sort of idea for which Cuny was famous. It seemed like fantasy, but so had building a water-purifying plant in Sarajevo. Cuny's patrons at OSI headquarters in New York were excited by the memo and kept their fingers crossed, hoping that Cuny had come up with yet another humanitarian coup. He had not. Pavel Grachev, the Russian defense minister, who several months earlier had boastfully declared that the Chechen rebels could be wiped out in "two hours with one parachute division," now ruled there would be no more ceasefires, not even to save Russian grand-mothers.

Cuny returned to the United States, where he met with many govern-ment officials to describe what he had seen and learned. He briefed Strobe Talbott, the deputy secretary of state, and many others at the departments of State and Defense. He also met with old contacts at the CIA and the Defense Intelligence Agency. In between the rounds of conferences, Cuny worked on "Killing Chechnya," his article for the *New York Review of Books*. Normally, Cuny would have provided his information solely to the highly influential decisionmakers. At an earlier time, he might well have consid-ered an article like this one, with its critique of Russian policies and unmis-takable sympathy for the Chechen predicament, to be indiscreet. It would, after all, become readily available to the FSB and other organs of Russian intelligence. But in this instance, he defended writing the piece, saying that in the absence of significant international media coverage it was nec-essary for him to widely share what he had learned.

It was this article that set off Goldfarb's alarm. He obtained a copy before it was published and found it troubling and naïve. The two men had never gotten along. Now that Cuny was focusing on Chechnya, Goldfarb may have felt he was encroaching on his territory. For the ISF under Goldfarb's direction had been operating a mobile trauma unit based in Ingushetia, Chechnya's neighboring Russian republic, where most Che-chen refugees had massed. Goldfarb feared that Cuny's outspoken written criticism of the Russians might compromise his organization's staff and undermine its work. However, his complaints went beyond that. Goldfarb felt that Cuny, who was not an expert on Russia, was incapable of under-standing the depth of feeling that the Chechen conflict had aroused throughout the country. He did not think that Cuny had considered how the Russian enemies of the Soros foundation—the people in the FSB who had tried to portray his science project as a secret-stealing effort of the CIA, or the ultranationalists and the anti-Semites—would exploit his written views to attack the entire Soros operation in Russia. He felt that Cuny's swaggering boasts of connections to high-level figures in the American defense and intelligence communities were serious liabilities in a culture long sensitive to the threat of spies.

He wrote a memorandum to Neier citing his complaints and demand-ing that Cuny's project in Chechnya be terminated. Within OSI the memo touched off a rancorous debate. After heated arguments with Neier by telephone, Goldfarb flew to New York from Moscow to press his demands in person. At the time Cuny was also in New York, preparing to leave for Chechnya. Neier raised Goldfarb's issues with Cuny and Cuny offered his rebuttal. Neier, who regarded Goldfarb's manner as boorish, took Goldfarb's arguments seriously but ultimately backed Cuny. Soros certainly knew about the conflict, but kept in the background. In the past, both in business and philanthropy, he had often treated feuding rivals with parity. Some associates even claimed that he liked to maneuver his aides and subordinates into positions with overlapping authority, on the assumption that this would stimulate beneficial competition. In the end, according to several accounts from within OSI, Soros did finally side with Cuny and Neier. Goldfarb's intervention had created an unpleasant atmosphere at Soros headquarters, where the details were widely known. Goldfarb had gone behind a colleague's back to snipe at his project.

"I was apprehensive about him going back," Neier would tell Scott Anderson, Cuny's biographer. But Neier was swayed by Cuny's personality. As he would explain in a televised interview after Cuny's death, "I was more than hesitant to tell Fred what he could not do," adding that Cuny "was much my better in terms of the capacity to deal with these kinds of situations."

By the time spring arrived, Cuny was back in the Caucasus. On March 30, 1995, he spoke with Neier on a portable phone as he drove from Grozny to Ingushetia. He told Neier of three new ideas he wanted to implement: to set up a small radio station to be used by scattered family members seeking to find each other, to establish an epidemiological center to track cholera, and to design and distribute a tool kit to people so they could repair their damaged homes. Cuny said nothing about his immediate plans.

The next day, Cuny, accompanied by his translator, Galina Oleinik, and two doctors who worked for Goldfarb's trauma unit, Andrei Sereda and Sergei Makarov, set off from Sleptsovskaya in Ingushetia with their driver in an ambulance loaded with medical supplies. Where they were going and what their mission might have been has never been fully established. One line of speculation is that Cuny was trying to reach the Chechen commander, Maskhadov, whom he knew from his earlier stay, to arrange an interview with the Chechen president, Dzhokhar Dudayev. Anderson, who retraced this last journey, wrote that the only certainty is that the ambulance was headed for rebel-held territory.

For several days there was no word of Cuny. Then on April 4, the group's driver brought a note to Cuny's base in Ingushetia. It was written in Russian by Galina Oleinik, the translator, from Cuny's dictation. He noted that they had been delayed by bad weather, bad roads, and detours to avoid areas of fighting. He asked that calls be made to Moscow to cancel appointments he had for that week. It was not particularly alarming, but the note ended with a paragraph that the translator had tacked on in her own voice: "Everything above I wrote under Fred's dictation and now I would like to say something for myself. We as always have gotten into a mess. The situation doesn't depend on us. If we're not back in three days, shake everyone up."

As later inquiries were to show, the group had been stopped by at least one rebel group, but then allowed to go on. They were stopped again and held while their driver went back on foot to deliver the note. He then drove back to the village but could find no trace of his passengers.

It took a while for the reality to sink in, both at Soros headquarters and among Cuny's closest friends. This time Cuny was not late for his appointments because he was improvising some life-saving maneuver or visiting a girlfriend; this time he was missing in very ominous circumstances. Lionel Rosenblatt of Refugees International, who worked closely with Soros, raced off to Russia. A few days later Neier arrived in Moscow, where at a news conference with Rosenblatt he announced that Cuny was missing and appealed for information. Abramowitz generated pressure at the State Department. Thomas Pickering, the U.S. ambassador to Russia, who had been among those Cuny had briefed on Chechnya, set up a twelve-man task force at the embassy to monitor the case and twist arms in Russian ministries to find Cuny and the three others, or at least to learn what had happened to them. President Clinton was kept advised.

It was not until August 1996 that traces of Cuny and the three others were found in a bomb-damaged house in Stari-Atchkoi, a village to which the group had been taken after being stopped for the second time. There, wrapped inside a bloodstained skirt, were the passports and identity papers of Cuny, his translator, and the two doctors. With them was a letter scrawled by Oleinik to General Aslan Maskhadov. It said: "We tried to come to you, with the medicines and the two doctors we promised. Fred Cuny is with me, the American whom you already know—who came in order to hold the meeting which did not happen last time. I ask you to confirm that you are aware of us and our mission. With respect, Galina Oleinik." The note suggests that the group was headed to see Maskhadov, bringing an ambulance, medicine, and doctors. Were these goodwill offerings to induce a meeting with Dudayev? And if so, what did Cuny hope to achieve with such a meeting? The note, however, was never forwarded to the commander by the captors and no *laissez-passer* was forthcoming. Why the captors killed the four remains a mystery, though several theories have been advanced.

Some who have looked into the case believe the rebels simply wanted the ambulance, the medicine, and the money Cuny had with him. Others have pointed to a rumor campaign consciously orchestrated by Russian intelligence, which had used infiltrators to circulate flyers among Chechens portraying Cuny, the unmistakable tall Texan in cowboy boots, as an anti-Islamic spy. The rationale for this analysis was that elements in Russian intelligence, incensed by Cuny's pro-Chechen views, had manipulated Chechens into eliminating Cuny. Scott Anderson offers another explanation. He believes that Cuny and the others were killed on the orders of Dudayev after the group's roundabout journey brought their ambulance to the town of Bamut. The town was the site of allegedly empty missile silos that Dudayev wanted the Russians to think might still contain nuclear warheads. Anderson speculates that Dudayev, known for his paranoid outbursts, may well have assumed that Cuny had come to Bamut to learn what lay in the underground silos. Anderson writes that it could have been chance that brought the ambulance to Bamut, but he does not rule out the possibility that Cuny, having learned about the silos and their possible contents—perhaps during his discussions in Washington—had organized this last trip specifically to poke around Bamut. A colleague of Cuny's in relief work, Larry Hollingsworth, alluded to such a possibility on a *Frontline* television show about Cuny called "The Lost American." He said it was possible that "Fred's role was purely humanitarian and he was asked to do a little bit of moonlighting for Uncle Sam. But no one will ever know."

Cuny's death hung like a cloud over OSI. One consequence was that Neier soon relinquished responsibility for any of the programs in Russia, presumably to avoid contact with Goldfarb. There are a number of people at OSI who have not spoken to Goldfarb since then. The tensions were still apparent when, fourteen months after Cuny's documents were found, *Frontline* aired its program about Cuny's life and death. For the most part, it presented admiring recollections of Cuny from aid workers, diplomats, engineers, and military men who had worked with him all over the world. In the time since he disappeared, Cuny's reputation had grown. Before his death it was presumed the MacArthur Foundation had awarded him one of its genius grants.

But on the television program, Goldfarb offered a striking dissent. More than two years after sending his protesting memo, he was still angry at Cuny. Referring to Cuny's views of the Chechnyan conflict, the scientist declared: "He was very encouraged by the fact that he found that the military in the field didn't want this war. [He] didn't understand Russian military, didn't understand what this was about and he thought he had the formula to resolve the crisis."

At another point, Goldfarb said that Cuny "invented himself" in his boasts of his connections to high military figures and national security agencies in the United States. "He kind of liked to present himself that way and that was very dangerous. Russians generally are paranoid about spies."

He explained why he had raised his objections with Neier. "Fred was obviously carried away and there was no point talking to him. So I talked to people in New York. . . ."

Soros did not appear on the program, though it was he who had commissioned Cuny's work, nor had he rushed to Moscow to join in the news conference where Cuny's disappearance was announced. Five years later, when asked about Cuny, his reply was measured and laconic. "He was a genius, but in Chechnya I think he got carried away. He certainly transgressed his mission, and caused a fair amount of trouble for the foundation, because there were people in the Russian government who vouchsafed for him, so to speak. And he did have, I think, a delusion, or an ambition, to meet with the president, and arrange a settlement somehow. He went beyond his mandate, and, of course, got killed, but so did the interpreter and the two doctors." He did not comment on unproved suggestions that Cuny may have been "moonlighting." Soros seemed uncomfortable with the subject.

Soros had been cutting losses all his life. He could be sentimental but he could also walk away, from stocks and from people who had enriched him. He had always taken risks but he kept his eye on the exit. In wartime, he had learned from his father that the trick, the real trick, was to survive, to move on, to pursue new goals. Often that could be accomplished by confrontation, but sometimes, as with the case of Fred Cuny, it could mean walking away and not saying very much at all.

CHAPTER 25

HAVING IMPACT

IN CONNIE BRUCK'S profile of Soros that ran in *The New Yorker* in January 1995, at about the same time Cuny was first setting off for Chechnya, she quoted Morton Abramowitz as saying "People in government used to sort of dismiss George—this crazy guy interested in Hungary. He's now become a player—but it's very recent, a new phenomenon. He's untrained, idiosyncratic—he gets in there and does it, and he has no patience with government. As I frequently say about George, he's the only man in the U.S. who has his own foreign policy—and can implement it."

Becoming "a player" in international affairs, a role he would sometimes describe as that of a stateless statesman, marked another shift in Soros's priorities. In a sense it was a logical synthesis of his earlier personas: philosopher, financier, and philanthropist. But it significantly raised the stakes and left Soros more vulnerable.

For pursuing stateless statesmanship meant proscribing and advocating policies, favoring some leaders and chastising others, steps that would inevitably attract both controversy and enemies.

But as he first ventured into this realm in 1992, quite consciously exploiting his notoriety in England to present himself as a promoter of specific public policies, very few were ready to receive him. Perhaps no one openly laughed now, but the response of the professional policy experts was markedly cool. Like the trained philosophers who had dismissed Soros as a dilettante, many in the foreign policy establishment considered him an oversimplifying dabbler. Within the community of experts, the very idea of an independent and rich outsider backing causes with his own money was unsettling, evoking images of a busybody and kibitzer, or a bull in the china shop. It did not help that Soros was not rooted in any sphere where meddling in world affairs was considered appropriate, either academia, diplomacy, military life, or journalism. He did not view the world through the prism of government service and, despite his wealth, he was not a financier seeking profits, though there were always those who suspected that his altruism hid mercenary motives. He, of course, denied this and contended that his rationale was moral and principled. And such assertions also bothered at least some of the specialists who regarded the notion of foreign policies based solely on principles as being preposterously and even dangerously naïve. Among the most widely cited modern quotations on the subject is Henry Kissinger's paraphrase of Cardinal Richelieu's maxim "governments have no principles, only interests." Implicit in the aphorism is the idea that foreign policy ought be a matter for governments alone.

Bill Maynes, now the head of the Eurasia Fund, recalls the opposition that surfaced when he first nominated Soros for membership in the Council on Foreign Relations, the inner sanctum of the American foreign policy establishment. "Despite his work in human rights and his record in philanthropy, there was considerable sentiment against him." Maynes said that much of this was summed up by the view that Soros was "just another rich man."

Slowly such attitudes changed. Information about Soros's projects spread. It also became apparent that he was writing his own material and that at the increasing number of conferences and lectures that he attended, he asked probing questions and offered useful comments without the prompting of advisers. Just another rich man would not be doing that. "Eventually he was accepted by the council but it took quite a long time," said Maynes.

Kissinger himself came to appreciate Soros. "I once said publicly that I take George Soros seriously as a financier but I don't take him seriously as a political expert, but then he decided he would shift and make political work the focus and he became a worse financier." Kissinger said that when he first met Soros, he had been concentrating on human rights. "In those days he was just an agitator at meetings."

But according to the former secretary of state Soros has grown significantly. "Generally a characteristic of rich people is that they are about as good at foreign policy as I am at making money. George Soros is much better than that. Most of the time I disagree with his conclusions, but they are not trivial conclusions. They are serious positions with which I happen to disagree. Like all dilettantes he thinks problems are easier than I think them to be, but on the other hand, you don't get great changes made unless somebody thinks they are easier to achieve than the experts. So I have great respect for George Soros and I think on the whole he has stood for good things and he has done good things even in areas where he oversimplifies. His input is important and I respect and admire him."

By 1995, Soros was getting his phone calls returned very quickly. He noted that many rich people contributed to political parties in order to get this sort of access but that he made relatively few political donations and they were usually modest. "Even so, people tend to answer my calls," he said.

That year he appointed John Fox, a former State Department officer, to serve as an unofficial "ambassador" for the Open Society Institute, working out of an office in Washington. Fox steered foreign visitors from Soros's more favored nations, Ukraine among them, to the appropriate American officials or helpful contacts at the International Monetary Fund and the World Bank, as he also tracked key policy initiatives through government labyrinths, pushing for or against some of them, in accordance with Soros's views.

In Morton Abramowitz and Mark Malloch Brown, Soros acquired two very savvy allies and advisers. Before Abramowitz became the head of the Carnegie Endowment for International Peace, he had been a shortlisted candidate for CIA director. He was very well connected. From his office at the World Bank, Malloch Brown was in regular contact with many government leaders and senior executives of the largest international organizations. Both men often consulted with Soros and members of the Open Society board in New York.

As the twentieth century entered its final months, Soros reflected about his maturation into "a player," recalling the messianic ideals that had gripped him since childhood. "I have had these illusions, or perhaps delusions, of grandeur and they have driven me. And, basically, I have no regrets. Because, first of all, they've made my life rather interesting. I mean, it was a great adventure that wouldn't have been available otherwise. It was such a fantastic adventure that, if I had more time to savor it, I could have made even more of it, but things happened so fast that I didn't even notice them, because the next thing was coming. So it's a great adventure, pushing to the limits of the possible, and also acting on this desire to be on the side of the good rather than the bad, which I think comes from my father."

He continued in an outburst of confessional candor: "Yes, I do have a foreign policy, and now I have it more consciously. My goal is to become the conscience of the world." The words sounded less pompous in conversation than they appear in print. Perhaps the hubris was modulated by a wink or smile. "When I talk about being engaged in policy issues, that's really what I mean. I think that creating a global open society should be our goal. There ought to be a development strategy that is clearly guided by the striving for an open society. And that is what is missing. I mean there is plenty of money for waging war, and there is absolutely no money for waging peace." He explained that though his foundations have achieved a great deal, larger looming challenges could not be confronted without the involvement of major sovereign states and international agencies, and that he continued to be increasingly eager to propel such powers and their leaders toward his goals. "So that's what I'm all about. I am a kind of nut who wants to have impact."

Once more he spoke of how ten years earlier, in 1989, he had desperately been looking "for something where I'd make my mark; I wanted to be included in the councils." Then his ideas were laughed at but "through a process of selection, trial and error, I built up connections. I have empowered other people whom I have come to trust and it is now true that I do have access. It is a 180-degree change from the beginning, when I had absolutely no access, when I couldn't get to Margaret Thatcher, couldn't get through to Bush."

His approach has remained the same from the start. When in the early eighties he wanted to find out about Russia and the Helsinki movement he found Ed Kline and through him made contact with Sakharov. When China began to interest him he had read a book and invited Liang, its author, to lunch. When he began to see the possibilities raised by Solidarity in Poland or Charta 77 in Czechoslovakia, he sought out people who were involved. For a while the direct approach did not work as well with people in power as it did with needier dissidents. Thatcher and Bush had rebuffed his initiatives, but that was before Black Wednesday. Afterward, even the powerful were willing to meet and listen.

One way he has increasingly sought to influence public opinion is through his writing. As a child he imagined himself a journalist or historian, and he has always written, whether philosophical works or economic analysis. But by the early nineties he began focusing on essays and op-ed pieces that went beyond economic subjects. His tone became less theoretical as he offered specific policy recommendations for various parts of the planet. The scale of his interests was evident in the headlines on a sampling of his contributions: "Joint Ventures: A Way to Make Perestroika Work" (*Financial Times*, 1988), "How to Help Poland" (*Washington Post*, 1989), "Can the Soviet Economy Be Saved?—Not without U.S. Aid" (*Wall Street Journal*, 1990), "The Situation in Russia Has Ceased to Concern Only Russians" (*Izvestia*, 1992), "Help Macedonia and Pressure Greece If Necessary" (*International Herald Tribune*, 1994), "Postpone the Bosnian Elections" (*Wall Street Journal*, 1996), "Immigrants' Burden" (*New York Times*, 1996), "The Capitalist Threat" (*Atlantic Monthly*, 1997), and "The Drug War Cannot Be Won" (*Washington Post*, 1997).

In these Soros was expressing positions he has backed with his philanthropy. When he wrote of the need to support Russia and Poland in their economic transitions, Soros was doing just that by assembling international teams of economic specialists to serve as consultants. He supported similar efforts in Ukraine, lobbying in support of the largest new country to appear on the map of Europe as a result of the convulsions of 1989.

But, as usual, it was Russia that preoccupied Soros. In 1990 he managed to obtain the agreement of the feuding Gorbachev and Yeltsin to have a team of preeminent economists advise on a pending Soviet proposal to restructure the economy, which became known as the Shatalin plan. Soros brought in people like Roman Prodi, who had headed Italy's conglomerate of state-owned companies, and Guillermo de la Dehasa, the Spanish official who oversaw his country's privatization program after Franco's death, as well as economists from Hungary, Israel, the United States, the IMF, and the World Bank. Soros flew them to Moscow where they shuttled between the Shatalin plan's designers, who were hoping to redistribute political power away from the center to the regions, and a rival group intent on scuttling any such program. Later Soros flew the Russian Shatalin proponents to Washington for meetings with senior officials of the World Bank and the IMF. He exchanged memos with Yeltsin and Gorbachev and worked most closely with Grigory Yavlinsky, the driving force behind the plan and the man many considered to be Russia's foremost democrat. Unfortunately for Soros and the Shatalin plan, and more importantly for Russia, even Yavlinsky's talents and boldness proved insufficient in the face of politicians and bureaucrats who were reluctant to prune the branches of centralized power on which they had long roosted.

Disheartening as it was, Soros's involvement with the Shatalin plan proved to be a significant step in his pursuit of stateless statesmanship. Yavlinsky would later write Soros, saying, "You have done many wonderful things for my country—more than anyone else." Soros had gone far beyond funding foreign foundations as they searched for and implemented relatively limited goals. In those instances Soros had cautiously distanced himself from various projects. He was backing men and women whose priorities and ideas he found interesting, but he carefully emphasized that they were not necessarily his ideas. Now that distinction was becoming blurred. He was increasingly prepared to openly support some leaders as friends, oppose others as enemies, and, at times, turn his back on those he supported as his view of them changed.

His politics were becoming more candidly personal. There was, for example, an instance in 1992 when several right-wing commentators associated with Hungary's then ruling party, the Hungarian Democratic Forum, attacked Soros in party newspapers using anti-Semitic phrases and innuendo. Soros has never worn his Jewishness or his survivor status on his sleeve, but he was alarmed by the resurgence of ultranationalism in several parts of Europe. He wrote an angry letter to Hungary's prime minister Jozsef Antall and then submitted a copy to the *New York Times,* which published it as an op-ed under the headline "Termites Are Devouring Hungary." He wrote: "Leading members of your party have accused me of nothing less than taking part in an international anti-Hungarian conspiracy whose origins can be traced to Israel and whose goal is to extinguish the Hungarian people's national spirit, making them susceptible to foreign domination." He said that the writers of the articles, among them Istvan Csurka, a prominent playwright, were seeking to establish a closed society under the guise of nationalism. "In order for them to succeed, they need first and foremost an enemy against which they can mobilize an entire nation, and if there isn't an enemy about, they must invent one. This is an extremely dangerous process whose ultimate consequences we have already experienced in the Nazi era, and can once again witness in the former Yugoslavia."

That same year, Soros traveled to the new country of Macedonia, which was then the object of propaganda attacks by its larger neighbors, notably Greece, which claimed that by usurping the very name of Macedonia from ancient Greek territory the new state signaled its covetous and irredentist designs. Soros knew little about the situation when he arrived, but he quickly determined that given the outside and inside pressures, the Macedonian government of Kiro Gligorov was at least rhetorically more supportive of pluralism and multiethnic power sharing than other countries in the region. Impulsively he gave Gligorov a critical $25 million loan to help tide the government over a tense and difficult period. Some years later, when he became convinced that Gligorev was failing to protect the

country's Albanian minority, he openly criticized him. He did the same
with Leonid Kuchma, the president of Ukraine, with whom he had earlier
cooperated closely on many projects, including one in which Soros was
paying to retrain more than 70,000 midlevel Ukrainian military officers for
civilian jobs in a privatizing economy. That cooperation did not prevent
Soros from attacking Kuchma for his 1999 re-election campaign. Immediately after Kuchma was voted in, Soros dashed off an op-ed article for the
Washington Post, charging his erstwhile Ukrainian ally with having taken a
page from Yeltsin's playbook by providing favors and resources to his own
country's clubby oligarchs in exchange for the support of their newspapers
and television stations. Soros wrote that supportive Western governments
should put the re-elected president on notice that they would no longer
tolerate the status quo.

In 1995, as Soros was increasingly concentrating on foreign policy
issues, he wrote to all his foundations urging them to pare down their
expenditures and to focus on eventual exit strategies, for at least some of
their programs. He set the year 2010 as a target date for winding up the
network. If he was still alive then, he would be eighty years old. He had
never endowed any of the foundations, and though he emphasized that he
was committed to maintaining them for the next fifteen years, he hoped
their leaders would begin looking for alternate partners and new donors
for their programs. Suddenly people in the foundations were looking for
what they called "OPM," or other people's money. By 1995 Soros was also
shifting some of his spending to the United States, where he was becoming
concerned with issues like education, attitudes toward death, and the pernicious effects of anti-drug laws.

The warnings of eventually diminished funding, the rise of the U.S.
foundations, Soros's continued admonishments against escalating bureaucracy, and the ensuing loss of mission aroused disappointment and dismay
within many of the older foundations. Nor were many of these old-timers
placated by Soros's assurances that he was still eager to start new foundations in places like Africa. At the annual gathering of all the national foundations in Budapest in 1996—the so-called Jamboree, which was meant to
foster synergy—a presentation about the new American foundation's programs drew fewer than 10 of the 250 delegates. Among those were many
who interpreted Soros's warnings about reduced funding simply as proof
that their patron's interest, which had been so great during the period of
transitional turmoil and promise, was now flagging as relative stability
took hold. George, they told each other, was getting bored with them and
looking elsewhere for excitement.

They may have overstated the case, but they were not wrong. Stateless statesmanship offered challenges and excitement. For example, in the spring of 1996, the Hague Tribunal investigating war crimes in Yugoslavia found itself at a critical impasse. Richard Goldstone, the South African jurist, was about to conclude his term as chief prosecutor, but there were many who felt that the tribunal's work had reached a highly sensitive stage and that its credibility and work would be endangered unless his departure could be postponed until the fall. Goldstone had earlier promised Nelson Mandela that he would preside over the final stage of the drafting of South Africa's constitution, which was taking place that summer. In the end, Soros quietly intervened to provide Goldstone with a chartered plane so he could shuttle between the Netherlands and South Africa and tend to his double duties.

There were other similar moments. For instance, two years later, in 1998, Mandela wrote to Soros, this time asking how South Africa should deal with currency speculators like Soros himself. Writing back on September 21, 1998, Soros said it was always futile to defend any indefensible exchange rates and instead urged the South African leader to avoid excessive short-term debt and to maintain stringent supervision over local banks.

Earlier that year Soros had flown to Seoul, where in order to avoid the press he registered in a hotel under the name of James Brown. He then spent several days with South Korea's president-elect, Kim Dae Jung, a once-imprisoned dissident, advising him on how to avoid the economic dangers then looming in much of Asia.

On November 21, 1998, Soros accompanied Hillary Clinton on an official trip to Haiti, introducing her to members of his foundation on the island. He also prevailed on Mrs. Clinton to host a White House meeting on halting the spread of multi-drug-resistant tuberculosis, another campaign in which OSI has been deeply involved.

Just two months earlier, on September 15, 1998, he had testified extensively before the House banking committee on the dangers facing the global economy. In remarks that he later greatly expanded into a book, *The Crisis of Global Capitalism*, he contended that the meltdown of the Russian banking system and the failure of the West to intervene, along with the Asian financial crisis touched off by Thailand's economic collapse, posed ominous challenges for the world economy and global capitalism. Once again he pointed out the need to enlarge the almost fifty-year-old Bretton Woods financial institutions that his hero, Keynes, had helped to conceive. In the winter of 2000, in another book, *Open Society: Reforming Global Cap-*

italism, he would recant some of his earlier dire predictions of collapse, saying he had gone overboard. Reveling in self-criticism and in his Popperian obligation to correct himself, he asserted his right to be wrong and told the *New York Times,* "I goofed."

He did not, however, bite his tongue. When in the early spring of 1999 the Albanian population of Kosovo was set in flight by Serbian forces, Soros urged forceful internationalized military responses, pointing out the dangers of acquiescence or appeasement, as he had done earlier during the Bosnian conflict. Since then, he had become a strong proponent of the "stability pact," an idea that would provide assistance to those Balkan states willing to adopt democratic practices and eventually usher them into a Europe that appeared to be consolidating around the euro. To that end Soros has been involved with scores of other players, including Javier Solana, the NATO secretary general; Martti Ahtisaari, the influential former president of Finland; and Paddy Ashdown, the leader of Britain's Liberal Democratic Party. In another initiative, Soros has strongly backed the formation of an international organization of democratic states, and delivered the welcoming address at the group's first meeting in Warsaw during the summer of 2000.

Clearly Soros has gained the influence he craved. But as he became more outspoken, he also gained enemies. "I have always taken sides, I've never been neutral," he says. "I have a desire to push to the limit, but to not go over the limit. It's a delicate balance. It's my survival instinct. Occasionally I do go over the limit, but then I pull myself back, and so far, I've been able to avoid falling on my face. Actually I have been very lucky in my enemies."

He has, in fact, crossed rhetorical swords with a sizable portion of the world's autocrats, dictators, and despots. Before Milošević was finally toppled by chanting throngs in Belgrade, he repeatedly sought to have Soros's foundation evicted, angered by its benefactor's support for the few outlets of independent media that had managed to survive. In Croatia, Franjo Tudjman, the late nationalistic strongman, similarly tried to punish the Soros foundation in Zagreb by bringing suits against the foundation's grantees. In Belarus, Aleksandr Lukashenka, the dictatorial and unreconstructed Communist leader, succeeded in forcing Soros to shut his foundation in Minsk by threatening criminal investigations against its local staff. In Slovakia, the former political boss, Vladimir Meciar, endorsed a press campaign that sought to smear Soros with the same sort of anti-Semitic slurs that had been used in Hungary. In Russia, Soros has criticized many powerful figures, including Boris Berezovsky and members of Yeltsin's family, and has in turn been criticized and assailed in media attacks. In the United States he has also come under attack, most notably from leaders of the country's "war on drugs," who deplore Soros's arguments for dealing with narcotics as a public health, rather than a criminal, problem and have attacked him for supporting referendum campaigns in five states where citizens have voted to legalize the use of marijuana for medicinal purposes.

But so far, Soros's most dramatic confrontation has been with the long-time president of Malaysia, Dr. Mohamed Mahathir. That showdown took place in late September 1997 in Hong Kong, but it had been building throughout the summer as Asian economies went into a nosedive. Malaysia, which under Mahathir's rule had seen per-capita income grow from several hundred dollars a year to $5,000 and which was the home of the world's tallest building, was suddenly being swamped. Within two months the Malaysian ringgit plunged by 20 percent against the dollar, the Malaysian stock market crashed, and the country's banking system showed signs of incapacity. Mahathir responded to the challenges by blaming the international financial system for the Asian crisis and his own country's difficulties. If he had stopped there, Soros might well have agreed with him. As Soros was to write of the Asian collapse in *The Crisis of Global Capitalism*, "It is difficult to escape the conclusion that the international financial system itself constituted the main ingredient in the meltdown process." In congressional testimony he declared that the financial markets had behaved like wrecking balls swinging from one country to another in irrational overreactions.

But Mahathir had not stopped there. Instead he pointed a blaming finger directly at currency speculators, notably at Jewish traders, and specifically at Soros. Through July and August he kept lobbing rhetorical grenades at Soros. "We have definite information that he is involved," said Mahathir of Soros's alleged role in bringing down the value of the ringgit and setting off a flight of investment capital. "He is not the only one but he started it. He has wiped out billions from our economy." That was soon followed by Mahathir's observation that "all these countries have spent forty years trying to build up their economy and a moron like Mr. Soros comes along with a lot of money." The ethnic slurs came next. First the Malaysian leader wondered aloud "whether the [Michael] Milkens and [Ivan] Boeskys and Soroses of the future will be more considerate than the present models," linking Soros to two notorious financiers and felons who like him happen to be Jewish. Then, in another interview, he declared, "The Jews are not happy to see the Muslims progress. The Jews robbed the Palestinians of everything, but in Malaysia they could not do so, hence they do this, depress the ringgit." And, when his comments brought accusations of anti-Semitism, he kept the controversy raging by responding, "We are not anti-Semitic. The Arabs are also a Semitic people, but when a person of Jewish origin does this kind of thing," meaning currency speculation, "the effect is the same as when a Muslim carries out something that is akin to terrorism."

Mahathir perceived another, more specific motive for the actions Soros had allegedly taken against his country. He pointed out that Soros had actively backed Burma's repressed democracy movement and its Nobel Peace Prize–winning leader, Daw Aung San Suu Kyi, while opposing those who had nullified her party's electoral victory and kept her under house arrest—the military officers of the State Law and Order Restoration Council (SLORC) who ruled the country they had renamed Myanmar. Earlier that year, Soros, along with the United States government, sought to dissuade the Association of Southeast Asian countries (ASEAN) from accepting Myanmar as a member. At the group's annual meeting, held in Kuala Lumpur, Malaysia's capital, with Malaysia acting as chairman, Myanmar and SLORC were seated. Mahathir dismissed the reservations about the country's poor human rights record that had been raised by Soros and others and went so far as to urge that the United Nations Declaration on Human Rights be repudiated since the standards it set, which Soros promoted, were designed in the West and served to inhibit economic development in countries with a colonial past. Now, as Malaysia's and Asia's crisis deepened, he suggested that Soros had triggered the crisis out of vengeance over Myanmar.

When reporters called Soros's office for comment, he called the charges absurd. He had not instigated the crisis, and, though he had supported Burma's pro-democracy movement through the Burma Project that he financed, he was not seeking to use the market to avenge ASEAN's acceptance of the country. In fact, at the time Mahathir was accusing him of driving down the Malaysian currency, the Quantum Fund was buying ringgits, on the mistaken assumption that the currency was bottoming out. Like other speculators, Soros had been surprised by the extent of the Asian decline, and, far from having set off the wave, his people were scrambling to catch it. What bothered Soros most were allegations that he was mixing his politics with his business. He had always tried to keep the two spheres distinct. He contended that his philanthropy and his statesmanship were driven by moral criteria, while his financial undertakings were amoral. Soros said that in seeking to make money he obeyed existing rules and regulations, even though he might agree that some of those rules needed to be changed in the interest of fairness.

Soros was aware that in September the World Bank and IMF were to hold a major joint meeting in Hong Kong. Mahathir would be there, along with other Asian leaders, finance ministers, and economists. With the help of Malloch Brown, Soros obtained an invitation to speak. Mahathir spoke on September 20. He did not mention Soros by name, but no one in the audience was left unaware whom he had in mind when he spoke of those "whose wealth must come from impoverishing others." He went on: "I am saying that currency trading is unnecessary, unproductive, and totally immoral. It should be stopped. It should be made illegal. We don't need currency trading."

The next evening belonged to Soros, who insisted that any effort to limit the free movement of capital, a major tenet of liberal economics that made currency speculations both possible and inevitable, would choke off investments and prove far more harmful than the practices that Mahathir sought to eliminate. "Dr. Mahathir's suggestion yesterday to ban currency trading is so inappropriate that it does not deserve serious consideration. Interfering with the convertibility of capital at a moment like this is a recipe for disaster. Dr. Mahathir is a menace to his own country."

Then Soros carried forth his attack with plain and undiplomatic language, declaring that Mahathir, and not the world economy, was Malaysia's main problem: "He is using me as a scapegoat to cover up his own failure. He is playing to a domestic audience, and couldn't get away with it if he and his ideas were subject to the discipline of an independent media inside Malaysia."

Almost a year after his duel with Mahathir, Soros offered another economic prescription that also aroused a serious contretemps. This time it was Russia that was at issue. Starting in the last week of July 1998, Russia's financial markets went into an accelerating tailspin, reversing gleeful proclamations that an IMF rescue mission had taken hold. Three weeks later, on August 13, Soros wrote a letter to the *Financial Times* suggesting a ruble devaluation of 15 to 25 percent to be followed by the creation of a currency board that would fix the ruble rate to that of the dollar, an emergency step that in some limited measure echoed Mahathir's rejection of free floating rates. He called for an emergency infusion of $15 billion from the major industrial countries to augment Russian and IMF reserves and wrote that "unfortunately, international financial authorities do not appreciate the urgency of the situation." Soros concluded by warning that the only alternatives to his proposal would be default or hyperinflation and that either would have devastating financial and political consequences.

The next day, the Russian markets went into meltdown, leading one analyst to write in the *Financial Times* that Soros's prophecy had "appeared self-fulfilling." There was a storm of protest. Soros may have thought he was speaking out as a well-informed and neutral observer, as a stateless statesman perhaps, but as his critics were quick to point out, for many his words were simply the ringing of an alarm bell by the man who moved markets: they accelerated a stampede for the exits. Moreover, in Russia there were those who were happy to have an outsider to blame for precipitating what by then was an irreversible development. There were also suggestions that Soros's funds would have benefited from the devaluation he had recommended. The day after his letter ran in the *Financial Times*, Soros released a statement: "The turmoil in Russian financial markets is not due to anything I said or did. We have no short position in the ruble and have no intention of shorting the currency. In fact, our portfolio would be hurt by any devaluation." The next day he issued a longer statement branding as false a TASS article claiming unprecedented trading by the Soros fund in London. He declared, "I have been deeply hurt by the attempts to blame me for yesterday's events. I am trying to help Russia and will continue to do so. I shall not abandon my foundation in spite of the malicious attacks on me."

Soros says that he has since learned that the Russian central bank had deliberately targeted his letter to deflect attention from themselves. "But that doesn't matter," he says. "The fact is, it is claimed that the letter had a negative impact, which shows that actions have unintended consequences and how dangerous it is to do something."

He had obviously been chastened by the reactions to his letter and its interventionist proposals. In his writings since then, he has repeatedly acknowledged that his predictions about a meltdown of the Russian economy in 1998 and its impact on global capitalism were erroneous.

But he was not truly embarrassed. Intellectually, he has always reserved the right to be wrong. He admits to his mistakes regularly, some would say even enthusiastically. He concedes, however, that it was much easier to own up to his mistakes when he was more anonymous and relatively few people knew who he was. But, of course, the *Financial Times* would never have printed his recommendations on its front page or editorialized about them if he had been unknown. Being wrong, he knew, was inevitable. Being wrong in the glare of publicity could be embarrassing. It was the price of having impact.

CHAPTER 26

BALTIMORE

O N APRIL 28, 2000, George Soros was planning to be in Baltimore,
Maryland, to attend the annual meeting of the Open Society Institute's board of trustees. Until 1996, Soros had largely confined his contributions to those foreign countries emerging from prolonged periods
of dictatorial rule. He had kept his contributions in the United States
to a minimum because the country was clearly an open society: in fact, it
provided the most attractive model of openness for the world's aspiring democracies. But as Communist rule shriveled and a bipolar world
gave way to one dominated by the United States, the single remaining
superpower, Soros focused his critical thinking increasingly on his own
country.

As he wrote in an article for the *Atlantic Monthly*, "The Capitalist
Threat," he had come to the conclusion that "if an open society is to serve
as an ideal worth striving for, it can no longer be defined in terms of the
Communist menace; it must be given a more positive content." Even earlier, when he had argued for a Marshall Plan–like commitment to the post-
Communist East, he claimed that by affirming common democratic
values, the West would gain a sense of purpose and cohesion. In the
Atlantic article and a follow-up piece entitled "Toward a Global Open
Society," Soros deplored what he considered to be divisive policies that
overvalued market discipline and sought to apply it in areas where it lacked
utility. This impulse radiating from a triumphant and triumphalist America, he said, revealed the sort of fatalistic historicism that had characterized
so much of Marxist thinking. Soros worried that just as millions had

regarded Marxist-Leninist laws of historical development with a quasi-religious faith, others were now stampeding toward a belief that unregulated markets would prove to be the sole determinants of progress in all spheres, social, political, and educational as well as economic. He saw such smug assumptions as posing the prime challenge to the principle of fallibility he regarded to be the foundation of all open societies. Soros's articles drew considerable attention, much of it focused on the apparent irony that someone whose great wealth had been built through speculation in financial markets would argue against extending the mechanism of his enrichment to the broadest reaches of political and social life. Soros did not find it ironic. He had always insisted that though he had gotten rich playing by the rules, he had not made those rules; indeed, he had often favored changing some of them.

Beyond such theoretical musings, Soros was also examining concrete problems of American society, notably the ways in which issues of death, drugs, and race were being dealt with or ignored. He held discussions with experts, considering what philanthropic role, if any, he could or should play in the country where he spent most of his time. Even after concluding that it was a logical extension of his philanthropy to go from helping to establish open societies where they had been absent to defending them where they existed, he found the challenge puzzling. In Hungary, when he had started, and in the other countries where he had set up his foundations, there had been virtually no other foundations, few NGOs or elements of civil society. By contrast the United States had hundreds of thousands of such associations. What, Soros wondered, could he do with his money that would be meaningful and distinct without duplicating the work of other groups?

On February 23, 1996, Soros invited eight people to spend the weekend with him in Bedford and discuss approaches and programs in America: Aryeh Neier; Leon Botstein, the president of Bard; three philosophers—Alan Ryan, from Oxford and Princeton, T. M. Scanlon from Harvard, and Bernard Williams of Oxford and Berkeley—rooted in moral philosophy and ethics; Seyla Benhabib, a professor of political theory at the Center for European Studies at Harvard, who has written on feminist theory, ethics, and citizenship; David Rothman, a physician who directed the Center for the Study of Society and Medicine at Columbia University; and Ethan Nadelmann, a former Princeton professor who had attracted Soros's attention with his writings about the inefficacy of treating drug addiction as a crime rather than a disease.

For two days the guests met and talked. The setting was elegant and the food and wine were excellent. But the discussion dealt mostly with poverty, misery, and injustice. As Soros took notes on a yellow pad, the guests traced the ways that inner-city problems were hardening social divisions along lines of race and class. They cited the sharp rise in prison populations, misdirected drug policies, the failure to provide assistance to fragile families or encourage community support for health and education. In keeping with Soros's skepticism about the overemphasis on market considerations, some participants pinpointed areas such as medicine, law, journalism, and culture where standards of professionalism needed to be bolstered to offset the growing reliance on supply and demand. There was a pressing need, they contended, to reinvigorate professional, civic, and political ethics as well as a spirit of community service.

Within two months, at least some of these ideas were translated into the Open Society Institute's American programs. An office was established in New York, and a director, Gara LaMarche, was chosen. He had worked with Neier at the ACLU and at Helsinki Watch, where he had consciously patterned himself after his boss, emulating his high-energy, low-ego approach. "I majored in Aryehology," he explained.

Prior to the "philosophers' meeting" Soros had sponsored two distinct initiatives in the United States. Inspired by his mother's death, he had funded the Project on Death in America. To administer the board of this grant giving effort, he chose Dr. Kathleen Foley, an oncologist and pain management specialist at New York's Sloan-Kettering hospital. Operating with a three-year $5 million budget, she was charged with stimulating a national discussion about dying and end-of-life care. Grants were made quickly, focusing on such objectives as reforming medical school curricula to introduce death and dying as subjects for study, fostering research on nursing home and hospice care, and supporting more open discussion of death and dying in journalism, the arts, and popular culture.

Soros's second American project concerned what he considered the country's counterproductive drug policies. In the spring of 1988, he had come upon an article in *Foreign Policy* attacking the direction of America's war on drugs and arguing that legalization of drugs coupled with expanded medical treatment of addiction would greatly benefit societies in the United States and drug-exporting countries. Soros had an article of his own in the same issue of the magazine, one in which he analyzed the stock market crash of 1987 and urged the establishment of an international central bank that would issue a true international currency. The two articles were very different in subject matter and tone, but they shared a visionary if utopian activism. Soros was so impressed with the drug policy piece that he contacted its author, Ethan Nadelmann. By 1993, with Soros's financial backing, Nadelmann established the Lindesmith Center, a policy institute named after Alfred Lindesmith, a sociologist who in the 1930s and 1940s had opposed harsh policies of drug prohibition in favor of medical treatment of addicts. Nadelmann, both brash and persuasive, identified the center's mission as seeking "harm reduction," which he defined as "an alternative approach to drug policy and treatment that focuses on minimizing the adverse effects of both drug use and drug prohibition."

Soros's earlier shyness and avoidance of publicity had vanished under the impact of his psychoanalysis, Susan's influence, and the positive results he achieved by stepping into the limelight after Black Wednesday. Now he was quite prepared to speak out on the controversial subject of drugs as well as financing Nadelmann's operation. Writing in the *Washington Post*, Soros flatly declared, "I firmly believe that the war on drugs is doing more harm to our society than drug abuse itself." In this op-ed piece he insisted that by unrealistically seeking to eliminate all drug use, government policies were encouraging social polarization. As usual, in his writings, he fleshed out his arguments with personal and even confessional touches. "I have no use for drugs. I tried marijuana and enjoyed it but it did not become a habit and I have not tasted it in many years. I have had my share of anxieties concerning my children using drugs, but fortunately it was not a serious problem. My sole concern is that the war on drugs is doing untold damage to the fabric of our society."

After the philosophers' weekend, new components were created to expand Soros's philanthropy in the United States. A Center on Crime, Communities, and Culture was established in 1996 and soon started channeling grants to organizations providing direct services in jails and communities, while supporting advocacy groups pressing for legal and political reforms. Soros underwrote the formation of his Emma Lazarus Fund, which supported groups that provide legal services to immigrants. From the beginning, OSI's American programs also focused on providing grants in the areas of education and youth development, eventually focusing on nationwide efforts to establish after-school programs that would provide children with educational tutoring, health services, and cultural training after regular classes. Other grant-making divisions included one dealing with governance and public policy, which supported research and advocacy on such issues as campaign finance reform and the transfer of public responsibility from central to local authorities and the private sector.

In 1996 Soros was devoting $81 million to the American programs out of his overall annual contribution of $362 million. In 1997, he spent $57.2 million on the American programs out of an overall philanthropic outlay of $428 million. By 1998, when the total expenditures rose to $574.5 million, the American programs were consuming $118.5 million. The following year, the cost of the U.S. programs dipped slightly to $93 million out of a total commitment of some $560 million.

In addition to identifying objectives of philanthropy, the participants at the philosophers' weekend had also discussed the possibility of targeting a particular city for a high concentration of programs and assistance. The idea was to select an urban center that might serve as a social laboratory where programs could be tested to reveal useful approaches or flawed hypotheses. The board members considered New Haven, Connecticut, and San Antonio, Texas, but ultimately chose Baltimore, with its 650,000 inhabitants, just forty miles from the nation's capital. Parts of the city, notably the downtown area and the waterfront, were experiencing a resurgence, but large poor and overwhelmingly black neighborhoods were languishing. Because of these areas Baltimore ranked very high in all the indicators of urban misery: unemployment, school dropouts, drug addiction, crime, hepatitis, unmarried mothers, incarcerated youth, fatherless children, shootings. The scale and depths of such problems attracted Soros, but he was also impressed by the man who, until he returned to private life in 2000, had spent twelve years as Baltimore's mayor. In 1987, when Kurt L. Schmoke, a black former federal prosecutor, first won election to City Hall, he gained attention by calling for the legalization of drugs as the best way to confront the pathology of profit, crime, and addiction. During his years in office, he found it politically impossible to win the necessary statewide support to carry out his ideas, but Baltimore remained the only large city in the United States where legalization had respectable public support.

In 1996, a special office of the Open Society Institute was opened in Baltimore. It operated similarly to the foreign foundations, staffed as it was by local people who had considerable discretion in establishing priorities and approving funding. There were about fifteen employees supervised by director Diana Morris, a lawyer. Grants and programs costing around $13 million a year were concentrated in five related areas: drug addiction treatment, criminal justice, workforce development, education and youth, and access to justice.

In spring 2000, as the fifth year of Soros's American program was being shaped, Soros, Neier, and LaMarche thought it worthwhile for the national board to hold its annual meeting in Baltimore, combining the formal gathering with onsite visits to programs in schools, ghetto neighborhoods, and jails. On the appointed day of April 28, the board members arrived, including Botstein, Neier, Rothman, and Scanlon, who had been at the philosophers' meeting. The newer additions included LaMarche, John Simon, a law professor from Yale; and Herb Sturz, the founder of the Vera Institute of Justice, a former deputy mayor of New York, and a former editorial writer for the *New York Times*. Sturz was supervising two Soros megaprojects: the South African mortgage guarantee scheme, which was helping to provide modest houses for close to half a million urban blacks, and the after-school programs in the United States.

LaMarche announced that Soros would not be coming until the afternoon. He said that George had called him at seven o'clock that morning to say he had to deal with an emergency. This was highly unusual, but no one said anything about it except for someone who muttered, "It must be the markets."

The group piled into vans that took them to jails, schools, and slums. At one detention facility a nun who ran a halfway house for paroled prisoners expressed gratitude for funding that enabled her to double the number of beds, from sixteen to thirty-two. A young junior high school teacher explained how he was using his Soros fellowship to devise a curriculum on violence. He said he was moved to do this after seven pupils in his school had been killed in separate shootings. Inside a women's jail, the board learned details of a program in which twenty women with long histories of substance abuse were being treated with a combination of acupuncture and intensive therapy. Several of the women said that though they had been pressured into the program by threats of longer sentences, their recent experiences convinced them they could change their lives.

The acupuncture program, devised at a hospital in New York a decade earlier, was generating good results. It was cited as part of an approach called coercive treatment. Essentially the idea was to force treatment on all addicts who passed through the correction system, in either jails, prisons, or youth facilities. There were believed to be 65,000 addicts in the city, and most, if not all, spent time in custody or were on probation. The reformers argued that instead of warehousing addicts and then returning them unchanged to the streets, intense treatment should be provided while the authorities had physical control of the addicts.

Of the thousands in custody in Baltimore who were eligible, only two hundred women and five hundred men were in the acupuncture program. While some other inmates and detainees were receiving other forms of drug counseling, the overwhelming majority of those in confinement were receiving no treatment. Despite the commitments of the old Schmoke administration and of the new mayor, Martin O'Malley, to deal with addiction as a medical problem, the city had not been able to find the funds needed to enlarge upon the programs that OSI was financing as pilot projects.

It turned out that the visitors had come at a critical moment in the struggle to find such funding. Peter Beilenson, the city's health commissioner and a leading figure in the fight for massive drug treatment, had appealed for $25 million in state aid, which is what a comprehensive program would cost. He was so confident of what might be achieved at that level of funding that he predicted the city's overall crime rate would be cut in half within two years of such an allocation, and pledged that if that didn't happen, he would quit. A few days before the Soros board visit, the governor had approved only $8 million for the program. Beilenson did not hide his unhappiness from his visitors.

The dramatic high point of the visit was a stop the board members made at the Rose Street Community Center. To get to the center the bus carried the board members through block after block of abandoned and ravaged houses that seemed to have spewed streams of trash onto sidewalks and gutters. Signs of death outnumbered signs of life; house after house bore daubings declaring "R.I.P." above the name of some remembered victim and the date of his or her violent death. Here and there the mourners had painted pistols and knives.

Within this wider wasteland, the Rose Street Community Center lay at the heart of a small oasis, where there was no trash, no houses turned into tombstones. Neighbors greeted each other on the street and children played. Two years earlier, the area around Rose Street had looked like the other blocks. It was actually the epicenter of the blight. The corner at which the board members were standing had been the heart of an open-air drug market that flourished night and day. As police turned a blind eye, a drug gang patrolled the neighborhood on horseback while its dealers maintained a wholesale operation servicing much of Baltimore and the suburbs. But all this changed because of three men, Elroy Christopher, Clayton Guyton, and Vincent Richardson, who lived in the neighborhood and decided to take it back from the drug gangs. Looking at the three helps to explain their success. Christopher, a retired lineman for the electric company, is seven feet tall and cannot fit into any phone booth. Guyton is a powerful prison guard. Richardson is a retired marine. They put out beds and slept on the corner. They organized trash removal, bringing out hundreds of Dumpster loads. They confronted neighborhood youths, gradually winning their allegiance from the drug gangsters who had become the neighborhood's sole employers.

"Rose Street was so far down that not only had the city given up on us, withdrawing police and sanitation services, but so had the churches," said Guyton, explaining that this started to change when the center received help from the Open Society Institute. Day after day, the three large men occupied the critical corner alongside the dealers. They challenged behavior they felt was harmful. "It was zero tolerance," explained Christopher. "If we saw people throwing garbage we'd ask them to pick it up, or we'd get them to turn down their radios." Steadily they steered some of the young runners into programs of tutoring and counseling and helped them find lawful employment. Today about forty of the center's most active members are former gang figures. Guyton explains that at one point the center was able to expel the major drug lords from their headquarters; that house is now the base of the center's operations.

As the board members heard of these developments, Soros was deeply involved in his own drama. At a hurriedly called news conference at Soros offices in New York, he was announcing that Quantum, his legendary fund which had once moved markets, was down 21 percent for the year, and that the aggregate worth of all his funds had fallen by $7.6 billion since August 1998, when they had reached their high-water mark of $22 billion. Despite the humiliating nature of his information, he presented it placidly, even affably. He told reporters that Druckenmiller, who was sitting at his side, was resigning after twelve years. Soros said he planned to reorganize his funds, operating within more conservative parameters. "We will accept lower returns because we will cut the risk profile." It was obvious that the reorganization flowed from the losses. Druckenmiller, who over the previous two years had twice been talked out of leaving by Soros, said, "I'm tired, it's a lot of pressure." He noted that "it would have been nice to go out on top, like Michael Jordan, but I overplayed my hand."

The fund had become ensnared in the competing currents of the new technology and the old economy. For much of 1999, Druckenmiller had shied away from the Internet and biotech boom, which Soros believed would end badly. During this period Quantum's value dipped by some 20 percent. But in July, Druckenmiller reversed his strategy, acquiring new technology shares despite their high prices and selling short some old-economy shares. He caught that wave right, and at year's end, the fund had registered a pleasing 35 percent gain. In 2000, as the old economy rallied and many of the new technology stocks faltered, Druckenmiller clung to his old positions, assuming that the new economy would maintain its ascendancy over the old one for a little longer. Soros disagreed, but he had long ago ceded responsibility to Druckenmiller; Druckenmiller had made a great deal of money for Quantum over a twelve-year period and had engineered the reversal of 1999.

Early in the relationship Druckenmiller had fought Soros over second-guessing him and looking over his shoulder. Now, differences again emerged and the impassioned voices of the two men were sometimes heard in the corridors. One of their arguments reportedly involved an Internet company called VeriSign, whose stock Druckenmiller had acquired a year earlier at $50 a share. By late February it had risen to $258 and in March, when it had fallen slightly to $240, Druckenmiller doubled the fund's stake in the company by spending another $300 million on the shares. By early April, the NASDAQ shuddered and VeriSign fell to $135. According to the *Wall Street Journal*, Soros told Druckenmiller, "VeriSign is going to kill us. We should take our exposure down." Druckenmiller disagreed and Soros, who had the authority to countermand him, chose not to; the shares fell further to $96.

But, whatever the history of tension between the two men, by the time of the news conference there was no sign of any conflict. They referred to each other with respect and admiration. Druckenmiller was leaving at his own request. And, of course, Soros knew better than anyone how punishing were the burdens that his protégé had endured for more than a decade. It was a graceful withdrawal—no epaulettes were snipped but Soros was once again separating himself from someone in order to survive.

Soros acknowledged that the new shape of the stock market, driven by technology shares, had proved bewildering. Just two months earlier, Julian Robertson, Soros's only rival as a hedge-fund operator, had shut down his own Tiger Fund after its value plummeted from a $21 billion peak reached nineteen months before. Warren Buffett, another titan of the old-guard investors, was also going through a bad patch. Soros smilingly confessed to the reporters, "Maybe I don't understand the market. Maybe the music has stopped but people are still dancing."

Soros knew that news of his fund's humiliating reversal would inevitably be on the front page. Moreover he was certain that many of his shareholders, who had grown accustomed to high returns, would decide to cash in their shares and move their investments elsewhere. Indeed, within a week some $1 billion would be withdrawn. The entire experience was a bitter pill that had to be swallowed. Probably Soros had waited too long. He had been thinking about reorganizing his funds for some time, realizing that their huge size was limiting the flexibility of their managers. It was far easier to pull off high-yielding intuitive coups when your stake was relatively small and when no one was watching your every move. What had once been a responsive and nimble vessel had become a gigantic aircraft carrier. With so much mass, each change of direction took a long time to execute.

In terms of aplomb and grace, Soros's conduct at the news conference was a tour de force. He announced his defeats, assumed responsibility, and saluted his fallen lieutenant. The performance was all the more remarkable for having been hurriedly scheduled just three hours before the newsmen were summoned.

Originally, Soros and Druckenmiller had planned to make their announcement on May 1, which would have left Soros time to attend his board meeting in Baltimore. Despite the weight of the impending news, Soros went about his business without showing any stress or anxiety. The day before the Baltimore meeting, Neier had five meetings with him. They discussed a new foundation they were setting up in Indonesia and plans for observers to monitor Peru's presidential election. "In each instance he was totally focused," says Neier, "and, of course, I had no idea of what was happening."

By late Thursday evening, Shawn Pattison, who handled public relations for Soros Fund Management, received a call from Kathy Burton, a reporter who covers hedge funds for Bloomberg. Was it true, she asked, that Nicholas Roditi would be leaving as the London-based manager of Soros's Quota Fund? Pattison confirmed this but told Burton that if she was willing to hold off on the story he might have something bigger for her. Pattison then informed George that the story was leaking. It was obviously important for Soros to keep control of the story. It was one thing if Soros and Druckenmiller disclosed the changes and the declining values, and quite another if the account came from outside, making it appear that there was disarray or a vacuum of leadership. In such a scenario, it was likely that more shareholders would head for the exits than if they heard the news from Soros.

Sometime after eight that evening, Burton again called Pattison, saying that she had learned the whole story from her sources. Pattison asked if she would give him time to alert the fund's directors. Such notification was legally required prior to any public announcement of such magnitude. Pattison made sure the directors were informed of the forthcoming changes and went home around midnight. He was back at the office four hours later. Clicking on his monitor he saw that Burton's story had gone out on the Bloomberg wire at 3:37 a.m. Pattison immediately called Soros and Druckenmiller. At seven o'clock that morning, Soros decided he and Druckenmiller needed to hold the press briefing. He told Pattison to invite reporters to his office at 10 a.m. and he called LaMarche to say he would be late for the Baltimore meeting.

As soon as the press conference was over, Soros caught the Metroliner for Baltimore. He slept for most of the trip. By three o'clock that afternoon, Soros had caught up with his touring board. He arrived at the waterfront facility of the Living Classroom Foundation, where young people who have had trouble in school or trouble with the law worked with artisans to learn skills and were introduced to potential employers. With the help of craftsmen the students have built large schooners and sailed them to New England. In smaller projects they have also built and sold a line of wooden furniture. Along the way, the students, many of whom were routed into the program by juvenile courts or guidance counselors, have come to understand and apply the math and science they had earlier failed to grasp in conventional classrooms.

With invited guests from the mayor's office nibbling cheese and drinking white wine, Soros smiled and nodded as a number of speakers explained the program and thanked him for his help. But as soon as the predictable niceties subsided, as all the nametagged guests turned to each other, Soros approached four sixteen-year-old boys who were standing alongside wooden rocking chairs they had made.

"Did you work as a runner?" Soros asked one of the boys about his earlier experience.

The boy, tattooed, his hair in cornrows, acknowledged that he had worked for a drug gang, making deliveries and serving as a street-corner lookout.

Soros kept talking to him, and he wasn't just making conversation. How much money was there in drug running, he wanted to know. The boy told him the pay had been "pretty good." Then he laughed and said, "But this ain't so bad either and it's a whole lot less risky." He explained that he had hopes of getting a well-paying union job. Soros spent close to thirty minutes with the young men. Three hours earlier he had told the world that the fortune managed in his name had declined by $7 billion. Now he was totally absorbed by the problems of Baltimore and the lives of these boys. He was not playing to the press—there was no press. He was an inquiring philanthropist eager to understand Baltimore's problems and to help solve them. There was unmistakable empathy in Soros's questions as he asked the boys about the dangers, risks, and rewards of life on the street. He too had been streetwise—on Wall Street, of course, but also when he was a teenager trading bits of broken gold and changing money at the Mienk Café.

He moved on to Beilenson, the health commissioner, who brought Soros up to date. At Baltimore's harborside, Mayor O'Malley then toasted Soros for all he had done for the city. "I just want to say that you had the leadership and courage to invest in this city when others were not wise enough." He said people financed by Soros were playing vital roles in every aspect of the city's plans for growth and development. In passing, the mayor politely acknowledged the governor's decision to partially fund drug treatment.

Taking the microphone, Soros offered no perfunctory pleasantries. "I wish to express my disappointment at the grant that the mayor referred to. I am less of a politician than he is. In setting up the OSI program in Baltimore it had been our hope that the program would serve as an example to the state and eventually to the whole country. And we have shown that there is a way of dealing with the problems of drugs that had not been tried at the time. If we could get 60,000 people into treatment we would have real statistics. There has to be a systemic approach to the problem. I hope you [will] do whatever it takes to make treatment available to everyone who needs it."

The evening continued with a cruise through the inner and outer harbors, during which Soros engaged several municipal boosters on how the growth they were counting on might affect the lives of those who lived in blighted and drug-ravaged areas. He asked if the young people from those areas would be swept up in the renaissance or if their neighborhoods would be sealed off from good fortune.

Finally, when it turned dark, Soros hosted a dinner for his board and the Baltimore staff. He led a discussion on strategy, raising the question of whether the state government, fearful of anti-Baltimore and anti-drug addict sentiment in the politically important suburbs, was holding back on vital funding in the expectation that OSI might pick up the shortfall. Had the state developed its own attitudes of entitlement? He wanted to know how the political ambitions of Maryland's lieutenant governor, Kathleen Kennedy Townsend, were likely to figure in the situation. It was almost midnight. The day that had started so badly for Soros was drawing to an end, but he showed no signs of fatigue. He lifted his glass and toasted the directors who had come from New York and the staff people from Baltimore, some thirty-five people in all. "On behalf of the founder," he said with a broad smile, "I'd like to express my appreciation to all of you. We have done well."

At breakfast the next day, the directors read about the news conference in a front-page story in the *New York Times* headlined "Huge Losses Move Soros to Revamp Empire." Then they went into another few hours of meetings during which they took up plans for funding the Project on Death in America for another three years. Soros made it clear how pleased he was with the project and with its director, Dr. Kathleen Foley, and quite casually he approved its budget. He never mentioned the reorganization of the fund or the losses he had spoken of so publicly twenty-four hours earlier, and neither did anyone else.

CHAPTER 27

SOROS AT SEVENTY

O N AUGUST 12, 2000, four months after the board meeting in Baltimore and the reorganization of his fund, George Soros celebrated
his seventieth birthday. To mark the occasion he invited five hundred
friends and associates to a party at Southampton College, near his beachfront home. Surprisingly, the theme was strongly Hungarian. Soros, after
all, had often said that there was little beside the language that had tied
him to his native country, and Susan, who helped plan the party, had never
been drawn to Magyar life. Yet the food and wine and the entertainment
were all Hungarian. Four chefs had been flown in from Gundal's,
Budapest's exclusive restaurant, but before a lavish meal was served, Soros
led his guests to a campus theater for a performance of music and dance.
He sat quite relaxed in the middle of the audience, several rows back from
the stage, with Susan next to him and Annaliese nearby. Annaliese had
given him a small party at her house the night before.

The program opened with a macabre but compelling musical piece
called "The Hanged," in which four percussionists used mallets to tap complicated rhythms on a dozen wooden mannikins that lay prone on special
stands. A string quartet accompanied the tappers through movements entitled "Fear," "Aggression," "Death," and "Bereavement," and two women
in black keened in harmonized anguish. The piece ended with each of the
effigies being slowly hoisted in turn by the ropes around their necks as a
bell pealed.

Thanatos, the embodiment of death, was powerfully present—not
exactly the usual guest in a funny hat who might be expected to sing

"Happy Birthday" to the party boy. But as a woman from the Soros foundation in Hungary had said in introducing the program, "We all know of George Soros's fascination with death." Soros had watched the work intently. Perhaps it had recalled the sight that had so impressed him at fourteen when he saw two hanged corpses on a Budapest street. Or the hangings of the wooden puppets may have suggested the executions of those who in 1956 had risen against Russian rule. Hungarian history, as well as his own, provided ample allusions from which to choose.

The party did not maintain this dolorous tone throughout the night; the tragic strains gradually gave way to more jubilant expressions as a Gypsy band played and danced in joyful frenzy and a willowy modern dancer took the stage masked and topless, drawing her inspiration primarily from Eros rather than Thanatos.

But it was clear that Soros, who had made his mark on the world by constantly looking forward, by identifying and taking on new challenges, studying and anticipating changes, was focusing somewhat less on the future and considerably more on the past. As the party ended and the guests left, each was given a copy of a newly published English translation of Tivadar's Esperanto memoir of war, *Maskerado: Dancing around Death in Nazi Hungary*, which told a key part of George's story.

Soros was clearly in the throes of recapitulation, summing up and setting things right. He was providing for the time when he would be gone, speaking more candidly about his legacy. A week before his party, at his apartment in New York, he acknowledged how much his life was changing as he prepared to blow out his seventy candles. He looked quite well, relaxed and tanned. He still played tennis regularly, beating men who were decades younger, and with some excitement he was awaiting the publication of another of his books that blended philosophy, finance, and moral prescriptions, *Open Society: Reforming Global Capitalism.**

"You know, when you are seventy you are sort of exempt, you are superannuated, and the standards are lowered for you. You are not expected to perform the same way as you did up to that point." He laughed and added that he had already lowered his standards.

"I've done that in terms of performance and in terms of pushing myself to the limit." As a moneymaker and fund manager, he explained, he had achieved this more relaxed status twelve years earlier when he first turned over responsibility to Druckenmiller. "But I was pushing myself very hard

---

*New York: Public Affairs, 2000.

on the foundation side, because I felt the pressures of time. Now I don't feel that anymore."

He then reviewed the state of his fortunes and ambitions, persona by persona. As a financier, he was no longer interested in generating huge profits, but was rather seeking steady, more risk-averse growth for his holdings and for some smaller groups of clients. "The hedge fund is no longer in existence. It has become the Quantum Endowment Fund. I still go to the office but it's now a different kind of operation. Essentially it's meant to administer my estate in an efficient manner. It's a fund of funds and a lot of it is farmed out to other hedge funds to manage, with lots of outside managers. The whole concept is to set up an operation that will continue after my lifetime. So now I consider myself the executor of my own estate; in that respect, my personal career has ended." A funny idea occurred to him. "I guess I could put it this way," he said, laughing, "that I am preparing for death. But I am trying to avoid a fate worse than death, which would be to become simply a client."

He spoke of his children. "Robert is taking a more active role. I think my other son, Jonathan, might also take a more active role. It will be their estate, so they'll have to look after it. And Robert is doing a very good job. I've been his sharpest critic and I have to recognize that he's rising to the occasion."

And what of his role as philanthropist?

There, too, he had altered his emphasis and reined in some of his enthusiasms. By creating his endowment fund, he was establishing a stream of capital that could be used to support a few of his projects beyond his death. A year later, he set aside $250 million to endow the Central European University.

As for the rest of his foundations, his plan had been to wind up his donations by that 2010 date. He had repeatedly warned the foundations of eventually diminishing flows and had encouraged them to find additional resources to supplant the steady shrinkage of his contributions. Now, however, he was not so certain about that deadline. He was re-evaluating the proposal in light of his new book. "In the book I propose that the democracies, or the open societies, of the world have to cooperate with some kind of alliance, with the dual purpose of, one, fostering the development of open societies inside the countries, and, two, creating the institutions and the laws which are necessary for a global open society."

His foundation network has for many years been pursuing the first objective, and now, he declared, he was tempted to redirect his philanthropy toward the second. "In other words, to develop some capacity to foster development of international institutions." He said that, for example, he was thinking of setting up an international institute for judiciary reform, and he was interested in sponsoring policy-shaping work on reforming international economic institutions.

As for the old national foundations, two relatively small ones, in Estonia and Slovenia, have essentially mutated into policy institutes operating at about a quarter of their old budgets. Soros had established a new Open Society foundation in Indonesia, which he was thinking about at the time of the Baltimore meeting. He was also considering opening others in Southeast Asia and the Middle East.

"I still aim to spend as much money as I can in my own lifetime, but I recognize there will be some left over, and that's part of my plan. We have cut the old budgets to some extent, but we're looking to be more engaged in policy, where we are increasing our commitments."

Soros has no illusions about sustaining the original vitality and spontaneity of his foundations. He knows that the process of bureaucratization that he feared at the outset has sapped their creativity. One of the networks' oldest employees remarks sadly that where once one simple message was enough to have the Russian foundation offer its resources to a handful of democrats trying to reverse the coup against Gorbachev, she now has to process as many as ten forms before a routine $2,000 grant is approved, and the check often arrives two months late. Soros is aware of such changes and contends that to an appreciable extent they are inevitable.

"There is no solution. If you set up an institution you always have a chance that somebody will emerge with a sense of mission, which may last for a while, but entropy is operative."

Nonetheless, he was pressing on as usual on three fronts, claiming that his seemingly disparate activities were quite integrated. His efforts to consolidate and perpetuate his fortune beyond his death were closely linked to his desire to sustain and extend his philanthropies, which in turn had driven him to prune and reform his foundations. And at the same time, his philosophical thinking was pointing the way to new areas of international philanthropy.

The impulse that had first goaded him to write "The Burden of Consciousness" in his thirties had not withered. Despite the critical attacks he endured for his writings from economists and philosophers as undisciplined, sloppy, and banal, he has not retreated to his garden. If anything, as the financial innovator and the philanthropic donor trimmed their sails, the contemplative thinker was asserting himself. He calls *Open Society: Reforming Global Capitalism* a work of "applied philosophy."

As he waited anxiously for its final galleys just before his birthday, he described one of the book's core ideas as an elaboration on the notion that though states were indeed driven by interests rather than principles, democratic states were also responsive to their electorates. Thus, an electorate with principles could induce governments to accept its ideals and advance them through sovereign power.

"So civil society has an important role to play in pushing governments. The weakness is that civil society is not terribly interested. I mean there is no great belief in open society as a universal principle. So it is difficult to mobilize civil society. However, here I am, and I am very interested. So I might as well do what I preach. You can look at the book as an extrapolation of what I'm doing or would like to do. And then you can look at the future of the foundation as an implementation of the program."

One could also look at the book as yet another attempt by Soros to articulate his basic philosophical ideas and confront the criticism of the people he respected who described *The Crisis of Global Capitalism* as erroneous and prosaic. Of course he wrote that earlier book in a feverish mood, eager to forestall or minimize what he viewed as the approaching collapse of an increasingly interwoven global economy. Certain that his insights were valid and that no time could be spared in sounding his urgent alarm, Soros was incredulous when Random House proceeded to edit his manuscript on a normal schedule, meaning that it would take months to appear. Irritably he withdrew the text and turned it over to Public Affairs, whose publisher, Peter Osnos, was able to produce the book within a month, so that it appeared at the end of 1998.

As we now know, it might have been better had Soros been less impetuous. His pessimistic scenario did not materialize. Soros would later acknowledge that he let himself get carried away. On a more personal level, Soros was confronted by extremely harsh criticism. He had been prepared for the more ideological reviews, in which market fundamentalists found it ironic and somehow even hypocritical that a man who had made his great fortune by engaging boldly in an unfettered market was now calling for some form of regulation. But what wounded him more were the belittling comments of people and publications he respected.

The tone of these responses was set by a short and anonymous review in the *Economist*, which said in part: "Because of who he is, there will always be buyers for his books, publishers for his books, and cash-strapped academics to say flattering things about his books. None of this alters the fact that his books are no good."

The essence of the argument, that Soros was an extraordinarily good man but a failed and even silly thinker, was soon widely repeated even by many of the "cash-starved academics" who weighed in on the work. For the most part the critics sounded like the academics Soros had invited to his estate to debate philosophy and who had ended up chastising him for being a dilettante and an autodidact. For example, Rudiger Dornbush, the Ford Professor of Economics and International Management at the Massachusetts Institute of Technology, wrote in the *Financial Times:* "Mr. Soros has no clue about what is done in financial economics research and his ramblings on the subject are at best an incoherent rendition of some common themes."

Perhaps the most withering attack came from a another MIT economist, the Nobel Prize winner Robert Solow, who offered his comments in an article contemptuously entitled "The Amateur": "I have to report that Soros has written an embarrassingly banal book."

To be sure, there were a few positive responses. "On the issue of globalization I think he was right," said Kissinger in an interview in the fall of 2000. "As always he was a little premature so that his predictions of catastrophe have not yet happened, but there he's right. I would tell him not to pull back too easily. History works in longer cycles. He thinks like a speculator and he looks and sees what happened and he thinks he was probably wrong. I think he was probably right, but so much new technology has developed that the cycle is longer."

Critical reviews by people like Dornbush and Solow hurt. Still, Soros has always appreciated criticism. Indeed, in contrast to the conventions of academia where errors can so easily derail careers and reputations and are thus feared, he has always treasured the feedback that exposed his mistakes. That is perhaps one way in which his appreciation of fallibility was less banal than it appeared to Solow and the others. He had, as we know, always claimed the right to be wrong, even exulted in it. It had been a part of his methodology all his life, whether he was making huge amounts of money or giving it away. He had tested markets and conditions, made mistakes, learned from them and refined his actions. He had made huge mistakes. He had lost as much as $600 million in a day. He had erred with his foundations in China and Russia, but dealt with his errors, staying in the game. It was in the same impulsive manner that he had felt compelled to write *The Crisis of Global Capitalism* to address his critics and refine his arguments.

There is yet another factor that none of the professors grasped, or at least mentioned. While they all praised Soros for his extraordinary accomplishments in finance and philanthropy, they lamented his need to be a philosopher, to think like a Central European intellectual, to dabble in ideas and to try to become a philosopher king, as if such unreachable aspirations detracted from his other achievements. In fact, it was precisely his yearning to make sense of the world and history, and to attain philosophical understanding and stature, that had spurred him to achieve his practical successes. A man of parts in every sense, Soros is indivisibly the financial, philanthropic, and philosophical speculator. His gestalt is formed in the dynamic relationship among all three personas. His ability to recognize his mistakes quickly and to reverse them established his success as a financial speculator. That same self-critical reflex led him to cancel his false starts in philanthropy and move into new and innovative areas. But a hesitant philosopher and a serially recanting visionary? That can be problematic. By turning his faith in fallibility and indeterminacy on his own thinking to proclaim his errors and offer corrections, he was being true to his most deeply held ideals. But it did tend to undermine his credibility with others.

Of course, Soros would not defend himself in psychological terms. He had cast his book as a rational argument, and he appreciated his rationalist critics for pointing out his shortcomings within their disciplines. He acknowledged that he had represented certain of his ideas poorly and he decided to weigh the criticism and respond to it in what he first envisioned as a second edition of *The Crisis of Global Capitalism*. That too was a characteristic act. Instead of shrinking in the face of scorn, he was forging ahead. He wrote, in longhand as usual, and steadily the effort turned into a totally new book, one that both elaborated on his first principles and took account of his critics, and went on to explore how moral visions originating outside sovereign concerns might be grafted on to the political life of nations.

Awaiting the new book's publication, Soros gave interviews in which he conceded the lapses and errors of the preceding work. But Soros would write it all once more, hoping this time to capture both the underlying principles, repay his debt to Popper, and reveal how his contemplative analysis applied to the real world. Just before his seventieth birthday he described the effort. He said he had just reread his father's memoir of war and determined that his father was a bad writer, adding, "I'm just like him, a very bad writer, because a good writer can conjure up an atmosphere, and that means expanding, and I am always condensing."

He said he sent early drafts of the work seeking critical comments from a number of philosophers and at a seminar at the CEU that was convened to consider the manuscript. "It was useful because, you know, I'm well short of a disciplined thinker. People sent in a number of papers. About the conceptual framework, about economic theory, and so on, I'm pretty convinced that I'm on the right track, that in a kind of broad-brush way, I've got the right idea. But in putting it in a form that would meet the standards of scientific proof, it ain't there."

Quite cheerfully, he explained how the Hungarian philosopher Janos Kis pointed out key failures in Soros's understanding of reflexivity. But if he was pleased by this criticism, he was even more delighted by the correspondence he had with another, even more demanding scholar.

"There's a philosopher in Britain by the name of Brian McGee who wrote a book, *Confessions of a Philosopher.* And he's a Popperian. And I think it's a brilliant book. Well maybe not brilliant, but a really first-class read in the field of philosophy. So I sought him out and asked him to read my manuscript and give me his honest opinion. I was hoping that I could maybe get him to collaborate in some way. Well, McGee was not interested—he was doing his own thing—but he gave me a really scathing evaluation. He said the book was unreadable and if it weren't that I was a public figure no publisher would take it, and he suggested that I should really get a ghostwriter to write for me. And his criticisms on style hit home, because I felt the same things. I think it was directed at the first chapter or two, which I had belabored too much because of all the criticisms. So it didn't have the natural flow of the rest." He added that McGee told him he had stopped reading the manuscript. But clearly Soros was grateful:

> You know, it was devastating. But it reaffirmed my own judgment that I ought to work on it, which I did. McGee said: You have something important to say. The points you are making are important points, and surely you want to make them well. You want them to stand up long after you are gone. And the way it is now, you know, the book will be published, and because you are a public figure, people are going to pay some attention. But it will not have the quality of a book that's read, you know, for eternity.
>
> And there he actually touched a real ambition in me. I wish I could write a book that will be read for as long as our civilization lasts. I mean, it's not new and it's not because I'm seventy, but it's

a very real thing and it has prompted me to work to try to make it better. At the same time, regretfully, I have to accept that, probably, I'll never do it. In other words, I just don't have that kind of creativity. Once I gave a lecture which I called "A Failed Philosopher Tries Again." That is still alive. In that respect I would consider that a superior kind of survival, because the myth that grows up around me is—how shall I say—outside my control, and people will make of it whatever they want and there is nothing I can do about it. However, if I can put things, ideas, into words, those words will be there. And even though people may misinterpret them or don't understand them, the words will still be alive, to be looked at and reconsidered. And even if that is not me, it's close enough to me that it really matters.

Then Soros acknowledged that in his life he had gained significant satisfaction in the sphere of action. "But you know—how shall I say it—the real me is the contemplative one. It's pretty eternal stuff, because it has to do with the human condition and questions of consciousness and death. And that is the dominant interest. But it created a vacuum around me. By doing I broke out of the vacuum. I filled the vacuum. And so, the doing fulfilled a need that I couldn't fulfill by contemplation, you know?"

Acknowledgments

Over the last five years I have spoken with some 130 people who provided the information and shaped the insights contained in this book. Of these, the most indispensable to my efforts was obviously George Soros, who patiently presented me with the details of his life, established their context, and provoked lines of inquiry I pursued with him and elsewhere. He offered me manuscripts from long ago, provided photographs, and gave me the names of people who had known him at various stages of his life. He was unfailingly gracious. When at the outset of my researches he wrote me that he would not attempt to influence or alter what I wrote about him, I did not completely believe him, but he fully kept his word. The only instance in which he refused a request of mine was when he declined on the grounds of privacy to let me see the list of guests he had invited to a New Year's party marking the advent of the new millennium.

I am also grateful to Susan Weber Soros for the candid openness she showed in talking to me and responding to my questions. Robert Soros, George Soros's oldest son, was extremely forthcoming, while always tactful, in talking to me about his father, and Paul Soros provided valuable information about the lives he and his brother led in Hungary before, during, and immediately after the war. I would also like to acknowledge those family members who elected not to meet with me. I am highly respectful of their decisions, and I simply want to note for the record that I never spoke with Jonathan or Andrea or their mother, Annaliese Soros.

As for the genesis of the book, I owe special thanks to my daughter Susan, who played a catalytic role in getting me to stop talking about Soros and to start writing about him. Kris Dahl, my agent, knew just when to nudge and when to leave me alone. From Prague, Jan Urban sent me encouraging messages that ultimately helped me decide to end a forty-year career at the *New York Times* and go off to write this book. As always, Rebecca, my wife, supported my choice and chased away the hobgoblins of doubt. I also want to express my thanks to Aryeh Neier for his discreet vote of confidence at the outset of this project. I am grateful to Marianne Szegedy-Maszak for first tipping me off to the Soros story fifteen years ago and for helping me to better understand Magyar ways.

In regard to the writing, I was greatly aided and abetted by Jonathan Segal, as subtle, clear-thinking, and quick-witted an editor as any writer could hope for.

This leaves the many sources from more than twenty countries whom I interviewed, ranging from Soros's childhood friends to wartime protectors, business associates, and confederates in philanthropy and world affairs. Many of these I have mentioned in the text, and I trust my gratitude for their help emerges as implicit. As for those I did not cite but who nonetheless helped me carry out my project, I now tip my hat and bend my knee in appreciation. Yvonne Sheer and Darinka Radic, Soros's secretaries, were always helpful and splendidly efficient. Shawn Pattison, the former director of public relations at Soros Fund Management, and Frances Abouzeid and Michael Vachon, who were his counterparts at the Open Society Institute, steered me to what I was looking for.

Others within the Open Society network who aided my understanding included Maureen Aung-thwin, who works on the Burma project; Tereece Bassler, who helped create the Albanian Educational Development project; Abby Gardner, who was deeply involved with ISF, and Gordana Jankovic, who passionately supported the growth of independent media in many countries. There was also Fron Nazi, who was the first head of the Soros foundation in Albania. Good luck led me to Lenny Bernardo, Deborah Harding, Stuart Papperin, Jonathan Peizer, Anthony Richter, and Amy Yenkin at OSI headquarters in New York. All of them helped me comprehend a welter of programs. Among the people at OSI-Budapest who shared their expertise were Katalin Koncz, who administers the European network, and Frances Pinter, who set up an extensive book-publishing operation. Stephen Holmes, who directed the Soros-financed Institute for Constitutional and Legislative Policy, covering the former Communist realm, often stimulated my thinking, as did Roman Frydman and Andrzej Rapaczynski, the co-directors of the Soros privatization project studying economic transitions. I learned about Soros's interests and activities in Africa from Michael Savage and Cedric DeBeer of the South African foundation.

In another category, I want to credit people outside the network who helped me to grasp elements of Soros's work and story. Adam Michnik, the Polish essayist and former dissident, and Fatos Lubunja, the Albanian novelist, were particularly insightful in describing Soros's role in the post-Communist transformations. Gyorgy Bence and Miklos Haraszti alerted me to specifically Hungarian aspects of those transitions. Finally, I need to express my gratitude to Harry Falk and Lawrence Malkin, who patiently demystified some elements of finance for me.

Though the book relies most heavily on the testimony of those in a position to have closely observed Soros's life, I also benefited from a number of books by him or about him or about periods and issues important to his life. Here is a partial list:

Black, George, and Robin Munro. *Black Hands of Beijing* (New York: Wiley, 1993).

Chernow, Ron. *Titan: The Life of John D. Rockefeller, Sr.* (New York: Random House, 1998).

Dahrendorf, Ralf. *LSE: A History of the London School of Economics and Political Science, 1895–1995* (Oxford: Oxford University Press, 1995).

Harrod, Roy. *The Life of John Maynard Keynes* (London: Macmillan, 1951).

Korey, William. *NGOs and the Universal Declaration of Human Rights* (New York: St. Martin's Press, 1998).

Langer, Susanne K. *Philosophy in a New Key* (Cambridge: Harvard University Press, 1942).

Lefevre, Edwin. *Reminiscences of a Stock Operator* (New York: George H. Doran, 1923).

Liang, Heng. *Son of the Revolution* (New York: Alfred A. Knopf, 1983).

Lukacs, John. *Budapest 1900* (London: Weidenfeld and Nicholson, 1993).

McCagg, William O., Jr. *Jewish Nobles and Geniuses in Modern Hungary* (Boulder, Colo.: East European Monographs, 1986).

Neier, Aryeh. *War Crimes: Brutality, Genocide, Terror and the Struggle for Justice* (New York: Random House, 1998).

Nielsen, Waldemar A. *Inside American Philanthropy* (Norman: University of Oklahoma, 1996).

Nikitinski, Leonid. *Trudno Delat Dobro (It Is Hard to Do Good)* (Moscow: Open Society Institute, 1997).

Popper, Karl. *The Open Society and Its Enemies* (Princeton, N.J.: Princeton University Press, 1962).

Schwager, Jack D. *Market Wizards* (New York: Institute of Finance, 1989); and *New Market Wizards* (New York: HarperBusiness, 1992).

Sidelsky, Robert. *John Maynard Keynes: The Economist as Savior* (London: Macmillan, 1992).

Snow, C. P. *The Two Cultures and the Scientific Revolution* (Cambridge: Cambridge University Press, 1959).

Soros, George. *The Alchemy of Finance* (New York: John Wiley & Sons, 1987); *Opening the Soviet System* (London: Weidenfeld and Nicholson, 1990); *Underwriting Democracy* (New York: The Free Press, 1991); *Soros on Soros* (New York: John Wiley & Sons, 1995); *The Crisis of Global Capitalism* (New York: Public Affairs, 1998); *Open Society: Reforming Global Capitalism* (New York: Public Affairs, 2000); "The Burden of Consciousness" (unpublished manuscript).

Soros, Tivadar. *Maskerado: Dancing around Death in Nazi Hungary* (Edinburgh: Canongate, 2000).

Stephens, Philip. *Politics and the Pound* (London: Macmillan, 1996).

Walker, Samuel. *In Defense of American Liberties* (Carbondale: Southern Illinois University Press, 1990).

—MTK, April 2001

Index

A NOTE ABOUT THE AUTHOR

Michael T. Kaufman spent close to forty years at the *New York Times* as a reporter, foreign correspondent, columnist, and editor. An earlier book, *Mad Dreams, Saving Graces*, anticipated the final collapse of Communism in Poland. He has won the George Polk award for foreign reporting and has received a Guggenheim fellowship. Born in Paris, he lives in Manhattan with his wife.

A NOTE ON THE TYPE

This book was set in Janson, a typeface long thought to have been made by the Dutchman Anton Janson, who was a practicing typefounder in Leipzig during the years 1668–1687. However, it has been conclusively demonstrated that these types are actually the work of Nicholas Kis (1650–1702), a Hungarian, who most probably learned his trade from the master Dutch typefounder Dirk Voskens. The type is an excellent example of the influential and sturdy Dutch types that prevailed in England up to the time William Caslon (1692–1766) developed his own incomparable designs from them.

Composed by North Market Street Graphics, Lancaster, Pennsylvania
Printed and bound by Berryville Graphics, Berryville, Virginia
Designed by Robert C. Olsson